VV 0

D0279657

Leabharlanna Fhine Gall
BALDOYLE LIBRARY
Inv/04 : DON0904 Price ε
Title: Leading the Way manag
Class:

371. 2

LEABI

STOP

Items should
below. Items
telephone or
Fingal Librar
ticket numbe
are charged (
in recovery.
borrower

Date D:

05 FEB

24. FE

24.

Eileen Doyle

Leading The Way

Managing Voluntary Secondary Schools

WITHDRAWN FROM FINGAL
COUNTY LIBRARY STOCK

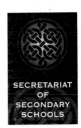

SECRETARIAT
OF
SECONDARY
SCHOOLS

Copyright © Secretariat of Secondary Schools

Published by:
The Secretariat of Secondary Schools,
Emmet House, Dundrum Road, Dublin 14

June 2000

ISBN 0-9538625-1-8

Written by Eileen Doyle

Produced by Andec Communications
Cover Illustration by Brian Fitzgerald
Designed by Alison Burns
Printed in Ireland by Print World

Text 10 on 13.5 point Adobe Garamond
Chapter headings and decorative type Gill Sans Light

*All rights reserved. No part of this publication may be reproduced,
stored in a retrieval system or transmitted, in any form or by any means
whatever, electronic, mechanical, photocopying, recording or otherwise,
without the prior permission of the copyright owners.*

contents

ACKNOWLEDGEMENTS

The Council of Management of Catholic Secondary Schools (CMCSS) commissioned this book. It is their Millennium Project. The intention was to provide a history of the voluntary education system that is led and managed by the Council and by the Joint Managerial Body. It is hoped that the result will be a cause of celebration as well as a resource for anyone interested in denominational schools or in the history of education.

George O'Callaghan, General Secretary, and Bernadette Kinsella, Principal Officer, acted as the steering team on behalf of the patrons. Without their support and expertise the task would have been difficult to complete. They helped to clarify issues and source material when necessary, yet they never attempted to influence the content or emphasis. They generously read successive drafts of chapters as did a number of other people.

The demands of the work on Bernadette Kinsella were considerable. Her professionalism in responding to innumerable requests, her good humour and persistence in clarifying issues and her enthusiasm for the outcome proved a challenge and a support.

Chapter Two was part of a PhD thesis and I deeply appreciate the supervision and encouragement of Ms Susan Parkes of Trinity College Dublin.

To others who read chapters, offered advice and access to private papers, I am grateful. Some have asked to remain anonymous. I salute those and Brother Declan Duffy, Liam Murphy, Sr Patricia Rogers, Don Herron, Dr John Harris, Liam Kelly, Dr Margaret McCurtain, Moira Leyden, Margaret Purcell, Professor Áine Hyland, Dr Michael Murray, Mary Anne Halton, Margaret Walsh, Sr Marie Céline Clegg, Seán Burke, and Sr Teresa McCormack.

Much of the primary resource material is located in the Secretariat of Secondary Schools. Other sources are with the Christian Brothers and a number of religious congregations. The records of the Conference of Convent Secondary Schools are extensive and not catalogued. There are copybooks, notes, minutes, record books, handouts, brochures, booklets and even memos on envelopes. In addition, material was made available by a number of individual religious and clerics: I am grateful for the use of that data. Moira Leyden, Assistant General Secretary at the Association of Secondary Teachers Ireland, was always helpful. I am indebted to her and to Charles Lennon, General Secretary, for access to the library, and research facilities.

Finally, this work is a tribute to the men and women in the many managerial organisations that were the basis of the Council and Joint Managerial Body of 2000. By their decision to commission this book, the Council of Management of Catholic Secondary Schools and the Joint Managerial Body has sought to acknowledge the roots and challenges of the voluntary school sector. Knowing what the Council and Joint Managerial Body stand for is essential if a vision of denominational education in a pluralist Ireland is to inform future decisions. It is the author's earnest hope that an understanding of the past may help to explain the present and give courage to those who will lead the voluntary schools forward.

Eileen Doyle
March 2000

ABBREVIATIONS

AIH	Association of Irish Headmistresses
AMCSS	Association of Management of Catholic Secondary Schools
APPTI	Association of Post-Primary Teachers of Ireland
ASTI	Association of Secondary Teachers Ireland
CHA	Catholic Headmasters' Association
CEO	Chief Executive Officer
CCSS	Conference of Convent Secondary Schools
CMCSS	Council of Managers of Catholic Secondary Schools
CMRS	Conference of Major Religious Superiors
CORI	Conference of Religious of Ireland
CEB	Curriculum and Examinations Board
EPG	Education Planning Group
FCLS	Federation of Catholic Lay Secondary Schools
FUE	Federated Union of Employers
IBEC	Irish Business and Employers Confederation
ICTU	Irish Congress of Trade Unions
INTO	Irish National Teachers' Organisation
ISA	Irish Schoolmasters' Association
IVEA	Irish Vocational Education Association
JMB	Joint Managerial Body
LRC	Labour Relations Commission
NAPD	National Association of Principals and Deputy Principals
NCCA	National Council for Curriculum and Assessment
SEC	Secondary Education Committee
SSPAI	Secondary School Principals' Association of Ireland
TBA	Teaching Brothers' Association
TUI	Teachers' Union of Ireland
VEC	Vocational Education Committee
VTA	Vocational Teachers' Association

PRESIDENTS CMCSS / JMB

Brother Adrian McGrath	01/10/87 - 1990
Liam Murphy	01/10/90 - 1997
Sr Marie Céline Clegg	1997 - 20/01/00
Mgr. James Cassin	2000 -

GENERAL SECRETARIES

John Hughes, SJ	1972 - 1975
(No appointment)	1975 - 1977
Brother Declan Duffy	August 1977 - July 1996
George O'Callaghan	August 1996 -

MINISTERS FOR EDUCATION

J. J. O'Kelly (Second Dáil)	26/08/21 - 09/01/22
Michael Hayes	11/01/22 - 09/09/22
Fintan Lynch (Provisional Govt.)	01/04/22 - 30/08/22
Michael Hayes (Acting)	17/07/22 - 30/08/22
Eoin Mac Neill	30/08/22 - 09/09/22
Eoin Mac Neill	09/09/22 - 24/11/25
John Marcus O'Sullivan	28/01/26 - 09/03/32
Tomás Derrig	09/03/32 - 08/09/39
Seán T. Ó Ceallaigh	08/09/39 - 27/09/39
Éamon de Valéra	27/09/39 - 18/06/40
Tomás Derrig	18/06/40 - 18/02/48
Richard Mulcahy	18/02/48 - 14/06/51
Seán Moylan	14/06/51 - 02/06/54
Richard Mulcahy	02/06/54 - 20/03/57
Jack Lynch	20/03/57 - 24/06/59
Patrick J. Hillery	24/06/59 - 21/04/65
George Colley	21/04/65 - 13/07/66
Donogh O'Malley	13/07/66 - 10/03/68
Jack Lynch (Acting)	11/03/68 - 26/03/68
Brian J. Lenihan	27/03/68 - 02/07/69
Pádraig Faulkner	02/07/69 - 14/03/73
Richard Burke	14/03/73 - 01/12/76
Peter Barry	02/12/76 - 14/07/77
John P. Wilson	15/07/77 - 30/06/81
John Boland	01/07/81 - 09/03/82
Martin O'Donoghue	09/03/82 - 06/10/82
Charles J. Haughey (Acting)	06/10/82 - 27/10/82
Gerard Brady	27/10/82 - 14/12/82
Gemma Hussey	14/12/82 - 13/02/86
Patrick Cooney	14/02/86 - 10/03/87
Mary O'Rourke	11/03/87 - 13/11/91
Noel Davern	14/11/91 - 11/02/92
Séamus Brennan	12/02/92 - 12/01/93
Niamh Bhreathnach	13/01/93 - 17/11/94
Michael Smith (Acting)	17/11/94 - 15/12/94
Niamh Bhreathnach	15/12/94 - 26/06/97
Micheál Martin	26/06/97 - 27/01/00
Michael Woods	27/01/00 -

FOREWORD

This book represents a very welcome and valuable addition to the corpus of educational debate and discussion in Ireland. As we embark on the twenty-first century it stands as a timely reminder of the significant role played by the management of voluntary secondary schools in the development of Irish education over the past thirty years. The CMCSS/JMB is a relatively young organisation. However, representing as it does those who are charged with the responsibility of managing voluntary secondary schools, it is the inheritor and guarantor of a rich educational heritage. Voluntary secondary schools comprise 60 per cent of the post-primary schools in Ireland and educate more than 60 per cent of the second level school-going population.

This book represents another milestone in the development of the association in its role of representing the interests of school management. Our history defines us, telling us who we are and what we are about; it illustrates our reason for being as well as recording how we have changed and what we have achieved. This is the first attempt to encapsulate our organisation in a written history. In this the millennium year it is appropriate to examine the role played by secondary school management in the rich tapestry of events that have occurred in Irish Education, particularly since the introduction of free education in the late 1960s. But this book takes a longer vista as well in examining the background, going back to the nineteenth century. In a comprehensive and wide-ranging examination the book explores the background of the managerial groups representing the various interests in voluntary secondary schools and expertly knits the strands of a complex web of events and organisations.

School management today faces many challenges in attempting to fulfil its responsibility of providing the best education for the children in our care. The challenging educational landscape characterised by development and reform of the curriculum, the changing mores and structure of society, and the decline in the numbers of religious in our schools continues to focus the energies of school managers on creating a vision and exercising leadership in Irish education. But there have always been serious challenges to be faced and in this book in what is a fair and balanced account we see how such challenges have been successfully confronted and sometimes not so successfully dealt with.

We are indebted to the hard work and dedication of Dr Eileen Doyle for bringing together in a well written and accessible manner the history and involvement of the voluntary secondary school managers in the developments that have brought about what is acknowledged to be a successful educational system - a system that has contributed in no small way to the current economic prosperity. Our association was delighted that Eileen Doyle agreed to undertake the task of writing this book and we are indeed indebted to her for producing such a fine, rigorously researched work. It is not only scholarly in content but gives a fascinating account of the events that have helped to shape the Irish education system that we have today. The wide breadth of matters covered are characterised by an impressive attention to detail, underscored by keen observation of the people who played an important part in the events and by astute analysis of the impact of the issues involved.

This book will serve not only as an important record of events and developments in Irish education over the period but also as testimony to the hard work and struggles faced by voluntary secondary school managers in their attempts to improve the lot of their schools and to influence educational policy at national and local level. The work and dedication of those who manage our schools and those who represent their interests have sometimes been undervalued. This book goes a long way to helping redress that situation.

George O'Callaghan

GENERAL SECRETARY CMCSS/JMB
SECRETARIAT OF SECONDARY SCHOOLS

April 2000

INTRODUCTION

In many ways it was a quiet revolution - the intrusion of the state into second level education in the 1960s - but before long the system had become a political maelstrom, pushed forward by a line of young, energetic Ministers beginning with Dr Patrick Hillery. Before that decade the managerial organisations of voluntary secondary schools were clear in their vision of education. The schools under Protestant management provided quality education for a scattered population. In the diocesan colleges the aim was to prepare future candidates for the priesthood and to pursue high academic standards. The convent schools educated girls in the certain knowledge that most of them would be wives and mothers and some of them nuns. The Christian Brothers offered an academic programme to boys, some of whom would join the brotherhood and others would be prepared to earn their living - many of them joined the civil service and some worked in the Department of Education.

Only the secondary schools prepared pupils for the Leaving Certificate, so a vocational school education would not offer the possibility of access to university education. Secondary schools had a monopoly on academic education and coincidentally educated the majority of those who comprised the Association of Secondary Teachers Ireland (ASTI) and the other two teacher unions.

Free education disturbed the established order. But the change did not come about at the mere whim of Minister Donogh O'Malley. It was informed by wide-ranging research. The work of the survey team on Investment in Education had exposed the reality of educational provision, and the political leaders knew that economic prosperity was achievable if education and training could be provided for the nation. The future of the country was at stake.

Chapter One presents the historical context in which the managerial organisations developed. Some of these were founded in the nineteenth century when Ireland was not self-governing. The change-over to the Free State in 1922 did not unduly disturb the voluntary secondary schools. They retained their independence and the focus of their work which was essentially one of mission. But free education changed everything and state provision of comprehensive and community schools was an important part of that change.

Most of the voluntary secondary schools were owned by religious orders, so developments emanating from Rome would always affect their members. For that reason, Chapter One explores aspects of the Second Vatican Council. The way of living within religious community was challenged by Rome in the 1960s - even the language of the prayer of the Church gave way in 1965 when the Mass in the vernacular was introduced. The voluntary schools were church schools, therefore changes in the institutional church whether it was the Catholic Church or the Church of Ireland would have an impact on them.

The role of the Minister for Education developed a new status in the 1960s and, inevitably, the foundation of a stronger Department of Education was established. Some Ministers had a greater effect on the managerial organisations than others; these are considered as three principal players emerge.

The managers, the ASTI and the Department of Education formed a triangle, though not an equilateral one: the remaining chapters are therefore explorations of the interaction of those three players.

The longer established managerial organisations are examined in Chapter Two. The fact that the schools under Protestant management went through a process of rationalisation was significant. Meanwhile, the authority of the diocesan colleges and clerical schools was related to their association with the bishops - in a male-dominated church, that helped to give them a leadership role in relation to the nuns. The emergence of the nuns as a more independent managerial group is identified from the early 1960s.

In the 1950s the number of managerial organisations increased and this growth is the subject of Chapter Three. One of the reasons for the succession of groups was a lack of clarity about the role of management at this stage. Principals and managers in the convent schools were more concerned with the curriculum and were slower to become involved in management issues. Even in the late 1960s there was some ambivalence in their approach. By 1968 all the Catholic groups had formed one umbrella body although the individual organisations continued to function. They had also combined with the Protestant groups in another managerial body.

The Catholic Hierarchy was an important part of the new developments and, along with the major religious superiors, the bishops became more involved in the voluntary school sector. From 1973 both bishops and major superiors were urging the managerial organisations to rationalise, yet nobody was prepared to take responsibility for the decision. The wish for rationalisation was not realised until 1987.

The next three chapters explore a number of issues that pre-occupied the managerial bodies. In Chapter Four teacher salaries and posts of responsibility are examined. The context is the Ryan Tribunal, the teachers' industrial action, and the subsequent agreement between managers and union about the implementation of posts. Attempts by the managerial organisations to re-organise the system of posts of responsibility are given in detail, a recognition of the relevance of this issue for the voluntary schools over a period of approximately thirty years.

The uncertain economy features in Chapter Five because it is the context of the work of the managerial organisations until the late 1980s. The identification by the managers of 'productivity' in 1980 is important because it becomes their principal aim in subsequent negotiations with the ASTI. For almost five years during the 1990s the Joint

Managerial Body pursued the principle of productivity in relation to posts of responsibility. Eventually, the Department of Education and Science, the teachers and the managers agreed a new direction in middle management in voluntary secondary schools from 1998. The work of the JMB negotiators throughout the period is considered in this chapter.

The final Chapter is a reflection on adult education and lifelong learning and here the arbitrary distinction between adult education and in-service or professional development is avoided. Adult education is not something that voluntary secondary teachers may 'do' to other adults. Rather it is an aspect of lifelong learning for all concerned. The Murphy Report (1973) acknowledged the involvement of the churches in the education of adults. That meant in some instances the formation and training of religious personnel: it was part of adult education or lifelong learning. The partnership between the Christian Brothers and parents from 1970, the interest of the clerical headmasters in Aontas, and the growing commitment of the major religious superiors to adult education form part of this chapter.

From the beginning of the earliest managerial organisations to 2000 is a long time and there have been many changes during this period. The ASTI is now in a strong position to ensure a healthy tension with management and the Department of Education and Science, and all in the context of legislation. Ultimately, union and management have a common aim, the continuation of the voluntary school system. Many parents now have a greater choice of second level school than in the past and the basis of their choice will be affected by the commitment of ASTI, the CMCSS and the JMB to a vision of denominational education. An effective working relationship between union, management and the Department of Education and Science is part of the macro picture, while collaboration between principals, boards of management and staffs in creating learning communities remains an important aspect of lifelong learning.

The major superiors, as the Conference of Religious of Ireland, maintain a commitment to Catholic education. However, their role will focus on lifelong learning for all in the context of social justice. Alternative forms of involvement in education will be part of that role for CORI, while the participation of the bishops and CORI in the CMCSS will facilitate the necessary interaction between trustees and those who lead the management of the secondary schools.

The CMCSS and the JMB are in a leadership position to support the management of voluntary secondary schools in the years ahead. Having established a clear identity as leaders and managers they cannot ignore the challenge to initiate a debate on social policy and voluntary education.

Historical Perspective

CHAPTER 1

The 1960s began a period of dramatic changes in Irish education. In a sense the decade was a watershed between a past where a child's access to secondary schooling might be limited by ability, money and geographic location and a future where those handicaps no longer mattered. Parents and children were deeply affected by the changes in educational provision and so too were the existing secondary schools.

This chapter is a consideration of the historical realities that affected the evolution of secondary schools in Ireland. It introduces the managerial organisations associated with these privately owned and managed church institutions and offers some statistical data. The 1960s were critical years and are therefore examined in some detail. During that decade the various players on the stage of education emerged, but in order to appreciate the context in which they worked it will be necessary to look back to some developments before the 1960s. The metaphor of a symphony is apt for this chapter as the attention moves from one group of players in Ireland, to the Second Vatican Council, to individual Ministers for Education, to an analysis of how all combined to sustain denominational secondary schools.

Leabharlanna Fhine Gall

The Main Players
in Secondary Education

At the beginning of the 1960s most of the secondary schools in Ireland were small, with less than 150 pupils, and generally provided an academic education. They were for the most part single-sex schools, some of them with boarding facilities. From the foundation of the state in 1922, up to 1961, there had been a gradual expansion in the number of privately-owned secondary schools in the country (Coolahan, 1981:19-80). The greatest expansion occurred in the 1950s and by 1957 the religious owned 401 secondary schools.[1] A further 78 were either diocesan colleges or schools owned by male clerical orders. There were 42 schools under Protestant management and 38 owned by lay Catholics. These secondary schools were the result of private, not government, initiative, and in a certain sense were élitist.

> *Even in 1960 the pupils in secondary schools represented only about*
> *16 per cent of those enrolled in national schools.*
>
> (COOLAHAN, 1981:79)

There were three principal players in the drama that was secondary education: the managerial bodies individually and collectively, the Association of Secondary Teachers Ireland (ASTI) which represented the teachers, and the government Department of Education, established under the Ministers and Secretaries Act, June 1924 and responsible under the Minister for Education for:

> *Primary, secondary and university education, vocational and technical*
> *training, endowed schools, reformatories, and industrial schools, and*
> *all powers, duties and functions connected with the same.*
>
> (HYLAND AND MILNE, 1992:3-6)

In all there were seven managerial organisations involved in the provision of secondary schools in Ireland. The Schoolmasters' Association, later the Irish Schoolmasters' Association (ISA), was founded in 1869 and consisted of the headmasters of Irish Protestant secondary schools. The Association of Irish Headmistresses (AIH) was established in 1882 for heads of girls' schools under Protestant management. The Board of Education of the General Synod of the Church of Ireland was founded in 1875 but is not presented here as a distinct managerial organisation since it tended to work through the ISA and the AIH. In 1965 the General Synod appointed a Secondary Education Committee (SEC) representative of the Church of Ireland, the Presbyterian and Methodist Churches, and the Religious Society of Friends (the Quakers). The primary function of the SEC is the disbursement of grants. It also assists in formulating a common policy for the schools under Protestant management. It is the policy-making body, not the managerial organisation, for the schools of those four combined church groups. There is a separate group of Governors of Secondary Schools.

The Catholic Headmasters' Association (CHA), which was founded in 1878, initially represented the heads of the diocesan colleges which were under the direct control of the Catholic bishops in whose dioceses they were located. The Conference of Convent Secondary Schools (CCSS) was set up in 1929 to represent the religious orders of women who provided secondary schools. In practice the majority of the members of the CHA and the CCSS were principals and managers of schools. The owners of lay Catholic schools formed an association in 1952. It was called the Federation of Catholic Lay Secondary Schools (FCLS) and included principals and managers.

In 1964 the Catholic religious and lay managerial organisations and the Protestant groups came together as a Joint Managerial Body (JMB) to represent the shared interests of secondary education. By 1987 the JMB schools catered for sixty-two per cent of all post-primary students in the Republic of Ireland. It was the main decision-making and negotiating body for secondary school management. It was an ecumenical body and came into existence while the Second Vatican Council (Vatican II) was in progress. The JMB did not exist in 1960 but in less than thirty years it was a key organisation in voluntary education. Numerically strong, the Christian Brothers acted independently of the other orders of teaching brothers; they worked through their Education Committee. In 1965 they were co-founders with other brothers of the Teaching Brothers' Association (TBA) but their Education Committee remained in existence. Until that year some of the orders of teaching brothers had been members of the CHA but the Christian Brothers never joined.

During the 1960s the Catholic groups loosely combined as a Joint Committee of Catholic Managers, then as the Catholic Managerial Consultative Committee, later as the Catholic Managerial Committee from which came the Special Committee. From 1968 the title in use was the Council of Managers of Catholic Secondary Schools. From the late 1970s the unitary system of school management was gradually being replaced by a board. One result was that the Council of Managers gave way to the Council of Management of Catholic Secondary Schools (CMCSS) which developed regional and central representative structures. In 1987 these structures were clarified: the manager or chairman of a board along with the school principal were automatically members of the regional group. The combined regional groups formed the Association of Management of Catholic Secondary Schools (AMCSS). The AMCSS forms the managerial basis for the CMCSS, the governing body of the Secretariat of Secondary Schools. Throughout this book the term 'the managerial bodies', 'the managerial organisations', 'the managerial groups' and 'the managers' will be used to refer to the Catholic and Protestant managerial groups. Whenever a specific reference is to the JMB, the SEC, the CMCSS or any other it will be so stated.

If 'actions override rhetoric' (Handy, 1985: 2-5) then close examination of the role and function of these managerial organisations as they interrelated with each other, with the union, and with the Department, is warranted. Behind each of these three players there were other activists whose roles were sometimes obvious and front stage. At other times they were unseen by the public and heard only by their front players. There were occasions on which they did the acting unknown to their own lead players. For example, the Catholic bishops were powerful and often unseen participants and leaders. The two provincial superiors of the Christian Brothers were usually main players even before they joined any of the managerial organisations. One outcome of negotiations by the ASTI in the earlier part of the twentieth century was that the brothers had their own contract of employment. This made them different from other managers as employers. They also had their own managerial voice through the Christian Brothers' Education Committee from the early 1950s. Even though they collaborated in forming the TBA and were active in it, there were times when the Christian Brothers went their lone way regardless of the managerial bodies with whom they willingly associated. They had every right to do so. The autonomy of each religious order was fundamental. Such power and independence had ramifications for relationships between the managerial bodies, the Conference of Major Religious Superiors (CMRS), and the bishops. One might therefore anticipate tensions in the struggle to provide for Catholic education. Meanwhile, behind the Protestant managerial organisations was the SEC, always active on behalf of the schools under Protestant management.

The Conference of Major Religious Superiors (CMRS)

From 1960 the major superiors of the religious orders of men and of women formed the CMRS of Ireland. This was a significant development because for the first time religious superiors from different congregations were meeting together, though the openness with which they discussed common interests of leadership, spirituality and apostolic works took some time to flourish. Through the CMRS the owners or trustees of the religious schools had a structure, funded by all the orders, within which support and development became increasingly available. The interaction of the CMRS and the Catholic managerial bodies since the 1970s has contributed to the high level of close co-operation which exists today. There have, of course, been healthy tensions at times as individuals and organisations worked towards an understanding of trusteeship and management; the distinctiveness of the roles took time to identify and actualise. There were no models of effective practice because the genesis of involvement by the churches in secondary education was unique; so the process was one of trial and error, reflection, and further attempts to find appropriate ways of interaction between trustees and managers.

By 1997, despite depleted resources in religious orders, the Conference of Religious of Ireland (CORI), formerly the CMRS, had found a new confidence. Opportunities were being grasped to articulate a 'ministry of influence with regard to public policy' (CORI Education Commission, 1997:51), and not only in education. A proactive approach by the religious superiors recognised the need for:

> *A radically different approach - one which is discontinuous with the*
> *past and involves a quantum leap into the future, or, as some would*
> *have it, a paradigm shift.*
>
> (IBID., 1997:65)

Thus, at the beginning of the twenty-first century, the owners of the majority of the voluntary secondary schools have come a long way and much of the current work of CORI is in helping orders to develop alternative forms of trusteeship for Catholic schools (CORI, 1996; 1997; 1997a). The fundamental aim of the religious orders, which led them to provide secondary education from the nineteenth and through the twentieth centuries, remains unchanged but now their approach is quite different as various groups work in close collaboration to ensure the future provision of Catholic education.

> *There is no solid basis for believing that the continuation of Catholic*
> *education depends on the direct involvement of religious. The*
> *provision of Catholic schools is, in fact, a responsibility of the whole*
> *Catholic community. According to this kind of thinking, religious,*
> *having made a valuable contribution to establishing a network of*
> *Catholic schools, can move on to identifying and meeting urgent*
> *educational needs which cannot be met by others. Therefore, many*
> *religious believe, that, even if the decline in membership of*
> *congregations was not taking place, it would be appropriate to begin*
> *to devise forms of trusteeship based on partnerships between*
> *congregations and others.*
>
> (MCCORMACK AND ARCHER, 1997: 4)

By 1960 the CMRS represented orders that owned primary, secondary and special schools, hospitals and hospices for terminally ill patients, orphanages and homes for young offenders. For the first time, significantly, members of teaching orders were coming into contact with religious in works other than teaching and running schools. Initially the organisation worked in two separate and distinct groups, one for male religious and the other for nuns. It was in the area of education that the two groups began to collaborate and this proved to be an important factor when the Minister for Education proposed community schools in 1970. Members of the CMRS, especially the nuns, were involved in a wide variety of apostolic or Christian works and had access to houses of their orders in countries outside Ireland. From the mid-1950s the government began to look outside Ireland at economic models and at educational provision, and in the early 1960s the possibility of joining the EEC was under consideration.[2] At the same time some of the religious orders were founding communities in other countries and towards the end of the 1960s superiors were allowing some Irish members to go abroad for study purposes. The insularity of Irish education was thus affected and undermined. In a number of ways religious would contribute to educational developments in the 1970s and 1980s partly because they had been exposed to new thinking in curriculum in the UK and the United States, especially in the area of religious education in the secondary school system.

A number of orders like the Ursulines and the Loreto Sisters, the Christian Brothers and the Marist Brothers were concerned mainly with education in schools though the Christian Brothers provided orphanages and some special needs education for the deaf (Coldrey, 2000: 7-18). Priests like the Cistercians in Roscrea in County Tipperary and those in the diocesan colleges were often involved in parishes and retreat work, in addition to running schools. A small number of female religious orders like the Religious Sisters of Charity and the Daughters of Charity (the French Sisters) had more schools than the numbers of teaching sisters may have warranted. They had significant involvement in nursing, care of the sick and elderly, care of orphans, home visitation which was an early form of social work, and 'home school liaison'. The wide variety within the CMRS thus provided the organisation with the potential to become a powerful lobbying group in church and state.

The Second Vatican Council

On 25 January 1959, three months after his election, Pope John XXIII announced his intention to hold a diocesan synod or meeting of all bishops and an ecumenical council. The Second Vatican Council (Vatican II) was an event of universal significance to the Catholic Church and had an influence on the majority of the managerial organisations mentioned in this book. The synod took place in 1967 and was to be the first of a series. The council and the synods necessitated the absence of Irish bishops from the country for lengthy periods of time throughout the 1960s and encouraged greater collegiality among them as they were drawn into closer contact with each other. The purpose of the long-established practice of councils in the Catholic Church was to re-affirm and formalise statements of belief and doctrine and to consider matters related to ecclesiastical discipline. What was unusual about Vatican II was that it was to be an *ecumenical* council [3] to which all other Christian churches were invited. It was an effort to promote unity and heal the religious division of centuries. Part of its work was to update the Code of Canon Law, or the written law of the Catholic Church. This was an enormous and complex task because so much of it was out of date.[4]

Pope John XXIII defined the Council as an energetic reminder to the 'whole world' of the command to 'teach all nations' through example and service in various apostolic works or 'apostolates'. The first session was held on 11 October 1962 and was attended by thousands of cardinals, bishops and a solitary layman, representatives of the Protestant Churches and the Orthodox Church. There were no women either participating or observing. After the death of Pope John XXIII his successor Paul VI admitted eight women as non-voting observers to the final full session which took place from 14 September to 8 December 1965.[5]

Among the owners of most of the voluntary secondary schools in Ireland, Vatican II brought a sense of excitement, expectancy, anticipation, fear of impending change and some cynicism about its effects. The CCSS records make frequent reference to members who wondered what Vatican II would say about Catholic education. Speculation was fuelled by the ecumenical nature of the Council and after 20 May 1963 following the announcement by the Minister for Education of his intention to establish comprehensive schools, by questions regarding the future of denominational education in Ireland. Shifting sands is an image that may accurately be applied to the experience of the managerial bodies of the voluntary secondary schools at this point. Catholic members might have seen their traditionally unchanging church beginning to move but few could have suspected the scale of the change. In the event the state schools made less of an impact on the religious managers than anticipated and religious did not have long to await a statement on education from Vatican II.

The Declaration on Christian Education (*Gravissimum Educationis*) was promulgated on 28 October 1965 (Flannery, 1975: 725-37). The Church position was clearly enunciated in a vision of educational provision informed by values. At the same time there was a call for a review and evaluation of existing provision so as to bring it into line with 'the church in the modern world'. The 'inalienable right' of all children was to a Christian education which 'should be suitable for the particular destiny of the individuals, adapted to their ability, sex and national cultural traditions'. Ensuring that such an education was available was 'a very grave obligation' on the Catholic bishops. While the family was the 'principal school' the Catholic school was to be where

> *true education is directed towards the formation of the human person in*
> *view of his final end and the good of the society to which he belongs and*
> *in the duties of which he will, as an adult, have a share*
> (*GRAVISSIMUM EDUCATIONIS*, PAR.728).

Gravissimum Educationis placed a strong emphasis on the importance of teachers, of Catholic training colleges and of appropriate teacher education in the Catholic universities. In many ways Vatican II simply affirmed the teaching of Pope Pius XI in 1929 in *Divini Illius Magistri* (31 December 1929) on denominational education [6] and it was no accident that in 1959 John XXIII had used the thirtieth anniversary of that document to remind bishops and teachers of the importance of education (*Acta Apostolicae Sedis*, 1930: 49-86). The fact that this affable pope died before the Council had finished its work did not impede the process that he had begun. His successor was Cardinal Montini, described as his 'right hand man'. The new Pope Paul VI was crowned on 21 June 1963 and immediately announced his intention of proceeding with the Council on 14 September.

The flux of the 1960s and early 1970s are encapsulated in the work of Paul VI. The divisiveness that followed his encyclical on birth control, *Humanae Vitae*, was unfortunate, if inevitable. It also cloaked the more liberating achievements of this suffering pope who died in 1978. He brought Vatican II to a close and set up a synod of bishops to advise him on the implementation of conciliar decrees. He brought about one of the most significant changes, the Mass in the vernacular, to replace Latin, hitherto the universal language of the Catholic Church.[7] The significance of 'abandoning' Latin as some people perceived the change or of using the 'language of the community' as others saw it, is easily forgotten in the twenty-first century. The change was indeed significant but its symbolism as a harbinger of even greater change was how believers read it. Pope Paul VI's declaration on contraception was the focus of attention during his pontificate, while other declarations were given less coverage, e.g. the statement of acceptance, and not condemnation, of the Jews. There were his many social teachings on justice that would affect the future role of religious in Irish education, his decision on obligatory retirement of ministers at age seventy-five and ensuring that cardinals over eighty years of age would not vote at future papal elections.[8]

Gravissimum Educationis spoke authoritatively about the limits of state involvement in education and its obligation to facilitate parents in their choice of schools by supporting the churches. The Council's vision of a relationship between church and state that facilitated and supported denominational education was clear. There were other documents from Vatican II that were to affect the thinking of religious in education and to have a strong impact on the CCSS and the TBA, as their records indicate. One related to the 'up-to-date renewal' of religious life (*Perfectae Caritatis*, 1966) and queried the wisdom of some religious who by the time of Vatican II were opting out of mainstream education in schools in favour of less structured apostolic work. In fact this had not yet begun to happen in Ireland and it is impossible to claim that the idea sowed seeds of discontent or creativity among some religious in the managerial bodies. But the nuns in the CCSS took the document of renewal seriously, a fact that did impinge on educational developments throughout the late 1960s and the 1970s.

Finally, the consistent theme in several conciliar documents on the importance of 'the laity' in the life of the church, in education and in schools was a sign of future developments.[9] Vatican II expressed concern about the falling numbers of religious and priestly vocations in many parts of the world. But the emphasis on 'the laity' was not in that context. The vision was of a more inclusive idea of the church. Theologian Hans Küng in 1965 called it 'the people of God', a phrase that was to become a byword for the work of the Council. It was the 1970s before the managerial bodies faced the issue of decreasing religious personnel. Vatican II promoted a new image of the Catholic school. No longer could it function as an institution. The emphasis in future would be on the school as a community, and many of the issues of the future - teachers' pay, contract of employment, redundancy, promotional prospects for lay teachers and shared management - would provide opportunities to exercise greater inclusiveness in denominational education.

For major superiors and religious owners of schools in Ireland, Vatican II ushered in an uneasy decade in the 1960s. It also gave most of the Irish bishops their first opportunity to learn about the needs of the universal church. For some the experience highlighted the relativity of issues in Ireland when compared with the struggle for survival which was witnessed on a daily basis by bishops from other parts of the world.[10] Throughout the lengthy conferences in Rome they were faced with proposals and arguments for change. But they belonged to an Ireland where change was moving with all the rapidity that a confident government on the crest of economic prosperity could effect. Between the censuses of 1951 and 1961 emigration from Ireland was at its highest since the late nineteenth century (Cullen, 1960). After the worst year of 1957-1958 the exodus rapidly declined and there were implications for employment, for educational provision and inevitably for the Catholic bishops, for all the Churches, and for the managerial bodies.

Irish Education and Vatican II

In the 1960s there were twenty-six Catholic dioceses and thirty-six bishops in the whole of Ireland. Three times each year the bishops met in conference in St Patrick's College, Maynooth, the major seminary or training place for priests. Four archbishops formed a standing committee and one member of the hierarchy, usually whoever was archbishop in Armagh, was elected as president of their conference for a five-year renewable period (Keogh, 1994). Three Archbishops of Armagh, Cardinal William Conway[11] until 1977, Cardinal Tomás Ó Fiaich[12] and Dr Cahal Daly,[13] covered most of the last century from the 1960s and each was deeply interested in education. One immediate effect of Vatican II was that the bishops set up a number of Episcopal Commissions including one on primary and one on second level education. It was an acknowledgement of the complexity of educational change and of the bishops' intention to be involved. In 1966 they established the Episcopal Commission on Post-Primary Education. Twenty-six secondary schools were owned by bishops of various dioceses;

these were called diocesan colleges and will be referred to later. The existence of such schools meant that the bishops shared a vested interest in developments in secondary education that would be promoted by the newly established Episcopal Commission.

According to Canon Law a bishop has a remit to ensure the provision of Catholic education in his diocese.[14] The existence of the religious teaching orders enabled the bishops to fulfil this obligation without significant financial or personnel involvement.[15] Yet the Episcopal Commission would expect to be a voice for all Catholic secondary schools. Such a commission would not be entirely satisfactory for the religious orders. Some years later, in the early 1970s, the bishops set up the Education Planning Group (EPG) chaired by the Archbishop of Armagh, Cardinal William Conway, and including a small group of major superiors who were well informed about education. The EPG was, according to one of the principal members, a 'policy group that didn't exist and that had no official minutes of meetings'.[16] Its establishment was a silent admission that the bishops' Education Commission was not sufficient to respond to the pace of educational change.

Traditionally in the Irish church the religious orders of men and of women zealously and sometimes jealously guarded their autonomy as distinct foundations that did not belong to the local bishop.[17] This was as true of the nuns and brothers, none of whom was an ordained cleric or priest as it was of priests who were members of religious orders, e.g. the Benedictines in their school at Glenstal Abbey in Limerick or the Jesuits (Society of Jesus) who owned Belvedere College and Gonzaga College in Dublin, Clongowes Wood College in County Kildare, St Mary's College in Galway and two colleges in Limerick. The majority of the priests who became bishops had never been members of religious orders with vows or promises related to community living. Religious priests were not usually appointed bishops and when a male member of a religious order was appointed he might cease to be a member of his religious order. Such an example was Dr John Charles McQuaid the headmaster of Blackrock College in Dublin and a member of the Holy Ghost Order[18] who was named as Archbishop of Dublin in 1940. Likewise in 1984 when Dr Brendan Comiskey, a member of the Sacred Heart Fathers and general secretary of the CMRS, was appointed an auxiliary or assistant bishop of Dublin he ceased to be a member of his order and was no longer under the jurisdiction of his religious superiors; he then came under the authority of Archbishop Dermot Ryan of Dublin. This practice does not suggest antipathy or disharmony between the bishops and the religious orders. The relationship was always a delicate one, not peculiar to the Irish church but for the most part it worked because bishops and major superiors respected their different positions, contributions and roles. It was perhaps inevitable therefore that in 1966 the CMRS established its own Education Commission (CMRS Education Commission). From the early 1970s in particular its members became increasingly involved in the politics of education and they were also important in the work of the Catholic managerial bodies.

The very fact that both the bishops and the major religious superiors each established separate commissions to deal with second level education is indicative of the complexities of developments in the 1960s and the seriousness of their intention to be main players. Now in addition to the seven managerial organisations there were two commissions from the bishops and the major superiors, as well as the bishops as a group called the Catholic Hierarchy and the religious superiors in their body the CMRS. The Episcopal Commission met occasionally with the major superiors in what was known as the Joint Education Commissions. Add to these the Board of Education of the Church of Ireland, the Boards of Education of the Presbyterian Church, the Methodist Church and the Society of Friends, and the Christian Brothers when they acted as a separate body. In all there were sixteen groupings or organisations. Each one was interested in and committed to secondary education from a particular perspective and cultural heritage. Bearing in mind that the SEC is representative of the four churches, it could also be added, giving a total of seventeen representative groups involved in secondary education. An organisation of parents was notably absent though the Christian Brothers would initiate change in that area during the 1970s.

Such a scattering of vested interests could enrich a process of change depending on its effectiveness as a dynamic web-worm and net-working agent. By definition a web-worm is a gregarious caterpillar spinning a large web in which to sleep or to feed on enclosed foliage. Networking through effective communication and united action may be necessary for successful results in an organisation but so too is the form of web-worming that ensures the future of the particular body: research for planning and development and the setting of achievable targets are crucial. The records of the CCSS and the nuns in the CMRS in the 1960s and 1970s show that a process of renewal was moving rapidly in response to Vatican II, and the 'spiritual diet' of the particular web-worm that was the religious teaching orders began to open up new possibilities for involvement in education, including opting out of state systems. This had important consequences for the CCSS as an organisation that rationalised itself out of existence in the 1980s.

A study of developments in Irish education from the 1960s onwards evokes images of networking and web-worming which come and go in the context of ever shifting sands. Being paid-up members of any of the managerial bodies or of the CMRS, along with regular attendance at meetings where lines of action might even be agreed, did not necessarily guarantee a united front. Each major superior was autonomous in her or his order and what might suit a congregation with plenty of teaching religious might be impossible in an order where schools constituted one apostolic work among many. The call of Vatican II to religious to go back to their roots and the fundamental aim of founders and foundresses sharpened what might be seen as division or distinctness between orders. In terms of leadership in education the religious were clarifying their understanding of the vision of the particular order or congregation in relation to education. From that vision would proceed a more defined sense of mission and purpose for the second half of the twentieth century. For example, the Religious Sisters of Charity and the Mercy nuns began to voice their aim to 'work with the poor' in education and other apostolates. They also saw themselves as distinct from orders such as the Loreto, St Louis, Ursuline and Sacred Heart Sisters who generally provided schools for wealthy families. It was not that one group saw themselves as better than the other. It was a matter of clarifying the intention of the founder or foundress in the light of the teaching of Vatican II for religious to become more attuned to the needs of 'the church in the modern world'.[19]

What resulted therefore was that at the very time that the orders needed to present a united front, as for example when Donogh O'Malley as Minister for Education proposed the free education scheme in 1966, there was division partly because of the variation in the perspectives of religious orders. Had the owners run the schools as profit-making ventures the managerial organisations might have imposed sanctions or even dismissed recalcitrant or inactive partners. The secondary schools were not the brainchild of business tycoons, yet as organisations for learning they had to be managed in a businesslike way. The churches saw secondary education as one way of ensuring that their particular religious beliefs and practices lived on in future generations. That was part of the explanation for the opposition of the Catholic bishops to schools provided in the eighteenth and nineteenth centuries by other church groups. For the nuns, brothers and religious priests their work in education was an inherent aspect of their vocation to follow God in a particular religious order or congregation. Each order, whether Sacred Heart nuns or Presentation Brothers or Holy Ghost Fathers or any other in education, believed they had something unique to follow and promote in their schools. The Religious Sisters of Charity and the Mercy nuns may both have welcomed the children of poorer families into their schools but each order saw itself as quite distinct. It had to do with the intentions of the founders of the orders and what members in the twentieth century understood those plans to be.

This is not to intimate that the lay secondary schools that had not been founded by the churches were less idealistic, mere business ventures without vision and idealism. On 4 September 1939, the day after World War II was declared, Bernard Sheppard opened a small private Catholic school in 17 Clyde Road, Dublin, with ten pupils. He chose as patron St Conleth, a fifth century Irish saint and moulder of precious metals.[20] When Mr P. Cannon opened Sandymount High School in Sandymount, Dublin in 1947 what spurred him on was a vision of a co-educational Catholic school.[21] The founders of many of the small schools in the south and south-west of Ireland (O'Donoghue, 1990) were visionary men and women. They wanted to provide secondary education in areas that were not served by religious orders, as for example the Hamilton High School opened in 1940 in Bandon in County Cork whose founder Seán Hamilton was instrumental in setting up the FCLS. The heads of the secondary schools, whether members of religious orders or not, ran schools because they had a vision and a philosophy of education.

The Teacher Unions

Three teacher unions represented their members in primary, secondary and vocational or technical schools. The Irish National Teachers' Association (later Organisation) was founded in 1868 and remains the only union representing teachers in primary schools in Ireland north and south. As such it is the largest of the three unions. Two unions represent the teaching profession at second level. The Association of Secondary Teachers Ireland (ASTI), the larger of the two, was founded in 1909 for lay teachers in secondary schools. The Vocational Teachers' Association (VTA) emerged from a number of technical associations as a formal body in 1955 to represent teachers in the vocational or technical schools (Logan, 1999; Ó Buachalla, 1988:133). In 1973 it was renamed the Teachers' Union of Ireland (TUI).

The three unions in their individual and at times united struggle for improved teacher salaries interacted variously with the managerial bodies. However, the ASTI as the union for secondary teachers is more important to the managers than either of the other two unions. From the late 1960s membership of the ASTI was steadily increasing, with the first peak in 1984 when there were approximately 10,600 members. One year later numbers had jumped to 11,700. There was a slight downturn between 1985 and 1988 though membership that year was 11,400. As the number of pupils staying in schools up to the senior cycle continued to rise so too did membership of the ASTI: it grew between 1988 and 1997 to 15,520 (ASTI, 1998:13) and is now approximately 16,000 strong.[22]

Traditionally teachers who were members of religious orders of men or women were not admitted to any of the three unions. Since the late 1970s the INTO has welcomed religious teachers. The TUI admitted religious from the mid-1980s. The ASTI continues to eschew religious members. On various occasions between 1970 and 1984 the question of admitting religious to the union was on the agenda of annual general meetings or conventions. On one such occasion a motion to admit religious was defeated by a narrow margin. Since 1984 there has been no earnest effort either on the part of the union or of religious teachers to gain admission. In the late 1960s a number of religious women who were neither principals nor managers came together to discuss educational concerns. Their experience was that lay teachers had their union, principals and managers had their managerial organisation, but the teaching religious was, according to one founding member, 'voiceless'. By October 1971 an Association of Post-Primary Teachers of Ireland (APPTI) had been formed. The President of the Association was Reverend Thomas Flynn, a teacher in the Diocesan College at St Nathy's in Ballaghaderreen in County Roscommon.[23] APPTI was insistent that it was not a 'trade union' and the CMRS upheld that fact.

In some parts of the country APPTI flourished for a number of years. It provided opportunities to meet for religious teachers among the nuns, brothers and priests and other religious who worked in schools as ancillary staff. The Association organised seminars on topics that included Catholic education, Vatican II, pastoral and student support topics, the teaching of religion. Members were helped to cope with the sense of 'isolation' experienced by some religious who were in a minority in their school. As representatives of APPTI pointed out to Dominic Ó Laoghaire, Secretary at the Department of Education in the 1970s, they were 'the people teaching and working in the schools yet they were outside the process of decision making'. The Secretary was sympathetic and told them on 13 October 1971 that he regretted they were not party to discussions on the new community schools. As numbers of religious in schools dropped and as more opportunities for religious to attend in-service courses increased after Vatican II and throughout the 1970s, the need for APPTI dwindled. On 24 February 1978 they told the managerial organisations that APPTI would cease to exist from 1 March 1978. They never saw the Association as another ASTI or TUI but its existence for almost a decade fulfilled a need for numbers of religious in schools. To that extent the Catholic managerial bodies facilitated meetings and communication. When it no longer served a purpose the very religious who had been among the founders brought it to a dignified end. Did the managerial bodies learn from the decision of APPTI that an organisation may outlive its purpose?

The Association of Secondary Teachers Ireland (ASTI)

The early years of the ASTI were taken up with attempting to improve the work conditions of members. Since 1929 the union had representation on the standardising committees of the Department of Education and members were involved in some aspects of the public examinations including the marking of scripts. Peters and Waterman (1983:31) suggest that

> *the basic philosophy of an organisation has far more to do with*
> *its achievements than do technological or economic resources.*

By the time the ASTI celebrated its golden jubilee in 1959 it had gained significant achievements in professional salaries, conditions, status and security for its members (Coolahan, 1984). Until the late 1970s membership of each of the three teacher unions was open only to lay teachers. Religious teachers were debarred because they were religious. The ASTI saw them as part of the management of the secondary schools and therefore distinct from 'lay teachers'.

From the 1960s onwards the growth in union membership was remarkable (Coolahan, 1984). In 1964 there were 2,242 recognised lay secondary teachers. The membership of the ASTI grew rapidly for two reasons: increased enrolments following on the free education scheme after 1966 and a decrease in numbers of religious.[24] Between 1968 and 1974 union membership grew from 2,242 to 5,809.[25] By 1982 there were 9,700 ASTI members in the voluntary secondary schools.[26] By contrast, in 1970 religious in receipt of incremental salaries accounted for approximately one-third of the total teaching force. But in 1974 they constituted little more than one quarter or 2,740 and by 1982 the total number of nuns, brothers and priests in the schools was 2,000. By 1993 when ASTI membership was more than 15,000 there were only 1,000 religious in the secondary schools.[27] A basic management skill in relation to trade unions is that of seeking co-operation in order to accomplish the task of the organisation or workplace (Rees, 1990: 260-90). The free education scheme meant that religious schools were increasingly dependent on the ASTI and this marked the beginning of a shift in the balance of power between religious and lay in the secondary schools. By the 1970s it was clear that lay principals would have to be appointed in a number of religious-owned schools. That issue brought the ASTI into closer contact with the CMRS. So too did the question of boards of management and thus the need for a harmonious working relationship between union, managerial bodies and the CMRS became more important. The 'lay teacher' had moved centre stage.

The 'Lay Teacher'

The term 'lay teacher' is peculiar to Irish education and is in itself a statement about the history of the secondary teaching profession. The adjective 'lay' means non-clerical or not ordained into the clergy. It can also mean not professionally qualified (*Oxford Dictionary*). From its foundation in 1897 the Association of Intermediate and University Teachers in Ireland, which included intermediate or secondary teachers, had worked for some system of registration to enhance the profession.[28] At the time the CHA feared that standards in teaching would drop because the profession was not highly regarded (*Irish Educational Review*, 1907: 2). The ASTI had been preoccupied with problems of pay and conditions of work,[29] but nevertheless a secondary Teachers' Registration Council had been established in 1918 and teachers who had the required degree and teaching qualification became 'recognised'. So by the 1960s a recognised lay or religious teacher was also a qualified one. Thus 'lay' did not mean unqualified for the task of teaching. The term merely marked the distinction between priests, religious brothers and sisters or 'nuns',[30] and those teachers who were graduates, usually with a diploma in education, but who were not priests or brothers or nuns; they were people, men and women, who were teachers by profession. The lay teacher did not belong to the trustees of the schools. Most of the secondary schools were owned by religious orders whose dominance remained unchallenged until the late 1960s. For the most part a lay teacher could not become a principal in a secondary school, and as long as secondary teaching was overly associated with religious and those religious teachers were numerous it would be difficult for the ASTI to encourage its members to such a position.

Some events in the earlier decades of the union are important in understanding inherited attitudes evident in the 1950s and early 1960s. For example, the union was only ten years old in 1919 when a committee[31] reported on the uninviting nature of the secondary teaching profession (Coolahan, 1981). The abortive attempt to introduce the Education (Ireland) Bill, 1919, following reports from two committees on Irish education, succeeded in burying temporarily the dissatisfaction of the teachers with their pay and conditions of service. The almost vehement public reaction to the first and only reading of the bill brought into the open the polarisation of school managers and lay teachers. The authorities of Catholic secondary schools (McElligott, 1966; 1981) were clear on their role in education: it was to ensure 'full Catholic control of the choice of teachers, retention of teachers, and removal of teachers'.[32] In a published letter the leader of the Catholic bishops, Cardinal Logue of Armagh, opposed the bill of 1919 on the grounds that it would interfere with the rights of parents to educate their children (*Irish Ecclesiastical Record*, 1919:252-53). Ó Buachalla points out that the unsuccessful bill also delayed the appointment of a Minister for Education until August 1921 by which time a compromise had been reached between state and church (Titley, 1983; Ó Buachalla, 1988).[33] From then on the policy of successive governments was one of 'hands off' schools where aspects of ownership were concerned.

One might also see the controversy surrounding the bill as setting the atmosphere for relations between the owners and managers of secondary schools and the teacher unions. Due to the determination of the ASTI a salary scheme was worked out with the government in 1924, school managers were obliged to employ a quota of recognised teachers on contract in 1925, and a pension scheme was set up in 1929. By 1940 conditions of work improved when the union succeeded in negotiating a contract of employment and a limited appeal procedure in a threatened case of dismissal; the CHA and Archbishop McQuaid had played a leading role in the contract development. In so far as the graduate with a teaching diploma could become 'recognised' by the Registration Council it might be said that status had improved too. However, the lay teacher in the secondary school was not on a level with the religious teacher. The lay teacher was hired and paid to teach whereas the unpaid religious was working in the equivalent of 'the family business', because the order or congregation to which the religious belonged was the owner. Vatican II promoted a new role for the 'laity' in the Catholic Church though it would be slow in developing in Ireland.

In summary, therefore, the lay teachers in Catholic schools at the beginning of the twentieth century were only beginning to be organised into the ASTI. By the 1960s their position regarding salary and contract had improved though it was not fully satisfactory. By the 1970s lay teachers were numerically strong and religious managers depended on them in the secondary schools. By the end of the 1980s, 66 of the 460 religious- and clerical-owned schools had lay principals. Initially slow, the pace of appointing lay principals has increased rapidly to date. The fact that they are nearly all members of the ASTI points to a new direction for principals and union. It also helps to focus on the work of leadership and management by the CMCSS and the JMB, and on leadership and administration by the principals.

The School System

In his study of Irish schooling from 1922 to 1960 Akenson (1975: 9) claims that 'the way in which people school their children is culturally diagnostic'. The school system in Ireland had its main roots in the late eighteenth and nineteenth centuries. In 1831 under British rule the bishops of the Catholic and Presbyterian churches had begun to assert themselves in relation to primary education, and ultimately they got what they wanted, a denominational system funded to an increasing extent by government. There were national or primary schools where attendance was compulsory from age six to fourteen. A system of payment by results was abandoned in 1900 and gradually the method of paying teachers improved. The initial arrangement whereby the local clergyman or parish priest administered payment on behalf of the state eventually gave way in the 1950s to a quarterly and then a monthly cheque paid directly to the teacher. Payment based on capitation or enrolments rather than a personal salary was preferred by many religious orders with primary schools.[34]

By the twentieth century with the setting up of the Irish Free State in 1922 and the Department of Education in 1924, the churches were long experienced in knowing what they wanted in a national school system. The new state did not attempt to interfere with the denominational nature of the primary schools or with the powers of the local manager, usually a priest or clergyman. A 'primary certificate examination' was introduced initially on a voluntary basis but from 1943 this was obligatory for all pupils in the sixth class. Even when rules for national schools were drawn up by the Department of Education they made no mention of denomination, leaving the local manager of the school responsible. When those rules were revised in 1965 the denominational aspect remained intact (O'Connor, 1986: 107). The reality was that the primary schools were in effect denominational; until the late 1970s there was no 'non-denominational' state primary school in Ireland and the establishment of a multi-denominational primary school was not any easier to achieve (Alvey, 1991; Cooke, 1997). By the 1960s, therefore, the churches were long accustomed to non-interference by the state. The Department of Education was involved in the curriculum and in the recognition and inspection of teachers but even the most senior civil servants would not presume to interfere with the teaching of religion which technically was 'permitted' for thirty minutes daily in national schools.

The bishops had little worry about the secondary system apart from their own diocesan colleges whose main aim was to provide future candidates for the priesthood. Since the early nineteenth century there were schools run by religious and attended by children whose parents could afford them. The term 'voluntary secondary school' applies to them because they were established by voluntary or private organisations. That was also true of the many lay secondary schools. The Intermediate Education (Ireland) Act, passed in August 1878, became the political mechanism by which funds could be made available for intermediate education. An unpaid board of seven commissioners of mixed denominations would

> institute and administer a system of public examinations in secular subjects
> on the results of which fees would be paid to school managers who
> fulfilled the board's regulations, while prizes, exhibitions and certificates
> would be made available to successful pupils.
>
> (COOLAHAN, 1981: 62)

'Intermediate' meant that the Act dealt with the period of education after basic primary or elementary instruction and before higher or third level education (McElligott, 1981; 1966: 59). Denominational schools therefore were in receipt of state funding though it was never adequate and trustees had to find the money for buildings and maintenance. Religious education as a subject could not be examined under the Act. This became an issue for the churches and the JMB in the late 1970s and early 1980s though by the end of the twentieth century it had been resolved. The work of the board was to control the examinations. Inevitably, the curriculum in terms of what was taught and how it was taught in schools was affected: there was a certain pressure to achieve. In short, the denominational schools received state aid through a system of payment by results. It also meant that a uniform curriculum developed in the schools because texts were set for the three levels of examinations. The result was the growth of public confidence in the examination system under the Intermediate Education (Ireland) Act of 1878. Under the Intermediate Education (Ireland) Act of 1914 a Registration Council was established. It was given power to regulate for a register of 'intermediate' teachers and to provide for the first Teachers' Salaries Grant under certain conditions which school managers had to meet.

Before Free Education

The Irish Free State, established on 1 February 1922, introduced another method of funding the secondary schools. It was a combination of capitation grants for 'recognised' secondary schools and incremental salaries for 'recognised' teachers. Capitation was conditional on pupils following an approved course of study for 130 attendances in the year. School managers were required to hold entrance examinations at the beginning of each school year in Irish, arithmetic and another subject (usually English). The new system did not interfere with the denominational nature of the secondary schools but it did affect curriculum.[35] Under the Intermediate Education (Amendment) Act in June 1924 the Free State put an end to payment by results.

Enthusiasm for the Irish language was strong in the new state and in 1924 the rules and programme provided for three categories of secondary schools. A Grade A school was one where all subjects apart from English were taught through the medium of Irish. An additional grant related to the capitation payment was made to 'A schools'.[36] A school where some subjects were taught through Irish and where the Irish language was informally used became a Grade B school. The Grade C school was one where Irish was taught as a school subject. Any student who answered the public examination papers through Irish was awarded ten per cent bonus marks.

On 31 March 1925 the new government dissolved the Intermediate Education Commissioners and transferred the education funding to the Minister for Finance. In 1925 a system of incremental salary payments by the state for teachers was established. The Registration Council that included representatives of the managerial bodies would decide the requirements for recognition as secondary teachers. The school managers who would employ the teachers would pay a 'basic' salary. This two-party involvement of state and school in the secondary teacher's salary became an important issue during the 1960s and again in the 1980s and 1990s when it was finally resolved.

As regards the public examination system under the Free State, it was decided to establish two certificate examinations. Thus the Intermediate and the Leaving Certificate Examinations were established on 1 August 1924. A pupil could sit the Intermediate after three years in a secondary school and the Leaving Certificate after a further two years. A small number of scholarships were made available to candidates on the results of the Intermediate Certificate Examination. The Department of Education published the examination results and the name of the school, though not the names of the candidates. The voluntary secondary school system therefore had a monopoly on the public examinations and thereby on access to the universities. Many of the secondary school fees were small but not within the reach of all families. The Report of the Survey Team *Investment in Education* showed that in 1961 there were 332 secondary schools with fees under £15 a year. Ninety-five schools sought between £15 and £25 while seventy-five, mostly in Dublin, charged more than £25 (1966: 310).

In 1963 there were 557 secondary schools for 84,912 pupils (*Tuarascáil*, 1964:19). Orders like the Presentation Sisters, the Religious Sisters of Charity and the Mercy nuns opened schools for girls where fees were either very low or waived. As the Catholic Church asserted its position, bishops invited or welcomed religious orders to their dioceses to open secondary schools. This enabled a bishop to meet the requirements of Canon Law that there would be provision for Catholic education in his diocese. A number of orders provided 'secondary tops' which were continuation classes in primary schools; there were eighty-one of these in 1959.[37] Within the religious secondary schools there were differences. Orders like the Ursulines, the Sacred Heart, the Dominican, the Loreto, St Louis, the Jesuits, the Benedictines attracted parents who could afford higher fees. Families with less disposable income might be able to pay the lower fees charged by the Presentation, Mercy, Holy Faith, Brigidine, Marist sisters and the De La Salle, Marist and Christian Brothers. It is possible that most religious schools lowered or waived fees in individual cases of need. Yet the reality was that parents selected in or out in accordance with their ability to pay school fees and accompanying overheads. Sometimes parents did not send children to secondary school because they were not 'bright enough' (O'Meara, 1958:16), though the decision may also have been that fees and allied expenses were beyond what was possible for the families. The diocesan colleges were voluntary secondary schools, mainly boarding and fee-charging.

The Vocational Schools

From 1899 a state system of technical schools had developed and in 1930 these were the nucleus of the new vocational schools. In 1957 there were 260 vocational schools in the state with 23,000 day pupils and 58,000 evening students (*Tuarascáil*, 1957). An important responsibility under the Vocational Education Act (1930) was for 'continuation education' which was intended to provide for pupils aged fourteen to sixteen after their primary education. Vocational schools were also involved in various forms of adult education.[38]

The vocational system was organised through thirty-eight local and representative Vocational Education Committees (VECs). In 1930 two aspects of vocational education concerned the bishops:[39] that the work of the schools might not be confined to 'technical' education, and that they would be co-educational (Logan, 1999:62-92; McCarthy, 1988:74-5; O'Connor, 1986:27). On both issues the Catholic bishops got the assurance of the Minister for Education that the new system would not infringe on what was being done in primary and secondary schools. Moreover, in 1942 the position of religion in vocational education was enshrined in *Memorandum V.40*, a document of the Department of Education to school authorities. This clarification in writing became important in the 1970s and 1980s. From 1947 the vocational schools prepared their pupils for a Day Vocational (Group) Certificate at the end of two years which usually meant that candidates were approximately sixteen years of age.

A Divisive System

The reality was a divisive system of second level education. Intelligent children continued from primary or national school into a secondary school if their parents could afford the fees, or the particular religious order waived them and the children passed the entrance examination. Often the less academic and those who could not pay fees attended the vocational school or 'the tech' as it was called colloquially. An eminent educationalist, bemoaning the divisiveness of the system, described the latter as 'dead end kids' who were forced to attend 'educational dustbins' (O'Meara, 1958: 16). One other significant factor in accessibility to second level education was the uneven geographic spread of both secondary and vocational schools. Regular transport was not available and even if it had been not all families could afford it. In 1960 a visiting professor had the courage or the temerity to ask the CCSS at their annual general meeting whether or not schools contributed positively to Irish society. He found that Irish teachers were more 'efficient' than their colleagues in the United States but that there was

> a degree of class difference and an acceptance of the doctrine of class
> difference so shocking that I am impelled to refer to it in unjustifiably
> strong terms and call it a caste system [which is] in particular in the
> secondary schools [and] completely incompatible with Christian life.[40]

According to the professor of education at University College Dublin at that time, 'the anomalous position [was] that with the exception of the Preparatory Colleges every secondary school in the country is privately owned'. He challenged the complacency of the system in a series of articles:

> What is basically wrong with education in this country is that enough
> people, teachers and parents alike, will not sit down and ask themselves
> some simple questions about our schools, questions beginning with
> why? and what? and how? and try to work out the answers. It is
> easier to drift than to steer, but you are more likely to end up circling
> lazily around in some backwater. And there are a lot of stagnant
> backwaters in Ireland.[41]

But change was coming, though not from the nuns, as the lecturer advocated, nor from the teachers and parents as the professor of education had urged. It came from a

Minister for Education who was not a teacher and the context was the emerging economic prosperity in Ireland. The gloom of the economy was past by the late 1950s and a 'golden age' was heralded (Ó Gráda, 1997:25-9). Investment in education was to become central. Economists now agree that such investment is a fundamental principle of development.

> *Education investment in human capital is at least as important*
> *as investment in physical capital for a country's long-run success.*
> *Thus, one way in which government policy can enhance the*
> *standard of living is to provide good schools and encourage the*
> *population to take advantage of them.*
> (MANKIW, 1998:528)

A recognition of the relevance of education to economic growth was growing in the 1950s with the work of economists like Solow and Schultz (1961:1-17). Successive Ministers for Education promoted and supported such theories and one report in particular, *Investment in Education* (1966), energised development in Ireland and led to a positive interface between research and policy.

Ministers for Education

Twenty-five Ministers for Education have served the Irish education system from 1957 to date (March 2000). Sixteen of these belonged to the largest party in government, Fianna Fáil. The longest appointment, Dr Patrick Hillery, lasted nearly six years, the briefest, Taoiseach Charles J. Haughey was Acting Minister for less than three weeks. That is not to suggest a correlation between length of service and impact of work accomplished. Ministers come and ministers go but the officials in the various departments of the civil or public service go on regardless. Any Minister for Education is dependent on the senior official in the Department who was called the Secretary and now the Secretary General. It was fortuitous that during the 1950s and 1960s two experienced and prudent men filled that post in turn: Torloch Ó Raifeartaigh from 1956 to 1968 and Seán MacGearailt until 1973. These two and one other official who would succeed MacGearailt from 1973 to 1975, Seán O'Connor, formed a strong team which was very active throughout a period of great change in the system (O'Connor, 1986). Between 1956 and 1989 six men held the office of Secretary at the Department of Education. On average the period of office lasted five years but Dr Ó Raifeartaigh was there for twelve years working with six ministers. Dominic Ó Laoghaire was Secretary from 17 April 1975 until 11 November 1979 and Liam Lane followed him until 9 October 1984. Next was Declan Brennan who came from the Department of Finance on 17 October 1984 and left the office on 13 July 1989. By that time the managerial organisations had been restructured and the CMCSS and JMB were the leaders of the voluntary school sector.[42]

Because of the politically structured relationship between minister and department the Secretary's role is limited (Harris, 1989:7-26). The powers of the Minister for Education derive from the Ministers and Secretaries Act, 1924 and from the Intermediate Examination Acts 1878 and 1924 which enable 'rules and programmes for secondary schools' to be issued. The Education Act, 1998 gives further powers to the Secretary General. Under the Ministers and Secretaries Act, 1924, the civil service that developed was centralist and directly controlled by the relevant ministers.[43] This prevailed although ministers in the 1980s began to select personal advisers who sometimes succeeded in mediating the influence of established civil servants. Loyalty to the minister in office may well cloak the creativity and perspicacity of a Secretary. Since the 1950s all but two of the secretaries were already long experienced in the Department of Education before taking up the senior post. Perhaps inevitably, familiarity with one department only and with the power of vested interest groups in education stifles creativity, but these men could not be faulted for loyalty.

> *Ils étaient imprégnés de la culture du ministère de l'éducation.*
> *Ainsi, ils ne pouvaient que garantir une certaine protection des*
> *traditions et du rôle de l'Eglise Catholique.*[44]

From the end of the 1960s, as the managerial bodies began to interact more with the Department of Education, the person who held the post of Secretary was important to the JMB.

Up to the 1950s education was not seen as a very high profile ministry. The Department itself was an inward-looking, Irish speaking unit in the centre of Dublin. Its civil servants had few opportunities for looking outward to other educational systems. But by the end of the 1960s the dismal profile of the ministry and the Department had changed. Economic development, government programmes and a number of young and energetic ministers helped to put education centre stage. The future growth of Ireland demanded a better education system and one that would be more accessible to a greater number of families.

Likewise, up to the 1950s, the role of the Minister for Education tended to be that of a benign onlooker who occasionally attended to the system to ensure that it continued. General Richard Mulcahy who held office from 1948 to 1951 and again between 1954 and 1957 described the role of the Minister for Education as that of an 'oil can man' in 'dungarees'. His job was simple maintenance and non-interference with vested interests (Whyte, 1971; OECD, 1991:39; Ó Buachalla, 1996:10-20). But three Ministers for Education in particular helped to change that notion, and as a result a different image of the ministry emerged by 1968.

The dominance of the churches as providers of secondary education was challenged by the entry of the state into a number of areas. These were: the comprehensive schools in 1963, the introduction of capital grants for voluntary schools in 1964, the provision of a free education scheme which succeeded in bringing most of the voluntary schools into its network by September 1967, and the announcement of community schools in 1970. The long-term effects of the free education scheme were the most significant for families and for the country. The glory of that announcement belonged to the fifth in the long line of ministers already mentioned, Mr Donogh O'Malley. The readiness for change had been created by Dr Patrick J. Hillery[45] a thirty-six year old medical doctor who was appointed Minister for Education on 24 June 1959 and remained in post until 21 April 1965. Dr Hillery's diagnostic skills were acute when applied to the education system. He viewed with concern[46] the symptoms of a divisive and selective secondary school system, ill-equipped to provide an educated and skilled population that would meet the demands of the government's plans for economic development. He knew that the managerial bodies were badly organised and lacked a representative spokesman. He was aware that the bishops had never taken a centre-stage role in the voluntary secondary schools apart from their twenty-six diocesan colleges. He was conscious that the technical or vocational system was inadequately distributed to cater for rural communities and that many families could not afford an education. In short, a national policy on second level education was needed and that entailed getting factual information about the system and devising some means for extending provision.

We now know that Dr Hillery also realised the intractable problems he would meet if he attempted to change the existing pattern of educational provision. Confrontation with the churches, the managerial bodies and the VECs would be inevitable if the Minister, in an effort to cater for the national needs, tried to develop the voluntary secondary schools in tandem with the vocational schools. But Dr Hillery also recognised problems within his own Department of Education where the results of a low status ministry were evident in poor morale and a degree of unhelpful cynicism about the role and function of the state in education.[47] Within three years of taking up office he had a structure in place that effectively enabled a policy of strategic planning to develop, and not just at second level. His successors in office would benefit from his work.

In 1960 Dr Hillery appointed a Commission on Higher Education to examine all aspects of third level education. Although the report was not presented until 1967 when Dr Hillery was no longer in office, it represented the beginning of a process of considerable change (Coolahan, 1981). Lemass had promised that his party would bring about an

> overhaul of the nation's educational system, including the considerable
> extension and improvement of facilities for secondary, vocational and
> higher education.[48]

It was important that young people should have greater access to university and third level education, particularly if the number of pupils increased at second level, and it was with this in mind that the Minister appointed such a commission.

Recognising the central position of the Irish language in the curriculum, Dr Hillery introduced an oral Irish examination in the Leaving Certificate Examination in 1960 though it was in fact the previous Minister, Jack Lynch, the first of the new breed of young, energetic ministers, who had made the decision.[49] Since 1926 there had been six Preparatory Colleges where native Irish speakers and others could be educated and sit the state examinations within four years; many of these students automatically entered the teacher training colleges. In 1961 Dr Hillery closed five of these colleges. He did so decisively, 'with one sweep of his pen,' according to an inspector then in the Department of Education.[50] In fact the ministerial decision was made in 1961; it took a number of years for the colleges to close and some of them continued as Grade A schools from 1967.

The ability to make a decision was a feature of Dr Hillery's leadership style. He was fortunate in that his term coincided with that of Seán Lemass (Horgan, 1997; *RTÉ*, 25 March 2000)[51] as leader of the government at a time of emerging prosperity in Ireland. Change was in the air, not least because the New Year 1961 was the planned launching of Radio Telefís Éireann, the national television network. The Education and Social Research Institute (ESRI) was established that same year, 'a symbol and a symptom of change in Irish life' (Farrell, 1986:143-51). More significantly for the Minister for Education, one of his officials in 1961 attended the OECD Washington Policy Conference on *Economic Growth and Investment in Education* (OECD, 1962; O'Connor, 1986; Ó Buachalla, 1996; O'Donoghue, 1996), and the Conference resulted in an undertaking by each participating country to appoint a team to study its education system. Thus, in 1962, Dr Hillery appointed a team of two economists, a statistician, an inspector and a civil servant as secretary to carry out the *Investment in Education* survey in Ireland. In the early months of that year two tasks were being pursued quite separately, one of them secretively in the Department of Education. The team to carry out the survey was being selected. At the same time and unknown to the men who constituted that team, Dr Hillery appointed the 'Duggan Committee' named after its civil servant chairman to advise the Minister on future educational developments (Hyland and Milne, 1992:556-60; Bonel-Elliott, 1994).

Dr Hillery pressurised the Duggan Committee for results,[52] and an interim report was presented to him on 8 December 1962.[53] The Department of Education knew nothing of this privately commissioned report, and neither did the bishops or the managerial bodies.[54] The report recommended free secondary education for children aged twelve to fifteen and the raising of the school leaving age from fourteen. These recommendations were put forward as a national necessity for both social and economic reasons. An extension of the vocational education system and a general development of local control in education were also recommended.

Clearly, the Duggan Committee saw the need for restructuring in the education system, but the churches might have been pleased had they known about one aspect of the report: the most important subject on the curriculum was religion; Irish was relegated to second place. On the need for change and the ending of a divisive secondary school system [55] paragraph four of the report was adamant:

> We can no longer allow traditional patterns to unduly influence
> educational planning and provision in a world where a social,
> political, economic, scientific and technical revolution has taken
> place and is still proceeding.

Comprehensive Schools

One year later, on 20 May 1963, Dr Hillery announced his intention of making second level education more accessible by establishing a number of comprehensive schools. These would be well placed geographically so as to cater for areas that were isolated and badly served (Barber, 1989:6; Barry, 1989:133-62; O'Sullivan, 1989:241-43).[56] A uniform curriculum and terminal examination would open up possibilities for those who had formerly chosen vocational education. The Minister wanted to ensure a safe passage into the secondary system of these new schools: he had previously assured Cardinal Conway and the bishops that the existing voluntary school system was not to be endangered (Cooney, 1999:358; 385). The comprehensive system never mushroomed: three schools were announced for 1966; by 1977 there were only fifteen in existence. And strangely a sixteenth was opened ten years later, in 1987, in the constituency of the then Minister for Education, Gemma Hussey: it was a 'Protestant comprehensive' for Wicklow town, an area of the country where there were many Church of Ireland families. It appeared odd because it was widely believed in the 1980s that the era of comprehensive schools was past. Closer examination however suggests that the 1987 school was an example of good church/state relations: the state recognising and supporting the needs of a minority church. The Church of Ireland authorities asserted a preference for a type of school with which they were familiar and satisfied, having carefully considered the community school option in the 1970s and finding it unacceptable. They could not afford to provide complete funding for their own denominational school in Wicklow: they needed state support: a 'Protestant comprehensive' was the only logical possibility and the state accommodated.

But although the comprehensive school system never flourished, two significant developments were achieved by Minister Hillery's initiative. A number of areas hitherto badly served were provided with schools. More significantly in terms of policy and the Department of Education, the Minister had succeeded in bringing the state into second level education in a unique way in Ireland and had made the churches his allies, not his opponents, thus forging a new, positive, church/state relationship. On 28 May 1963 Dr Hillery assured the Dáil that the 'relevant religious authority' would be represented in the new schools. The management structure facilitated five comprehensives under Protestant management once the three pilot schools at Cootehill, Shannon and Carraroe had been established. The Jesuits who helped to create Crescent Comprehensive in Limerick in 1971 succeeded in having three representatives of the order on the management board and this in turn proved a headline for the Protestant comprehensives (O'Flaherty, 1992:118-39). It was a new departure for the managerial bodies who now witnessed an easy alliance between church and state.

But there was another aspect to it. The Minister had carefully prepared the way, to obviate any opposition from the Catholic bishops. He had not consulted the managerial bodies, arguably the most powerful education lobby in terms of size. Neither had he consulted the teacher unions, as they publicly complained (*The Irish Times*, 21 May 1963). Leadership necessitates keeping the end or aim constantly in view. Dr Hillery did that by dealing directly with the bishops and by ignoring the managerial organisations that would almost certainly have delayed the implementation of his decision. In an interview with Dr Hillery in 1991 one researcher quotes him as admitting that his approach was designed to 'outrun the inertia of the government and the bishops' in Irish education in the 1960s.[57] The records of the CCSS and the CHA are interesting. The CHA complained of not receiving 'a copy of the Minister's press statement' of 20 May 1963 when he announced the comprehensive school plan. The CCSS appear not to have complained at the time. The nuns later referred to the fact that Dr Hillery had ignored them at a significant time of 'state intrusion into secondary education'.[58] The ASTI too played a part, by securing guaranteed posts for their members where comprehensives resulted from assimilations of existing schools. Thus managers and union were being drawn into new ways of managing schools as a result of strategic planning by the catalytic role of Dr Hillery and his Department. It is important to emphasise that development. The small number of comprehensive schools means that they are often overlooked in the story of Irish second level education. But they marked the first entry by the state into the school system at second level. The process was a learning opportunity for the churches, the managerial bodies, and the ASTI.

Thus, 1963, the year in which President John F. Kennedy visited Ireland, was also the year in which the Irish education system was opened up to new possibilities as a result of an effective liaison between the churches and the state. The comprehensive schools marked a new beginning in secondary education and significantly affected the social and educational reality in Ireland. Parents would not have to pay fees and these schools would be co-educational and provide a curriculum inclusive of academic and technical subjects, leading to the public examinations. Young people could continue on from them to university or third level education, whereas attendance at vocational schools precluded entry to the universities up to the late 1960s.

A unitary management structure was never considered for the new schools. They would be managed by boards of three or five persons who were representative of the bishop, the Minister for Education and the VEC. Inclusion of the relevant church authority obviated criticism from the denominational managerial bodies. The presence of the VEC, usually through the Chief Executive Officer (CEO), brought the vocational sector and local structures on side.[59] The Minister's involvement through a nominee was a testament to state partnership in an unprecedented manner. It was a policy of inclusiveness that had been adapted from comprehensive models in northern European countries. The board had all the responsibilities of the single manager to which the Irish secondary system was accustomed: the hiring and firing of teachers, intake of pupils, discipline and general running of the school, allocation of the state funding, maintenance of the plant. There was no teacher representative on the boards, a fact that proved a learning point for the ASTI a decade later. When the question of boards of management was raised by the CMRS in the 1970s the union was quick to insist on a role for their members.[60]

Dr Hillery had made a successful beginning for state involvement in post-primary education. Subsequent Ministers for Education in the 1960s and early 1970s built on that 'platform' (Starratt, 1996). Dr Hillery had buried the image of the minister as an uninvolved politician in Irish education and had put the ministry in the driving seat of 'fundamental policy'. On 28 May 1963 he made it clear in the Dáil that there could be 'no question of (his) submitting to outside bodies' of bishops, managers or teachers.[61] However, when there was opposition to the management model, as for example happened with the Jesuits in Limerick in 1971 who sought greater representation than the one nominee suggested, the Minister for Education Pádraig Faulkner happily agreed to three nominees. This proved useful to the Church of Ireland bishops who consulted the Jesuits: thus each of the five boards of the Protestant comprehensives subsequently had three nominees of the bishop.[62]

As Minister, Dr Hillery had laid a foundation for changes in Irish education that no previous holder of the office had even envisaged. Shifting the traditional relationship between church and state through the introduction of comprehensive schooling was a cross-road that tends to shade his other achievements. He had sensed the need for strategic planning as shown by his appointment of the Duggan Committee and the team to survey the country's investment in education. He had taken little notice of the *Report of the Council of Education on the Curriculum of the Secondary School* (1962), seeing it as irrelevant to his plans and the needs of the country.[63] The records of the CHA and the CCSS indicate that these organisations also gave very little attention to discussing the *Report*. It is possible that the religious managers and principals were satisfied that Dr Hillery was well aware of the importance of religion on the curriculum of their private schools (*Council of Education*, 1962:246-48). One smaller decision that would become a thorn in the side of the managerial bodies was the creation in 1963 of a scheme of grants of £150 for any science graduates who would be employed by schools. It gave rise to 'head hunting' of these teachers by some members of the managerial organisations.

Free Education

The return of the eighteenth Dáil and a continuation of the Fianna Fáil Party in government on 21 April 1965 brought with it a promise of equality of educational opportunity for all families. Dr Hillery's successor as Minister for Education was George Colley, a solicitor and politician who was appreciated for his affable manner. Appointed to Education on 21 April 1965 he remained in office until 13 July 1966. A new edition of the rules for national schools was published during his time as Minister and he received the *Investment in Education* report in December 1965. His tenure of office may have been short but it contributed to unease amongst the managerial bodies despite his friendly and inclusive approach and his ambition to establish a consultative council to provide a forum for all the education groups to work together. Thus he highlighted a major weakness, the absence of a forum for discussion on education. The various managerial organisations had not developed the level of trust necessary to enable them to speak with a united voice. The complexity of the human activity of management was very evident at this stage.

It is in the Dáil speech on the budget estimates for education that the Minister for Education may indicate or reveal aspects of policy. George Colley was the first Minister to list his educational priorities as he presented his estimates. In his introduction of the education estimate for 1965-1966 on 16 June 1965, he promised a significant increase in the number of local authority scholarships that provided free secondary education for the recipients. In order of priority he wanted free transport, collaboration between vocational and secondary schools, the establishment of an advisory council from the existing groups and the rationalisation of smaller schools (O'Connor, 1986:96).[64] The Local Authorities (Education Scholarships Amendment) Act, 1961 had almost doubled the number of awards from 2,668. The Minister planned to double that number again.

The CCSS welcomed the additional scholarships.[65] The limitation was that children had to prove their ability to gain these awards and many 'failed', so the potential for continuing a divisive system of second level education was actually fuelled by the scholarship scheme. Colley was very interested in education and believed that the state needed to be more proactive in the light of what had been revealed by *Investment in Education* (O'Sullivan, 1989:219-74). For him the provision of post-primary education for all was desirable (O'Connor, 1986:109).

Two other proposed changes by the Minister had potential. One was the introduction from September 1966 of a programme of civics education for pupils in the first three years of second level schooling, a development with which the managerial bodies complied perhaps too readily and without adequate preparation of programmes and teachers. The other was the establishment of a Development Branch within the Department of Education which was to ensure that the research work begun by the *Investment in Education* team would continue. The Minister's plan to make comprehensive schools widely available had a logical basis. The report from the survey team on *Investment in Education* [66] highlighted the inequality of educational provision and participation throughout the country, but only slightly more than fifty per cent of the 13 to 17 age cohort were in full-time education. Resources of teachers and facilities were not efficiently utilised. The relationship between the curriculum and the needs of a growing economy was out of balance. If an increasing number of pupils was to be served in the existing secondary and vocational schools the three-year Intermediate Certificate programme would need to be provided in all schools and not restricted to the secondary system. This provision would also contribute to lessening the distinction between the academic type of education in the secondary schools and the vocational or technical curriculum in the VEC schools; as it stood, the existing curriculum in vocational schools was too narrow (Owens, 1989:163-90).

George Colley suggested a programme of rationalisation of schools. He envisaged that 'equality of educational opportunity' would result from collaboration between 'the 600 secondary schools and 300 vocational schools in the country'.[67] But he failed to appreciate the complexities of relations between the various interests when he wrote to the school authorities asking that they meet in local groups in order to plan for rationalisation of provision. This time the managerial bodies could not complain of being ignored by a minister. Indeed the contact was valued for its courtesy and recognition, as the records of the CCSS and the CHA show. Randles (1975:202) is correct in stating that the local meetings of principals and managers from the vocational and secondary schools after January 1966 distracted attention from the findings of the *Investment in Education* team. However, the records of the CHA and the CCSS show that some of the survey team's findings were discussed. No difficulty was found with the survey recording that 388 of the 608 secondary schools had less than 150 pupils. What bothered the managerial bodies was the suggestion that viability of school provision should be related to school size: a viable junior school should have an enrolment of 150 pupils; a senior school would need between 320 and 400 on roll. Closure or rationalisation of 'non-viable' schools and the provision of transport to viable education centres was interpreted as a threat to the future of denominational education. There was criticism by the managers that the Department viewed pupils as 'mere statistics'. Dr Hillery, the Minister who had initiated the *Investment in Education* survey, had never intended that the work of the team would be one of policy. Almost thirty years later he still insisted that their task was a fact finding one[68] and indeed that is clear from the introduction to the report:

> This Report, therefore, is essentially a technical study
> of trends in Irish education and of the use of human
> and material resources in that system.
> (*INVESTMENT IN EDUCATION*, 1965:XXIII)

With the benefit of hindsight and the knowledge now of his appointment of the Duggan Committee referred to earlier, Dr Hillery's insistence on the non-policy role of the *Investment in Education* recorded by the team would serve to inform policy. In 1966 George Colley was already in trouble with the Catholic Bishop Michael Browne of Galway over the policy of rationalising small primary schools (O'Connor, 1986:124-28). These school closures were frequently discussed at CCSS meetings and in the context of the Minister 'striking next' at the small voluntary secondary schools.[69] There were some religious who saw signs of opposition to *Catholic* education in the Department of Education's rationalising. So the meetings of local principals and managers encouraged by Mr Colley became a boomerang to strike his earlier positive profile among the managerial bodies. When the ASTI complained about their exclusion from the local meetings the Minister agreed that they could attend. But that did not save him from their suspicion and criticism (*Official Programme*, 1967:66-8).

Seán O'Connor as a retired assistant secretary from the Department of Education ranked Mr Colley as 'a major figure in Irish education' (1986:135) and an important Minister. So too does Ó Buachalla (1996:11-12). Historically, Mr Colley is sandwiched between two ministers who made very public changes in the education system and whose contributions therefore tend to enmesh whatever he may have done. So what did he do? In the 1960s there was little awareness that change is a process. Perhaps Mr Colley's contribution was to heighten that process of change, quietly begun by Dr Hillery's introduction of comprehensive education. Dr Hillery's contribution was to be the catalyst. Mr Colley continued to nudge the system towards change and to heighten the Minister's profile as a key political leader whose sense of purpose would have ramifications for the country. Like his two previous colleagues, Jack Lynch and Dr Hillery, he ensured that education was part of the *political* agenda, thus raising the status of the ministerial office and perhaps the morale of the Department of Education.

These Ministers gave evidence of leadership and a sense of purposefulness in their approaches to education. They also revealed that there was a cadre of civil servants in the Department of Education who were skilled in dealing with the intricacies of church/state relations. These officials had accomplished important research work on *Investment in Education* and had the ability to inform the work of ministers by solid information about Irish educational provision. Quiet ripples of change often precede noisy streams. In this case some noise resulted from George Colley's attempts to bring school authorities together at local level to initiate a form of rationalisation of school provision. In July 1966 there was a re-shuffle of cabinet ministers within the government and Colley's successor as Minister for Education was Donogh O'Malley. Mr O'Malley's term in office was to bring waves of change in the Irish education system and the managerial organisations were to be swept along in the aftermath. The voluntary secondary school system would never be the same again.

Donogh O'Malley, Minister for Education

Donogh O'Malley was appointed Minister on 13 July 1966 and died unexpectedly on 10 March 1968. He was less than two years in office. Experienced in the Office of Public Works and as Minister for Health, O'Malley was criticised by opposition deputies for hasty action and praised by supporters for his courage.[70] According to one civil servant he had a reputation as a 'hell raiser' (O'Connor, 1986:139). What was meant by this remark was that O'Malley's determination to accomplish a task would often rouse emotional reactions even in those who worked with him. Seán O'Connor at that time was responsible for secondary schools and the Development Branch in the Department of Education. The year 1966 was an eventful one. The Catholic bishops were lately returned from the final full session of the Second Vatican Council in Rome. Alert to the forthcoming *Report of the Commission on Higher Education* (1967) they decided that lay students would be admitted to the university at St Patrick's College, Maynooth. At second level came the announcement of free post-primary education. As Minister, Mr O'Malley took it upon himself to make that historic announcement to journalists on 10 September 1966 (Atkinson, 1969:172-76; Akenson, 1975).

The implications for the managerial bodies were enormous. What the Minister envisaged was free education for all pupils, free transport, a free book scheme with certain limitations, and the equalising of educational opportunity. The fact that the Common Intermediate Certificate programme commenced in the schools in September 1966 added to the sense of impending change.[71] Minister O'Malley's civil servants had prepared options (O'Connor, 1986) which he ignored, probably wisely according to Seán O'Connor in a radio review years later (*RTÉ*, 1988). The speed of the announcement and of all that followed gave little opportunity to the managerial bodies to examine the implications of free education. Only scant attention was given at one CCSS meeting in November 1966 to the alternative proposal from Fine Gael, the opposition party in government (Downey, 1998:67).[72] Their suggestion was for government to give sufficient funding to the schools to enable the managers to offer free education. It was a model that would not have directly involved the state. The O'Malley scheme envisaged a more obvious role for the State (*The Irish Times*, 10 September 1966). The CCSS records show that the nuns were much more concerned with the statistical data that many of them had received from the Development Branch of the Department of Education.[73] Clearly the work begun by the *Investment in Education* team was being pursued. The Development Branch was promoting the concept of 'post-primary centres' where collaboration between schools was the aim. The CCSS saw this as further encroachment by the state into privately-owned and denominational schools. One headmaster in the TBA at that time interpreted the Department's strategy as that of threatening the managers with something worse than free education in the hope that they would agree to the O'Malley scheme.

In the event O'Malley's approach engulfed most of the managers who by September 1967 opened their schools to provide 'free' education. Donogh O'Malley had succeeded in pushing an agenda of equality of educational opportunity for all as never before in the history of the country. But he could not have delivered the innovation without the collaboration of the majority of the managers of existing privately-owned schools; that some managers were reluctant in their conformity mattered little. How willingly did the managerial bodies embrace the scheme? What effect did it have on the voluntary schools? Within seven years, by 1974, there was a twenty-five per cent increase in school enrolments (Coolahan, 1984:272). The free scheme not only gave every child the chance to access post-primary education, it also ensured the continuation of voluntary secondary schools.

Before the year had ended there were other changes. The Primary Certificate Examination would be discontinued from 1968.[74] In theory the holding of 'entrance examinations' which had been laid down in 1925 to ensure that a child was fit to secure a place in a secondary school would cease.[75] There would be a new approach to the teaching of the Irish language in primary schools.[76] The allocation of marks in the revised Intermediate Certificate Examination[77] would be replaced by grades from A to E and to No Grade and all candidates would receive a certificate of attainment from 1969. At third level a number of regional technical colleges were to be provided and Mr O'Malley proposed that a merger should take place between Trinity College and University College Dublin. An Educational Research Centre (1972) would be established on the grounds of the male primary teacher training college in Drumcondra, Dublin to promote research throughout the system. The changes, like the Minister's energy, seemed endless and about to have an impact on every aspect of education. In December 1967 he appointed Professor Louden Ryan, an economist at Trinity College Dublin, to chair a tribunal on teachers' salaries, the findings of which would have a profound effect on the voluntary secondary schools, as will emerge. The following year 1968 brought more innovations. The Development Branch introduced a publication, *Oideas*, which has lasted to date and has proven a useful conduit for educational thinking. Grants were introduced on a means-tested basis for third level education and a Higher Education Authority was established (Clancy, 1989:99-132).[78]

Between January and March 1967 the Department of Education tried without success to initiate a revision of the Leaving Certificate programme. Although ten working groups including representatives of teachers and managers were set up, O'Malley had agreed that the findings would not be published until the various associations had seen them (Kirkpatrick, 1967:6-7; O'Connor, 1986:189). The idea of reviewing the Leaving Certificate was a logical move after the announcement of free post-primary education for all. Secondary schools would be accepting pupils some of whom up to September 1967 would have been considered academically unable and more suited to technical education in the vocational schools. It was a case of too much change too quickly for the CCSS and the other managerial bodies did not co-operate either. A further attempt was made by the Department in 1969 and again in 1972 (Kirkpatrick, 1967; O'Connor, 1986:144-45). The Department wanted Leaving Certificate students to select from five groupings of subjects. This would have facilitated planning in the curriculum of commercial and technical subjects, but although the ASTI at one stage gave 'a qualified acceptance' to the proposal nothing happened because the managerial bodies held back.

In line with the interpretation by the *Investment in Education* survey team of a viable size of school, the Department of Education proposed common enrolment in areas where two or three small schools existed. The hope was that school principals would accept joint responsibility for enrolment. Sharing of facilities and teachers would follow. Predictably the teacher unions were concerned, the ASTI fearing a strengthening of the VTA membership.[79] This attempt by the Department of Education and by Donogh O'Malley as Minister to soften the traditional distinction between secondary and vocational schools and to create viable education centres was abortive, though it would return to be a source of annoyance and distraction to the ASTI in the seventies.[80]

The year 1967 had been one of pressure and hard work for the managers who had to decide whether or not to participate in the free education scheme. For them it was a walk into the dark because they saw how inadequately the Minister and his Department were prepared for the scheme. But the year had been one of pressure and hard work for the Department of Education too. The school transport scheme to accompany free education had to be established. Responsibility for this was delegated to the VECs, the only local structure available to the Department. The necessary local meetings between VECs and principals and managers of schools were sources of considerable anguish to many of the voluntary school managers as the records of the CHA, the CCSS and the TBA show. Fear of the unfamiliar and the complexity of the human activity necessary for effective management, leadership and administration was very evident in the creation of the school transport scheme in the1960s. Yet between April 1967 and February 1968 the scheme was designed and in operation though at enormous financial cost to the country (Randles, 1975:268-71). In spite of its problematic start the school transport service stood the test of time. By the late 1970s the JMB initiated a review of the system as it affected the voluntary schools. Issues were then pursued with the Department in the 1980s where transport frequently featured on the agenda of the Dublin and the Cork Advisory Councils on Post-Primary Education.

To some of the managers it seemed that as a result of the transport scheme the VECs were becoming more powerful and involved in secondary schools. A religious member of the CHA at that time said that he had 'never even met a CEO' until September 1968 when he had to attend meetings regarding 'the school buses' which were 'destroying' the secondary schools in the area. The cause of the 'destruction' was the route followed by the buses. The secondary schools were last, thus causing pupils to be late for morning classes on occasion. It was no consolation to the headmaster or the teachers that the bus did the evening or home journeys in reverse order. The ability of human beings to become accustomed to a development is well illustrated in most instances of initial frustration regarding the free education school transport scheme. Donogh O'Malley had been fearless in pursuing educational change. In so far as the majority of the secondary schools became part of his scheme of free post-primary education, it could be said that the managers made an impact at times in spite of themselves.

The announcement of free education was to have a significant effect on the nature and provision of the education offered by the voluntary secondary schools. If Minister O'Malley was a 'hell raiser' perhaps it was because he brought to the surface the inequality of the second level system and did something about it. His vision and sense of purpose tended to ignore the obstacles to achievement. That it worked in relation to the introduction of free education may have as much to say about the eventual willingness of the managerial bodies to collaborate. Mr O'Malley followed three Fianna Fáil colleagues in the ministry, each of whom had contributed to the readiness and the process of change. But he displayed fearlessness in pursuing the vision of free education. He died in the same year as Martin Luther King, the black activist from South Carolina. King's statement on the eve of his assassination might be a fitting epitaph for Donogh O'Malley, though not all the secondary managers would have rejoiced in the words: 'I'm not fearing any man,' said the charismatic black leader. The

O'Malley scheme came when it did because the Minister had no fear, no fear that cabinet would let him down, no fear that his civil servants would not remain loyal no matter what they might think of the timing, and no fear of the managers of the private schools. None of the ministers who came after Mr O'Malley would have the opportunity to impinge on the system and on the managerial bodies in quite as powerful a manner.

Brian Lenihan succeeded Donogh O'Malley on 27 March 1968 and had the unenviable task of facing a teacher strike on pay-related issues in 1969 [81] and a leak in the public examination papers that led to students having to repeat some papers in June 1969. There is one publication that emerged during Mr Lenihan's time that is worth mentioning because it is both a summary of achievements and a first bridge to parents in education. The publication was delivered to every household in Ireland and it was the first time that parents and the general public were given formal information about the education system. *Ár nDaltaí Uile*, or All Our Pupils, was a booklet that described primary, post-primary and third level educational opportunities (Downey, 1998:59-64). It bore witness to a newly confident Minister and Department and to the entry of the state more obviously into educational provision. At the time it was published a pilot stage of a new curriculum was in progress in a number of primary schools.[82] In many ways the publication is a summary of the far-reaching changes begun by Dr Hillery, hastened by George Colley and radically brought to fruition by Donogh O'Malley. However, there were indicators about developments in the senior cycle, or final two years, in post-primary schools that did not come to pass. It is interesting that the publication was discussed at some length at a meeting of the CCSS in June 1969 and the implications for senior cycle curriculum were welcomed.

Pádraig Faulkner who replaced Brian Lenihan on 2 July 1969 as Minister for Education continued in office until 14 March 1973. During his time the compulsory school-leaving age was raised to fifteen years, in 1972.[83] He was in office when community schools were proposed (Coolahan, 1984:341-44). In 1970 he introduced the Vocational Education (Amendment) Act, 1930 that enabled the VECs to work with other educational partners and to contribute to the cost of managing shared resources (McGinley and Donoghue, 1999:235-76; *The Irish Times*, 12 November 1970). It was in short a conjoint management bill that enabled them to participate in the boards of management of community schools. Management boards for primary schools were encouraged by the Department of Education Circular 73/74 of July 1974; they were introduced into all primary schools in 1975 and all Catholic primary schools came under the patronage of the bishops.[84]

By the early 1980s a new model of school under the VEC emerged. The concept of the community college was the outcome of a VEC request to Archbishop Dermot Ryan of Dublin in 1979. The VECs in the Dublin archdiocese were concerned at the growth of new community schools and the emergence of such schools from the amalgamation of vocational and small secondary schools. The resultant 'Dublin model' deed under section 21 of the Vocational Education Act, 1930 and the (Amendment) Act, 1970 for a community college has proven successful in the Archdiocese and has been replicated in other dioceses. While the community colleges were similar to the community schools in offering a wide academic and technical curriculum, the structure of the board of management was different. The 'Dublin model' was formally agreed in 1980 when John Wilson, a former classics teacher from the Jesuit private school, Gonzaga College in Dublin, was Minister for Education. Less than twenty years after the introduction of the comprehensive schools by Dr Hillery in 1963 the variety in the models of provision of second level schools was greater, the state was more involved in the provision and management of schools, and the churches had found appropriate ways of being involved. The Minister for Education was directly represented on the board of the comprehensive schools while the VECs had direct representation on the boards of the community schools and community colleges.

The 1970s bore the fruit of the vision of four successive Ministers for Education, beginning with Jack Lynch in 1957. Five regional technical colleges opened and the National Institute of Higher Education (NIHE) at Limerick was established. It would become the first university since the founding of the Free State in 1922, when legislation in 1989 gave it university status as the University of Limerick and its sister NIHE in Dublin became Dublin City University (Clancy, 1989:99-132). The Catholic Hierarchy lifted the ban on Catholics attending Trinity College Dublin in 1970. A different education system prevailed on many levels from what had existed in 1960. By 1970 it was clear that the common Intermediate Certificate programme for twelve to fifteen year olds did not suit all ability levels. The percentage of those who passed the examination dropped from 87 per cent in 1968 to 74.6 per cent in 1969 which was the first year of the common Intermediate Certificate Examination in secondary, vocational and comprehensive schools.[85] In 1970 the percentage dropped further to 73.5 and the Minister for Education, Pádraig Faulkner, appointed a committee to be chaired by Paul Andrews SJ, headmaster of Gonzaga College in Dublin and a member of the CHA. The task of the committee was to

> consider the form and function of the Intermediate Certificate
> examination and to advise on new types of public examinations.

In 1972 the National Council for Educational Awards (NCEA) was established to provide a means of recognition and accreditation for third level programmes outside the universities. The NCEA was given statutory basis in 1979 (Harris, 1989:13-14). To Minister Faulkner belongs the credit for the setting up of the first Teacher Centres in 1971 that were to be managed by primary and second level teachers as centres of research, in-service and support for the profession.[86]

During the Fine Gael and Labour Party coalition government from 1973 to 1977, 'the government with all the talents' (RTÉ, 7 March 1998), the Minister for Education was

Mr Richard Burke, a former secondary teacher at Blackrock College, a private fee-charging boys' secondary school in Dublin. He became Minister on 14 March 1973 and remained until 1 December 1976.[87] Peter Barry succeeded him and was Minister until 4 July 1977. At that stage the coalition government was replaced by a Fianna Fáil single party government again.

Boards and Management

A number of issues that concerned the managerial bodies emerged in the 1970s. These will be explored in subsequent chapters so it will suffice to mention them here. *A Report of the Committee on Adult Education* (1973) gave impetus to the managerial bodies to become involved in adult programmes. The transition year from junior to senior cycle in schools was introduced by Minister Burke. Other proposals were not so successful: the regionalising of educational structures and establishing a Teachers' Council or professional body at national level in 1974. Mr Burke was more successful in getting agreement from the bishops and religious to establish boards of management in the national schools, in 1975. Sharing management was related to increased funding by the state. Many of the religious orders involved in the managerial bodies, and the Protestant churches, ran primary schools. The CCSS, the TBA and the Christian Brothers had frequent discussions about the primary school boards. It is reasonable to suggest, therefore, that the primary boards helped to create some readiness for change among the managerial bodies. They also formalised the patronage of the bishops with all Catholic primary schools. Richard Burke suggested to the ASTI that the secondary schools also should establish boards with teacher and parent representatives (ASTI *Annual Convention*, 1975). At the time he was aware from friends among the Christian Brothers that the religious orders were looking at models of management of Catholic schools in other countries.

Mr Burke's time in office coincided with developments of the Draft Deed of Trust for community schools. However, what most affected the managerial bodies was his attempt to rationalise provision at the senior level in schools where enrolments were small. Only some schools lost their senior classes, for example Dominican College and Caritas College in Ballyfermot in Dublin. But the CCSS records in particular abound with the anxiety and disagreement of the nuns about a policy of rationalising educational resources. The CHA and TBA had few discussions and no disagreement. They had no intention of ceasing to provide for senior classes. So, for example, the De La Salle Brothers in Ballyfermot refused to end their senior cycle and succeeded in maintaining it.

The Dominican nuns and the Daughters of Charity, who owned the other two schools almost side by side with De La Salle College, spent many subsequent years seeking to restore their senior cycles. They eventually succeeded but they had been a salutary case study regularly cited at CCSS meetings up to the 1980s.

The ICE Report 1975

There was far less discussion by any of the managerial bodies of the work of the committee on the form and function of the Intermediate Certificate Examination or their Final Report (ICE Report) in 1975, although the chairman was a CHA head-master. Appointed by Mr Faulkner, the committee presented its Report to Minister Richard Burke in 1974 and it was published a year later. This radical report proposed alternative forms of assessment to the Intermediate Certificate Examination which had been shown to be failing numbers of pupils. Nothing came of the report for several reasons. The proposals for an alternative assessment system were radical and the government did not accept them. Moreover, the first oil crisis in 1973 and the second in 1979 brought the beginning of a period of economic recession and education was to suffer for some time. It was fifteen years before serious consideration was given to the development of a unified examination system to replace the Day Vocational Certificate and the Intermediate Certificate Examinations. Yet a single examination system should have followed the introduction of free education. It was 1989 before the Junior Certificate Examination became the terminal assessment of compulsory education, thus ending a dual system of assessment that was often discriminatory.

Challenging Times

In the internal CMRS Focus for Action Report (1974) the importance of the continual provision of Catholic schools was recognised. There was also a definite challenge

> to many religious to work in other kinds of schools where their witness
> is of great importance. New fields of work awake a natural response of
> new enthusiasm (1974:15).

Community schools were not mentioned by name, though members of the working party have assured the author that these were discussed. Four other emphases in the report are related to the managerial bodies. There was concern about the quality of 'the teaching of religion' in secondary schools and the importance of developing a policy of home school liaison as part of the 'school mission'. Schools needed 'to provide education for living' programmes that would be 'beyond mere sex education' and the report noted the gap in such programmes 'for boys in particular'. There was a strongly worded recommendation that

> CMRS should encourage and collaborate in the drafting of growth and
> development programmes for schools, and Catholic schools must ensure
> that they are fully implemented.

What is of interest in the recommendations is the collaboration envisaged between the CMRS and the managerial bodies in developing curricula. Furthermore, there was anxiety that 'schools are far too productivity oriented' and that

> the accent, in partly misplaced responses to the parents' requirements,
> falls heavily on examinations and scholastic achievement.

There was a plea for involving lay teachers in 'Christian education', an admission that the necessary trust 'has been far too slow in coming' because 'attitudes of paternalism and over-protectiveness have generated corresponding reactions of immaturity among laity' (Focus for Action, 1974:54). However, this did not mark the beginning of appointing lay principals in the religious schools. The process of involving lay teachers in the running of the schools was to be slow as will emerge in later chapters in this book. In the light of the *Report from the Commission on Adult Education* (1973) there was a recommendation that

> religious should make the education of parents and other
> adults in personal growth and in religious and moral
> development a central concern in their activities.

The chairman of the Focus for Action working party was the provincial of the Marist Brothers who had already agreed to work with the Holy Faith Sisters in one of the first two community schools in Dublin, the Tallaght school. It was possible therefore for the working party to familiarise themselves with the 'community' education aspect of the new schools. It was this fact as much as the challenge of Vatican II to develop 'adult catechesis' that encouraged them to suggest detailed approaches to adult education in the secondary schools. There was a definite focus on the use of school premises by the local community and on the role of the CMRS in supporting religious personnel whose work would be in adult rather than child education.[88] The Christian Brothers were already involved in adult education through their Parents' Federation since 1970.

When the Irish Hierarchy attended a synod of bishops in Rome in 1970 they had been urged by eighty-year-old Pope Paul VI to implement the teachings of the Second Vatican Council in their dioceses, 'in a world that was rapidly changing'. There was a sense in the early 1970s of battening down the hatches in the face of stormy times to come in education in Ireland. Cahal Daly as Bishop of Ardagh and Clonmacnoise thought it necessary in view of the Minister for Education's announcement about the new community schools to remind people that the Catholic Church had made 'a considerable investment in education' both in personnel and finance (*The Irish Times*, 22 April 1971). This was a direct reference to church involvement in primary schools and, through the religious orders, in secondary schools. But a changing Ireland was becoming more confident in the1970s. Relaxation of the censorship laws (1967) a few years earlier had galvanised the CCSS [89] though not the other managerial bodies into a campaign for 'moral literature'. In 1972 an amendment to *Bunreacht na hÉireann*, 1937 (the *Constitution*) lowered the voting age to eighteen years (Casey 1982:267-80). The nuns, the CHA and the TBA considered this to be too young because there were students aged eighteen in their schools. The fifth amendment to the *Constitution* modified *Article 44* by deleting 'the special position' of the Roman Catholic Church and those who did not understand the fine points of the law perceived an element of threat in the change. The CCSS urged their members to be 'vigilant' about religious and moral 'formation' in their schools. A referendum in 1972 had resulted in an over-whelming majority vote in favour of joining the EEC to which Ireland had failed to gain admission in 1961. Membership for Ireland, along with the UK and Denmark, became effective from January 1973 with an almost immediate impact on agriculture and a feeling among some of the managerial bodies that Ireland would be adversely affected by European influences. In 1974 *McGee vs. the Attorney General* (Whyte, 1980; Casey, 1982; Hogan, 1987:47-96) a woman successfully challenged the Supreme Court to protect her right as a married person to the availability of contraceptives (Whyte, 1980:403-06). One eminent legal scholar declared this to be 'a watershed in church/state relations' (Hogan, 1987:69).

Change was in the air and bishops, major religious superiors and managerial bodies were becoming alert to its effect on public attitudes to church/state relations. The northern bishops among the Hierarchy were concerned about political violence since the 1950s and matters came to a head there on 'Bloody Sunday', 30 January 1972. But the setting up of the secretive EPG already mentioned was an indication of the concern of bishops about the future involvement of the church in schools. From the report of their own Research and Development Commission (1974) in Maynooth there was evidence of disaffection from religious practice among young people in the eighteen to twenty-five year group, and many of these would be the future parents. The FIRE Report had shown that the Catholic Hierarchy could no longer presume on nuns, brothers and priests to continue providing Catholic education because their numbers were decreasing. Strategic planning was needed. The bishops went to Mulrany in County Mayo in March 1974 where they prepared the Mulrany Report (1974) which was a blueprint for future developments in the Catholic Church in Ireland. So, two confidential reports were prepared in 1974, one by the CMRS, Focus for Action, and one by the bishops from Mulrany. There is much that is similar in the two documents and both include concerns and signposts for the future development of Catholic schools and adult education.

Perhaps the most practical outcome of the Mulrany Report and the Focus for Action Report was the series of seminars held around the country for religious including teachers, principals and managers. Although these seminars were organised by the CMRS some of them were presented in the context of spiritual retreats for religious. A number of bishops participated, including Bishop Cahal Daly who would become Archbishop of Armagh in 1990, and the seminars were presented by members of the committee who had prepared the Focus for Action Report. The report encouraged religious to 'focus' in planning future works by reviewing current commitments and taking note of personnel and other resources available. While such an approach may appear logical at the beginning of the twenty-first century, it must be remembered that religious were not accustomed to the use of strategic planning for their apostolic works. These were the people who were in the majority among the managerial bodies of the secondary schools. They were being asked to think differently about their work, about the future development of education, and about themselves as religious.

Strategic planning would have been considered as distrustful and lacking in that 'blind faith' which many of the constitutions and rule books of the religious orders stressed.[90] It is true that by 1974 all the congregations represented in the CCSS and many of the brothers in the TBA were in the process of up-dating rules and constitutions as directed by Vatican II. But the process of change is slow and takes longer than does the re-wording of documents. By asking the teaching religious to review and evaluate their complex roles (Fullan, 1991; Hargreaves, 1995:14-19) in a secondary school system that was traditionally focused on examinations, the Focus for Action process was being radical. Would all the thinking and discussion lead to change in the secondary schools? Perhaps the religious owners of the schools would initiate a process of planning for the future of denominational education. The religious were urged by the Focus for Action team to plan new models of community living including smaller units, particularly where religious might become involved in the community schools that were then under negotiation.

The community schools were to provide a comprehensive education for the children of an area. The community aspect would be evident in the provision of adult education and in the use of facilities by the local people. Capital expenditure would be provided by the state with a local contribution. That contribution became a matter for lengthy negotiation by the religious congregations who chose to be co-trustees in the new schools. Funding was to be either directly to the school or through the VEC. The state would pay the running costs of these schools. From the outset the plan was that some community schools would result from local amalgamations of perhaps a voluntary school and a vocational school. Other new schools would be 'greenfield' in the sense that no previous institution had existed in an area. Management would be shared. In effect, the boards of the community schools were comprised of representatives of the religious authorities, the VEC, elected representatives of the parents of pupils and elected teachers from the permanent staff of the school. The principal would attend board meetings (Grogan, 1990:377-80; Coolahan, 1981; O'Flaherty, 1992).

There was heated reaction at times from religious who believed that participation in community schools would be to the detriment of the private voluntary institutions. The Christian Brothers were very opposed to religious involvement in the community schools. Were religious thereby indicating a lack of confidence in the secondary system they had developed? Focus for Action urged religious to develop adult education programmes in their schools and the CCSS and the CMRS Education Commission undertook to support this development by research. For the managerial bodies, the 1970s may not have been as dramatic as the 1960s in terms of educational change, but the pace of change was increasing. Members of the CHA, CCSS and TBA were becoming involved in a variety of discussions, seminars and workshops related to denominational education as a direct result of Focus for Action (1974). Originally written for the male religious orders, three factors ensured that the Report had an impact. All but one of the religious members of the working party were involved in secondary schools. The women's section of the CMRS had not contributed to the Report but they readily agreed to attend the seminars and retreats. This ensured that the CCSS, the TBA and the CHA were discussing the future of the Catholic secondary schools in 1974 and 1975. Finally, the findings of the Mulrany Report (1974) from the bishops gave greater credibility and a sense of urgency to the task of planning future developments in Catholic education.

A result was seen in the willingness of a number of orders of brothers, nuns and priests to become involved in community schools. In retrospect, some of the religious leaders of the 1970s have told the author that the community school challenge had been 'a lost opportunity' for the majority of the religious congregations. On another level, however, the review and evaluation done by many of the teaching orders as a result of both the FIRE Report and Focus for Action contributed to readiness for change. Developments in adult education, in curriculum, in in-service and in home-school links in the voluntary school system may be attributed at least in part to what emerged in 1973 and 1974 from those Reports. They were not officially presented to the Ministers for Education because they were designated 'confidential' and 'internal' to the religious superiors, but it is true that Ministers who were promoting community schools found more religious orders interested after 1974.

White Paper 1980

John Wilson replaced Peter Barry as Minister for Education under a Fianna Fáil government on 5 July 1977 and remained in office throughout the duration of the government until 29 June 1981. In February 1978 it was known by the EPG that preliminary work had been done in preparation for a government White Paper on education. This knowledge gave added importance to the work of the Cardinal and the group. Members of the EPG had discussed the provision of Catholic secondary schools in areas where community schools or vocational schools might be an alternative. They had considered the wisdom of the church taking over the management and operation of secondary schools where religious orders were withdrawing due to shortage of numbers.

The EPG had also discussed the minimum investment possible by the church so as to ensure that a Catholic school would be regarded as a voluntary one and therefore retain its independence. Would the church authorities only have to provide the school site? Or would they also have to contribute to the capital cost of the building? There was also the possibility that the Department of Education could be asked or allowed to pay 100 per cent of secondary teacher salaries. In other words, the basic or school element of pay would cease if the diocese were to become a school trustee.[91] Rationalisation by religious with depleting numbers was accepted as inevitable and the bishops were responsible for the provision of Catholic education. A memorandum of 23 February 1978 prepared by a member of the EPG communicated the importance of planning:

> *The prospect of the large scale loss of Catholic secondary schools*
> *at a critical period of our development could constitute a serious*
> *loss to the Church in Ireland. If a model could be developed which*
> *would allow for an orderly transfer of control from the religious*
> *order to representatives of the local Church, then this would*
> *represent a real contribution to the Church.*

One possible model was for the bishop to become trustee of a school from which religious were withdrawing. A board of management would then be set up to ensure continuity of a Catholic school. If the EPG could develop this model each diocese would have a plan and an option 'at the appropriate time'. Moreover, the memorandum stated that such an approach 'would ensure a greater participation by lay Catholic teachers, as in national schools'. In relation to government plans for education, the EPG model would strengthen the Church position 'in seeking greater financial support from the Department in the coming White Paper'. An insight into relationships between the churches is in a *note bene* addition to the memorandum:

> *When we have resolved the above problems we might then seek*
> *discussions with the Protestant Churches to seek jointly with*
> *them the right to continue (a) to run voluntary secondary schools,*
> *(b) to run denominational secondary schools in any future*
> *legislation which is contemplated.*

By April 1978 a detailed memorandum was prepared for the bishops regarding the 'decision by a religious congregation to withdraw from a school managed by their institute'.[92] A bishop's involvement might be that of patron. Certain conditions would be essential:

- *that the Catholic ethos of the school would be maintained*

- *that there would be adequate provision for Catholic education (instruction and formation) in the school*

- *that the school would be financially viable and not dependent on diocesan or parish funds*

- *that there would be appropriate arrangements for the gift/rent/lease/ purchase of the property from the religious congregation withdrawing from the school*

- *that there would be acceptable management structure especially to ensure the calibre of the Catholic teachers employed*

- *that there should be a careful examination of the situation in other local secondary schools. The purpose of this exercise is to ensure that any alternative plans proposed for the school which is in difficulty will not result in threatening the viability of any existing school in the locality.*

On the one hand, every effort should be made to keep a school open. Otherwise, the Department of Education should be consulted in relation to the possibility of a community school being established. Three years before the first Deed of Trust was signed, the satisfaction of the bishops and CMRS with the community school model was evident. The EPG had ensured that the Catholic Church submission for the White Paper (1980) was both relevant and proactive in terms of denominational education. The appointment of Brother Declan Duffy to the Secretariat of Catholic Secondary Schools in 1977 had unintentionally acted as the lynchpin between the bishops, the CMRS and the managerial organisations.

The submission to the White Paper from the Church of Ireland Board of Education, 14 September 1979, was in two parts. The second dealt with youth work and was ahead of its time. The first concerned provision for voluntary schools. Like the Catholic Church, the Church of Ireland sought continuing support from government and wanted that to be recognised in the forthcoming White Paper. The Board of Education advocated

> *the continued safeguarding of the existence of the Church-linked schools, whether national Schools, Voluntary Secondary Schools or Comprehensive Schools, to be built into the White Paper.*
> *By existence we mean not simply survival but being on an equal footing with other types of schools in terms of real availability to our Church members, and in terms of the standards to be maintained.*

The submission also proposed the setting up of a small, permanent Education Commission with a wider network of consultative members. The Commission would include the Minister for Education, Minister for State, and educational spokespersons of the other main political parties. It would also include senior officials from the Department of Education and managerial representatives from primary, post-primary and third level. The teacher unions, the Irish Congress of Trade Unions (ICTU), and the Federated Union of Employers (FUE) would be included. In addition, there would be representatives of second and third level students, parents, the Industrial Development Authority and AnCO, the Higher Education Authority, educational psychologists and curriculum development personnel. In different ways, the EPG and the Church of Ireland were trying to ensure the future of denominational education.

The government *White Paper on Educational Development* was published in December 1980. Expenditure on education over the previous decade was an indication of the importance that successive governments attached to an educated population. In 1970 expenditure on education was £78 million. In 1979 it was £443 million (Hyland and Milne, 1992:52). In January 1980 the JMB welcomed the fact that substitute teachers for recognised absences would be fully paid by the Department of Education. The *White Paper* (1980) stated the need for a curriculum council to advise on developments[93] It also proposed that religion would become an examination subject for the Leaving Certificate (1980:6.16). Six months later the government fell, only to return again as a single Fianna Fáil party.

Professor Martin O'Donoghue, an economist and former member of the *Investment in Education* (1965) team, was Minister for Education from 9 March 1982 to 6 October 1982. Despite the short life of the government its new economic plan, *The Way Forward*, published in October 1982 was an indication of harsher economic times to come. The emphasis was on maximising the use of resources and seeking to lessen the national debt. However, the idea of the curriculum council as proposed in the *White Paper* (1980) was reiterated (Hyland and Milne, 1992:61). It would be realised under a different government, in a differing shape, during a period of economic recession, and by the first woman to hold the post of Minister for Education, Gemma Hussey.

Change and Little Money

A coalition government of Fine Gael and Labour was in power from December 1982 until February 1986 and again, following a general election, from February of the same year to March 1987 under Garret FitzGerald as Taoiseach. In their unpublished though agreed Programme for Government, December 1982, the two parties made a short statement on education. The focus was on reform and development with an emphasis on skills for the workplace. It reflected the economic reality much as earlier fiscal programmes in the 1950s and 1960s had done. To that end a 'curriculum and examinations board' was to be set up to restructure the examinations system. The new government also stated its intention to establish a National Parents' Council (NPC) and to promote co-education and integration of people with disabilities into the main school system (Hyland and Milne, 1992:61-64).

Traditionally the Catholic Church had emphasised the primacy of the role of parents in education and Vatican II reminded the owners of schools about this challenge. The Christian Brothers had led the way in the 1970s in establishing a vibrant parent support group, the Parents' Federation, in all their schools. The Parents' Federation had worked with many CCSS and some CHA schools to assist in the establishing of Parents' Committees or Associations that combined to form the Catholic Secondary School Parents' Association. Before announcing the NPC, there was no attempt on the part of the new Minister, Gemma Hussey, or her officials to glean from the experience of the parents. A number within the managerial organisations believed that the denominationalism of the second level school system became an obstacle to political intervention to formalise parents as partners in education. It was a token of the separation of church and state. The ASTI in 1973 had refused to attend parent meetings after school hours and the holding of meetings during the school day went on uneasily until the union sought additional payment for such work. The issue had not been resolved by the time the NPC was established.

Parent/teacher meetings was one of three items in the first of two 'packages' for negotiation between the CMRS, ASTI and the CMCSS. The first 'package' in the 1980s involved complex negotiations about boards of management for secondary schools, redeployment of teachers who were extra to school requirements and the resumption of parent/teacher meetings. As a result there were many in the CHA and the CCSS who believed that the announcement by Minister Hussey of the NPC (Hussey, 1990:163) could not have come at a less appropriate time.[94] Gemma Hussey proved a controversial minister for some of the bishops, and only partly because she questioned an all- male Catholic priesthood. Many of the managerial bodies came to view her with disfavour and she also ran into conflict with the teacher unions. Had she not been in office at a time of severe economic pressure and consequent cutbacks in education would her impact have been different? Perhaps she lacked a sense of the history of the vested interests represented by the churches, the managers and the teacher unions. Maybe she under-estimated the power of the officials in her own Department.[95]

Gemma Hussey was appointed Minister on 14 December 1982 and left office on 14 February 1986. Negotiations over teacher pay had been difficult and she had offended the teacher unions by publicly denouncing as immoral (*The Irish Times*, 22 August 1985) their day of strike action planned for 15 October 1985. She had antagonised the religious managerial bodies by the decision to close Carysfort College that was owned by the Sisters of Mercy who had invested so much in Irish education and whose patron was the Archbishop of Dublin.[96] She had followed the example of another Fine Gael Minister for Education, John Boland,[97] in appointing a personal adviser from outside the Department of Education. Gemma Hussey chose Dr John Harris, who was then headmaster of Sandford Park School in Dublin. She was also the first former Minister to publish a diary about her years in the cabinet.[98] The appointing of the first Curriculum and Examinations Board (CEB) in 1984 where parents were included,[99] and the first NPC were logical outcomes of the *Programme for Action in Education*, 1984-1987. The aim was to 'initiate a constructive debate on the educational system' so as to ensure a 'rational and complementary development of the secondary, vocational and community/comprehensive sectors' (*Progranne for Action*, 1984-1987:22). The idea of the CEB was not dissimilar to the education council proposed in the Fianna Fáil *White Paper* (1980) already mentioned. Gemma Hussey underlined the roles for parents, teachers and managers in the development of the system. A full partnership between all the interests involved was to be promoted by greater delegation and by the introduction of thirteen Local Education Councils and boards of management in all second level schools in an effort to de-centralise the work of the Department of Education (*Green Paper*, 1985).

The managerial bodies were not supportive of the suggested councils. The CMCSS was already in protracted negotiations with the ASTI and their 'package' included boards of management. Neither the CMRS nor the managers were excited at the ministerial suggestion about shared management. Because of the serious economic situation in Ireland in the 1980s, the Minister's programme had an air of unreality, yet there were some positive outcomes though Gemma Hussey would not receive the plaudits for them at the time. What was aspired to was an emphasis on an education that would be relevant to the needs, abilities and potential of all citizens in the context of a rich Irish cultural heritage. There was a need to modernise educational provision in a technological age and to ensure equality of educational opportunities between the various socio-economic groups in society and between the sexes. The work done by Dale Tussing for the ESRI (1978) had already alerted the managerial bodies to such needs. Government policy was documented in *Building on Reality*, 1985-1987, but it was severely criticised as being full of aspirations with no strategic planning. However, government intentions for educational development were stated. The emphasis at second level would be on curriculum reform. Additional funding from the European Social Fund (ESF) had been negotiated and would enable 19,000 pupils to follow alternative programmes to the traditional academic ones in 1984-1985. This development would include an allowance of £300 for the participating pupils, a payment that caused concern to the managerial bodies and the ASTI.

A ministerial discussion paper on 'The Ages for Learning' (June 1984) led to the publishing of *Ages for Learning: Decisions of Government* (May 1985) where it was stated that pupils should have access to six years in post-primary education. All the managerial bodies were preoccupied with the implications and the possibilities inherent in a six-year cycle although some schools under Protestant management and a number of CHA and CCSS fee-charging schools provided six years at that time. In effect, the government decision would raise the school leaving age without making it compulsory, thus lessening temporarily the numbers on the live register of unemployed. The poor economy was encouraging more young people to stay in school. *Ages for Learning* (1985) offered three options after the third year in post-primary school. Pupils might follow a transition or bridge year, free of examinations, before entering senior cycle for two years leading to the Leaving Certificate Examination. Pupils could enter the two-year programme immediately after the Intermediate Certificate Examination which ended the three junior years; such pupils might then leave school after their five years or could choose to repeat the Leaving Certificate programme in one year to improve results. The third option would enable pupils to follow a one or two year Vocational Preparation and Training Programme. Pupils who might complete a five-year cycle could choose a further year in the vocational training programme; those who might not wish to follow a Leaving Certificate programme could opt for the two-year vocational programme on completion of the junior cycle.[100]

There was divided opinion within the managerial bodies about the implications of *Ages for Learning*. The Minister was criticised by some for ignorance of what a six-year optional cycle would mean for principals and managers. Smaller schools might have difficulty in planning appropriate timetables. Any implication that might affect timetables tended to be unpopular with the school principals. Both the CCSS and the CHA expressed doubts about the ability of the economy to fund six years in all schools and there was a fear that only some schools would be able to provide for six years.[101] Size of school and pupil enrolment was relevant. Some feared a return to a government policy of rationalisation of schools based on pupil enrolment. There was considerable discussion in the CCSS and the CHA about a 'liberal government agenda'[102] that was not favourable to denominational education.

Managerial response to extending the transition year to all schools was more positive as was their welcome to the CEB *Guidelines for Schools* (January 1986). Introduced in 1973 by Minister Dick Burke (Egan and O'Reilly, 1977), by 1985 there were 115 voluntary secondary schools, many of them fee-charging, providing a transition year. Some thirty of these schools, including the all Irish schools, had retained four years in the junior cycle, thus enabling pupils to spend their first year as a transition one from the primary school system and a subsequent three years to the Intermediate Certificate Examination (*Rialacha agus Clár*, 1976). The remaining schools devoted three years to junior and three to the senior cycles. In some instances the first of the final three years was a transition year but many schools used the extra year to prepare for the Leaving Certificate Examination. Of itself this was discriminatory against the majority of pupils in the country who had two years to prepare for the same final public examination.

A few fee-charging schools did not do the Intermediate Examination, preferring instead to design their curriculum in keeping with the educational philosophy of the owners of the schools. Some of these schools prepared pupils for the General Certificate in Education (GCE), the terminal examination of the English system in the fifth year, and for the Leaving Certificate of the Irish system in the sixth or final year. Seven schools provided a seventh year though this was considered to be quite unofficial as far as the Department of Education was concerned. Only one school in the free education scheme from 1967 had prepared the pupils for GCE but that Dublin school closed as part of a rationalisation plan in 1977.[103] Two schools under Protestant management prepared students for the International Baccalauréate, the senior examination of the European school system.

By enabling all pupils to follow a transition year Gemma Hussey was equalising opportunities between the 114 schools referred to and all secondary, vocational, community and comprehensive schools. In October the earlier doubts of the nuns and the CHA about financial support were allayed when a circular (M85/85) from the Department of Education to 'the managers of all post-primary schools' stated that forthcoming structures would enable all schools to effect the changes decided by the government. The managers' relief was short-lived. In 1986 they were angered by a limitation which was put on the number of schools to be involved some months later when the Department of Education issued its own Guidelines (1986).

The Department had the unenviable task of telling the managers that only 150 additional schools would be admitted to transition year and that the whole process would develop in phases. The fact that only ninety schools pursued the option in 1986 did not serve to ease managerial displeasure. Inevitably they blamed the Minister for her lack of awareness of the school system and for what appeared to the JMB to have been inadequate planning by the Department of Education regarding the cost implications of a six-year cycle. Some within the managerial organisations believed that the ESF scheme of allowances to pupils following the vocational preparation programmes could have been re-directed to enable all schools to offer an extra year.

It was unfortunate for the work of the CEB that Gemma Hussey's period as Minister for Education was one of uneasy relations between the managerial bodies and the ASTI. Her approach to curriculum and examinations was more radical than that of any previous minister. As a result of her leadership there was the beginning of some debate about curriculum and education. Was she in the wrong ministry? She had been a successful business woman and owner of a private language school before becoming a politician. Perhaps she lacked the patience to struggle with perspectives that were hewn out in the slow-moving traditions of education. Perhaps she belonged to a government which was associated with a 'liberal agenda' and a 'constitutional crusade' (Hogan, 1987:92), with the referendum on abortion in 1983, with debates on divorce and with a strong pro-Europe approach to politics.[104] She was unfortunate that some bishops and many among the managerial bodies perceived her as unsympathetic to Catholic education. There is no evidence to suggest that such a perception had any foundation. Her determination that sex education would be included in the school curriculum did not serve her well with the Catholic managerial bodies.

The New Ireland Forum was established in April 1983 to facilitate consultations between political parties north and south of the island of Ireland. One commentator wrote that the 'highlight' of the Forum was the appearance of the Irish Episcopal Conference Delegation led by Bishop Cahal Daly (*New Ireland Forum*, 1984; Hogan, 1987:92-95). The delegation was questioned carefully about the south being 'a confessional state' and members enunciated their enthusiasm for a 'separation of church and state'. It is possible that the government and the new Minister for Education were too optimistic in their interpretation of the anxiety of the Catholic Hierarchy to change.

Reports and Reports

Reports and publications related to education came in quick succession in the 1980s. In 1985 the *Report of the Committee on Discipline in Schools* was published. This committee was a ministerial response to the reaction of teacher unions and managers when on 26 January 1982 Minister John Boland had prohibited the use of corporal punishment in schools. The main implications for the managerial bodies were the recommendations that each school should have a written code of discipline and should liaise effectively with its feeder primary schools. These demands could be a test of leadership and the necessary organisational skills to meet the concerns expressed by teachers in relation to discipline. Ultimate sanctions of suspending or excluding a disruptive pupil temporarily from school, or of final expulsion, were to be used with great care, according to the *Report*. The professional warnings of the *Report* had implications for the management of schools.

Other reports emerged: *The Place of the Arts in Irish Education* (1979), *The Arts in Education: a CEB Discussion Paper* (1985) and *Access and Opportunity: a White Paper on the Arts* (1987) each of which should have interested the managerial bodies. In addition, the decade had brought the interim report from the Review Body on Teachers' Pay (1980) and reports on educational broadcasting (1980). The report on the child care services (1980) was of considerable concern to the Christian Brothers, the Mercy nuns and the Religious Sisters of Charity, all of whom were involved in homes and institutions for children. *The Report of the Pupil Transfer Committee* (1981) led to energetic debate among the managers. There was also the *Final Report on the Public Examinations Evaluation Project* (1980) in which the CCSS was particularly interested. The Kenny Report on adult education (1983) was relevant to those voluntary secondary schools mostly in the CCSS and the TBA that were providing adult programmes.[105] *The Report of the National Youth Policy Committee* (1984) called for regionalised structures for more effective provision for youth, including appropriate guidance services. Indeed there were echoes in it of the recommendations of the Church of Ireland Board of Education in advance of the *White Paper* of 1980. Increasingly since the mid-1970s some of the religious orders of women had become more involved in youth apostolic work outside schools so the *Report of the Youth Policy Committee* was of interest to them and it was widely discussed within the CCSS.

The CEB from September 1984 published a stream of documents and discussion papers that challenged the managerial bodies and all interested in educational development to respond. In November 1985 Gemma Hussey issued *Partners in Education: a Green Paper* which proposed the establishing of thirteen local education councils in an effort to de-centralise and develop the education service. This too had direct implications for the managerial bodies and their schools. There was an avalanche of reports and suggestions throughout the late 1970s and up to 1987. Reports impose demands on leadership and organisational structure. The managerial bodies during this period were tested on their ability to interpret, to respond, to challenge and to select what was crucial for them as leaders and owners of schools.

Patrick Cooney succeeded Gemma Hussey as Minister for Education from February 1986 to the fall of the coalition government in March 1987. He was an astute politician and legal expert. As such he was well placed to interact with the CEB on the proposed *Curriculum and Examinations Board Bill* (1986) though time and the change of government aborted what might have become the first curriculum act and provided a legal framework for much of the work of the managerial bodies.

By 1987, therefore, when the CMCSS was coming to the end of a re-structuring process as an organisation, the legal position of the voluntary secondary schools was unchanged from what was enshrined in the *Constitution* of 1937. Three *Articles* (42-44) - on education, private property and religion - remained relevant. The family is acknowledged as 'the primary and natural educator of the child' (*Article*, 42) and parents cannot be forced to send a child to school if alternative provision is made for education. The issue of school attendance in 1987 was governed by additional legislation and it had implications for the work of the managerial bodies. From 1963 and the introduction of comprehensive schools the managers became more familiar with the constitutional position relating to schools:

> *Every religious denomination shall have the right to manage its own affairs,*
> *own, acquire and administer property, movable and immovable, and maintain*
> *institutions for religious or charitable purposes.* (CONSTITUTION, 44:2,5)

The attitude of keeping a respectful distance between church and state as maintained by a Minister for Education like General Richard Mulcahy in the early 1950s might be seen in the light of that *Article*. The model for the comprehensive schools, including what was always referred to as 'the Protestant comprehensive', showed Dr Hillery's ability to develop the school system while maintaining appropriate relations with the churches. And so the following *Article* from the *Constitution* (1937) was observed:

> *Legislation providing state aid for schools shall not discriminate between*
> *schools under the management of different religious denominations, nor*
> *be such as to affect prejudicially the right of any child to attend a school*
> *receiving public money without attending religious instruction in that school.*
> (IBID., 44:2,4)

Similarly, the many drafts of the Deed of Trust for Community Schools and the years taken before its finalisation give some insight into the efforts of Ministers Pádraig Faulkner and John Wilson along with the Catholic Hierarchy and the CMRS to achieve the best possible outcome in the Irish context.

The Vatican Congregation for Education had published *The Catholic School* (1977) and *Lay Catholics in Schools* (1982), each of which stressed the importance of justice and inclusiveness by employers and managers. Inevitably the records of the CCSS and the TBA show that the nuns and the brothers were discussing both documents. The test of the effectiveness of these discussions would be the extent of the involvement of lay teachers in the management, leadership and administration of the religious schools. By the early 1980s the CCSS was preoccupied with the future of their managerial organisation but they were also concerned at the volume of educational publications and reports and the scarcity of time to consider them.[106] Each member was either a full-time secondary school principal or a part-time manager with other functions in a religious community or both. Members of the CCSS executive at the time wondered if the pace of change in education could possibly continue. Perhaps the fact that the Vatican Congregation published yet a third book, *The Religious Dimension of Education in a Catholic School* (1988), within a ten-year span is itself a statement about the pace of change in education and society. Ball (1997:257-74) has written about 'the major transformation in the organising principles of social provision right across the public sector' in most Western and many developing societies from 1982. Jessop (1994) sees such changes as part of a more profound move from one form of 'welfare statism' to another. In Ireland, though not strictly a welfare state, membership of the EU and of a more global economy have affected the changes that have happened between the late 1950s and the 1980s in

> *the forms of employment, organisational structures, cultures and values,*
> *systems of funding, management roles and styles, social relationships*
> *and pay and conditions of public welfare organisations.*
> (BALL, 1997:258)

The tension between Christian values in education and at times the actuality of the experience of teachers, pupils and managers became more marked after Vatican II and particularly towards the end of the 1970s when nuns, brothers and priests had studied the council documents. The test would be whether that tension would result in positive outcomes. How might the managerial bodies contribute to denominational education? In other words, what theory would be evident in their practice?

The oil crisis in 1979 was followed by a return of economic problems in the early 1980s. These years brought with them an unprecedented number of committees and reports. It was as if the education system was forcing a period of reflection upon itself at a time when there was little money available for educational development. The early 1980s also offered opportunities to the managerial bodies to participate in debate and reflection on their role as leaders and managers.

In February 1987 Fianna Fáil and the Progressive Democrats, a new political party that had formed on 21 December 1985, came into government. The national debt was more than twenty-five billion pounds, the equivalent of nearly twice the GNP. Unemployment was almost one-fifth of the work force and would reach 201,000 two years later. A government *Programme for National Recovery*, October 1987 was an attempt to redress the economic situation and high emigration. A particular focus in education was to be on the vocational preparation and training programmes which had been introduced in 1977 and subsequently funded from the ESF (Leonard, 1990:33-46). Some of the managerial bodies were already providing these courses in their schools. Mary O'Rourke of the Fianna Fáil party was appointed Minister for Education on 10 March 1987 where she remained until 14 November 1991. A former secondary school teacher, she was a pragmatist and a politician rather than an educationalist. She decided to change the personnel and title, though not the work, of the CEB. In a clever political move, she persuaded Dr Edward Walsh and the author to continue as chairman and vice-chairman of the new body. Their appointment had the advantage of ensuring continuity in the work of curriculum development. The National Council for Curriculum and Assessment (NCCA) was appointed in November 1987 and would ensure that the unitary system of assessment as designed by the CEB would be implemented. Pupils who entered first year in comprehensive, community, vocational and voluntary secondary schools in September 1989 were the first to sit the new Junior Certificate Examination. This replaced both the common Intermediate Certificate and the Group Certificate which had been available mainly in the vocational schools.[107] Perhaps this should have been the logical outcome of free education in the 1960s.[108]

More than twenty years after the introduction of free education the OECD (1991) noted the growth in the number of Leaving Certificate candidates in Ireland. From under 10,000 in 1963 to 60,000, the figures hid the vision, courage and hopes of the many players who had contributed to this achievement. Of the Ministers for Education who held office from 1957 to 1987 a number emerge as more significant than others in relation to the managerial bodies of the voluntary sector. It is evident from what has been written about the ministers that the following holders of the office will figure more than others: Dr Hillery, George Colley and Donogh O'Malley who between them catapulted Irish education into a more comprehensive and available mode; Pádraig Faulkner who was involved in the outcome of the Ryan Tribunal on Teacher Salaries from 1969 and who along with John Wilson was associated with the development of the community schools and community colleges; Gemma Hussey who led the way in systemic reform and Mary O'Rourke who was there to see it to a partial conclusion. The managerial bodies in their separate organisations, in their occasional combining of forces in the 1950s and early 1960s and in their ecumenical umbrella body, the JMB from 1964, were in a state of continuing interaction with the ASTI. On one level they were partners because between them they delivered a system of secondary education. On another level they were opponents in an employer-employee sense. Charles Handy (1985:35-6) questions the distinction between leadership, management and administration in schools, between educational policy and execution. His musings raise similar issues regarding Irish education because an important aspect of the role of the managerial bodies was in their dealings with successive Ministers for Education and the Department of Education.

The denominational aspect of schools and the independence of managers in the selection of teachers were important to the various churches and were not interfered with by the Free State from 1922. Indeed, the *Education Act*, 1998 has protected them. By the 1960s the managerial bodies had inherited a public examination system that was respected in the context of their private secondary schools. Moreover, the state advocated entrance examinations to ensure that pupils were suited to the academic curriculum in the voluntary schools. Children who were unsuited might attend vocational schools that were geared to technical education and training under the legislation of 1930. The secondary schools had been accustomed since 1940 to following the curriculum set by the Department of Education. Public perception of secondary education was to change after 1966 when Donogh O'Malley introduced the free scheme that enabled the vocational schools to admit younger pupils and to provide programmes similar to the secondary schools.

By the 1970s there were secondary schools, vocational schools, comprehensive schools and community schools, all providing for the Intermediate and Leaving Certificate Examinations. Everybody gained from the 'investment in education'. The free education scheme extended the secondary system and gave more funding than many religious orders had ever earned in fees. Increasing enrolments put additional pressure on managers and teachers to prepare pupils for success in examinations. Inadequate funding of third level colleges meant there were never sufficient places to meet demand: this in turn added to the pressure on teachers and schools to attain in public examinations.

The Investment in Education (1966) report revealed the inability of the secondary school system to meet the needs of families and the developing economy. The report has been unfairly criticised for too great an emphasis on 'quantity' rather than 'quality' in schools (Clancy, 1988). However, Minister Hillery's quest was for information about the existing system and as such the *Report* was unique.

The free scheme enhanced the position of the ASTI by a dramatic increase in membership and for the first time the VTA was competing for membership (McGinley and Donoghue, 1999:238). Families deserved access to second level education. Ireland needed well-educated people but the system that the voluntary organisations had established could not have met the demands in 1967. Proof of the vision of some religious orders was apparent in 28 community schools that were catering for local populations before the Deed of Trust was finally agreed.[109] The managerial bodies concerned with schools under Protestant management made an important breakthrough for their denominations in negotiating comprehensive schools. The 1960s may well have begun 'the best of times' for the churches in education.

Seventeen groups were involved in the provision of second level education. The total was nineteen from 1970 if APPTI and the EPG are added. That does not include the Department of Education and the ASTI. Such a web of organisations breeds complexity if not tension. Managers, religious, bishops and laity also struggled with the 'structural shift' (Hannan and Breen, 1987:100) occurring in the economic and social life in Ireland from 1960. By the 1980s there was also evidence of a shift in attitudes and values.

In 1960 parents were not heard in matters of education, but free education meant that parental expectations of schools would change.[110] The Christian Brothers were the leaders in formalising parental involvement in schools in 1970. Gradually from the mid-1970s the nuns and other managerial bodies followed their example. Parents were on boards of management in the primary schools since 1975, in the community schools after 1981, in some vocational or community colleges after 1980, and on comprehensive school boards by the end of the twentieth century. To Gemma Hussey as Minister goes the credit for establishing and funding the NPC by 1987. So, twenty years after free education, a national body of parents emerged alongside the other organisations. At the beginning of the twenty-first century parents are recognised as partners in education and acknowledged in legislation, not as NPC, but as 'parents of students of a recognised school' (*Education Act*, 1998:VI, 25).[111]

The lowering of the voting age to eighteen in 1972 meant that some schools had 'adults' in the senior classes. There was no facility for giving them a voice though the Board of Education of the Church of Ireland recommended significant developments in youth work in 1980. In the mid-1970s voluntary schools introduced student councils of varying types and that variation continued to the end of the twentieth century. The

Education Act, 1998 (VI:27) charges the boards of management with establishing and 'maintaining procedures for the purposes of informing students' of 'the activities of the school'. Students 'may establish a student council' and the board 'shall encourage' them to do so. A new interface may need to be found between management and the school community. In the twenty-first century, one of the challenges for the CMCSS and the JMB is to promote models of effective practice for voluntary schools as these develop and are evaluated.

Reflection

From 1922 to the 1960s the owners and managers of secondary schools enjoyed relative independence to run their schools without interference from the Department of Education. Their freedom to hire and fire teachers was untouched by legislation. The Christian Brothers had their own contract. In the 1950s the CCSS accepted the contract of employment negotiated by the CHA and the ASTI but they managed to retain considerable independence through the use of temporary contracts. The need to employ a lay teacher was seen as 'a temporary little arrangement' by the nuns and brothers until a religious was available.[112] That attitude contributed to tensions with the ASTI. Before the advent of free education many schools operated without lay teachers but escalating enrolments and decreasing vocations to religious life resulted in greater numbers of lay teachers from the early 1970s. Thus, the managerial bodies were forced to confront the legality of being employers. The CMRS Report on Religious as Employers in November 1978 was an effort to improve the situation in schools in the light of need and the challenge of Vatican II for greater inclusiveness of the laity. Developments in employment legislation in the late 1970s curtailed the power of the managers and legislation against varying forms of discrimination (1998) and for equal status (2000) forms part of the leadership and management context at the beginning of the twenty-first century.

Unlike the Catholic Church, the Church of Ireland had rationalised provision and had set up the SEC by 1965. Although the SEC may be best described as an *ad hoc* arrangement it provided a structure that proved useful. The schools under Protestant management were able to negotiate a block grant in their response to the free education scheme in 1966. The SEC subsequently managed grants to parents to assist them in paying the school fees. The Catholic bodies lacked that structure because of the position of the bishops, the newness of the CMRS and the relative independence of each religious order. The Irish bishops were happy to allow and even invite the religious orders to provide secondary education. Unlike the bishops in the US and Australia, providing Catholic schools did not cost the Irish bishops money or personnel. Thus the canonical requirement on a bishop to provide for Catholic education was generally met by the religious.[113] The diocesan colleges were different because they were the source of future candidates for the priesthood.

The challenges that faced the managerial organisations before the 1960s were never daunting for them because the churches were unchallenged in their unique position as providers of secondary education. Few would have questioned the meaning of 'a Catholic school'. By and large, there was no reason to fear a decline in candidates for convents, monasteries and seminaries and the future of the schools seemed assured. The struggles were mainly financial and therefore external in nature. Community living simplified overheads since individual nuns and brothers never handled money for personal use. It was the job of superiors to ensure a continual supply of religious in the schools. Individual religious who were waiting to train or follow a degree could still contribute to the work of the 'family business'. And there was no concept of an age of retirement, so older religious continued to teach, to supervise boarders and day students and to provide extra curriculum. In the teaching orders there were individuals who could not become teachers either because they lacked ability or belonged to 'the lay sisters' or 'second degree sisters'.[114] The CCSS, and sometimes the CHA, occasionally complained of the influence of the public examination system on the curriculum. Nevertheless, principals had the authority to ensure as wide a curriculum as desirable. In the case of the nuns and the brothers, their formation as novices and young religious inculcated in them the 'custom and practice' of the particular order; in turn, this had an effect on the curriculum in the secondary schools. The educational philosophy was one of personal discipline, conformity and loyalty to the Catholic Church. Educational experience was predictable in the best sense.

The role of the religious orders in the secondary schools became more complicated through the 1970s and 1980s. The problem for the nuns and others in the managerial organisations was that the 'external environments' were continually changing. The comprehensive schools had not lessened the hold of the religious on education because the bishops and Dr Hillery, Minister for Education, had reached an accommodation. But parental demand for second level education outran the ability of the voluntary sector to provide.

Community schools were a different matter and many religious orders declined to become involved at the initial stage. The real state of vocations was recorded and shared among them for the first time after the completion of the FIRE Report in 1973. The Report was a record of religious 'investment in education' and it provided statistical information just as *Investment in Education* (1966) had done for the country. In retrospect, religious could take pride in what had been achieved. In prospect, there was need for concern. The FIRE Report (1974) was a cerebral statement and many religious did not want to know. The old adage 'God will provide' meant that vocations would increase again, rather than that other means of providing Catholic education should be developed. But times were changing: Vatican II had called for greater lay involvement and Cardinal Conway contrasted the strong lay leadership in the north with the reality in Irish voluntary secondary schools.

Investment in Education in 1965 ultimately changed the ground under the religious in secondary schools because it heralded national educational opportunity. The singularity of voluntary secondary schools ended when every family in Ireland could access the public examination system through education. The separateness of the religious orders in education began to break down in the wake of the work of Focus for Action, but the danger of demoralisation in the face of so much change was perhaps lessened by the possibilities envisaged in the Focus for Action Report and the Religious Employer Report (1978).

Individual members of the CMRS and some religious in the managerial organisations were far-seeing and a new cosmology of post-primary education was coming into view. The orders that participated in the community schools after 1970 did so because they understood the 'external environments'. They also appreciated the safeguards for Catholic education offered by the Deed of Trust. Involvement in these schools was a learning opportunity for CMRS who quickly saw that their voluntary secondary schools needed new structures to ensure their future. The concept of shared management was learned from the community school model though Cardinal Conway had already explored it within the EPG. Thus emerged the document on boards of management for secondary schools. Many CCSS principals were deeply unhappy about boards of management. Some individuals believed them to be unnecessary while others held that they would engulf the principals in additional work. Either way, the CMRS and some of the bishops had a sense of the bigger picture and of the importance of ensuring the continuation of Catholic schools. Dr Donal Murray (1991), bishop of Limerick and a foremost member of the Hierarchy in 2000, in a reflection on a philosophy of Christian education, re-iterated what the bishops had said in the New Ireland Forum (1984). The Catholic Church does not obstruct parents who may want multi-denominational education; the virtue of tolerance is a mark of belief. At the same time, he affirmed Church expectations of Catholic teachers. From the 1970s to the end of the twentieth century there was a shift in attitude regarding the role of denominational schools - it was a move from protectionism and lack of tolerance towards a vision of the potential of church schools, and respect for difference and alternative forms of education.

The three-tiered structure of the schools under Protestant management developed in 1965 and the subsequent decades offered opportunities for review and clarification of how and when the trustees, the SEC and the ISA might interact. The chairman of the SEC is from the Church of Ireland. The position of vice-chairman rotates among the other churches. In the 1990s the SEC established a 'committee on management'. There are representatives of the SEC, the ISA, the Secondary School Council of Governors and Compass which is the body that represents parents of schools of minority religious groups including the Jewish community. It was the 'committee on management' that interacted with the Department of Education and Science on such issues as the Education Act, 1998, legislation on Education Welfare (2000) and adult education. For the Catholic schools at the beginning of the twenty-first century there is CORI and the CMCSS. The bishops are represented in both organisations. The presence of principals and managers or chairmen of boards in the CMCSS may at times blur differentiation between the responsibilities of trusteeship and management but the work of CORI since 1996 has contributed to greater clarity of roles. The interface between CORI and the CMCSS is that which pertains to the religious-owned schools, though the CMCSS also includes the Catholic lay schools that are not owned by members of CORI. CORI has outlined the legal and moral basis of the responsibilities of the owners or trustees (1996:4):

> *The legal basis derives, in part, from the fact that the congregation is*
> *the owner of the school in two senses. First, the title of the 'real'*
> *property (land and buildings) is usually registered in the name of*
> *members of the congregation. Secondly, the congregation owns the*
> *enterprise of the school itself in the same way that an individual or*
> *a company can own the 'good name' of a particular business.*

The legality of ownership is clear, but other aspects of ownership are more complex:

> *As legal owner, the congregational leadership or its nominee(s) is obliged*
> *to hold the school property in* trust *for the purposes (mission) to which*
> *the congregation is currently committed - hence the use of the term*
> Trustee. *Trustees have a fiduciary relationship towards other persons*
> *(beneficiaries) and are obliged to honour the trust* (1996:5).

In the 1970s the CMRS (CORI) initiated discussions on boards of management. The major superiors needed a structure where management decisions would be shared 'while taking account of the distinctive responsibilities of trustees' (1996:7). When the 'package' was finalised with the ASTI and the Department of Education by 1987, the structure was identified and agreed in Articles of Management for Catholic Secondary Schools (1989) that are signed only by trustees. The relationship between trustees and school management is based on the fact that the trustees are ultimately responsible for the school, and

> *The school is most likely to be effective when its day-to-day management*
> *is carried out in partnership between trustees, parents, teachers and the*
> *wider community, and when its future is planned through dialogue among*
> *all the partners* (1996:7).

Under the Articles of Management, the boards are entrusted with the property and are responsible to the trustees for the conduct of the school 'in accordance with the religious and educational philosophy' (Article 2c). It is clear that the leadership and management role of the CMCSS is inextricably linked with aspects of the work of CORI. In the twenty-first century when CORI are supporting a number of religious orders to implement new structures of trusteeship, it is inevitable that the CMCSS will be challenged to review its leadership role and management functions. The CMCSS is distinctly the management organisation of the Catholic voluntary secondary schools. The JMB is uniquely the management organisation of all the voluntary secondary schools. The interface between both organisations has been effectively reviewed and developed, but the evolution of the National Association of Principals and Deputy Principals (NAPD) at the end of the twentieth century may challenge the CMCSS and the JMB to re-evaluate the structure created in 1987 in the light of the Education Act 1998, proposals on boards of management and declining numbers of religious.[115]

2

The
Managerial
Organisations

THE MANAGERIAL ORGANISATIONS

In 2000 the CMCSS remains the representative of Catholic management. The SEC does not enjoy as structured a position in relation to the schools under Protestant management because a number of churches are involved. There is an essential interface between the CMCSS and CORI and between the SEC and the Board of Education. The AMCSS is simply the name given to the ten regional groupings of principals and managers. The present structure of the management bodies in secondary education emerged in 1987 resulting from a lengthy process of reflection, negotiation and rationalisation by the constituent organisations. The purpose of the next two chapters is to trace the origins and development of the various groups who today form the CMCSS and the JMB.

The Schoolmasters' Association 1869

On 29 June 1869 the headmaster of the Church of Ireland diocesan school in Monaghan, Maurice Hime[1] proposed to a number of colleagues the setting up of an association which would be a source of support to the principals and would represent secondary schools. The outcome in December 1869 was the founding of the oldest of the managerial bodies, The School Masters' Association (Schoolmasters' Association). Members were headmasters rather than managers of Irish Protestant second level schools. However, from the beginning the Association acted in a managerial capacity. Under the *Rules of the Schoolmasters' Association*, amended in December 1877, membership was restricted to heads and assistant masters of 'diocesan schools, endowed schools, and private schools of high social standing,' and who held a university degree. Only nine assistant masters could be in the Association at any one time. It was not therefore an early example of 'middle management' in the schools. Nevertheless the existence of nine assistant masters suggests awareness of the importance of involving teachers in management. A century later when the appointment of 'vice-principals' of schools was under discussion in 1970, a member of the JMB referred to this early collaboration between headmaster and teacher.

In the Rules of 1877 there were two quite specific aims in the Schoolmasters' Association: to advance the interests of 'upper-class schools in Ireland' and to afford members 'the advantages of mutual counsel and support'. In 1916 when the purposes of the Association were reviewed their first aim was changed 'to advance the interests of secondary education in Ireland'. Applying the criterion of a clear mission or purpose, the Schoolmasters' Association is exemplary. It was the only group among the managerial bodies that set out to give human support to its members. Was this an early recognition of management as a complex human activity? Following the introduction of the Intermediate Education (Ireland) Act in parliament in June 1878, the Schoolmasters' Association invited the principals and managers of Catholic secondary schools to join them, but in the context of the nineteenth century and a Catholic Church that was concerned to protect its denominational interests, the invitation was not accepted.

The Schoolmasters' Association pursued its interest in educational developments and played a part in the early history of the Association of Secondary Teachers Ireland (ASTI) founded in 1909. It supported the campaign for teacher salaries and improved funding for schools. It also favoured the proposed legislation in the Education (Ireland) Bill of 1919 (the MacPherson Bill) to which the Catholic bishops were opposed (Titley, 1983). The professor of education at University College Dublin was clear on the role of the authorities of the Catholic secondary schools: it was to ensure 'full Catholic control of the choice of teachers, retention of teachers, and removal of teachers'.[2] After 1922 under the Free State the Schoolmasters' Association lost its northern colleagues as separate education systems evolved in the two parts of Ireland. In 1968 the name of the organisation was changed to the Irish Schoolmasters' Association (ISA). The new name should not disguise the fact that their female colleagues in the girls' schools often attended the Schoolmasters' meetings. In the 1970s when the system of posts of responsibility was introduced the ISA showed a keen awareness of the importance of associating the posts with organisation and management in their schools, and when the posts system was under review in the late 1970s the Schoolmasters were insistent that appointees should be

> the best members of the staff of any school, and that it should not
> encourage automatic promotion solely by seniority, which it seems to
> do at present.[3]

The Association of Irish Headmistresses 1882

The parallel Protestant group for women, the Association of Irish Headmistresses (AIH) was founded in 1882

> to promote the higher education throughout Ireland by affording a means
> of communication between schoolmistresses and other ladies interested in
> education and by watching over the interests of girls, especially with
> regard to Intermediate Education and the Royal University.[4]

The schoolmistresses showed leadership and vision in forming their association at that time. In 1879 one year after the Intermediate Certificate (Ireland) Act, the Royal University was established. It was an examining board that awarded degrees and did not provide a college where students would take courses. The senate of the Royal University consisted of equal numbers of Catholics and Protestants. It was not an ideal solution to the need for university education but it was less objectionable to the Catholic Hierarchy than the Queen's University that had been a similar type of examining body since 1850. The Royal University continued to be funded by parliament to examine and award scholarships and fellowships until it was replaced by the Irish Universities Act in 1908.

The story of these early years of the AIH is not unlike that of the Dominicans: the nuns in Eccles Street and Dominican Hall in Dublin also encouraged girls to pursue studies, qualifications and awards from the Royal University. Part of the heritage of the AIH was a strong sense of a mission to have as many young women as possible achieve third level awards. The association had contributed to other aspects of education by its interest in the Teachers' Registration Council and in the improvement of teacher salaries and curriculum. Their original aims had been re-drafted. In addition to communication and co-operation were added: 'to promote the liberal education of women in Ireland' and 'to encourage women to undertake administrative posts'. Up to 1987 the AIH was unique among the managerial bodies in promoting women in management. This proactive approach has not been taken up by the present managerial organisations. Recent research (Warren and O'Connor, 1999) highlights the anomaly and the decreasing number of female appointments to senior posts in education.

Membership of the AIH was open to 'headmistresses, lady principals or managers or vice-principals, and senior mistresses' involved in administration. They became active members of the increasing numbers of subject associations that had formed by 1960. The nuns and the headmistresses met frequently from the mid-1950s to share concerns about curriculum development. The AIH formally joined with their male colleagues in the ISA in 1968 though the two associations continued in existence until October 1981. The women's group published a newsletter, *AHEAD*, concerning school affairs. They contributed to the founding of the Council of the Status of Women and were one of the ten organisations of women who volunteered in 1968 to investigate discrimination against women in Ireland. In March 1970 when the Council of six men and six women was established with Dr Thekla Beare as chairman, the contribution made by the AIH was publicly acknowledged.

The beginning of the ISA had been marked by a concern for mutual support in their work as headmasters. The AIH on the other hand was a response to political decisions regarding education as much as to the vision of the headmistresses for the education of women. The emphasis in both was on service in denominational schools.

The Board of Education

An important part of the structure of the schools under Protestant management is the Board of Education of the General Synod of the Church of Ireland that had been established in 1875.[5] The Board had moved through different phases in its development and by 1904 was concerned with 'the promotion of Secondary and Technical Education, and all matters relating thereto'. The following year primary education was included in its responsibilities. By 1917 the Board was 'to embrace all matters religious and secular relating to primary as well as secondary education'. At this stage the ISA was represented on the Board though the schoolmistresses were not included. However, the Board had supported the efforts of the secondary schoolmistresses along with the ISA in the work of teacher registration, improving salaries and curriculum. In 1951 the Board appointed an education officer. It was an organisational decision that distinguished it from the Catholic managerial bodies in the 1950s and 1960s. Another review of the Board took place in 1955 and the organisation of schoolmistresses, then seventy-three years in existence, was represented for the first time. In the 1960s a sub-committee of the Board prepared a revised Constitution that was accepted in 1964.

From June 1964 an executive committee of the Board was appointed annually, with authority to establish sub-committees to carry out its work. Thus the Church of Ireland had a defined structure to support its education mission. Protestant secondary schools were managed by individual boards of governors who were generally responsible to the Church of Ireland Synod of Bishops. To some extent, therefore, the structure was simple when compared with the Catholic bishops and the many self-governing religious orders that owned the majority of the secondary schools. In 1959 there were forty-two secondary schools under Protestant management, most of them in Dublin. Of the 6,295 pupils on roll the majority, 4,368 were Church of Ireland. The schools varied in size. Wesley College in Dublin, for example, had 479 pupils of whom 218 were Church of Ireland. Wesley College is the only school actually owned by the Conference of the Methodist Church. A unique aspect is that the Board of Governors includes the principal as a governor. Bishop Hodson School in Elphin had twenty-five pupils none of whom was Church of Ireland.[6] The concern of the General Synod of the Church of Ireland was that denominational education should continue to be available for Protestants. In 1962 this led to the establishing of a special Advisory Committee on Secondary Education in the Republic of Ireland. By the mid-1960s the total number of recognised pupils in Church of Ireland secondary schools was 5,520.

The records of the 1950s and 1960s show the concern of the Church with the scarcity of teachers of their own denomination. Like the Catholic bishops, the Church of Ireland bishops could be expected to insist on the right to select teachers. In turn, that would necessitate a significant involvement in the management of schools. This clear vision of their role was evident in the negotiations for comprehensive schools in the 1960s and in their rejection of the community school Deed of Trust in the 1970s.[7] It also makes sense of their unwillingness to accept as suitable for schools under Protestant management the Articles of Management that had been agreed by the Catholic managerial bodies and the ASTI in 1984.

The Advisory Committee worked assiduously for three years and presented its Report to the General Synod in 1965, a report which was remarkable for its time as an analysis of educational provision for a denominational system. A total of twenty secondary and two comprehensive schools throughout the Republic of Ireland would be adequate.

The locations of the comprehensive schools were identified: one in west Cork and one in Donegal.[8] The setting up of the Advisory Committee in 1962 was fortuitous. By 1963 when the Minister for Education, Dr Patrick Hillery, announced the scheme for comprehensive schools, the Church of Ireland had already identified areas in the country where provision was inadequate. An important key to the success of the Advisory Committee of the Church of Ireland was in the leadership and organisational skills of the chairman, Right Reverend Dr Richard Perdue, Bishop of Cork, Cloyne and Ross.[9] The Report recommended collaboration and consolidation of resources if the Church of Ireland was to have viable denominational schools. Indeed the Report ended on a formidable note: 'Time is short, and the sands are running out' (1965:24).

Collaboration with a view to rationalisation of schools was actively pursued once the General Synod accepted the Report. Such a policy was possible because of the firm position taken by the Board of Education which was then the policy-making body of the Church of Ireland and responsible to the General Synod. A year later the General Synod set up a commission, the Secondary Education Committee (SEC), referred to earlier, consisting of eight Church of Ireland members, two Presbyterians, two Methodists and two of the Religious Society of Friends. Their task was to formulate 'a common policy for Protestant secondary education in the Republic of Ireland'. The group was also

> *authorised to enter into discussion with the Minister for Education, the*
> *schools, and other authorities, for the purpose of implementing their policy.*[10]

The SEC would become the structure for the effective administration of the free education fund. When the Protestant schools made representation to the Minister for Education, Donogh O'Malley, about the impossibility of functioning without the kind of voluntary and unpaid staffing that religious-owned schools had, a special arrangement was made. On the basis of a payment for each day pupil and additional payments in boarding schools the state would give a block payment to the SEC. In turn, the money would then be disbursed to the schools. The demarcation was clear between policy and the concerns of the ISA and the AIH even though both those organisations included managers of schools and regularly discussed leadership, management and administration. The making of policy was the responsibility of the Board of Education but the lines of communication were open between the Board and the two Associations.

Time has shown that the work of the Advisory Committee was admirably accurate in its prediction. By the end of the 1980s there were twenty-two secondary and five comprehensive schools associated with the SEC and by the school year 1999-2000 there was only one secondary school less. The Advisory Committee's planning could not have anticipated the number of Catholic pupils who would choose to attend their schools by the 1980s, particularly in Dublin. Neither could it have foreseen the changing pattern in the availability of boarding schools throughout the country. Diminishing numbers of religious in education, rising costs associated with running boarding schools, and the need for additional classroom accommodation from the early 1970s led to a decrease in Catholic boarding places. Yet the market for boarding schools continued and by the 1990s there was evidence of a new demand for boarding school provision for pupils on completion of the Intermediate or Junior Certificate Examinations. In 2000 schools of the SEC continue to meet such needs.

A Changing Catholic Church

By the mid-1960s, the Catholic managerial bodies had not attempted any type of review of their position but the Federation of Catholic Lay Secondary Schools (FCLS) was an exception. As a group of lay owners of schools the FCLS were familiar with the struggle to survive as private establishments. Unlike the religious bodies the lay schools did not have access to other members of a community to support their work. The FCLS therefore continually reviewed their position and on a number of occasions in the 1960s urged their colleagues in the religious bodies to carry out some analysis of the position of their schools. Perhaps it was the differing levels of accountability that made the FCLS review their situation at various stages. The individual members had an acute awareness of what was needed to keep their schools in operation. Religious and clerics, on the other hand, might be described as having a 'corporate' approach. Individual principals and managers were accountable for what they did in the schools, but the community aspect of ownership or trusteeship cushioned the religious to some extent. A lay Catholic school such as Hamilton High School was more vulnerable financially than, for example, the schools of the Mercy Sisters or the Christian Brothers, and the schools under Protestant management were in much the same situation as the religious bodies. The case of the lay Catholic school, therefore, was quite unique.

Research in any organised manner was not a feature of the Catholic managerial organisations in the 1960s.[11] Bearing in mind that the majority were members of religious orders or priests with promises of obedience to their bishops, the idea of reviewing or investigating the 'apostolic works' including education would have been unthinkable at that time. The practice of religious obedience did not include discussion or dialogue between superior and subject. The very terms 'subject', 'major superior' and 'superior' give some indication of the hierarchical structure that existed within convents and monasteries. The approach had been effective for decades and the impetus for change did not come from within the orders and dioceses. The documents that emerged from Vatican II were the catalyst, though the effects were not immediately evident among the managerial bodies. The process of change is often complex for the individual, and there may be further complications for institutions. Traditions, customs and practices, organisational structures and individual roles may add to the challenges of managing change. It was a combination of falling numbers of candidates for the religious congregations and the teachings of Vatican II that set in motion a chain of events that affected the picture of Catholic education in Ireland. At national level the community schools and the primary school boards developed during the 1970s. Sandwiched between the radicalism of free education and comprehensive school plans in the 1960s and the pressures of the dismal economy of the 1980s, there is a danger that this decade could be neglected. But it was during these years that a platform was built from which remarkable changes would take place among the CMRS, the Catholic managerial bodies, and their schools.

A series of reports by the CMRS[12] challenged the religious orders about their role in education. The FIRE Report was completed in 1973 and the Focus for Action Report was presented to the religious superiors a year later. In 1975 a CMRS report was published on *Adult Education and the Catholic School* and in 1976 the major superiors funded a research project on adult education that led to *The North American Report* (1977). Some unease about the role of religious as employers brought about the Religious Employer Report in November 1978.[13] All of these reviews and the Catholic bishops' Report from Mulrany (1974) were the result of deliberations by the bishops and major superiors after Vatican II. There was also the impact of the 'external environments' of education (Goldring, 1997) from the 1960s. The real effects of free second level education, comprehensive schools and the contentious issue of teacher salaries, posts of responsibility and contracts of employment were experienced in the 1970s. But it was the CMRS rather than the managerial bodies that took the initiative, by leading a response to the effects of increased state intervention in education.

By contrast, the Church of Ireland had successfully implemented a process of planning for change during the 1960s. There may have been problematic situations at local level, but the leadership was evident and the General Synod of the Church of Ireland was a decade ahead of the Catholic Church authorities in exercising effective management in relation to the voluntary secondary school system. The extent of involvement in schools is relevant in seeking to understand why one group would make an impact on the system ahead of the other. Those Catholic bishops who had diocesan colleges may have been acutely aware of issues related to school management but the fact was that the bulk of the secondary schools were owned by religious orders and for the most part the bishops maintained a trusting distance. The SEC on the other hand related to a smaller group of schools. It is true that there was some uncertainty about its role in the early years and perhaps a degree of suspicion about what it might seek to accomplish. But the clarity of the distinction between management and policy making is of fundamental importance. So too is the ability of the minority church group to establish structures to facilitate organisational development. The seeming inability of the Catholic Church groups is related to the complex human and organisational relationships between the bishops, the CMRS, the autonomy of the religious orders and the lack of interaction between the managerial bodies. It was 1987 before the much needed restructuring could take place.

The Catholic Headmasters' Association 1878

The Catholic Headmasters' Association (CHA) was founded in 1878. It owes its beginning to the Intermediate Education (Ireland) Act of the same year and to some extent the prior existence of the Schoolmasters' Association. Individual Catholic headmasters were concerned that opportunities would be lost to their schools under the new legislation that for the first time enabled the funding of secondary education. Reverend William Delaney was the Jesuit rector or superior of their novitiate - the training school for members of the order - in Tullabeg (Morrissey, 2000: 62-70). He wrote of his concern to a friend who was then President of the major seminary for training priests, St Patrick's College, Maynooth. The context of the letter was the invitation of the Schoolmasters' Association to the Catholic principals and managers to join with them in responding to the incoming Intermediate Education Act. Reverend Edward Raffé, CSSp, headmaster and President of Blackrock College in Dublin supported Delaney in his desire to do something. The rector was conscious of the lack of leadership and organisational structure among the Catholic schools where 'we are still, and I fear likely to be, scattered units, without a plan or a policy'.[14] His friend Dr William Walsh who was to become the future Archbishop of Dublin in 1885, responded by inviting the Catholic headmasters of the diocesan and secondary schools to a meeting in Maynooth, with the intention of establishing an organisation. Neither the nuns nor the Christian Brothers were invited to the meeting and there was no reference to them in the founding of the new organisation.

An intriguing fact in the context of the time is that Dr Walsh did not inform the bishops of the decision to meet until he had notified the headmasters. Perhaps this was because he was aware of the lack of unity among the school headmasters; it was a mirror image of some disunity and rivalry among the owners of the diocesan colleges and the religious priests at that time. As Dr Walsh wrote to his fellow bishops on 21 September 1878, the aim of the diocesan colleges was 'to provide young men for the major seminaries and priesthood', but the principle of payment by results had brought an element of rivalry and meant that schools were caught in competition with each other.

Dr Walsh's letter to the bishops outlined the objectives of the proposed organisation and a number of the bishops and forty-four headmasters attended the meeting at Maynooth on 8 October 1878. Archbishop Croke of Cashel was the chairman. Fr Delaney SJ, and Dr Coffey headmaster of St Brendan's Diocesan College in Killarney, acted as the secretaries. Structures were set in place to ensure effective work. A standing committee was formed: the rector and vice-rector of the Catholic University, the President and vice-president of Maynooth, four heads of diocesan colleges and four headmasters from other clerical schools. From its beginning therefore, the CHA had a close association with third level education and with the bishops.[15] The first task of the CHA was to prepare a list of textbooks suitable for Catholic schools and a draft examination programme. These were to be sent to the Board of Commissioners who would be administering the Intermediate Education Act. The objectives as stated by Dr Walsh to the bishops were accepted by the assembled headmasters as those of the new organisation. The CHA therefore in 1878 aimed for

> *mutual communication and interchange of ideas as regards methods of*
> *teaching, the best school books, the special training required in preparing*
> *students for the examinations.*

Their second aim reflected the inherited knowledge gained by the Catholic bishops since the 1831 legislation on primary schools. Anything that might interfere with the denominational nature of their schools or with the freedom of the managers to select teachers would be unacceptable. Part of the function of any organisation therefore would be to note those factors in any emerging legislation. The bishops in 1878 who were present at the founding of the CHA would ensure

> *careful consideration of the Rules of the new Act, with a view to seeking*
> *their amendment through the Commissioners so far as it may be*
> *thought advisable in the interests of our Catholic Colleges.*

The standing committee was to plan for communication between the diocesan colleges and the secondary schools. It would also deal with 'the leading publishers of school books'. The bishops were anxious to exploit the Act to the advantage of the Catholic Church and they were urged on by the exhortations of Pope Pius IX to protect the interests of denominational education. The very existence of this first Catholic managerial body therefore was the result of a political decision to extend a system of public competitive examinations to Ireland.

There was strength in unity. The bishops saw the organisation as a means of supporting Catholic education, and their leadership and organisational skills were evident in the structure of the new body. In time the CHA would become a managerial organisation but that was not envisaged by its creators in 1878. To be accurate, the bishops should have been members of the CHA: they were legally the managers of their diocesan colleges. There were variations among the other CHA members. The majority of the religious priests who were members were headmasters or principals, not managers, of their schools. For the first five years in the 1960s a number of brothers joined the CHA. The organisation distinguished between those brothers who were headmasters and managers of their schools and those who were simply headmasters, though the reason for clarifying the roles of the brothers (and not the priests) is not recorded.

The original Constitution (1878) urged members of the CHA to ensure that their schools would be the leaders in the competitive public examination system. Good results would draw parliamentary funding to the schools. From the nineteenth century the voluntary secondary system had developed a tradition of commitment to academic achievement and the Constitution of the CHA is a statement of such interest. At the end of the twentieth century and into the twenty-first that strong emphasis on academic attainment has persisted in CHA schools. This does not deny a long tradition in sports, debating and a broader educational experience for students. The CHA was also interested from its foundation in 'teaching methods' and 'special training' for teachers to help pupils to learn, but that aspect of their work tended to give way to macro-managerial issues particularly from the end of the 1970s. The test of time and a different era showed that the organisation was pragmatic in its responses to 'external environments': a new Ireland, a Department of Education and two different state examinations by the late 1950s, though under the Intermediate Education Acts of 1878 and 1924.

The diocesan colleges were originally junior seminaries or preparatory institutions for boys, many of whom would pursue a vocation to the priesthood. In addition to Maynooth as the major seminary there were minor or smaller seminaries in a number of dioceses, for example St Peter's College which was the seminary for the Diocese of Ferns. Dublin as an Archdiocese had its own seminary at Clonliffe College in Drumcondra, while the religious orders of priests had their own houses of formation. A clear aim of the CHA in 1878 was to ensure that the boys in the diocesan colleges would pass the entrance examination for Maynooth. The bishops wanted 'the alignment of the content' of the Maynooth examination to be planned with care. Moreover, the bishops knew the importance of interpreting legislative measures and directed the new CHA to give 'careful consideration' to the Act of 1878. It is evident that the bishops believed that the new organisation should be a watchdog and conduit for responding to educational legislation and developments. It was not intended to be a managerial body with responsibility for the school system, though it became such.

The need for clarification of role is crucial to effective management. The bishops who established the CHA were not confused: the headmaster, or president as he was some-times called in diocesan colleges, was in charge of the leadership, administration and managing of the school. One of the school aims was to prepare boys for Maynooth by ensuring the required examination standard. But the headmaster was not the manager. The bishops were the managers and patrons of their diocesan colleges and the intention was that the demarcation line between manager and headmaster would remain. Management theory has developed slowly and mainly in the twentieth century and so there was no job specification for either principal or manager. General practice in the religious schools up to the 1960s was for one person to combine roles. It is possible that the presence in the CHA of the religious priests and later of brothers who were principals and managers meant that discussion centred on the running of schools rather than on any separation of roles in management and administration. By the time of the establishing of the Department of Education in 1924 there was little evidence of a distinction between the role of manager and headmaster or principal. From the 1950s to 1987 the minutes of the bi-annual meetings of the CHA show that the work of manager and principal was of continual interest to the members. No additional payment was made to school principals until 1974. There was an expectation that the principals in the secondary schools were like those in the national schools where the *príomh oide* was the principal or leader teacher. Certainly, if a secondary schools had more than 60 pupils on roll the principal was not required to teach. The majority taught.[16]

No official publication or statement from the Department of Education recognised the need for management training until the mid-1980s when Gemma Hussey was Minister, although the managerial bodies provided training from 1973 and the Department organised occasional summer programmes related to school administration. Doubtless the fact that so many CHA men became bishops helped to blur the distinction between roles in the diocesan colleges. The combination of the headmasters of all the diocesan colleges, the close interest and support of many of the bishops and the contribution of the religious priests made for a small but strong CHA by 1909 when the ASTI was founded.

The story of the union struggle in relation to teacher salary and the contract of employment (Coolahan, 1984) records the close involvement and at times opposition of the CHA at many levels (Ó Buachalla, 1988:141). The CHA was a main player among the three managerial bodies even then. For a number of years the organisation had published the *Irish Educational Review* (1907-1914) but no other publication followed. The close association with the Catholic bishops would have encouraged communication. Would it also engender confidence within the managerial organisation at times of pressure as in the 1960s, 1970s and 1980s? During the 1960s and 1970s other managerial bodies might experience a sense of being excluded from 'a club'. In keeping with their Constitution one might expect the CHA to be watchful of official or ministerial pronouncements. Equally one might anticipate a keenness to interpret the external environment of secondary education.

By 1960 the original aims of the CHA had been revised a number of times. A constitution was formulated and organisational details were refined. However, the twin aims of 1878 remained unchanged apart from the inclusion in 1953 of the word 'secondary'. Another review was done in 1973 when four regional groups met to draft an education policy statement. The various regional reports show general agreement on the role of the schools in Catholic education and the increasing workload of the headmasters. One report recommended that the secondary school should provide adult education. In 1987 when the re-structuring of the managerial organisations was finalised the CHA Constitution committed members to

> the advancement of Catholic secondary *education and mutual aid*
> *in questions concerning the interests and educational problems of*
> *Catholic secondary schools.*

The composition of the standing committee had ceased to include representatives of the universities after 1925. At times individual bishops were voted honorary members and some continued to attend CHA meetings on occasion. That close relationship with the Hierarchy continued to 1987 though at times there were tensions. The custom of holding general meetings in October and April was followed from the beginning though from 1967 the second meeting was rearranged for the month of May. Since the 1970s these two annual gatherings were often planned to coincide with some significant sporting fixture. The social aspect was important to the CHA and continues to be part of the bonding of the members. In the early 1950s a number of teaching brothers sought membership and were welcomed into the CHA. By 1960 four orders of brothers had joined though not the Christian Brothers who preferred their own separate organisation. When the CHA made its submission to the Commission on Higher Education in 1961 it represented ninety-four schools with a total of 17,359 pupils. They did not include Catholic lay schools. In 1970, Liam Murphy, the first layman to be appointed headmaster in a diocesan college, became a member of the CHA. As principal of St Patrick's Classical School in Navan, he also functioned as manager. He subsequently became president of the CHA.

Throughout its history the CHA has been more reactive than proactive in relation to curriculum. The records show their responses to various changes in courses and in the 1940s and 1950s their input on choice of texts, particularly in Latin and English. Clarity about their mission in the schools comes across in the records of discussion by the priests on texts, courses and examinations. That ability to concentrate on the principal task was a mark of their effective management and leadership. The manner in which they appear to have dealt with the lengthy questionnaire on the curriculum of secondary schools from the Council of Education is of interest. They devoted two CHA meetings to the matter, one in 1956 to discuss the questionnaire and urge members to share suggestions and another to agree their draft response. But the year before the publication of the Council's Report the managerial body had discussed at length their much shorter submission to the Commission on Higher Education.

The vision and mission of Catholic education shared by the CHA is evident in this submission. They include a section on the aims of education and they envisage 'the spiritual formation' of their pupils continuing into third level. One of the recommendations formulated at the CHA meeting in the Gresham Hotel Dublin on 3 May 1961 encapsulated a fear that academic standards might be sacrificed to science in the schools. They subsequently wrote to the Commission on Higher Education:

> In the swing away from our previous neglect of science and technology we should, we think, be careful not to fall into the greater hazard of producing one-eyed monsters of science - a danger that has been realised elsewhere.

During the early years the CHA had fostered an association with third level and there is evidence of appreciation of the university system in their response in 1961. In fact they saw a possible liaison with third level as a useful way of implementing change in the secondary system. It is fair to suggest that these managers appreciated the need for structural change to facilitate curriculum development.

In 1962 Dr Hillery as Minister for Education sought the views of the CHA on the *Report of the Council of Education* which had been published that year.[17] There is no evidence of a similar request to the other managerial bodies. It is possible that the Minister's subsequent disinterest in the *Report* was influenced by the CHA response to his 'unofficial' request. Perhaps he was seeking confirmation of his own reaction to the lengthy and conservative *Report* at a time when the economy was highlighting the need for educational change. Dr Hillery was aware of the importance of the Catholic Hierarchy in education. Perhaps his approach to the CHA was another example of his understanding of the complex system of voluntary education in Ireland and the close relationship between this managerial group and the bishops. At their meeting in October 1962 the CHA discussed three items as requested by the Minister: the new science courses for Leaving Certificate pupils, the *Report of the Council of Education*, and the provision of texts in Irish for grade A or all-Irish schools.

The brevity of the CHA reply to the Minister in November 1962 nonetheless gives some insight into the managerial body at that time. They used the opportunity to remind the Minister of 'what has been done from private resources for the development of secondary education in Ireland'. They advised him that religion as a subject should be 'explicitly mentioned' in the Department of Education regulations dealing with the 'recognition of secondary schools' and that the 'most desirable age of entry' to secondary schools was 'twelve plus'. These two items, religion as a 'subject' and the 'age of entry', were to become important issues for the managerial bodies in the 1970s and 1980s. In 1962 the CHA reminded Dr Hillery that the *Report of the Council of Education* positively recognised that

> *a well balanced course must have a basic core of humanist and other subjects but that the balance should be in favour of the humanist group* (1962:170).

The managers believed in the secondary system that offered a 'general education' to Leaving Certificate level though they admitted the inability of some pupils to deal with honours mathematics. The 'secondary tops' (or additional classes at the top of the primary school system) were a 'temporary solution to a pressing need for secondary education'. Unknown to the managerial bodies the Duggan Committee was already (and secretly) at work in the Department of Education preparing policy that would result in free education. The need for textbooks in Irish for the grade A schools was declared by the CHA to be 'urgent'. While the new science courses were welcomed they cautioned against the 'quite undue influence' of the university on the curriculum of secondary schools. On this point the CHA wrote to Dr Hillery on 21 November 1962:

> *Preparation of students for the University is neither the sole nor even the primary function of secondary schools. The very great majority of pupils in secondary schools do not proceed to the University and the principle that secondary schools have as their purpose the giving of a balanced and general education must be maintained and protected.*

The CHA in their submission to the Council of Education in the 1950s had emphasised 'the determining influence on both the curriculum and the examinations' of the university. In 1962 their attitude was unchanged. It seems a strange omission that the CHA did not repeat to the Minister for Education their recommendation to the Commission on Higher Education a year earlier:

> *Since the foundation of the State we have had a Commission on Technical Education (1926), a Commission on Vocational Organisation (1943), and in more recent times a Council of Education to make recommendations on Primary and Secondary Education; now we have a Commission on Higher Education. Very few of the recommendations of these Commissions or Councils have been put into practice. We think that the most glaring need all the time has been for a Commission or Council to make recommendations on co-ordination and with real power to see that they are put into practice.*[18]

The CHA specified the kind of organisation they envisaged: a 'Board of Control' that was not 'an amorphous ephemeral body like the Council of Education'. They admitted the similarity between this proposed 'Board of Control' and that envisaged by the Council of Education for vocational schools. Perhaps they were wise in not telling the Minister for Education about their proposal. The priests were in agreement that the Department and the civil servants should not run the 'Board of Control', though they could be involved. It appeared at this stage that the CHA were of the belief that review of the school system was necessary.

The Headmasters also began to show a greater awareness of the need for structures in the Catholic school system though they continued to be concerned about standards in education. A few years later there was concern about proposed changes by the Department of Education in the Latin programme. The work of Dr Peter Birch, Bishop of Ossory and former professor of education in Maynooth, was mainly responsible for the energy with which the CHA again pursued the issue of set texts in the subject. Dr Birch's earlier experience as teacher of classics in St Kieran's College, Kilkenny set the context for his interest in Latin on the curriculum. 'The greatest need is for an enthusiastic teacher who would read Latin with his pupils,' he wrote on 29 July 1966 to Canon Mooney of St Jarlath's College, Tuam and secretary of the CHA. The interest of the priests in the Latin programme is understandable since this was the official language of the Catholic Church until the end of the 1960s.

In the thirty-year period up to 1987 there is little evidence in the records that the boys' schools were *developing* curriculum. They continued to pursue high academic standards, the public examinations, and a strong interest in sporting activities. On occasion they continued to bemoan the plight of pupils who were unfit for honours mathematics. As a managerial organisation they had been established to respond to a competitive examination system and they remained true to their roots. In spite of the fact that there were many priests including some former headmasters among the members of the VECs, the CHA distrusted vocational education,[19] and their attitude until the late 1970s can be summed up in the belief that an education where skills rather than intellectual training are emphasised would be an 'illusory freedom' (Jonathan, 1997). If it ever occurred to them that the secondary school curriculum did not suit all pupils, this concern does not appear in their records before 1973. The boys who came to their schools were fit to be there and would benefit from the academic education and the emphasis on sports. There are references to 'in-between pupils' in the context of discussions on the honours mathematics courses that should be

> the equivalent of two subjects. Boys who cannot cope with honours
> and are well able for pass level should have available an alternative
> programme or be enabled to be assessed in 'stages'.

But there was no attempt to develop such a programme. The priests appear to have had great confidence in their system of education and the doubts that arise in the 1960s are related to the intrusion of the state into second level education through the comprehensive schools. A logical response of the CHA therefore was a request to the Department of Education in 1968 for 'legal status':

> The CHA requires from the government that the relations between
> the state and secondary school authorities be set down in an Act
> of the Oireachtas.[20]

The CHA and the Nuns

Because there was no separate organisation for the nuns' schools the CHA acted as a kind of 'father caretaker', though the nuns never attended meetings of the organisation on a regular basis. The priests advised rather than consulted the nuns about the issues related to the teachers' salaries grant of 1914, the establishment of the Teachers' Registration Council in 1918, and the bishops' opposition to the proposed Education Bill of 1919. But awareness of the need for women to be more involved in educational developments was quietly growing in the convents where most of the secondary education for girls was provided.

The period during which Dr John Charles McQuaid, President of Blackrock College was chairman brought the CHA to the centre of the educational and political power (Cooney, 1999:82-5; 305-6). Until the early 1960s the CHA unofficially accepted responsibility for negotiating on behalf of the nuns and one such occasion is of interest because it involved Dr McQuaid who had recently succeeded in preventing the establishment of an Educational Advisory Council proposed by the INTO. Many convents had private junior or fee-charging primary schools attached to their secondary schools, though with a separate principal and staff. From its beginning in 1929 the CCSS included these principals and managers in the organisation. In September 1934 a circular from the Department of Education stated that junior departments in private schools which met the necessary requirements of inspection would receive certification. The Department justified its initial request for detailed information from the private schools on the basis of the School Attendance Act (1926) because the children were within the compulsory age. Some convents had already returned the necessary agreement form to the Department. Others resisted despite 'extreme moral pressure' from local inspectors.

The nuns believed that inspection was the beginning of 'serious and complete control of education by the state' and sought the advice of Dr McQuaid because Blackrock College also had a junior private school. His name was familiar to the nuns for his involvement in the on-going contract negotiations with the ASTI.[21] He told them to ignore the ministerial request for information because their schools were private and therefore did not require certification from the state. Those managers who had given their consent for the Department inspection were instructed to withdraw it.[22] In the light of subsequent historical developments in education perhaps what is of greatest interest is that this circular led to the first significant contact by the CCSS with Dr McQuaid in the CHA.[23]

In 1946 a 'commission' of the CHA was asked to report to the bishops on the salaries paid by the nuns' schools. A sample of forty schools was surveyed, a high proportion. At the time there were 110 schools in the CCSS. Eighty-eight schools employed a total of 235 full-time and 39 part-time lay teachers. Neither the bishops nor the CHA viewed the nuns as a main player in the leadership and management of the secondary system. Their approach was in keeping with the status and customary practice of religious orders of women at the time. This enhanced the role of the Headmasters' Association and led to more contact with members of the Hierarchy than the small group of male schools might otherwise have needed. From 1958 the records show the frequency of the discussions between John Hughes SJ, Mother Jordana OP, and certain members of the Hierarchy among them Archbishop John Charles McQuaid.

This interaction was rarely publicised within the CCSS or the CHA, but it helped to bring the nuns towards the centre of the stage for the renewed negotiations on the contract of employment from the end of the 1960s. Máire McDonagh was glad that 'the nuns had found a voice' in Mother Jordana OP in 1958.[24] Before the end of the 1950s the ASTI contacted the CHA rather than the CCSS when the question of finalising the contract issue was being pursued and, as late as 1968, officials of the Department of Education who believed that 'a new contract' for teachers was essential, directed the remarks to the CHA, not to the nuns.[25] The bishops also looked to the CHA to act on behalf of the nuns.

The CHA and the ISA

Individual members of the CHA kept contact with their colleagues in the ISA. They had occasional discussions about boarding schools, Leaving Certificate programmes and university education. Salary and contract problems were not a common concern between the CHA and the ISA. The ASTI rarely had problems with ISA schools and the contract issue was only relevant to the Catholic schools. In that sense the CHA as an organisation was more devoted to managerial concerns than the ISA, the AIH or the CCSS. In 1973 the Headmasters insisted that:

> *Catholic school authorities are not interested in retaining managerial*
> *or property rights for their own sake. We are concerned solely with*
> *providing the best possible education for all our children. We are*
> *ready and anxious to co-operate with everybody in this. And we make*
> *no apology for being in education. On the contrary, we have an*
> *obligation to be there. We see education as the highest form of*
> *Christian social action today.[26]*

This confidence appears to be based on a belief in the mission of the Catholic Church to educate and, while that conviction is also evident among the nuns in 1973 at the time of the FIRE Report, the difference is that the women are questioning and sometimes beginning to doubt their role in the secondary schools. Were the priests better at reading the 'external environments' to education? In the 1960s the CHA had explored the idea of a 'Board of Control' and a confidential policy document within the organisation in 1973 advocated 'an Independent Education Authority for Post-Primary Education representative of all interests'. The discussion was in the political context and the concern was that 'one-party rule can hardly be always said to have worked according to the highest objective principle'. To avoid the subservience of education policy to political parties the proposed 'Independent Education Authority' would advise on 'such matters as curriculum, syllabus, examinations, teacher remuneration etc' and, to ensure that all types of educational needs would be met,

this Independent Education Authority should strive to introduce the
principle of Regionalisation, on the same lines as Health, Tourism and
Industrial Development. The Regional Body would be best able to
explore the needs of a particular area and decide on such matters as
utilisation of existing facilities, the syllabi and curriculum best suited
to a particular area, co-education, multi-denominational education.

The Church of Ireland submission for the White Paper (1980) may have been influenced by individuals in the CHA and certainly the proposal to establish an Education Commission resembled the Independent Education Authority recommended by the CHA in 1973. More than twelve years before Gemma Hussey as Minister for Education proposed regional boards (*Green Paper*, 1985; Walshe, 1999) the CHA had recommended them.

The traditional academic emphasis in the curriculum of CHA schools was discussed frequently from 1973. The impact of free post-primary education was being experienced in classrooms and as a result some boys who might have gone to the technical schools before 1968 were now in the traditional academic schools of the CHA. Discussion about those who could not cope with honours level mathematics gave way in the 1970s to concern about pupils who were finding difficulty with a range of subjects. The realisation that 'a more comprehensive curriculum' is necessary was agreed though there is little evidence of attempts at development. In the north and north-west regional group of priest headmasters there seems to have been a sharper focus on the need to balance the academic emphasis in their schools with 'technical training' to ensure that pupils would work 'in Ireland'. There were misgivings that the CHA as a managerial organisation would attempt to prepare a policy document for the Catholic schools because

the CHA covers a very wide spectrum from the upper class boarding
school to the day school of the country town. Its members, however, are
mainly drawn from upper or middle class schools. On the other hand, if
there is to be a report at national level, this report must deal principally
with day schools, comprehensive, secondary and vocational from
which the overwhelming majority of Irish children receive their
education. The vast majority of the members of the CHA know little
of this side of Irish education.[27]

In their discussions about state involvement in education the CHA appear not to deviate from a belief that a shortage of priests, nuns and brothers should not deter the church from staying in management even if that necessitated a 'Catholic comprehensive' like the example set by the Jesuits in Mungret.

The CHA had decades of experience in dealing with the ASTI and the Department of Education. There were also many personal friendships between the priests and individual union members. When one of the CHA members initiated legal proceedings against the Minister (Osborough, 1978:147), both the ASTI and the CHA were supportive. The denial of service recognition to a priest in respect of overseas teaching experience had implications for union members too and winning the case was a victory for the CHA and the union.[28] As a managerial body the CHA did not initiate in-service training though they were willing participants with the other organisations. For instance when the CCSS organised the first training programme in pastoral care in the 1970s they were fully supported by the headmasters and teachers from CHA schools.[29]

The CHA was a small group that became smaller when the teaching brothers finally formed the TBA in the 1960s. The priests did not have any full-time officer. But like each of the managerial bodies the CHA fulfilled an important role for its members. In the absence of a review or evaluation of the organisation at any stage in its history it is impossible to quantify that contribution to its membership. Neither could one estimate the extent to which the CHA was an information resource for newly-appointed headmasters. The organisation lasted because members attended meetings and participated in its continuing negotiations on behalf of Catholic education.

The Conference of Convent Secondary Schools 1929

Though not the oldest of the managerial organisations the CCSS had a bigger membership than each of the others and the members were all religious sisters. The term 'the nuns' was commonly (though not accurately) used by the religious themselves and will therefore be used in this book. The CCSS records are extensive so there is more information about the organisation. The members met more frequently than any of the other managerial bodies and were the first to develop a regional structure, in 1966. The organisation had a president and a central standing committee. The structure helped to ensure meetings, communication and a wealth of archival material. The extent of the influence of the CCSS among the managerial bodies, in a Catholic Church that was dominated by men at every structural level, is of interest, but it is also difficult to assess. For much of the time the interest of the nuns was directed to curriculum rather than to managerial issues. Yet the impact of the Second Vatican Council (Vatican II) was more pronounced on the CCSS than on the other Catholic bodies and their educational values as an organisation are therefore well documented.

The contribution of the Irish Dominican nuns to the education of girls and to the history of the CCSS was considerable. St Dominic's Training College was opened in the convent in Eccles Street in Dublin in 1909 and within twenty years more than 100 nuns from several congregations had been prepared for their teaching diplomas. Thus the Dominicans were highly regarded among the female teaching orders as leaders in education, and when a managerial body for the voluntary secondary schools run by nuns was to be established, they were to the fore.

The organisation began with a meeting of a group of Dominican headmistresses in 1929 in the convent in Cabra. Their agenda was to examine the 'relations of the schools with various educational and government authorities' and particularly with 'the use and abuse' of examinations. The tradition of competitive public examinations (Coolahan, 1981) was given greater impetus from 1878 and 1924 under the two Intermediate Education Acts. Some of the nuns had expected that the new Department of Education and the introduction in 1925 of the Intermediate and Leaving Certificate programmes would have freed the system from the competitive aspect. They feared a diminution in the attainment of their ideals about the education of girls by too great an emphasis being placed on results.

> People judge us and our schools largely by our examination results. Therefore we keep up a high standard in results so that people may send their children to us. But it is in order that we may get hold of their children, so as to influence them aright that we aim at 'good results'. The results are not themselves the object of our work. This is sometimes lost sight of.[30]

The discussion in 1929 was to enable the headmistresses to 'assign each subject its true place in the curriculum' and to explore the 'particular means to be adopted to achieve our ideal in education'. It was an exercise in review and evaluation as well as an effort to renew their awareness of the Dominican mission in education and their quest for 'the truth' which was their motto. Time was given also at this meeting to discussing teaching methods and

> the relative importance of subjects in the development of the child with the Catholic mind and the intelligence to know what is right and the will to do what is right.

Two months later, on 26 March 1929, Dr W.F. Butler who had been Assistant Commissioner for Education from 1910 to 1924 and then principal officer in the secondary branch of the new Department of Education, issued a circular letter, Secondary School Certificate Examinations: Appointment of Standardising Committees. He was communicating a ministerial decision to establish the committees, initially to consider the examination papers in Irish, English, Mathematics, History and Geography in the forthcoming examinations. The committees were to be composed of representatives nominated annually 'by such recognised Associations and other bodies of Secondary Teachers, as, in the opinion of the Minister, afford representation to the different interests concerned'.[31] This role in conferring status on organisations would be a power used with effect by the Department of Education in the 1950s, 1980s and 1990s. The nuns had no 'recognised Association'[32] but Dr Butler who was friendly with the Dominicans in Cabra suggested to them that 'a few of the more important nuns' schools' be asked to send representatives to the meetings to be held in number 1 Hume Street. The three 'important' orders he named were the Ursulines, the St Louis and the Loreto nuns.

Thus it was in the context of the standardising committees that the nuns sought the necessary approval from Archbishop Walsh to form a headmistresses' association. A preliminary meeting of fifteen nuns from the three religious orders was held in Dominican College, Eccles Street on 26 April 1929.[33] At the request of the Archbishop a Vincentian priest presided. Subsequent to this meeting was a gathering of nuns from all the schools on 17 May in Dominican College, Eccles Street, with the intention of forming a headmistresses' association for convent schools. As on the previous occasion a Vincentian priest presided; it was a custom that was to continue for forty years in the CCSS and on some of those occasions the presiding cleric also chaired the meetings. In the 1950s the priest was often John Hughes SJ, chairman of the CHA. In 1959 when Mother Jordana OP was President the nuns decided to run their own meetings.

From its beginning the CCSS aimed

> to facilitate interchange of ideas and information on all school
> matters for example, teaching, examinations, internal management
> and organisation generally.

The caring aspect of management evident in their aim is one of the characteristics that Rothschild (1991) found in management by females as compared with males. The nuns never used the term 'action research' (Elliot, 1990 and 1991) though their interest in sharing their practices in internal management, organisational skills and leadership might be seen as an early example of reflection on work practice. Like the ISA, the AIH and the CHA, the nuns were committed to denominational education. They aimed

> to watch over Catholic interests in all matters concerning our schools,
> and to take such steps as may be considered advisable to procure the
> due consideration of such interests.

Seventeen convents could not send their two representatives to the inaugural meeting 'due to long distance'. Nevertheless, a total of 120 nuns attended, presumably representing sixty schools since no religious woman was allowed to travel unaccompanied. In his address the archbishop's representative hoped the meeting 'would prove the Educational Magna Carta of the Nuns of Ireland'. The invitation by:

the Ministry of Education to the convent schools to take part in the framing
of the programmes and examination papers, was a recognition by the
government of the importance of religious bodies in the educational work
of the country.[34]

Moreover, 'since the Examination Paper controlled the teaching', the presiding chairman thought that representation on the standardising committees would be very important and might be the way to end the system of publication of examination results and the consequent imbalance in the curriculum.[35]

The women in 1929 did not attempt to re-invent a wheel: they simply took the rules of the CHA, modified them and submitted the amended version to the archbishop whose approval was required before they could set up an organisation. At that first meeting they also used democratic procedures to elect their five representatives on the standardising committees and compiled a list of twenty-one lay teachers 'recommended as suitable to act as representatives'. Unfortunately the records do not contain the criteria for the selection of these lay teachers.[36]

The CHA was not the only influence on the new association. One enterprising Dominican in the Cabra convent had contacted a Vincentian priest in the Training College at Strawberry Hill in London regarding the Association of Head Mistresses there. The topics being discussed by the English counterparts of the CCSS were syllabi, salaries and superannuation, qualifications of teachers and teaching methods. The usual complexities of human interaction were not missing at the start of the CCSS. The presiding priest who chaired the early meetings wrote of

> *the many rival interests in this association of head mistresses though it*
> *runs smoothly. Naturally there is a healthy rivalry between the Sacred*
> *Heart Nuns, the Sisters of Notre Dame, the Nuns of the Faithful*
> *Companions, Sisters of the Holy Child and the Sisters of the Assumption*
> *all of whom have large schools in this country. Whilst there may be*
> *domestic differences they present a common front as Catholics when*
> *meeting the problems that arise in the educational world in which they*
> *move. I have omitted the name of the Ursulines but I may inform you*
> *that they have some live wires in the movement.*[37]

Some of the religious orders had convent schools in Northern Ireland. The ISA, the AIH and the CHA were all founded in the nineteenth century when the whole island of Ireland was part of the United Kingdom. Membership included colleagues in what became Northern Ireland after 1921 although gradually the organisations came to represent only schools in the south. The CCSS was founded in the Free State and in 1929 when preparatory work was being done by the nuns they considered including sisters from the northern schools as their representatives on the new standardising committees of the Department of Education. There is no evidence that this happened and in 1942 the northern convents established their own conference. From the 1970s the CCSS and the Conference of Catholic Schools of Northern Ireland were in regular contact with each other and with their counterpart organisation in England.[38]

The early records of the CCSS show that attention was given to a range of issues including the Teachers' Registration Council by 1935. That same year the nuns were the first of the managerial bodies to recognise the importance of school insurance.[39] They discussed contracts for lay teachers agreed with the ASTI in 1937 though it was ten years before they accepted them.[40] The nuns invested time and thought into problems consequent on the teacher contracts. By 1949 they were concerned about the hardening attitude of the ASTI on the rights of probationary teachers, salaries, school timetables, teaching hours and secondary tops. But they were slow to recognise the role of lay teachers in their schools. The fact that some thirty schools had no lay teachers at this time gives an insight into the slowness of the CCSS in interpreting the reality of the 'external environment' that not all teachers would be nuns.

A year earlier an article associated with Professor Alfred O'Rahily, editor of the *Cork University Record* accused the nuns of using lay teachers as 'a stop gap profession'.[41] In an unusual response the CCSS sought the support of the ASTI. The CHA had already reported at the request of the bishops on CCSS school salaries. Nevertheless from the publication of the article there is an increasing volume of letters to the CCSS President from the convent schools about the payment of lay teachers. It was not that the nuns chose to ignore what today is called 'social justice' so much as that lay teachers and in particular lay women were seen as 'stopping the gap' in a school. This might enable a nun either to complete training as a novice or qualification as a teacher. The nuns knew that few women teachers would remain unmarried and marriage would end a teaching role. The notion of career for women was undeveloped and the ban on married women in the public service was only lifted after 31 July 1973. By the 1950s the nuns were more concerned about the use of contract forms, the implications of the Unemployment Insurance Act (1920), and possible pension schemes.[42]

Throughout the 1930s and 1940s the CCSS discussed ways of improving the education of girls. It is in these years that a marked independence of the Department of Education becomes evident in the records. In May 1937 a circular from the Department declared an intention to standardise entrance examinations by setting the papers. It drew from the nuns a refusal to comply because of its 'undue interference in our schools'.[43] That year the nuns were more interested in discussing teaching methods in Irish and mathematics and the value of including philosophy as a subject on the curriculum.[44] Through the 1930s their attention was devoted to the importance of music, art, physical education and sports and all cultural activities including radio, cinema and drama, on teaching methods and 'how to improve learning'.[45] Guest speakers, usually lay women, were often invited to introduce topics for discussion. Among the issues addressed were physical culture for girls, games and girl guiding, the papal encyclical on Christian Education (*Divini Illius Magistri*, 1929), the Catholic tradition in education, the correlation of history and geography with other subjects, the place of traditional music in secondary schools. It was very rarely that the teaching of the Irish language was discussed though the learning of French and Latin featured and the nuns had sought an oral Irish examination in the 1930s. In 1933 and 1934 despite resentment that the newspapers knew before the nuns about Minister for Education Tomás Derrig's circular (25/33) on the importance of 'home exercises for pupils in secondary schools', the CCSS organised subject discussion groups to consider the 'quite contentious' topic.

The conscientious concern of those in the CCSS with girls' education was reflected also in the decision in 1943 to establish an internal commission to enquire into the 'failings in the present system for girls'. The report was completed in 1945 and identified as the chief failing the fact that 'many schools fail to train the girl for life in the world of today'. The CCSS consistency of aim is reflected in the report's criticism:

> It is said that (the girl) leaves school with mind undisciplined, judgement
> untrained, character unformed, and is often a prey to selfish individualism.[46]

The failure of the system was seen to be the result of

> the changed order in the world in which girls' greater freedom
> and independence (enables them) to leave home and enter
> into competition with men; this demands a two-fold education
> where schools should prepare a girl to be a wife, mother and
> a home-maker on his (sic) income.

This aspect of the CCSS schools was highlighted by Pope Pius XII on the occasion of the silver jubilee of the conference in 1954 when he appealed 'for the conservation, the preservation and the defence of the Christian family' as the priority in all educational activity. The convent schools valued 'training in self-control and in moral purity and dignity' as essential for girls whose main task in living was to become 'home makers'.[47] There can be little doubt that the teaching nuns found courage when the Pope told them to 'look forward, unafraid,' because 'the mission which is yours to accomplish' was their 'one light'. Two years earlier Seán Moylan, Minister for Education, had identified the source of the nuns' self-assurance about their role in the schools when he quoted the Taoiseach Éamon de Valéra who likened teaching to a religious vocation. And de Valéra, as Moylan believed and told the nuns, 'was right as he always is, in matters of spiritual significance'.[48]

Another Minister in the 1950s used the CCSS annual general meeting to challenge the nuns (Downey, 1998:68). Jack Lynch was eighteen months Minister for Education when he experienced some European incredulity regarding the Irish system of education.

He found the system 'hard to explain'. People were astonished that 'the directors of the secondary education in the country were largely in charge of privately-owned schools'; small wonder that 'our system has been described as excellent, fundamentally sound, and the worst in Europe'.[49] But Lynch was politically wise enough to recognise the power of the nuns and used the occasion to propose an oral Irish examination for the Leaving Certificate, though the format was not favourably received. He also urged them to make their pupils 'more politically aware'.[50]

At the same time the nuns pressed hard for the Department of Education to provide practical examinations in domestic economy; because that would be more helpful to pass-level pupils.[51] They wanted the Department to provide assessment for groups of subjects within the arts including 'useful hobbies' such as dancing. In 1943 the nuns had appointed a Committee on Education to prepare a series of discussion papers for their meetings and these papers provide an insight into schools and some curriculum evaluation being pursued by the CCSS.[52] The examination system was criticised because it was 'purely intellectual' and did little 'to prepare a girl for life'. There was 'no co-ordination between subjects taught'. The nuns advocated two separate Leaving Certificate courses, one to cater for 'the twenty per cent who would proceed to University', and the other to be 'of a practical nature'. They recommended that the Intermediate Certificate Examination should include practical and oral assessment.[53] There is evidence that, some years later, in 1948, when the CCSS was engaged in a review of the curriculum, they wanted to provide a 'second more practical stream' in their schools because the 'curriculum only suits forty per cent of the girls'. In 1943 when technical subjects were developing in some of the boys' schools the CCSS had tried in vain to persuade the Department of Education to allow girls' schools to teach horticulture. As early as 1939 and again in 1949 and 1952 the nuns were considering how psychology could help them deal with 'adolescent problems', but all the time the aim was to provide the best education for 'good mothers' for the future.[54] That education should be based on 'a balanced curriculum' of

> elementary logic and philosophy, art appreciation and history of art
> in addition to the existing art course, music appreciation and history
> of music in addition to the existing music course, the world's great
> literature in translation, world history, film appreciation and physical
> culture with games and team sport.

Alone among the managerial bodies until 1970, the nuns were continually seeking 'contacts with parents', though clearly the emphasis was on mothers rather than fathers and on 'mothers' meetings' and later on 'mothers' sodalities'.[55]

It was largely their concern for parents that led the nuns to oppose the government's proposed Public Health Bill in 1946 with its medical inspection scheme for school pupils. The letter of the CCSS President seeking the permission of Archbishop

McQuaid to write to the Taoiseach specifies five sections of the bill. The CCSS records show that the President had already been alerted to these sections by General Richard Mulcahy, Minister of Education, 'who felt sorry for her having to wade through the whole bill'.[56] Two years later the nuns welcomed the inclusion of parents on the forthcoming Council of Education to examine curriculum in national and secondary schools, though they themselves declined to take part.[57] The nuns' belief in their ability to prepare girls 'for Christian marriage'[58] led them to object to the Department of Education when it tried to replace the physiology and hygiene course with biology. In 1951 in the midst of concerns about the new superannuation scheme for teachers and unemployment insurance the nuns were consistent in their emphasis on preparing 'women for the family and motherhood'.[59] One may only guess at their impact on future families when one considers that in 1954 there were 24,500 girls in the 186 convent secondary schools.

The nuns put a remarkable emphasis on physical education and sport, especially 'open air sports', right up to 1959. This was remarkable when one remembers that recreational sport was not part of life in convents at that time. It was desirable in the education of girls because of its relevance to discipline. Homework was a means of training pupils in 'self-discipline' and 'control' and sports education was related to that basis for personal development. In 1955, in response to the Council of Education, the CCSS still believed that homework had a part to play in developing self-discipline, being as 'necessary for character training as for progress in studies', and that teachers should help pupils to learn how to learn.[60] The CCSS records show that at times the nuns thought they were making no impact on the system in relation to the 'centrality of physical well-being and sports'. However, by the end of the 1950s the Department of Education appeared to recognise the importance of physical education. There is insufficient evidence to claim that the CCSS as a managerial body influenced the development but it is possible. The nuns were affirmed by the aims and objectives expressed in the Syllabus in Physical Education for Girls for Secondary Schools:

> *to obtain a full and harmonious development of the physical and mental*
> *powers, to build up a sound constitution, thus securing health, the*
> *power of endurance, a high degree of bodily control, grace of movement,*
> *economy of effort, the development of obedience, ready response,*
> *co-operative activity and team work.*
>
> (RIALACHA AGUS CLÁR, 1958-1959:20)

Training in 'self-control' was believed to be a vital aspect of the educational work of the nuns. But it was not control for its own sake. Rather it was a cornerstone for future Christian family living.

Papal Influence

The impact of the leader of the Catholic Church on the life of religious is understandable since they have chosen freely to live extraordinary lives in loyalty to the teachings of the Church. Throughout the 1950s the major superiors of Irish orders of nuns began to travel to Rome, sometimes for conferences and meetings of international religious orders, and Rome was seen as the centre of the Church. Pius XII's many addresses and writings attest to his deep interest in the role of the Church in education at all levels and to the contribution that religious should make. With a speed that was admirable for the time papal addresses were translated into English as a result of the work of the Irish Dominican priests connected with *Osservatore Romano*, the Vatican newspaper. The papers found their way into Irish convents where they were read with respect and interest. In the 1950s and 1960s there was strong observance of the rule of silence in all the women's orders in Ireland including the teaching orders. A daily custom was the reading aloud of pious books during the silence of breakfast, dinner and more often than not the evening meal, except on feast days or days of particular celebration when conversation replaced the reading. Until the publication of the documents of Vatican II at the end of the 1960s, writings and addresses of Popes Pius XII, Pius XI and Leo XIII were regular reading for religious communities whose main work was education. The writings of founders and foundresses were also reminders of the vision and mission of the particular orders.

Papal addresses and teachings were a frequent topic of discussion and study at CCSS meetings. In 1957 the papal address on school discipline and boarding schools was discussed. Pius XII had called for a discipline that respected the individual pupil and avoided 'mass education' by the creation of a 'house system' where 'no more than fifty' young people would be a unit.[61] In the 1960s and 1970s an increasing number of CCSS principals attended summer schools in England and Wales. They found it easy to transpose the 'house' system of organising schools into year groups or 'mixed age groups' back into Irish schools particularly as enrolments escalated after free education. There is little doubt that Pope Pius XII influenced the development of Catholic education in Ireland and elsewhere. When in 1958, shortly before his death, he addressed the Office of International Education at their Rome Congress, attended by representatives from thirty different countries, he stressed the need for a 'profound study' of how Catholic schools were being adapted to the needs of 'the modern world'. Vatican II would take up the topic. He reminded teachers of a previous papal instruction that schools need more than religious knowledge classes and 'pious practices': schools need 'truly Christian teachers communicating to their pupils' formation of mind and character and the marks of their own deep spiritual life' (*Divini Illius Magistri*, 1929).

The emphasis urged by Pius XII was on liturgy and the sacraments, on the apostolate and Christian works, on the challenge of the missions and on the development of pupils' 'future careers not as mere jobs but as something done for the salvation of the world'.[62] It was in the 1960s that the nuns first, and then the other managerial bodies, began to express concern at the value of the competitive examination in religious knowledge required by the Catholic bishops. The consistency of the nuns' spiritual aim in their schools continued to be voiced in the CCSS. To the secretary of the Council of Education in which they had declined to take part they had stated that

> the function of all our education is to co-operate with Divine Grace
> in preparing our girls for life here and hereafter by the balanced
> development of all the faculties, i.e. of the personality as a whole,
> according to each one's capacity. The specific function of secondary
> education is to continue the formation of moral and intellectual
> habits begun in the home and carried on in the primary school.[63]

Vocational Guidance

The extent of CCSS involvement in the education of girls was acknowledged by Labhrás Ó Muirithí, Secretary at the Department of Education, in an address at the annual general meeting on 21 June 1954. The aim of the schools was still 'to prepare girls for their function as homemakers', but by then another aim was being expressed. The schools prepared girls for entry to the civil service, the banks, the Electricity Supply Board, the Corporation and other major bodies as well as for teaching, nursing, medicine, dentistry, and a small number for architecture.[64] Their schools needed to respond to 'parents' pressure for girls to pass examinations and qualify for positions'. Perhaps it was the vision and mission of the nuns in the education of girls that accounted for their unusual interest in vocational guidance by 1955 (Doyle, 1997). At the annual general meeting in June Archbishop McQuaid recommended that schools should choose suitable teachers to act 'as facilitators in vocational guidance for pupils'. No doubt his recommendation was informed by the *Report of the Commission on Youth Unemployment* (1951) which he had chaired. When the Department of Education introduced the first vocational guidance courses in Dublin and Cork in the summers of 1968 and 1969 the CCSS urged its members to ensure that there were nuns in attendance because of the importance of guidance for pupils. Again during the seven years that the Mater Dei Institute provided a full-time one year guidance course in the 1970s the CCSS encouraged schools to release 'a nun or a lay teacher' to attend. When that course finished in 1979 the nuns in the managerial body carried out research on guidance programmes that were related to work in schools; they recommended a course in Edgehill College in Liverpool that was pursued by a number of religious in the 1980s.

CCSS records from the early 1960s show that the nuns were developing contacts with colleagues in other countries and with the headmistresses in the AIH in relation to curriculum development. For three years the two organisations worked closely on programmes in mathematics, history and geography.[65] When both organisations sought to persuade the Department of Education to introduce some changes in the syllabi for girls they were told that no changes would take place while the report of the Council of Education (1962) was awaited. In 1958 the CHA and the nuns were asked by the bishops to represent Ireland at a conference in Rome organised by the Catholic International Office at the Hague. This organisation had 'the approval of the Holy See' and its aims were for

> the co-operation, the co-ordination of Catholic education throughout the
> world and also towards securing representation on, and collaboration in,
> the work of international institutions.[66]

The Office was to become an important resource in the 1970s and 1980s when the managerial bodies wanted information on denominational education and school management in other countries. It would also prove useful in providing information on alternative management structures for schools. The following year CCSS representatives attended the annual general meeting of the English Association of Convent Grammar Schools and this was to open up opportunities for the exchange of ideas and the possibilities of attending courses in England.

Mother Jordana OP, the President of CCSS from 1959,[67] insisted on frequent meetings of the committee and the organisation developed a new sense of its potential. It was from this point that the nuns became more actively involved in policy and negotiation. The era of dependence on the CHA appears to have passed though the two organisations continued to work together. For approximately twenty years individual CCSS members had contributed ten shillings and subsequently one pound annually to the CHA to 'defray expenses' incurred in the work of negotiating for the Catholic schools. From the mid-1950s the number of subscriptions had dwindled partly because there was no secretarial service to remind the nuns to pay. In October 1961 the CHA was informed that individual contributions would cease but that the CCSS would pay an annual sum of twenty pounds towards expenses.[68] It is perhaps symbolic of a shift in the balance of power between the two organisations and an effort by the nuns to become more active in management issues.

In 1961 the CCSS was thirty-one years in existence. It was an organisation of nuns who were confident about their educational values, their ability to meet the needs of girls, their proven and proactive role as guardians of 'sound curriculum'. As an organisation it had become more interested in the issues of salaries and school systems. The nuns were still unchallenged in their role as the sole providers of secondary education for girls in both boarding and day schools.[69] In 1951 the CCSS had not even considered entering the Conciliation and Arbitration (C and A) Scheme dealing with teacher salaries. In 1955 when Conciliation was made a permanent service the CCSS paid little attention to it. In 1959, along with the Christian Brothers, they decided not to become party to the process although the CHA recommended it. On 23 and 24 June 1960 when 400 nuns representing 217 convent schools met in Mount Anville, Dublin, for their annual general meeting they had a lengthy discussion about C and A. Four years later they joined.

The ASTI and the Nuns

The ASTI recognised the emerging role of the CCSS in issues related to union members apart from the question of the school salary. Teachers of domestic economy, art and music were already on the confined register because they did not have university degrees. In the 1950s the CCSS appears to have been ambivalent about the inclusion of teachers of physical education on this register. The nuns traditionally valued the role of this subject in a broad education and did much to ensure its status. However, the ASTI was opposed to allowing these teachers on to the open register because they feared it would degrade their members who had degrees. The nuns seem to have been influenced by such thinking and agreed with the union but when the union sought support for their Draft Scheme for International Exchange for Teachers there was division among the nuns about the wisdom of agreeing. The CHA supported the Scheme as important for the schools and the matter was settled when the standing committee referred it to the bishops - who were in favour.[70] Gradually the CCSS was interacting with the ASTI as it had not done prior to 1957.

Given the cloistered living practices of the nuns it was only as they came into greater contact with lay teachers that attitudes begin to change. In 1957 it was the nuns who objected to the inclusion of personal details of age, qualifications, and status on a new monthly incremental salary form from the Department of Education which teachers were required to sign. The forms were subsequently re-designed to respect the individual teacher's privacy. At the same time the CCSS was involved in accepting the general agreement on contracts as arrived at between the CHA and the ASTI (Coolahan, 1981). From this point the nuns seem to have pursued a more realistic approach to employment issues.

The nuns were founder members of the Association of Classical Teachers in 1958 and members of a number of other subject associations. They were therefore working with union members. The ASTI and the inspectors of the Department of Education valued the nuns' contributions on curriculum. The agenda of their general meeting in 1960

Leabharlanna Fhine Gall

included the contentious oral Irish examination, the addition of physical education teachers to the confined register, entrance examinations to teacher training colleges, Department of Education forms, a creative writing workshop, and the ongoing issues of decent dress and decent literature. The nuns were a powerful and formidable body by the early 1960s, not least because the key members on their standing committee represented Dominicans, Sacred Heart, Loreto and Presentation nuns, teaching orders who between them had centuries of tradition as teachers and founders of schools world-wide. Their commitment to curriculum, discipline and Catholic values persisted.

Youth Organisation for Decent Dress and Literature

At the annual general meeting of the CCSS in 1961 the papal plea to religious women was quoted; in their schools the nuns should strive to

> *counteract the immoderate pursuit of pleasure and lack of moral discipline with the education of self-control, of sacrifice and of renunciation.*[71]

It did much to explain the emphasis by the nuns on 'control' in schools. Writings on 'Forming the Christian Conscience of Youth', 'Integral Formation of the Adolescent', 'Ideals and Norms for Sodalists', 'Guiding Christ's Little Ones', 'Moral Dangers to the Girl of Today' and 'The Woman's Apostolate' were familiar to Irish nuns and were promoted within the CCSS. By the mid-1950s most Catholic secondary schools for girls had 'sodalities' or religious organisations for extra prayer and some form of Christian service. The CCSS standing committee had written to the Taoiseach Éamon de Valéra about the problem of 'evil and objectionable literature' readily available in shops.[72] Concern about dress and pornographic magazines led the CCSS in 1960 to try to establish YODL, Youth Organisation for Decent Dress and Literature. YODL was to be countrywide and elaborate in tackling the evil of indecency in dress and reading material. Each convent secondary school was to nominate three 'locally resident girls' who would be trained to address their peers on the importance for Catholic girls of wearing

> *jumpers that were not too tight to display the figure unduly, modest shaped brassières; ...[they must not wear] backless frocks or topless frocks where the cleavage was obvious, transparent or flimsy fabrics unless the skirts under them provide adequate coverage, skirts or frocks that are so tight as to emphasise unduly or immodestly certain parts of the body; slacks or jeans are not recommended at any time and beach suits were only to be worn while actually bathing.*

The nuns' campaign against 'bad' literature was even more demanding of the 'locally resident girls'. Trained teams of two or three were to be allocated a local newsagent's shop where they would 'make friendly contact with the owner'. They would then explain the purpose of YODL: it was to 'protect the ideals and morals of youth'. They would 'quietly look over the racks of magazines on that and similar occasions'. If 'anything objectionable' was found the leader of the small team would quietly bring it to the attention of the newsagent. If the owner refused to remove the offending literature the team was to leave silently because 'moral pressure can be brought to bear in other ways'.[73] It was the nuns' well-intentioned efforts to establish such groups that give some insight into their conviction about their role in secondary schools.

YODL appears to have had limited success; the records show that those principals and managers who initiated the movement were few. The nuns' vision was unquestioned by themselves because their mission and purpose in the education of girls was so strong. Vision and clear aims, those two essential features of effective management, were evident in the CCSS. Inevitably nuns also believed in their role as assessors of 'character' in pupils. This meant that not every girl would be deemed 'worthy' of membership of the sodality, for example. School was not about salaries or examinations or results. School was the greatest means the Church had of ensuring future motherhood in particular. An emphasis in the secondary school curriculum on training girls for that role demanded self-discipline and control in addition to education in literature and the arts. The nuns themselves were to be examples or role models of such discipline. When Pope Pius XII advised the superiors general of women religious in Rome in the 1950s about the need to improve the living standards of their nuns, he did so in the certain knowledge that nuns did not spend money on personal comfort.[74] A seemingly parsimonious way of living was as much a means of ensuring the provision of secondary schools as it was an expression of the vow or solemn promise made by nuns to live 'in poverty'. One specific concern voiced by Pope Pius XII was the fact that so many nuns slept in dormitories, like boarding school pupils; it was a practice that continued in some convent schools into the 1970s. His advice was that every nun should have a bedroom or 'cell' of her own as a necessary part of religious living. Inadequate living conditions were a reality in many Irish convents (and monasteries) for two decades after this because money earned or donated was spent on schools and other works.

Vatican II and the CCSS

Perhaps 1970 was a watershed for religious women as a post-Vatican II self-awareness began to emerge. Those who participated in the seminars and retreats following the FIRE (1973) and Focus for Action (1974) Reports were developing a sense of themselves that would affect the work of the CCSS as a managerial body. The main teaching orders in Ireland then began to talk more openly about the supporting role of the state in educational provision and the century-old belief by the nuns that they should live frugally in order to provide what they believed was good secondary education began to recede. Falling numbers of religious vocations and the beginning of a steady exodus from convents undoubtedly were relevant, but a 'newer' and more vocal group of nuns was beginning to emerge, many of whom had taken up post-graduate educational opportunities in Ireland and abroad.

Religious Education and Community Service

Understandably, the teaching of religion was an ongoing concern in the CCSS. Since 1879 formal examination in religious knowledge was mandatory by the Catholic bishops for senior classes in all secondary schools and this continued virtually unchanged until the 1960s. The implications of Vatican II and the unease of the CHA and the CCSS with the practice eventually led to its demise. There was a defined programme for religious education, with theologians setting the textbooks and examinations. The CCSS schools followed the prescribed programme but also tried to place an emphasis on social work aspects and the importance of active involvement in some form of Christian service.[75] This was more evident in the 1950s because of papal exhortations to which reference has already been made. It was revised again by some of the Christian Brothers' schools and then by the nuns in the 1980s when a new senior cycle catechetical programme was agreed by the bishops.[76]

The CCSS and CHA records from 1971 show that the issue of the 'teaching principal or headmaster' was being discussed. The managerial issues that emerged before the 1960s were related mainly to teacher salaries and contracts of employment: in both matters the CHA played the leading role and was encouraged to do so by the bishops. Moreover, if the ASTI had problems with individual schools they tended to deal with the manager and principal rather than with the managerial organisation.

In curricular matters however it is clear that the CCSS was much more creative and interested than the other organisations. In 1977 when the nuns conducted a survey to identify the extent of curriculum innovation in the convent schools, more than 300 projects of various kinds were listed. Included were programmes in transition year, vocational preparation programmes, special transition projects with first year pupils, pastoral care, personal development courses, senior cycle religious education projects, a variety of subject specific activities, alternative history, science and humanities programmes: it was a lengthy list. What was interesting was the extent of involvement by the principals in curriculum at the end of the 1970s. One reason why the members of the CCSS continued to be interested in curriculum was that the majority of principals or managers or both continued to teach. Some taught as much as a full-time teacher and they never lost contact with their professional role as teachers. But before the agreement on Posts of Responsibility was implemented in the early 1970s there was no financial allowance for the work done by principals, so they were seen by the Department of Education as teachers rather than as leaders, managers or administrators.

Sex Education and the CCSS

From the late 1970s public interest was honing in on the extent of education in sexuality in second level schools. It was an aspect of education that was frequently discussed at CCSS meetings and the approach recommended to members was to ensure that the religious education programme as laid down by the bishops was followed. Generally the nuns tried to plan for collaborative work between teachers of catechetics or religion and other related subjects in conjunction with parents and usually guest speakers. By and large it was an approach that was without undue controversy until the mid-1980s. From 1980 onwards a diminution of interest in curricular matters is evident in the records of CCSS meetings but the schools continued working on curriculum development.[77] In 1984 the tragic death of a young pregnant schoolgirl in convent grounds[78] led to renewed efforts to ensure that the nuns' schools offered appropriate personal development programmes which included education in sexuality. In 1985, in the wake of the tragedy referred to, when Gemma Hussey as Minister for Education was insisting that sex education be part of the curriculum she acknowledged that the girls' schools were already offering relevant programmes (Hussey, 1990).

When the managerial bodies were involved in in-service training with the Health Education Bureau in the 1980s the convent schools were the most interested in availing of a teacher training programme,[79] but their involvement was not without controversy. A small group of parents and a few priests raised fears that the Bureau was using the Catholic schools to promote secularism. It was the emphasis on 'personal development' and 'values clarification' with students that created the problem for the concerned group. They believed that 'health education programmes' emanating from the work of the Bureau were 'value free' and therefore unworthy of Catholic educational institutions. On the other hand some principals had experienced considerable pressure from individual parents who opposed pastoral care because of a false belief that the Bureau was promoting it.[80] The issue was discussed many times in the CCSS and it was a valuable lesson in the importance of open communication with parents.

The CCSS and Vocational Education

Prior to the 1950s there are few references in the records to indicate the attitude of the managerial body to the Vocational Education Act (1930) or to the vocational schools. Like the ASTI, however, by 1950 the CCSS was concerned at the expansion of the vocational sector (Ó Buachalla, 1988). The nuns believed that primary and secondary schools should be given freedom and funding to provide a vocational 'block' or 'section'. Had this happened it might have become an earlier type of comprehensive schooling. But like so many ideas in this managerial organisation it was never pursued. Inadequate support structures, the autonomy of the many religious orders within the CCSS and the social variation among the schools made it difficult to introduce systemic change. Reluctantly, the nuns accepted that vocational schools were 'here to stay'. They believed that these schools attracted pupils because they offered 'free education' in beautiful buildings with highly qualified teachers. Clearly, the CCSS records of many discussions in the 1950s suggest that there was little awareness of the reality of VEC schools at this stage. The negative aspects were that they were

> strictly lay and co-educational, completely undenominatonal, offering
> only one hour weekly of religious knowledge taught by a visiting priest
> or cleric who was not a teacher.[81]

Moreover, vocational schools were 'conducted on a principle of free discipline where attendance was voluntary' and 'all internal discipline was dependant on the personality of the headmaster or individual teacher'.[82] Staffed by teachers who were 'civil servants' and who therefore 'do not depend on pupil numbers or results for their jobs', the vocational schools were 'best suited to adults'. 'Disastrous results were inevitable if they were for children in the impressionable years of early adolescence'.[83] To allow the vocational schools to expand would be to allow 'the secularisation of education to expand still farther'. It did not seem to occur to the nuns that many of the vocational teachers would have been past pupils of convent secondary schools since only the voluntary schools enabled pupils to continue to university. There was perhaps some mixed motivation on the part of the nuns in their opposition to expansion of vocational education.

Technically the age of entry to the vocational schools was fourteen years. Individual principals had evidence to indicate that younger pupils attended and both the nuns and indeed the INTO were worried that their own enrolments would decrease as a result. The Mercy nuns and the Religious Sisters of Charity who ran most of the 'secondary tops' resented losing girls to the vocational schools. A consequence of the free transport scheme in 1967 was that the managerial bodies at local level had to collaborate with the CEOs who had responsibility for the administration of the scheme. Many local arrangements were made in a satisfactory manner and in general the scheme was effective, if costly to the state. But typically it was the problematic instances that were discussed at the meetings.[84]

Vocational schools had been restricted to the Group Certificate programme but the introduction of free education in the 1960s resulted in the common Intermediate Certificate and the freedom for all schools to provide for that and the Leaving Certificate Examination. This put secondary and vocational as well as the emerging comprehensive schools on a par, at least in theory. The 'external environment' (Goldring, 1997) was now changed and by 1967 the common Intermediate Certificate course had altered the status of the various bodies. Though the nuns welcomed the extension of educational opportunity it cannot have been an easy time for them: there was now a sense that their vision and mission in education was under threat. The confusion and uncertainty and lack of leadership that accompanied the announcement of the O'Malley scheme of free education in 1966 added to the questioning. The unexpected influx of pupils after September 1967 brought new pressures on the nuns and the records of CCSS meetings at local branch level show their anxieties: Classrooms were more crowded. Toilet facilities were problematic. Building extensions were not ready and the grant since 1964 was inadequate. Poor sports facilities in some co-educational schools and no halls for wet weather added to the problems. School buses were often late and teachers annoyed as a result. Lunch times without facilities and supervision were an additional pressure. In some places convent rooms were used as classrooms, with consequent intrusion into community living. In short, the nuns were experiencing the hallmarks of a scheme that had been precipitately announced.

The CMRS and all the Catholic managerial bodies were brought into closer contact with the VECs because of systemic changes in the 1960s and 1970s. The comprehensive schools, the community schools, the community colleges and the beginning of some policy on rationalisation and amalgamations in varying ways brought closer interaction and collaboration. By the 1980s the religious orders were in decline and the CMRS was beginning to explore new ways of exercising trusteeship of the schools. At the same time all of the managerial organisations were considering their future plans and, as the largest of the group, the CCSS had a leadership role to play. In 1977 the CCSS interest in curriculum focused on what they perceived as discrimination against the voluntary schools. The funding for vocational training programmes was to be directed towards the vocational schools in spite of the fact that the majority of all voluntary schools were in the free scheme and therefore open to pupils of any ability. Following representations to the Department of Education the matter was resolved and the first voluntary school to offer the one and two year vocational programmes did so in 1981.[85]

New Directions

That the nuns were learning from the complexity of managing schools becomes more evident through the 1960s. After Vatican II and the work of renewal of religious life nuns who had rarely been seen outside convents were given greater freedom of movement. In 1970 for example the Religious Sisters of Charity who had been the least cloistered of the teaching orders were allowed to go out unaccompanied by another nun; it would take four or five more years for some other orders to follow. Such freedom meant that individual principals and managers were able to attend summer and other courses more easily and it coincided with the availability of post-graduate programmes in school leadership and management. Inevitably the nuns began to become more involved in issues of management. From 1973 a number of CCSS principals became members of *AONTAS*[86] and attended summer programmes in 'adult education'. They subsequently initiated programmes in their schools.

In-service and the Nuns

In the 1940s and particularly in the 1950s the nuns were the leaders among the managerial bodies in what is now called teacher in-service.[87] However, the thrust of this was not leadership and management but matters related to curriculum and the Catholic school. The CCSS organised summer courses on a regular basis and from the late 1950s frequently requested the Department of Education to make courses available to update teachers in teaching methods. The courses run by the CCSS in the 1950s were not only about the teaching of Christian Doctrine, as religion was then called. They included the scriptures, ethics, teaching methods in languages, in literature, in art, music and domestic science. During the 1950s and early 1960s the Department of Education gave recognition to courses in domestic science organised by various religious orders of women in order to enable nuns to qualify as recognised teachers.[88] Up to the mid-1960s the common practice was for individual religious orders to provide courses for their own members, but in the greater openness that followed on Vatican II there was more communication between the orders particularly in courses related to teaching catechetics. After 1967 when Archbishop McQuaid established the Mater Dei Institute of Religious Education in Dublin, the religious generally attended courses there. In the 1970s the managerial bodies sought the support of the CMRS and the bishops who agreed to sponsor some Leaving Certificate pupils to train as catechists; the drop in religious vocations and a recommendation from Focus for Action (1974) helped to increase the level of sponsorship. This project was an example of effective collaboration between all these groups involved in Catholic education.

In 1973 the CCSS organised its first course for principals. Each subsequent year training courses were provided and by the end of the decade were being attended by principals from the other managerial organisations. The courses included sessions on dealing with the posts of responsibility, the Department of Education, and every possible aspect of the work of the principal.[89] From 1974 there was an emphasis on the importance of the probationary teacher and the need for principals to organise support for them in their early years in teaching. The CCSS prepared a number of publications for principals and these will be considered in relation to contracts of employment.[90]

The Role of the Principal

The theme of the CCSS annual general meeting in 1983 was 'the curriculum in the Catholic school' though discussion in the workshops was on the role of the principal.[91] While it cannot be claimed that the nuns had developed a clear distinction between the role of principal and management, the emphasis from 1977 was on management. Motions were forwarded from each annual conference to the JMB, to be pursued with the Department of Education. The list of school needs included increased capitation grants, additional library grants, caretakers and secretarial assistance, the introduction of continuous assessment in the public examinations, additional appointments to the inspectorate to support the schools. For the next four annual meetings the nuns emphasised the close connection between curriculum development and the support of the inspectorate.[92]

A survey was conducted in 1983 on Department grants. The CCSS was beginning to appreciate the importance of research in seeking funding for voluntary schools. It arose out of CMCSS discussions when the General Secretary was planning independent research on the funding of the voluntary schools (Nolan and Burke, 1991). The refusal of ASTI members to supervise was becoming a problem in an increasing number of convent schools and data was gathered to argue a case for additional funding. Supervision during break and at lunch time was one need. The other was to cover for absent teachers. Certified illness enabled the principal to appoint a substitute for whom part-payment could be recouped from the Department of Education but the real problem was 'casual absences' where a teacher might be unavailable for work for up to three days. A survey among the voluntary schools revealed the extent of the problem. Few convents in the 1980s could rely on older religious to supervise as in the past and the ASTI did not accept supervision as part of teaching duties, though members might volunteer their services and many did so.[93]

The managers and principals had two concerns: untaught classes and insurance coverage. Even when the Department brought the voluntary schools in line with the comprehensive, community and vocational schools in 1985 by paying the full cost of a substitute, it was on the basis of 'recognised' absence; the issue of 'casual absences' was not resolved. The records of the CCSS show that much time was spent discussing the problem and it was agreed that the only solution was the availability of a panel of paid substitutes. But few schools could afford this and the panel proved impossible to create. The supervision problem was frequently discussed at CMCSS and JMB meetings because the ultimate responsibility was a management one. Unsuccessful attempts had been made during the contract negotiations in the 1970s to find some resolution; it was a complex matter for union and managers.

3

Management
and
Leadership

MANAGEMENT AND LEADERSHIP

From the middle of the twentieth century a number of new managerial organisations came into existence and by 1987, through a process of rationalisation, the CMCSS and JMB had become the leaders in the management of the voluntary sector. The more simplified structure came from a vision and a hope about the future of voluntary secondary education. The membership of the CHA, CCSS and TBA were significantly affected by the re-structuring of the managerial bodies. None of the managerial bodies was unaffected, but they chose to collaborate in the creation of the CMCSS and this in turn had an effect on the JMB. The three Catholic managerial organisations took on a leadership role that involved tensions but the outcome showed the ability of the managers to lead. This chapter will trace the development and activities of the various groups from 1952.

Federation of Catholic Lay Secondary Schools (FCLS) 1952

Chronologically next among the managerial groups was the founding of the FCLS. It too was concerned with secondary schools and with bringing together the principals, who were usually the managers and often the owners, so as to influence educational development. Founded in 1952 to represent the lay secondary schools that were Catholic, the FCLS was for some years a contentious body (O'Connor, 1986). Before a lay Catholic secondary school was established the approval of the local parish priest and bishop was normally sought. The Department of Education did not have such a requirement in its Rules,[1] but the bishops were accountable under Canon Law for ensuring that Catholic education was available in their dioceses, so if somebody wanted to found a secondary school and call it *Catholic* it was reasonable to expect that the local bishop could acknowledge such a school. Religious orders had to receive the approval of the local bishop before opening a secondary school unless he invited them to do so and this practice was in keeping with Canon Law.

It is possible that the FCLS was considered to be questionable for reasons not associated with the Catholic bishops. As a lay group the Federation was more proactive in challenging successive Ministers for Education to support secondary schools. Four years before the publication of *Investment in Education* (1966) a member of the FCLS researched and published a study of the secondary education system in Ireland (Cannon, 1962). When one recalls its title it is small wonder that Dr Hillery who was Minister for Education appeared critical of the publication. It was called *Investment in Education in the Republic of Ireland* (Randles, 1975:83-87; Ó Buachalla, 1988:158-59). Whatever about the accuracy of some facts the publication was the first attempt by a managerial group to research the system.

The Federation was also the first of the managerial bodies to propose that the Department of Education should pay an allowance to school principals. This could be part of a system of posts of responsibility such as already existed in the UK. Viewed from the criteria of effective management it may be said that the Federation had a clear mission and aim 'to foster the growth and improve the quality of secondary education in Ireland' (Constitution, 1958). The organisation also displayed a sense of the external environment by seeking to compare the Irish system with another on the basis of funding, structures and participation rates. Perhaps the timing of this early investment report was unfortunate for the Federation. Its founder and president publicly and frequently criticised the Department of Education, the public examination system, the lack of government financial support for secondary schools, the poor investment in the teaching of science and in management structures in schools, and the indefinite policy on the Irish language. Apart from the Christian Brothers the FCLS was the only managerial body that consistently championed the language question.

On 25 April 1958 recognition was granted to the Federation only to be withdrawn again in 1962 when the Teachers' Registration Council refused to acknowledge it (Ó Buachalla, 1988:159). John Hughes SJ, as chairman of the CHA, was supportive of the group that then numbered forty-eight lay schools. He quietly used every opportunity to get the FCLS recognised as a representative group. George Colley as Minister for Education successfully negotiated their re-instatement in 1966 and in 1967 it became a constituent body of the JMB. The inclusion of the FCLS brought a lay view of the struggle to maintain Catholic secondary schools.[2] In 1987 when the other Catholic organisations were in the process of rationalisation, there was no question of uncertainty about the future role of the FCLS. In the twenty-first century, the Federation continues to represent the lay and privately-owned secondary schools as a distinct organisation and as a constituent of the JMB.

The Joint Committee of Catholic Managers 1959

Individual members of the CHA were alert to the need for united action by the managerial bodies and they began by seeking the co-operation of the nuns. The first formal meeting of the CCSS and the CHA took place in January 1959. Each was still a separate organisation and there was no structure for them to speak with one voice. There were two outcomes to their meeting. The CHA wrote to Minister Jack Lynch requesting an increase in the capitation grant and the restoration of the ten per cent cutbacks of the previous two years. The Christian Brothers had not been invited to the first meeting perhaps because they were not 'an organisation' of principals and managers like the CHA and the CCSS. But their support was sought before the letter was sent to the Minister. The letter of 26 February therefore emphasised that the Christian Brothers and the CCSS were 'fully behind' the CHA. To emphasise the unanimity of the request the letter proposed capitation payments of £18 for senior and £12 for junior pupils. This represented a modest increase of £2 to replace the previous £10.[3] The Minister's reply was prompt. On 2 March the restoration of the cutbacks was promised though no date was specified. It would become a lesson to the managers 'to get it in writing from the Department'.[4]

It is probable that the strong statement by the CHA that their request was supported by the other two Catholic organisations made an impact. Neither the Department of Education, nor Jack Lynch as Minister in a government that was only two years in office, wanted the combined opposition of all the Catholic secondary school managers.

The economy was only beginning to develop and much work needed to be done in Ireland to educate a workforce for the future. One might therefore describe the action of the managers on this occasion as effective. But they were still separate groups of voluntary workers whose principal activity was to run schools and teach classes. Perhaps if a structure had been in place to support their organisations, the potential of the Apprenticeship Act in 1959 [5] for pupils in some of their schools might have been appreciated.[6] The Act offered a possibility for schools to prepare pupils for entry to the trades. If the voluntary secondary schools had responded, a wider range of subjects could have balanced the academic curriculum. Even in the 1950s there were signs that the voluntary activity of the managerial bodies was unable to meet the needs of their school system.

Nevertheless, the combined approach on the matter of the capitation payment in 1959 helped the three religious and clerical groups to learn the importance of a united front when dealing with the Minister and his Department. John Hughes SJ, chairman of the CHA, told the nuns that the future of the managerial bodies was dependent on collaboration, everyone working together. He proposed that they establish a Federation of Catholic Voluntary Schools which would include the CHA, the CCSS, the Christian Brothers and the lay managers in the FCLS. A Federation of Irish Secondary Schools should encompass all the other managerial bodies. It is very likely that the germ of this idea came to John Hughes in 1958 from Seán Hamilton who was head of the lay managerial body at the time. Thus, the FCLS was the first among the managerial organisations to appreciate the need for solidarity on the part of all the voluntary secondary schools.

The aim of the new Federation would be 'to present a united front on major issues affecting secondary education in general'. The nuns brought the proposal to a CCSS meeting and discussions continued among them from February to May 1959.[7] The nuns were unhappy about being in a 'federation' with the lay managerial group but would willingly be part of a 'Joint Committee' of Catholic managers. The records do not specify the source of the nuns' problems. There was unease with the idea of including the lay group because such a combination would dilute the image of the religious and clerical schools. Why then did the CCSS go for a Joint Committee? One can only surmise that they made the fine distinction between a specific function that might be the aim of a committee and the more long-term inference of a federation for the constituent and independent groups.

On 5 June 1959 the nuns agreed to be part of the Joint Committee of Catholic Managers and the first meeting was held on 13 October 1959 with John Hughes SJ as chairman. To be exact, this Joint Committee could not become active unless the bishops approved it. During the meeting the chairman addressed the need for a single managerial group to act on behalf of Catholic education. The outcome was that the

CHA was in favour of the proposal and the CCSS would act in accordance with the response from the bishops. Thus, the Joint Committee agreed that the idea should be put to the bishops. Their response was that any such representative managerial body 'would be under the bishops'.[8] No doubt Dr James Fergus, Bishop of Achonry who was secretary to the Hierarchy, was aware that matters of policy regarding Catholic education warranted the attention of the bishops. The Joint Committee of Catholic Managers was at best a beginning on what proved to be a lengthy road towards a united managerial organisation.

The Department of Education would probably have accorded the status of 'recognition' to a Federation of Irish Secondary Schools. But it would not 'recognise' a Federation that was not in fact what the name inferred because the priests and nuns were not members. However, membership of the Joint Committee was important to the FCLS because it enabled them to have a managerial voice at a time when they were not recognised by the Department of Education. It therefore contributed to closer collaboration between religious, clerical and lay principals and managers of the Catholic secondary schools.

A Stream of Organisations

In 1963 the Joint Committee of Catholic Managers met with the Minister for Education, Dr Hillery, shortly after his announcement regarding comprehensive schools. The managers were anxious to learn more about the plan to make 'secondary education widely available'.[9] They reported on the meeting as 'unsatisfactory'. It was evident that the Department of Education officials themselves were not clear on the plan for comprehensive schools and the nuns still feared that expansion would result in a lowering of educational standards.[10] That the comprehensive schools might be the first step towards mass education never occurred to the managers. Neither did the Duggan Interim Report to the Minister and the later Report of the investment survey team envisage a free scheme for all pupils.

Further reflection by the Joint Committee on the system and on Dr Hillery's 'plan' was prevented by more immediate concerns. The ASTI problem of teacher salaries emerged again and the introduction of grants for modern language teaching and for buildings in 1964 (Circular 20/64) served to distract the managers from thinking out the consequences of either Dr Hillery's plan or any alternative which they might develop. If school authorities perceived their work as 'a spiritual trust', the state saw schools as part of a 'national investment' (Akenson, 1970). In a letter to John Hughes SJ,

'Headmaster', dated 9 October 1963 the Secretary to the Department of Education, Dr T. Ó Raifeartaigh put matters in perspective:

> *I think many of all our difficulties arise from the unique nature of the relationship between the state and the secondary schools here. This unique system of ours has its advantages, but also of course throws up some inherent problems. Its advantages will, I feel, far outweigh its difficulties, provided we do not unduly magnify the latter. In that regard it must at all times be borne in mind that the pressures for more and better education are constantly increasing and that these pressures are being brought to bear on the state rather than on private individuals or groups.[11]*

The Secretary was right: the relationship was 'unique'. But in 1963 there was no evidence to suggest that any of the managerial bodies appreciated the singularity of the relationship.

In his 'market model' of social institutions West (1994:247) suggested that at the end of the twentieth century Ireland was about to introduce state intervention for the first time. The proposed model offered only three ways in which the state might be involved in schools: by regulating and inspecting for minimum standards; by funding education for families who could not afford it; by selectively compelling children to participate in the educational opportunities. West might well be describing the 'relationship at a safe distance' that was part of the unique church/state reality in the Republic of Ireland. Before Dr Hillery introduced comprehensive schools in 1963 the managerial bodies had no other point of comparison with their secondary school system. The vocational schools might have 100 new buildings since the 1940s but they could not offer 'secondary' programmes and the CHA, CCSS and ASTI tolerated the 81 'secondary tops' as temporary solutions. But from 1966 when the first three comprehensive schools opened, the comprehensive school system provided a point of comparison, though once Dr Hillery had announced the plan in 1963 the managerial bodies were perturbed.

In 1965 when George Colley was Minister the managerial bodies sought in vain a statement from the Department of Education concerning secondary education. The records show their preference during the next three years for some type of legislation that might safeguard the voluntary system. This appears to be the first occasion on which any of the managerial bodies discussed an education bill. It was followed by a plea from John Hughes SJ to the bishops to establish 'a forum for decision making'. The Joint Committee agreed by the CHA, the CCSS and the FCLS did not represent all the Catholic schools since the Christian Brothers who owned seventy-nine schools were not involved. The sands were continually shifting under them and at times when they believed they were negotiating, the bishops had already moved. John Hughes seems to have been surprised to learn that the bishops had been 'in regular contact' with officials of the Department of Education.[12] And indeed the results of this contact were evident in the ease with which Dr Hillery introduced the comprehensive schools in 1963 and again three years later when the bishops received assurance from the Department that the diocesan colleges would 'fit' the O'Malley scheme.

The Joint Committee was a weak structure with no constitution or rules of procedure. Its three constituent organisations remained independent and their lack of unity was a serious flaw. But the founding of a separate managerial organisation by the Christian Brothers in 1965 was a cross-road for the Joint Committee and it became significant in strengthening the JMB in ensuing years.

The credit and foresight for proposing a managerial body that would represent the educational interests of all the churches is correctly attributed to John Hughes SJ. There had been informal interaction between them in relation to examination courses and curriculum, and members of the Joint Committee were encouraged by what appeared to be the changing attitude to other religions shown in Vatican II. A further source of encouragement in 1964 was the first of many inter-faith or ecumenical summer schools organised by the Benedictine monks in Glenstal, Co. Limerick. John Hughes SJ, chairman of the JMB, and members of the recently formed Dublin Council of Churches attended. At the same time the ISA was interested in developing a strong mouthpiece for voluntary schools.[13] From 1964 there were two representatives of the ISA on the JMB though it is not possible to assess the significance of their contribution: the records do not specify names of contributors at meetings. One aspect of their presence was the creation of an ecumenical image in the 1960s,[14] but the concept of the differing denominations working together needed time to develop. By constitution neither the ISA nor the AIH was management though technically it is probably true that the members are managers. The governing bodies of the schools under Protestant management do not operate as boards of management. The members of the ISA and the AIH therefore tended to function as managers and principals. By 1964 both the Catholic and Protestant groups shared many educational concerns and they also had a common mission in denominational education.

In the 1950s when the managerial organisations responded to the Council of Education they had hoped to find in the final Report (1962) answers to some of their problems. Their hopes were not realised. One commentator would say that the politicians had 'discovered' education (Akenson, 1970 and 1975). Ireland had joined UNESCO in 1961 and the consequent 'collaboration among the member nations'[15] would lead to the OECD in 1962 and the work of the *Investment in Education* survey team (1966). The potential of the JMB may have been limited by the reluctance of the Catholic Hierarchy to recognise the new organisation as the sole negotiating body for secondary education. By 1966 that attitude was unchanged. It is possible that neither the managers nor the bishops had a clear understanding of the difference between 'policy' and issues that affected the smooth leadership, management and administration of the schools. Both are related but at times they became distinct, as for example when the various models of shared management were being negotiated, or when religious studies as a public examination subject arose in the 1970s.

In the context of increasing state involvement in education in the 1960s the Catholic managerial bodies sent a memorandum to the bishops expressing concern about the future of their schools. The reply from Dr James Fergus of Achonry as Secretary to the Hierarchy is indicative of church role in educational policy:

> *their Lordships have been in contact with the Department of Education for*
> *the past two years through correspondence and interviews, in regard to*
> *most of the matters mentioned in the Memorandum ... and all these matters*
> *will continue to receive their closest attention.*[16]

The message did not lessen the anxiety of the managerial bodies. Sometimes unease is heightened by what people believe they do not know and that is what happened at this stage: the problem was a lack of communication partly because there was no structure to facilitate exchange. But the addition of another Catholic managerial organisation at this point proved helpful because it opened a channel of communication with the Christian Brothers.

The Teaching Brothers' Association 1965

The Christian Brothers had been recognised by the Department of Education as working through an official Education Committee of the Irish Christian Brothers, St Helen's, Booterstown in Dublin. The Christian Brothers in the northern province did not have a similar formal committee and the provincial council fulfilled that role. In the 1960s an education office was developed in their house on the North Circular Road in Dublin from where their magazine *Our Boys* was published.[17] The records of the ASTI show that the brothers in St Mary's northern province had to be negotiated with as a separate group until the 1960s when they joined the TBA. In the 1970s during negotiations about teacher contracts of employment the managerial bodies were careful to include a Christian Brother from both the northern and the southern province. This was not a constitutional requirement of any of the managerial bodies but it registered a sensitivity to the existence of two quite distinct and separate provinces of the same order; they might meet in the TBA but they remained two units. A member of the northern province also served on the EPG and on the Focus for Action (1974) team and provided a source of information about Catholic schools and boards of management in Northern Ireland.

The Education Committee of the Christian Brothers in St Helen's was a high-powered group. It consisted of the provincial who was the major superior in Ireland, the four masters of his advisory council who were also brothers with the status of superiors, and a group of teaching brothers appointed by the provincial chapter or meeting of delegates who met every six years to regulate the affairs of the province. It could not be described as a democratically-elected body but by 1960 it was the negotiating body for the owners of the largest number of boys' secondary and primary schools in the country. In 1987 and into the twenty-first century it still represents the biggest group of brothers' schools. In the 1960s it outnumbered the combined diocesan colleges and religious priests' schools. The founding of the TBA did not mean that the Education Committee ceased to function. For a number of years it continued to deal with the Department of Education in matters that related to Christian Brothers' schools. The Department might have reminded the brothers that the TBA was the recognised managerial body for the brothers' schools; that this never happened is a tribute to the respect of the civil servants for the Christian Brothers.

From the end of the 1970s the activities of the Education Committee were entirely concerned with reorganisation and rationalisation of the schools of the southern province of the Christian Brothers. What it brought to the TBA and the other managerial groups including the JMB was considerable experience, expertise and contacts developed by successive Christian Brothers over many years prior to 1965. The movement to involve parents formally in secondary schools was initiated by the Christian Brothers of the southern province in 1970 and during the following fifteen years before the setting up of the NPC all the Catholic managerial organisations benefited from the work of the Federation of Parents of Christian Brothers' Schools. The contribution of the Christian Brothers to the development of in-service for school principals, managers and bursars from 1978 marked a further stage of development for the organisations. They encouraged the Catholic managerial bodies and the JMB to organise courses in financial administration and planning for secondary schools and helped in the design and delivery of such courses.

In 1964 there were 1,328 brothers in the six groups of brothers involved in secondary schools. By the type of organisation they created, the two Christian Brother provincials, along with the provincials of the Marists, De La Salle, Franciscan, Presentation and Patrician brothers, showed strong leadership and an awareness of the complexity of management. There would be no confusion between makers of policy and those who would implement it. There would be two-way communication between the executive committee of the six provincials and ordinary members who included principals, managers, individuals who fulfilled the dual role, and brothers who were teachers. In 1965 the new managerial group emerged when the Christian Brothers and some other teaching brothers came together on 25 September and founded the TBA. The Marists, De La Salle, Presentation, and Patrician brothers did not join the TBA from its foundation in 1965 because they had joined the CHA in the 1950s, and they were familiar with the organisation - it met twice each year and provided a means of communication for them within the Irish secondary school system. There may also have been the fear that these orders of brothers, who were much fewer in numbers than the Christian Brothers, might be 'lost' in the new managerial body. There is nothing in the records to suggest this but it is possible given the powerful position of the Christian Brothers and their practice at that time of 'not mixing' with other orders. The bigger and more powerful the organisation the greater the tendency and perhaps the need to be self-sufficient. It may not be so much a policy of exclusion as one of looking inward: the web-worm image is useful in this context.

It was not until the CMRS and Focus for Action (1974) teams began to implement the teachings of Vatican II in the 1970s that the traditional separateness of the male religious orders began to break down. The Department of Education perhaps unwittingly ensured a future for the TBA as a managerial body by refusing to recognise it as long as other teaching brothers remained in the CHA. There is no evidence that this refusal was dictated by a refined appreciation of the inherent difference between the meaning of the religious brotherhood and the priestly vocation. Likewise, it cannot be claimed that the underlying aim of the Catholic bishops to see their diocesan colleges as preparatory places for entry to the seminaries in any way affected the attitude of the Department of Education. The bishops wanted to maintain some element of separation between their schools and those of the brothers and this is understandable in the context of the 1950s and 1960s when there was a certain competitiveness to attract the increasing numbers of boys who were opting for the priesthood and the brotherhood. There is no evidence that the bishops ever intimated to the officials of the Department of Education that teaching brothers would best leave the CHA in favour of an all-brothers' organisation. However, it was not unusual for members of the Catholic Hierarchy to negotiate privately, and independently of the CHA, with the Department. One may therefore wonder if the issue of a separate organisation for brothers was discussed.

The first meeting of the TBA had taken place in September 1965 but it was two years before the Department agreed to recognise the organisation. On 10 October 1967 the Marist, De La Salle, Presentation and Patrician brotherhoods withdrew from the CHA and joined with the Franciscan brothers and the Christian Brothers and the TBA was formally recognised.[18] According to one of the early Christian Brother members of the TBA, 'most of the Department officials were our past pupils so you could count on their interest if not their support'.[19] There had been some discussion between the

Christian Brothers and Department officials about the establishment of the TBA. A letter from the TBA to the CHA on 10 October simply recorded the fact that the new organisation existed and that all brothers in the teaching orders would be members. The aim of the TBA was

> *to discuss every aspect of educational policy, to ascertain the thinking of the different orders in matters educational, and to advise the Executive of the TBA on all such matters.*

The stated aim of the organisation reflected a wider vision of the role of management in schools and inferred a structural hierarchy in decision-making. Such a hierarchy existed in the CHA and the CCSS where the reality was that policy decisions were taken by the bishops and by the major religious superiors in the case of the nuns and religious priests. But the structure of these two managerial bodies did not reflect that reality. The TBA on the other hand left no brother in doubt; perhaps the provincials had the benefit of learning from the existing managerial bodies. Official recognition of the new organisations meant that before the end of 1965 there were three managerial bodies of religious and priests - the CHA, the CCSS and the TBA.

It is difficult to assess the effectiveness of the TBA because of its unusual structure as compared with the other managerial organisations. All teaching brothers including principals and managers were members of the TBA and the CCSS was similar until the end of the 1970s. What was unique in the brothers was the executive committee that comprised the provincials or major superiors of the six orders of brothers. The making of policy continued to rest with this group. The chairman of the TBA was not a member of the executive committee. He might be a principal or manager or a teaching brother; in the early years of the TBA he might be all three. The role of the brothers was to advise the executive. One of the criteria of management relates to a style of leadership that has vision, mission and the ability to communicate that to followers. The clarity of the TBA structure from 1965 is a good example of such a style. However, the Christian Brothers were the largest brotherhood in the TBA, since their two provincials comprised one third of the executive committee, and the Presentation Brothers were closely linked with them. It will be relevant therefore to examine how the Christian Brothers responded to the first capital grants from the Department of Education in 1964 for secondary buildings.

This first state contribution to capital expenditure for secondary schools did not interfere with the private nature of ownership, but the Christian Brothers were distrustful. The same Minister who introduced the building grants, Dr Patrick Hillery, had also brought in comprehensive schools. The brothers believed that the Department of Education had 'undeclared intentions' of somehow taking over the voluntary secondary schools and that the building grants represented stage one. [20] The brothers like all religious orders saw themselves as being 'entrusted' as 'trustees' with their inherited apostolic works where the commitment was to mind the 'family business' through which a religious community served pupils and parents. This in turn was part of the wider mission of the Church in education. From interviews with a number of the brothers the author is satisfied that their distrust of the growing role of the state in education had some impact on the early work of the TBA. The Department did not recognise the TBA until October 1967, so the Christian Brothers responded as an autonomous group to the O'Malley scheme in 1966 though they also worked with the other Catholic managerial groups as the TBA.

From the mid-1950s to 1968 an increasingly complicated web of groups and organisations and re-groupings emerged of those concerned with the private system of education. The Christian Brothers who became part of that complex activity would continue to manage their schools without seeking building grants. But the free education scheme was a bigger threat. Independently of the managerial bodies the Christian Brothers presented Minister O'Malley with a memorandum on his scheme in October 1966. It was a methodical tabulation giving details of the brothers' investment in education. It compared the suggested capitation and tuition grants unfavourably with the 1964 price index. The brothers' estimate was that capitation of £30 along with other grants was necessary to operate the scheme. They 'would advocate the abolition of the proposed building grant' in favour of more realistic grants for capitation and tuition. The brothers were long experienced in raising money for school buildings and rightly foresaw the weakness of the building grant. It would inevitably lead to 'a system of priority with consequent unnecessary delay, probably prolonged'. Ten years for repayment of bank loans was 'too short a period'.

No specific date had been set for the commencement of the building grant. Yet the link between building and the free education scheme was obvious to the managers and principals; increasing enrolments would demand additional accommodation. Although the Christian Brothers did not mention it there was cause for concern: a 'blanket clause' in the building grant circular said that 'the Minister may at his absolute discretion attach special conditions in any particular case' to the award of a grant. The brothers knew [21] that the CHA had discussed this at length with Dr Hillery and had 'failed to elicit any information as to what kind of condition might or might not be imposed'. The CHA had pursued the matter independently of the CCSS and the FCLS and the Christian Brothers likewise acted alone in October although the three religious managerial bodies had met in February.

It was therefore what was *not* known that gave rise for concern. Suspicion often follows lack of information and failure to secure clarification especially when dealing with official documentation such as that of the building grant scheme. There was no precedent of such state funding for private schools that might have allayed managerial suspicion. Dr Hillery did not appreciate the growing sense of vulnerability among the managers. The Christian Brothers did not waste time seeking information from Department of Education officials who would not or could not provide it. Instead when Mr O'Malley was Minister for Education they offered a counter proposal: the Department should abandon the building grant, increase capitation and tuition payments in the free education scheme, and pay 'the basic salaries of all teachers' without interfering with the role of the school managers as employers. The brothers were more worried about the building grant scheme than about salaries. Good organisation was evident in the depth with which the brothers had examined state funding of secondary schools. They were the first among the managerial groups to seek an end to the payment of rates: secondary schools should be free of them like the national schools and schools in the vocational sector. Aware of the cost of maintenance they sought sixty per cent of the upkeep for schools and grounds. In their thinking, the Department was a service unit not a policy maker. Above all the brothers wanted to protect their role in ownership. From the day that the building grants were announced the Christian Brothers were alert to any aspect of state involvement in secondary schools and they brought that watchfulness to the TBA in 1965.

The Catholic Managerial Committee 1966

We are now entering a period of fairly rapid responses to educational change by the Catholic managers. Their efforts were genuine attempts to protect their Catholic schools against what was perceived as state interference and they were fuelled by fear that denominational education was under threat. For the first time they began to acknowledge the role of parents in the voluntary schools. Fear often seeks out a focus for blame and the religious managers pointed to the Minister for Education and his Department: extreme measures were needed to deal with what they believed was a misuse of power by Minister and officials.

The three religious managerial bodies met on 1 February 1966 under a new name but keeping their separate identity as the CHA, CCSS and TBA. Thus was the unremarkable Joint Committee of 1959 replaced by the Catholic Managerial Consultative Committee.[22] It was subsequently shortened to the Catholic Managerial Committee. Undeniably the Christian Brothers in the TBA influenced the creation of this religious and clerical group. The FCLS was not included. Once again the religious and clerical managerial groups were withdrawing from involvement with the lay Federation.

There seems to have been much anxiety in the schools at Minister Colley's request that vocational and secondary school authorities should meet in local areas. The Catholic Managerial Committee was an attempt to unite the religious schools in opposition to the Minister. Their response was to resist the ministerial attempt at local collaboration and, to emphasise their opposition, the Christian Brothers sent a separate letter, also on 1 February, to Mr Colley. Unknown to the managers the bishops were meeting the Minister in February [23] to ensure their place on the boards of the comprehensive schools where they would work *with* the authorities of the vocational school system. The bishops saw the inherent weakness in having too many managerial groups but they were wise enough not to interfere with any one organisation. They might look at the situation at some future date. Meantime Mr O'Malley's free education was announced and had to have a response. Early in February the bishops set up two Episcopal Commissions on Education to deal with primary and post-primary matters - a step towards a more strategic form of management by the bishops.[24] At the same time the managerial bodies continued to function, sometimes separately, at other times in unity. An article in *The Irish Press* on free education, 1 December 1966, brought the opposition of the teaching brothers to the O'Malley scheme on to the centre of the stage.

Between 1966 and September 1967 when free education became operative newspapers frequently carried articles and letters about the scheme. The brothers' response to the article in December 1966 was swift and an example of a managerial body united in action. The six provincials of the TBA signed a 'memorandum presented to *An Taoiseach* and to the Minister for Education objecting to the Minister's statement' quoted in the newspaper.[25] The scheme planned a variation in the scale of fees (Randles, 1975:275-79) to be paid to schools, related to the fees schools had charged before free education. The brothers' vision of education was clear in the memorandum. They feared that the

> division of schools into various categories according to the amount of the
> grant paid to them is bound to establish an undesirable social distinction.

The six provincials hit hard. Schools that had charged low fees or often no fees were now to be punished under the Minister's scheme:

> It is unjust to give only minimum grants to schools which through
> the past years have striven to provide post-primary education to
> children of families in the lower income group. In order to ensure
> that such children would not be denied post-primary education, the
> fees in these schools have been kept at a low level, below the actual
> cost of providing such education.

This was more accurate of the Christian Brothers' schools than of the other brotherhoods. Their financial records for the two provinces show that at least half the education they were providing by 1966 was 'free'. The TBA memorandum presented a canvas that no Minister for Education could afford to ignore: parents would come under pressure if

chapter 3 | management and leadership

their children failed to secure places in the schools with higher free education grants:

> *Owing to the inability of these schools to accommodate all those who*
> *will apply, an undignified procession of rejected applicants must then*
> *be made to schools in lower-grant categories.*

Like any politician Donogh O'Malley was sensitive to potential voters in elections. The six orders of teaching brothers, owners of 124 secondary schools for boys, ended their memorandum by saying:

> *We, therefore, regret that we cannot accept the scheme as at present proposed*
> *and are unwilling to participate in it unless the same grant be made, without*
> *discrimination, to all secondary schools within the scheme.*

Their united response in 'a spirit of constructive criticism' sought a scheme that would be 'equitable and acceptable'. Donogh O'Malley was furious at what he saw was the refusal of the teaching brothers to collaborate with free education. Within days he sought a meeting with 'the TBA' - an interesting title since the brothers' organisation was not 'recognised' by the Department of Education until October 1967. The Minister said that the government was in no position to offer a state system of free schooling to the whole country and that the collaboration of as many voluntary secondary schools as possible was essential if the new scheme was to succeed.

The TBA notes of the meeting of six brothers with Mr O'Malley and three senior officials are the only account available to the author.[26] The incident gives some insight into church/state relations and indicates that change in the delicate balance was afoot. An emotive scene is described when 'before we were properly seated the Minister attacked'.[27] Doubtless O'Malley knew the TBA was no ordinary managerial body: these six men were the major religious superiors of all the teaching brothers. The Minister might as well have been dealing with the might of the CMRS of which they were also members. He was incensed at what he saw as TBA 'refusal' to take part in the free education scheme. Although he had not consulted Archbishop McQuaid of Dublin, the Minister and his secretary had met Cardinal Conway and Archbishop McQuaid in Maynooth a month after the announcement of the free education scheme (*The Irish Times*, 10 September 1986; Cooney, 1999:385). O'Malley might therefore have reasonably expected that the brothers would not be complaining to him.

If the brothers' record is accurate the Minister was in fighting humour and challenged them:

> *If it is your decision to remain outside the scheme then we must go*
> *ahead without you. We accept your challenge: we will tell the*
> *people that they have a free post-primary education but that you*
> *refuse to enter it. Owing to your refusal the people will be deprived*
> *of the free education for their children which they are paying for by*

their rates and taxes. They will be so informed. The scheme we offer
you will give you a much greater income than you were collecting
from fees and so you have no grounds whatever for refusing to participate.

In fairness to the TBA, the Minister was misquoting their memorandum and they so informed him. The displeasing document was sent for but Mr O'Malley read from it only the final sentence where the brothers declared their unwillingness to enter free education 'unless the same grant is paid to all schools'. He made no reference to their alternative proposals for the scheme. There were no winners at the meeting - the summary comment on the TBA record is 'no agreement whatever'.

The interaction revealed something about organisational policy making. The TBA had anticipated ministerial displeasure, but their inherited vision as providers of secondary education was stronger than any annoyance or impatience at offending retorts from civil servants. One of the Minister's group, Seán MacGearailt, was a past pupil of the Christian Brothers in Tralee where his parents had paid 'a fee of three pounds a year'. The TBA minute of the meeting describes being asked

if we could be prepared, next September, to go before the parents of the
Tralee pupils and tell them that we were refusing to go into the
Government's scheme by which we would be paid £15 per pupil per year
and that we would still continue to ask them to pay the fees for their
children. Did we think they would be satisfied? Books also - would they
be pleased to pay for them if they knew they could be got free?

It is now known that the civil servants in the Minister's Department were of the opinion that it was unwise to proceed with the scheme until 1970 when all details were finalised (O'Connor, 1986). They were broadly in agreement with the TBA though loyalty to their Minister prevented them from saying so. But Donogh O'Malley too had a vision and a political awareness: he may not have known the school managers but he had a sense of the environment external to politics. Seán O'Connor, his assistant secretary, admitted years later that had the Minister not doggedly pushed the free scheme through in 1967 'it would not have come'.[28]

By February 1967 details were sent to the schools (Randles, 1975:265). The deadline for entry to the scheme would be 16 May 1967 (Circular M32/67). Independently of the bishops the CHA wrote to the Minister on 24 February 1967 and expressed their willingness 'to recommend acceptance of the scheme to all the schools in our associations' (Randles, 1975:266). There was some tension among the managerial bodies at the way in which the CHA acted at a time when representatives of the bishops and the schools were considering a counter proposal to the Minister's scheme. The CHA had also acted outside the Catholic Managerial Committee that had been established in February of the previous year. It is probable that the closer contact between the CHA and the bishops gave them inside information that the free scheme was not going to cause problems for the diocesan colleges - and these colleges were the largest group within the CHA. The bigger membership in the CCSS would make it difficult to agree a united response to the Minister. Moreover, the autonomy of each religious congregation meant that a policy decision on entry or otherwise to the scheme would be decided by individual major superiors and of course the notion of going against the free education scheme was very difficult for a large number of religious. There followed nine months of wrangling about details of a scheme that lacked adequate preparation and for which the system and the churches were ill prepared.

Free Education and the Catholic Managerial Committee

The Catholic Managerial Committee sent a lengthy memorandum to the bishops for their pre-Easter meeting in 1967. Some of the anxieties of the principals and managers are clear in the document. Government policy to allow vocational and comprehensive schools to prepare pupils for the public examinations would mean that all were 'secondary' schools. Larger school units would inevitably mean separate junior and senior schools, co-educational institutions

>*and maybe in some instances, interdenominational; by the gradual*
>*elimination of the small local Church-linked parental schools.*[29]

The managers were convinced that the Minister and his Department intended 'the destruction' of their schools and that, as a result, there would be 'a loss of suitable recruits to the religious congregations directing these schools'.

The memorandum urged the bishops to seek 'An Act of the Oireachtas' in order to

>*control the, at present uncontrolled, power of the Minister and the*
>*Department. It is true that such an Act might be amended at some*
>*future date to our detriment, but this could only happen after* public
>discussion. *Regulations made by the Minister may indeed be challenged*
>*but they have already right of possession before any challenge can be*
>*brought against them.*

The managerial organisation was not opposed to free education. In fact, the members supported equalising educational opportunities, but what they were seeking was parity of funding with the vocational and comprehensive schools. In a final recommendation to the bishops the Catholic Managerial Committee asked that a working committee would be established which should include representatives of the managers and the bishops. Their task would be 'to review the whole present and future situation of our voluntary schools'. The managers hoped that the outcome of such a review would be

> *Provision for a revision of the relations between the state and the*
> *church-linked, parental, voluntary schools. We consider that such*
> *revision should involve formal legislation, as the securest method of*
> *ensuring that we may continue to serve the church, the people and*
> *the state in the years ahead.*[30]

The Christian Brothers met the Minister in December 1966. They were not 'opposed in principle' to free education but wanted practical details. Mr O'Malley asked them for memoranda on the issue of free books and free transport and after the meeting he asked a representative for 'an alternative to the basic state fee scheme'.[31] The managerial bodies had an opportunity to influence the operation of the free education scheme in 1966 but were not sufficiently organised among themselves to do so. The Christian Brothers did submit proposals for a free book scheme. However, they had no experience of organising school transport so did not make suggestions. If the JMB had been involved, the experience of the Church of Ireland in school transport might have been a resource.[32] The Catholic managerial bodies were opposed to accepting the scheme 'without stringent enforceable guarantees'. In theory, the Catholic managerial bodies might have made a financial arrangement like the SEC. In fact they could not have done so because they lacked the structures, the leadership and, most of all, the trust in each other. As has already been stated, the principal providers of secondary education were autonomous religious orders and, for the first time, the exercise of that legitimate autonomy emerged as a disadvantage during the introduction of the free education scheme.

The difference between the managerial bodies and the bishops was that the managers sought details out of their experiential knowledge of running the schools whereas the bishops viewed the scheme from another level of management and leadership. The ultimatum came at a meeting with the Hierarchy on 16 February 1967 when it was made clear to the managers that rejection of the scheme would 'be a disaster' for the church in education.[33] That meeting might secure the support of the Catholic managerial bodies for the bishops' stance on free education, but it would not necessarily ensure their approbation as emerged when the CCSS President and standing committee met the principals and managers in Dominican College, Eccles Street. Annoyance was expressed that the Minister had been the one to tell the school authorities that the managerial bodies recommended acceptance of the scheme.[34] The several hundred nuns present were mostly in agreement with the principle of free education but there was discontent at the lack of preparation. It was also clear that some religious schools would stay outside the scheme. Even the Christian Brothers had a few schools that would remain outside[35] as would a number of CHA schools.[36] What is important here is the extent to which the introduction of the scheme highlighted the weakness of the Catholic managerial bodies. By contrast the schools under Protestant management coped. Of course without the participation of the majority of the voluntary schools the O'Malley scheme would not have worked in 1967 and to that extent the managerial bodies had a significant impact on free education. But they proved unequal to exploiting the opportunity or influencing the scheme because they lacked an effective representational organisation.

In the end the bishops and managerial bodies went along with the scheme and the majority of all secondary schools joined (O'Connor, 1986; Ó Buachalla, 1988; Cooney, 1999). In September 1967 out of the total 551 secondary schools, 485 or eighty-eight per cent had opted in to free education. As mentioned earlier the schools under Protestant management had negotiated a separate arrangement through the SEC.[37] Their position was stronger than that of the Catholic managerial bodies - their rationalisation policy, already mentioned, which included re-location of a number of inner city schools to the suburbs in Dublin, assured the future of their schools. In spite of the tensions and difficulties for the Catholic groups, only twenty-six secondary schools remained outside the O'Malley scheme. One managerial participant of that time claimed that he and others envied the apparent ease with which the schools under Protestant management 'finally dealt with the free education'.[38]

The brothers, who had proposed alternative ways of funding the schools, were proven correct when pupil enrolments increased beyond expectations. The Department of Education had calculated on the basis of an increased enrolment of 7,000 in 1967, but the actual number was 15,000. As a result, the pressure on teachers and schools was enormous. The Christian Brothers perhaps experienced that pressure more than most because of the scale of their involvement in schools and their refusal to avail of the state building grant scheme. Some of the most creative forms of fund-raising in secondary schools date from the end of the 1960s. There was the Christian Brother superior of a school in a country town who paid for the building extension by persuading groups of small farmers to donate 'the price of a cow'. There was his JMB colleague, a Church of Ireland clergyman, who reared a herd of cattle as the fund raiser. There was the 'sixpence a week' donated by parents in a rapidly growing urban school of the Christian Brothers. The list is endless but the records also show the pressure on the brothers:

> *Bhí éileamh throm ar na Bráithre ó thaobh fuinnimh agus ama de agus*
> *na foirgnimh and na hachainní ba ghá chun cóir a chur ar an slua breise*
> *mac léinn á gcur ar fáil. Caitheadh mórchuid ama le himeachtaí chun*
> *airgead a sholáthar mar aon leis na cruinnithe agus na seisiúin phleanála*
> *a ghabh leo.*
> (Ó MUIRÍ, 1996:86).[39]

Financial pressures were not the only reality faced by the brothers who were long accustomed to competition with CHA schools.[40] The priests and the brothers looked to the boys in their respective schools for vocations. The records reveal the resentment of some CHA schools when the local brothers introduced Latin on the curriculum. The brothers felt that no boundaries should be put to what was done in schools. The traditional ecclesiastical and canonical distinction between priests and brothers has been mentioned.[41] A small but nonetheless telling image of that difference was the biretta or box-like black hat worn by priests and brothers: the Christian Brothers insisted on a four-cornered model so as to be distinguished from priests who wore the standard biretta which had three corners.[42] Division was never far beneath the surface in the complex human interaction of the managerial bodies and the manner in which free education was introduced did not lessen that division. Perhaps it helped by revealing the fact that the Catholic managerial bodies were not ready to deal with the implications. What was needed was an adequate enabling organisational structure. The JMB was too new by 1966, the SEC had ensured that their schools would have their own scheme within the free education plan, and the Catholic Managerial Committee that had come together in February 1966 proved ineffectual.

The Special Committee 1967

The Catholic Managerial Committee in 1966 was as inadequate as the Joint Committee had been in 1959. The CHA, CCSS and TBA tried to structure the Committee and draft a constitution, but it seems that no one of the three organisations wanted to take precedence over the others. They sought the assistance of the bishops who accepted responsibility for appointing a Special Committee; the members would choose their chairman. The task of this Special Committee was 'to draw up concrete proposals relative to Fr Hughes' memorandum and other problems of the secondary schools'.[43] This proved to be a turning point for the Catholic managers. Did the bishops foresee a rationalisation of the existing managerial bodies? On Friday 30 June 1967 at 3 pm the Special Committee held its first meeting in the Catholic Secretariat office that Archbishop McQuaid had established in Earlsfort Terrace, Dublin. The leadership had come from the bishops who were showing some sense of the external environments affecting Irish education. The task of the Special Committee was specific. The group of seven named by the bishops included two CHA men, one of whom was John Hughes SJ, two from the TBA which was then two years in existence, two from the CCSS including Mother Jordana OP, and Mr Seán Hamilton representing the FCLS. There were two significant differences between the Catholic Managerial Committee of 1966 and the Special Committee of 1967: the lay managerial body was back and the bishops had been directly involved.

Many members of the Hierarchy appreciated the Catholic lay secondary schools in their dioceses and, to them, excluding the FCLS, as the Catholic Managerial Committee had done, was unthinkable. The initial task of the Special Committee was to submit suggestions to the meeting of the Hierarchy in October and to that end they needed to forward their work in September when the preparatory work for the bishops' meeting was being done. A measure of the seriousness with which the Hierarchy treated the Special Committee of the managerial bodies is in the attendance of four bishops at a meeting on 29 August 1967.[44] John Hughes SJ had prepared a draft constitution for discussion and decisions were agreed on this though it would be brought back to the constituent associations. The bishops suggested that a Presentation sister be brought on to the Committee and it already had a representative from the Mercy order. Traditionally the bishops insisted on a member of these two orders being included in the CCSS executive in recognition of their contribution to Catholic education and of the diocesan nature of their foundations.

The bishops must have had concerns about the earlier letter asking the Department of Education for a statement on secondary education: they enjoined the Special Committee to make

> *no request for an Act of the Oireachtas to be passed regarding certain*
> *points between the Department of Education and the voluntary schools.*[45]

This is an interesting reminder of the care with which the bishops viewed legislation in education, having learned from the experiences related to vocational education. An education bill was not desirable in their view. Would time change their attitude?

The Council of Managers of Catholic Secondary Schools (CMCSS) 1968

Three decisions of consequence were made at the Special Committee meeting: a full-time secretariat was to be funded by the secondary schools; legal advice was to be sought on the proposed constitution; a representative Council of Managers of Catholic Secondary Schools was to be established. So the Joint Committee of Catholic Managers in 1959 gave way to the Catholic Managerial Consultative Committee and the Catholic Managerial Committee in 1966. Finally, the Council of Managers of Catholic Secondary Schools (CMCSS) emerged. At their meeting on 3 October 1967, the bishops welcomed the end of a lengthy gestation period. The hope was that the new organisation would prove its worth. Its aim was 'to promote unity among Catholic managerial associations'. To that end there would be a representative council from the various bodies. The bishops stated that there should be 'a clear distinction between matters of policy which should be reserved to the bishops and other matters'.[46]

By 4 December the draft constitution which provided for a representative of the bishops and one from the CMRS was ready for the approval of the major religious of the secondary schools; following their agreement the new CMCSS Constitution was ratified by 1 January 1968. The many meetings of the Special Committee that had begun the work showed the earnestness with which the bishops and the managerial representatives pursued the creation of a new structure.[47] The inaugural meeting of the new Council took place on 7 June 1968 at 3 pm in the Mater Dei Institute of Religious Education in Dublin. The CMCSS not only represented the Catholic school authorities, it also included the policy makers through the membership of representatives of the bishops and the major superiors and marked an important stage in the evolution of the managerial bodies.

The secondary schools had settled into the second year of the free education scheme when an article in the Jesuit quarterly *Studies* gave the new CMCSS and the JMB matter for discussion. It was written by Seán O'Connor, the Assistant Secretary to the Department of Education and head of the Development Unit set up in the wake of *Investment in Education* (1966). The title 'Post-primary education: now and in the future' had added significance because it was written by a member of the Department. The article may or may not have been O'Connor's personal opinions but it fanned the flame of uncertainty and mistrust among the managers. Thirty years later one of O'Connor's colleagues has revealed to the author the context of the publication.[48] It seems that the article caused a 'crisis meeting' in the Department before it was published - O'Connor was told he could publish but 'if his job was at risk that it was on his own head'. When the publication emerged it was not seen within the Department to be a cause of any embarrassment but the impact among the managerial bodies was another matter. The frequency with which it was discussed at their meetings is indicative of the anxiety caused. Managers who had only recently joined the free education scheme talked of the 'hidden Departmental plan' being revealed.[49] One principal among the nuns wondered 'why on earth did the Jesuits print it?' Archbishop McQuaid had tried to prevent its publication when he discovered that the new editor of *Studies* had actually commissioned the article from O'Connor (Cooney, 1999:396-7). The editorial of *Studies* was trenchant in detailed criticism of O'Connor's ideas (Troddyn, 1968:274).

Managerial displeasure at the article was more marked in the CHA, CCSS and TBA than in the JMB. The same edition of *Studies* printed a welcome to the article by the secretary to the Board of Education of the General Synod of the Church of Ireland and by the general secretary of the Vocational Teachers' Association. The Church of Ireland favoured rationalisation and had already begun the process.[50] Their secretary was correct when he wrote that

> the churches will be failing in their duty if they restrict their contribution
> to a re-statement of their rights, instead of pointing to the needs of men
> in a rapidly changing climate and engaging our minds in the vital
> discussions of how these needs may best be met.
> (STUDIES, 1968:269)

When O'Connor wrote that he wanted religious as 'partners' and not as 'masters' (1968:249; Cooney, 1999:397) many religious interpreted it as state interference with the structures of denominational schools. Others responded by emphasising the need to work together to protect the voluntary school system.[51] For the majority of principals and managers, the years from 1967 to the early 1970s were fraught with the consequences of free education and coping with pupil enrolments for which the system was ill prepared. They would survive the offending article (Barber, 1998).

CMCSS Leadership

Almost from the beginning of its existence the CMCSS bore the fruit of having a bishop and a major religious superior involved. There was a sense of purpose and a strategy about the way in which meetings were planned. Members of the constituent managerial organisations were asked to alert the Council about any local meetings that were then being organised by the Department of Education and the VECs. The double agenda of these meetings was local co-operation on the school transport scheme and collaboration between schools. In the 1970s amalgamations and community schools were added. Under its constitution the CMCSS met twice each term. It also met with the Episcopal Commission on Post-Primary Education on 12 June 1969 to review the first year of the Council and to discuss areas of importance in education. For the first time, review became a part of how the managers operated.

The contrast between this new way of working and the complex earlier history of the seven managerial bodies was striking. While there were tensions, the records indicate that satisfaction was increasing among the constituent bodies, with the CMCSS assuming a leadership role. The fact that members of the Council attended the sometimes controversial local meetings was important. On another level the Council had regular meetings with the Department of Education which had given it 'recognition' from the beginning. The level of preparation for these is evident in the copious notes of planning meetings.[52] In September 1968 the new Council had met Dr T. Ó Raifeartaigh, Secretary, and officials at the Department of Education. The agenda drawn up by the Council is a reminder of issues that would come to the fore in the 1970s: co-operation between the Department and the managers; co-ordination at local school level; common entry for pupils; amalgamations; the 'community school'. The Department promised it would 'shortly issue draft statements, for discussion, on these points', but in spite of frequent reminders from John Hughes SJ, chairman of the CMCSS, the Department failed to produce them. When the question of the community schools arose the Department had dealt with Cardinal Conway - successive Ministers for Education and the officials in the Department were clearer than the managerial bodies and the CMCSS on the source of policy in the Catholic Church.

The meetings between the CMCSS and the Department were not about 'policy' but about those 'other matters' as Bishop Fergus had called them in 1967: salaries, staffing, time tables, grants, posts of responsibility and appeal procedures, examinations, and the many managerial concerns of daily life in schools. Involving the church in community schools was 'policy'. The Department respected the role of the CMCSS and subsequently of the JMB in those 'other matters', one of which was the capitation grant. Inevitably from 1968 to 1987 the CMCSS and the JMB was constantly seeking improved funding for schools.[53] The Tribunal on Teachers' Salaries and the teachers' strike of 1969 brought the CMCSS into frequent contact with the Ministers for Education, Brian Lenihan and Pádraig Faulkner. Faulkner had agreed to the managers' request for monthly meetings with officials of the Department, a fact that enhanced the status of the CMCSS. Those meetings continued to 1987 and illustrate the manner in which the organisation of Irish education was now conducted.

Throughout the 1960s when so much was changing in Irish education the managerial bodies had no full-time support service - every activity was the result of voluntary work. But in 1971 a part-time office was replaced by a full-time secretariat and in 1972 John Hughes SJ became the first full-time Director of the Secretariat of Catholic Secondary Schools, established by the CMCSS.[54] His assistant was a member of the Church of Ireland, Miss Margaret Larminie, who also supported the working party that produced the FIRE Report in 1973. The Catholic schools contributed one shilling per pupil and the ISA made a subscription towards the cost of running the office. The JMB was serviced from the Secretariat. In addition to the provision of support, the new CMCSS met another criterion of effective management and leadership: the ability to undertake review and evaluation. In preparation for the annual review in 1972 the assistance of a consultant, Eoin McCarthy, was available.[55] His conclusions are useful because they give the perspective of a professional, an experienced manager but not in education, and a lay man. He described one aspect of the 'external environment' with which the managers had to deal because

neither the bishops nor the religious superiors realise that the shift

*of power has moved from the politicians to the bureaucracy. The
commitment of the state made by the various Departments is so far
planned that politicians have little say. Even the Taoiseach or his
Ministers can do little any more. The Department of Education
is the policy-making body and in this respect neither trustees nor
boards of management are important.*[56]

McCarthy's recommendations included the setting up of 'an Independent Education
Authority' that would be independent of the state and would represent all second level
schools. The CHA one year later was in favour of such a structures; presumably their
representatives on the CMCSS had promoted the consultant's thinking. McCarthy
believed that an education act would not be realistic because 'an Act is a major constraint
on government and so no government wants one'. Neither did the Catholic Hierarchy
want one. The consultant stated that a government White Paper on education 'would
be useless because it would be a fuzzy document similar to that for Local Government'.
Among the immediate practical advice he gave was that the CMCSS and the JMB
should not go to the Department of Education on 'minor issues without an alternative
plan of administration'.[57] He was advocating strategic planning for which the managerial
bodies had been poorly prepared.

The consultant's report highlighted the weakness of the system in the Catholic Church
in Ireland at a time when 'policy' was the responsibility of the bishops and major superiors.
Policy was artificially separated from leadership, management and administration and
the demarcation line might be indefinitely blurred. The difficulty in the 1970s as the
new managerial structures were in place was that the sands were continually shifting under
any work the CMCSS tried to do. From 1974 the voluntary secondary schools were
catering for the majority of all pupils in second level schools. Richard Burke, Minister
for Education publicly stated his wish

> *to allay the anxiety of the authorities of the voluntary secondary
> schools, both Catholic and Protestant, in regard to their future role
> in secondary education.*[58]

Minister Burke also favoured a public debate on an education bill when he addressed
the annual conference of the CCSS in 1976. In a lengthy speech he outlined matters
to be considered:

> *The legislation would make it possible for school authorities to have a
> clear understanding of their statutory duties and rights within the
> general framework of the system of education; it would enable the
> general public to be fully aware of the educational facilities statutorily
> available to them and accordingly put them in a better position to make
> informed decisions in relation to the education of their children;
> the voluntary secondary schools should not be discriminated against in*

the matter of the appropriate level of financial aid accorded to them in comparison with the amount of aid given to comprehensive and community schools and to vocational schools. A statutory instrument which did not seek to ensure that such discrimination would not exist could not be regarded as effective or useful.[59]

The CMCSS was more concerned that the ASTI were asking for a renewal of negotiations on the teacher contracts to include an appeals procedure for probationary teachers. The existing appeals procedure for permanent teachers was to the bishop or major religious authority, while the appeals procedure on the new posts of responsibility was between the ASTI and the JMB.

JMB Leadership

One outcome of the continuing confusion about the roles of the managerial organisations in relation to policy matters was the period of misunderstanding surrounding proposed boards of management in Catholic secondary schools (O'Flaherty, 1992:98-104). Having spent three years as director of the Secretariat of Catholic Secondary Schools, John Hughes SJ resigned and unsuccessful attempts were made to fill the post which had been advertised. It was a sign of the lack of effective leadership within the organisations that agreement could not be reached on a successor. The CMCSS was not opposed to the appointment of a layman. However, the prevailing opinion among the representatives of the managerial organisations was that it was too soon to do so. The vacancy coincided with the refusal of the ASTI to agree to the type of boards of management proposed by the CMRS. One positive result of the delay in filling the vacant post was that in 1976 a full review of the work of the Secretariat was conducted with the support of the CMRS and the bishops. The FIRE Report (1973) and Focus for Action (1974) and the planned sharing of management in Catholic secondary schools indicated that further developments in support structures were necessary. In 1977 Brother Declan Duffy, former chairman of the CMRS Education Commission and a member of the EPG, was interviewed. He was appointed secretary general (later General Secretary) of the CMCSS for a period of five years.[60] It had taken two years to find a successor to John Hughes SJ but the time had facilitated clarification of structures and communication between the bishops, the CMRS and the CMCSS.

Negotiations on the Contract of Employment

At this stage, it is appropriate to consider some aspects of the contract negotiations of the 1970s. The question of contracts is included here because they did not apply to the schools under Protestant management. The Christian Brothers had their own contract which was rarely a cause of grievance to the union, but this was not the situation with the nuns: ASTI records show that the union had far more problems with the nuns in relation to contracts than with all the other managerial organisations. Why?

In 1974 the CCSS prepared *Guidelines Regarding Teachers on Probation* to encourage members to support the beginner teacher in relating to 'management, staff, parents and pupils'. The six-page document was far-seeing for its time. It highlighted the responsibility of manager and principal for a programme of 'continuing professional development' for teachers. Each school staff was urged to develop a policy on 'induction' of new teachers; a 'problem class' should not be given to beginners; regular 'self-assessment' should be done with probationary teachers to enable them to 'reflect' on their progress and to encourage them to 'seek help if necessary'. The document included 'practical guidelines for teaching', the 'presentation of lessons', 'evaluation', and 'discipline'.

In 1957 the nuns had accepted the inevitability of the contract of employment. However, they had persuaded the CHA to increase their year of probation to two years. The nuns also insisted that an experienced teacher who came from another secondary school should do two years of probation. Understandably, it was an unsavoury situation for the ASTI, though they signed on 11 May 1957. Moreover, the union reluctantly agreed that marriage would be an acceptable reason for 'dismissal' or, as the CCSS would have said, for 'cessation of contract of employment'. To make matters worse for the union, they had failed to persuade the representatives of the 54 lay Catholic schools to accept the contract. The FCLS was more interested in learning from the schools under Protestant management how they coped without the complexity of a formal document. Wisely, the ASTI did not pursue the FCLS on the matter.[61]

A review of the contract was to take place every five years but that did not happen in 1962. It seems from the records that the ASTI did not press for it and the managers did not pursue the matter. In 1965 the union was pressing for 'longer holidays, shorter hours and a five day week'; therefore they needed to revisit the contract.[62] A letter from the CHA on 29 January 1966 to ASTI suggests that the managers were initiating a revision of the contract along with the CCSS and the TBA.[63] At this stage the union was tabulating 'dismissal cases', mainly from CCSS schools and wanted written termination of employment. 'Case E' is an example of what was causing concern in the union. Their member, a woman teaching in a convent school, had been three years on staff and was 'dismissed' in July 1966 without warning. The nuns had given no contract form and subsequently no reason for cessation of employment 'on the grounds that it was not necessary to do so'.[64] On 25 May 1966 the CHA exercised leadership by sending the union a list of managerial demands related to the proposed revision of the contract. The union appointed a sub-committee of four to deal with the matter. One positive outcome was agreement by the CHA and CCSS to tell teachers who had temporary contracts whether or not they were needed the following school year.[65]

For the union, the inherent weakness of dealing with several separate managerial bodies was apparent again in the response of the Christian Brothers who were unhappy about what had been agreed. The Brothers promised that the union proposals would receive the attention of the TBA because 'the points at issue could not satisfactorily be decided except as a general agreement between representatives of the managerial bodies and the union'.[66] The two provincials were not criticising their colleagues in the CHA and convent schools, but they were not pleased at the change. The lack of unity and the absence of a strong presence to negotiate for the voluntary schools were becoming more apparent as the ASTI was developing organisationally. For the union 1966 was a gloomy year, with dismissal cases emerging in rapid succession, and by October the managerial bodies were informed that class size would be an issue in re-negotiating the contract.

By 1967, the face of Irish education had changed dramatically. The majority of the Catholic secondary schools had begun to offer free education as part of the scheme. ASTI membership was set to increase and with it problematic contracts of employment. Throughout that year the spate of 'dismissals' continued in spite of the fact that a series of meetings took place between union and managers. Then, after a lapse of time the talks resumed in 1971 and continued intermittently until 1973.

The ASTI became more confident in its demands: to class size was added a demand for a maximum of 22 hours in the teaching week and an appeal procedure for probationary teachers.[67] A cause of frustration for the union was the existence of separate managerial organisations.[68] Until the 1950s the union was able to deal with the CHA, but the CCSS, as it became more independent, posed a greater problem for the ASTI. In 1968 Seán O'Connor told the CHA that a new contract was essential if secondary schools were to operate effectively within the free education scheme,[69] and as more lay teachers were employed the contract would become more significant. The nuns' use of temporary contracts was a cause of complaint, though there was an improvement by the end of the 1960s.

In 1977 the first *Guidebook for Principals* was prepared by the CCSS. The other managerial bodies expressed interest and were supplied with copies. The internal publication shows some insight into issues related to a teacher's contract. The six chapters of the publication also indicate the developments within the CCSS: the role of the principal, appointment of teachers and contracts, teacher formation, school discipline, posts of responsibility, and religious education in the schools. The importance of presenting the contract form to teachers was highlighted as was the need for clarity with teachers on the nature of the contract. The records show that there were instances where managers used probationary contracts where temporary forms were needed. Sometimes no form was presented and young teachers did not request a written agreement. In an effort to encourage teachers the CHA and the CCSS agreed that the ASTI office would supply forms on request.

The year 1977 seems to have marked a turning point for the CCSS. Coincidentally, the first of what would be a series of Unfair Dismissal Acts was enacted that same year. Negotiations with the ASTI on the contract of employment involving the CHA, the TBA and the nuns had resumed but little progress had been made because, basically, the managers had nothing to trade with the union negotiators. The ASTI was singular in its demand for an appeals procedure for probationary teachers. Appeal was a policy matter that was reserved to the bishops and major superiors and available only to holders of permanent contracts of employment. The managerial negotiators had been instructed that the issue was not to be discussed during negotiations. Both sides in the negotiation spent months analysing the minutiae in the contract forms. The union had made a unilateral decision that a maximum of 22 hours constituted the teaching week; the contract stated 26 hours. The union wanted their figure printed on the contracts; the managerial negotiators refused. Finally, the managers consulted Donal Nevin of ICTU and the Employer Labour Conference who agreed that the union had acted unilaterally.[70]

However, the weakness was systemic and involved the Department of Education. In fact, there were individuals teaching less than 22 hours; very few taught in excess and in 1978 no lay teacher was asked to do 26 hours, though detailed figures are not available. In some schools where individual lay teachers taught more than 22 hours there was agreement between the manager and the union that additional time would not be recorded on the official forms for the Department of Education. It was a quiet policy of collusion between union and managers. The basis for the managers was that the Department paid incremental salary for eighteen hours of teaching. Liam Murphy of the CHA, one of the contract team, described the situation as 'an impossible one for us as negotiators because of our powerlessness'.[71] The managers had nothing to give or to trade.

In September 1977 the CMRS Education Commission agreed to allow the contract negotiators include the appeals procedure in their deliberations with the union and that marked a new beginning for the managerial bodies.[72] But although the union and management teams completed their work on the contract revision and the appeals procedure, it came to naught because the ASTI rejected what had been worked out. The contract of employment did not become a matter for re-negotiation for the remainder of the twentieth century and custom and practice continues to prevail in 2000. However, the growth in employment law has been significant since the 1970s and has contributed to greater clarity in the area of rights and duties. Ireland is unusual in that teachers in the voluntary secondary schools are public servants who are employed by the manager or board of management on behalf of the churches; for the most part, the teachers are paid by the state (Glendenning, 1999:359). The 'privity of contract' between manager or board and teacher prevents interference by 'a stranger to the contract'.[73]

The Work of the Secretariat of Secondary Schools

The structure created through the CMCSS and the JMB ensured that issues were researched to enable informed negotiations to take place with the Department of Education and the ASTI. It appears that the advice given by the lay consultant for the FIRE Report in 1973 was now being followed. Brother Declan Duffy, the new General Secretary, had been chairman of the Education Commission of the CMRS and closely involved with the various internal reports of the 1970s. It is no surprise, therefore, that from the end of the 1970s the JMB and the CMCSS began to gather information about the voluntary schools. A survey on class size had already been done in 1976; this was reviewed and up-dated. Urged by the CMRS a new approach to find a common system of dealing with CMCSS school accounts was initiated from 1977. [74] Studies were conducted on the use of voluntary school premises for adult and community education.[75] Other areas included selection of pupil intake, examinations, curriculum development, the structure and work of Posts of Responsibility, principals and their work, staff in-service, home school links, school transport, the free books scheme, boarding school fees, fee-charging schools, ancillary staffing, finance. In short, every aspect of the secondary school system was reviewed in some way in order to build up factual information that would inform the CMCSS and the JMB.

In the twenty-first century such a process of review is not remarkable, but for the religious managerial bodies especially, it was a first move towards strategic planning. The gathering of information about the system was basic to future developments in private education. It was the first attempt by the combined churches to evaluate 'investment in education'. The past belonged to autonomous religious orders that owned schools and while they were still autonomous in 1980 there was a greater awareness of the need for collaboration. A unified approach by trustees and management to Catholic secondary education had been missing and despite earlier hopes of the bishops and the CMRS for a rationalisation of the Catholic managerial bodies only one had ceased to exist. Two other structures would emerge in 1987 though one was simply a development of the CMCSS set up in 1968.

Re-structuring the Organisations 1980

By 1980 the CCSS was acutely aware of the difficulties involved in meeting the demands of school management. Negotiations on the contract of employment had achieved nothing and the redundancy issue was unresolved. The ASTI was about to ban any form of parent/teacher meetings. There were impending problems with pastoral care and little development in a more effective middle management system in schools. Boards of management were being pursued by the CMRS and there was ambivalence among the principals about them. Dr Brendan Comiskey, Auxiliary Bishop of Dublin and a former general secretary of the CMRS, told the nuns at their annual general meeting that

> religious involved in primary and post-primary schools should have
> skilled and competent 'union' negotiators. It is of serious concern that
> religious have no team or individual at either primary or post-primary
> level who could engage full time in dialogue with lay colleagues in
> their professional associations. Without the goodwill and trust of our
> lay teachers I see no great evangelical dimension to our continued
> presence in Irish education.[76]

By the end of 1980 the CCSS were working in response to the Joint Commissions of the bishops and major superiors on 'a comprehensive view of the roles and functions of the various organisations'. Not for the first time the nuns discussed joining with the TBA to form one managerial group to represent the religious schools.[77] There was no question of not wanting the CHA, but the feeling was that the teaching nuns and brothers had more in common. Negotiations were continuing with the ASTI about redeployment of teachers and boards of management, though it would be another five years before a solution was agreed. The age profile of the religious principals and managers was relevant and the inevitability of more lay appointments was clear.

In the 1980s there was a growing concern among CCSS members at the increasing complexity of school management and the continuing lack of support systems.[78]

Redundancy, rationalisation, boards of management, staff development programmes, adult education - these were the topics of discussion at their meetings.[79] Nevertheless in 1984 the nuns were enthusiastic about the Curriculum and Examinations Board. Their last three annual gatherings received less and less media coverage although public relations firms had been engaged - youth culture, computers and time tables, transition year and assessment failed to gain headlines.[80] In 1982 when a CCSS manager dismissed a lay teacher for allegedly unacceptable conduct, it was the managerial role rather than that of the principal that came under a sharp light. The 'Eileen Flynn case' in the Holy Faith Secondary School in New Ross in Wexford [81] was a complex learning point for the CCSS. The nuns were prepared on the one hand to support a manager but the issues were yet again an example of the complexity involved in management. While the law courts upheld the school, the issues highlighted the weakness and isolation of a unitary system of management.

Since 1929 the CCSS had consisted of principals and individual managers; at the end of that year there had been eighty-four schools involved and a small standing committee ensured that numbers would increase. In 1961, as a result of requests from members, branches were formed in Cork, Tuam, Sligo, Athlone, Thurles, Limerick, Galway, Waterford, Killarney and Dublin. The standing committee was replaced by a central executive in 1966 in a deliberate effort to counteract a president becoming too powerful. By 1970 there were 315 schools in the organisation but as a result of school closures and amalgamations the number of member schools dropped to 286 in 1976. The nuns then decided to establish a standing committee again that year - the central executive was too big to be effective.[82]

As regards attendance at CCSS meetings, the teaching sisters attended until 1973 (primary teaching sisters had attended until 1949[83]). From the early 1970s APPTI was functioning so the CCSS decided to confine their membership to principals and managers. When APPTI ceased in 1978 the CCSS executive discussed re-admitting teaching religious, but the decision taken was 'that we remain a managerial organisation for religious principals and managers'.[84]

By the end of the 1970s the nuns had learned that management and leadership in organisations needed continual review and evaluation. In 1981 a committee was established to review the CCSS constitution for their 277 member schools. The only change was to allow teaching sisters to attend regional meetings though they would not have a vote. It was symbolic of the uncertain direction of the organisation at that stage.[85] In 1985 some CCSS schools already had boards of management and since the ASTI on 24 September had voted in favour of boards it was certain that many if not most of the nuns' schools would move to shared management. Like the TBA it seemed that the CCSS would be something of an anomaly as a 'convent' organisation. The JMB and the CMCSS already represented management and there seemed to be no further need for a CCSS.

The FIRE Report (1973) had called for rationalisation of the many groups involved in education and a subsequent Report on Religious as Employers (1978) had also suggested new structures. Between 1974 and 1978 there had been some discussion about rationalisation by the CCSS and the TBA but nothing came of the exchange. The CCSS was organised on a regional basis and the central executive encouraged the regions to seek opportunities to meet with local TBA and CHA members. Cork was probably the most successful because they established an Association of Principals and Vice-Principals of all second level schools and for the first time the vice-principals of the religious schools were included with their principals. This was important in recognising the team nature of school leadership and suggests that the voluntary system was learning from practice in the community school system. By 1982 this group of lay and religious was meeting regularly for mutual support and management in-service, reflecting a view that organisational skills could be learned and that review of their roles in schools would inform future professional development programmes. No other area of the country replicated the Cork model though some attempts were made in the west and south west as the CCSS regional reports show.

In the 1980s the CMCSS encouraged the principals to meet on a county level and this proved important when a national campaign on educational funding by union and voluntary sector was organised in 1986 and 1987. Also in the 1980s the complexities of school leadership, management and administration became more pronounced. This was partly the outcome of the employment legislation of the 1970s, a very strong ASTI, the protracted negotiations about models of management and policies on rationalisation already mentioned, and depleting numbers of religious in education.

The CHA, TBA and CCSS discussed rationalisation of the managerial bodies and it was felt that the JMB and the CMCSS that was fully supported by a secretariat and full-time general secretary since 1977 constituted the effective way forward. Once boards were agreed the managerial bodies would face a dilemma: whom would they represent - principals, managers or boards? A lot of time was devoted to discussing the future and meanwhile negotiations were continuing with the ASTI and the CMRS on the 'package' about boards, parent/teacher contact and redeployment.

What happened is an example of what Rothschild wrote about in 1991 when she examined the characteristics of feminised workplaces and found that the tendency of women is towards power-sharing and away from opportunism. The CCSS still represented the nuns who were principals or managers or both, and they systematically consulted their branch members. The CMRS had recommended rationalisation, on the grounds that Catholic principals and managers needed to have more effective managerial structures. In fact, the CMRS believed that 'the web of fourteen existing bodies is now a real problem'.[86] Should the CCSS merge with the TBA and the CHA? The understanding of the CCSS executive was that the brothers in the TBA were engaged in a similar process of consultation. There was some uncertainty about the CHA because of their close association with the bishops who had diocesan colleges in their dioceses. Under Brother Declan Duffy, General Secretary as chairman, a working party was established and representatives of the Catholic managerial organisations considered possible structures to ensure that the CMCSS would become a stronger managerial body. There was some opposition from the CHA and the CCSS to the idea that their groups would cease to exist. The nuns proposed that an Association of Catholic Education would replace all the managerial bodies but the idea was not popular.[87] In the end, the CHA continued in existence to support their boarding and day school headmasters. Traditionally, the CHA had two representatives on the Teachers' Registration Council - one from a diocesan college and one from a clerical school. Over the years that distinction was forgotten and the organisation simply had two representatives. Membership of the Registration Council was not a problem for the TBA because they did not cease to exist after 1987.

By analysing the objections to rationalisation over a period of time, agreement was reached on the composition of the new CMCSS in 1987. Finally, the central executive of the CCSS decided that the organisation would 'cease to be' because it had outlived its purpose and effective managerial structures in which the nuns' schools were represented were already in place.

The final annual gathering of the nuns in 1987

> was an historic occasion as earlier in the year the members of the CCSS
> had given unanimous approval to proposed new structures for the
> management associations of Catholic secondary schools. As a consequence
> of this, CCSS as a management association would cease to exist and the
> annual general meeting had the task of ratifying its dissolution and also
> deciding on a future association for sisters.[88]

Although a working party was established no other association emerged for the nuns and this created some difficulties after 1987 when 'the CCSS' representatives on the Teachers' Registration Council and nominations for other Department of Education groups as well as the European school heads' organisation (ESHA) were to be replaced.[89]

The need for an organisation to represent voluntary school principals was considered by the CCSS though nothing came of it. Their conclusion was that the new CMCSS and JMB structures were sufficient for the schools. This was perhaps a lost opportunity at the time but there was already an association of vice-principals and the nuns believed that any future development should include both principals and vice-principals.[90] The vacuum was filled before the end of the century when NAPD was established with financial assistance from the Department of Education and Science and the boards of management of the schools.[91]

Leadership by the CMCSS and the JMB was a gradual evolution. From 1977 meetings with the Department officials or the Minister tended to be by the JMB and not the CMCSS. This was not merely an ecumenical gesture. There was a belief that the Department treated the exchanges 'more seriously' when the combined denominational groups were present. From this point the JMB gradually came more to the centre of the stage as negotiator for the voluntary schools. All the formalities including a minute book and procedures were introduced. Each constituent managerial organisation had its own vision of education, there was much in common, and gradually an agreed sense of mission and purpose developed. A Committee to Monitor School Closure had been set up at the request of the ASTI in 1972 and its work continued under the CMCSS until 1981. The JMB did not need to be involved since the schools under Protestant management had already carried out rationalisation in the 1950s and 1960s and the SEC could assist each of the minority churches in monitoring educational provision.

The CMCSS and the JMB

The decade that began in 1980 was a period of reflection and discussion within and between the managerial organisations. It was a demanding time on the JMB as they tried to persuade the Department of Education to pay the full cost of substitute teachers, to provide caretakers and to increase grants. A lot of time was given to the JMB submission to the Review Body on Teachers' pay in 1980. Their 53-page submission showed the results of three years' research on the voluntary schools. At that time the JMB represented 530 schools that provided education for 70 per cent or 200,000 of post-primary pupils - there were 8,489 lay and 2,341 religious teachers involved. A substantial argument in their submission was the gap between a teacher's 22 hours of instruction each week,[92] the requirement of the Department that the school be in operation for a minimum of 28 hours, and the fact that the Department paid incremental salary based on 18 hours weekly. The ASTI was threatening to have its members teach only the minimum 18 hours from September 1980. In that context it was difficult for management to engage in either short- or long-term planning.

> Management is faced with the dilemma of having to win more working hours from teachers (that is, in excess of the 18 hours for which the Department of Education provides an incremental salary) while at the same time having nothing to offer as extra remuneration.
> (JMB SUBMISSION, 1980)

A central issue for the JMB was the fact that 'society recognises money' as a reward for work but the schools in the free scheme did not have money to give. In 1980 the CMCSS was acutely conscious of their impossible position in the contract negotiations with the ASTI. A member of the negotiating team wrote that the managerial representatives 'were effectively powerless to offer incentives to teachers. The Department controlled all salaries and related payments so the inducements normally offered in industrial relation negotiations were not available to the management side'.[93] The problem for the Department was that any change in payments to one group of teachers would begin a round of talks in C and A for which the agreement of the Department of Finance would be necessary. At school level in 1980, the principals were under increasing pressure. Boards of management, substitution, parent/teacher meetings were unresolved. From the surveys carried out the JMB was able to highlight school management needs in the 1980s - each constituent organisation had made a separate presentation to the Review Body.

The JMB final submission was a thorough exploration of the realities experienced by those who were running the voluntary schools. Under a section entitled 'the quality of the school service' it stated:

> It is essential that management will have available to it, adequate
> provision in respect of class teaching, supervision of pupils
> immediately before and after school, during normal school breaks
> and for school trips and field work associated with the school
> syllabus, and substitution for absent teachers (1980:19).

Little came of the exercise although the pay issue was resolved in 1981. What was important was the new approach taken by the CMCSS and the JMB in relation to putting their case. In that sense their involvement in the Review Body of 1980 marked a new stage in leadership by the managerial organisations.

There were other expressions of the new direction by the JMB in what proved to be difficult years in the 1980s. Professor Kevin McDonagh, Head of Education in Carysfort College of Education, and John Nolan the Registrar were commissioned to conduct a survey on school finance.[94] At the same time the ASTI decided to ban parent/teacher meetings of any kind and to threaten the work of class tutors and pastoral care.[95] There was a resolution of the pastoral care issue in 1981 and by December the 'package' for negotiation had emerged (O'Flaherty, 1992). Boards of management, parent/teacher meetings or home/school links and redundancy constituted the 'package' for negotiation by the CMRS, CMCSS, ASTI and the Department of Education but it took effectively nearly five years before each element in the 'package' was resolved and a further year before the redundancy aspect was implemented. Throughout that time the work of the JMB continued unabated. It is likely that the emergence of so many issues in the early 1980s, in the aftermath of the 1979 oil crisis, impending recession and rising unemployment, energised the managerial bodies into leadership.

The ban by Minister for Education John Boland on corporal punishment in schools, the ASTI ban on lunch-time supervision and the implications for parents led the JMB to engage a consultant on school insurance in 1982,[96] while increased awareness by the managers of the demands of employment legislation resulted in trial membership for one year of the FUE.[97] At the same time the CMCSS prepared a response to the Department of Education on the proposal to establish a National Parents' Council. Many of the voluntary schools had very active parents' associations since the 1970s and the Christian Brothers' groups were the most organised. The CMCSS was in a position therefore by 1982 to contribute to a debate. Their suggested model was not a top-down one as emerged in 1985 with the establishment of the NPC. Mindful of the existence of so many parents' groups, the Department was asked to wait for five years to enable all schools to develop parents' associations. Democratic elections could then follow, to create the NPC. Clarification of role was essential to obviate overlap and confusion.

> The CMCSS would maintain that the delegation of inappropriate powers
> to a national parent group could frustrate the direct contact necessary
> between the Department of Education, managerial representatives and
> teacher union officials. Given a well-constructed framework within which
> to operate, making allowances for the different sectional interests among
> its membership, the National Parents' Council would serve as an effective
> organ for consultation and exchange of information between the Department
> of Education, school authorities and Irish parents.[98]

In 1986 capitation grants were withdrawn from the fee-charging voluntary schools. This increased fees and the fears of the managers that the payment of the incremental salaries might be under threat.[99] It was clear to the CMCSS that the multiplicity of groups was not effective and that a stronger organisation was needed to respond to educational changes. The appointment of a number of lay principals raised questions about the nature of the CCSS and the TBA as representative bodies since the lay principals were already members of the ASTI. Was there a possible contradiction between membership of the union and of a managerial body?[100]

The old structures were falling apart and had become a very divisive base from which to negotiate with the Department or the union. The bishops and CMRS had urged rationalisation in 1973 and again in 1976. Overwork,[101] frustration, lack of direction, and a belief that there were difficult years ahead, eventually gave way to agreement by 1987 to establish a new CMCSS as an umbrella organisation for the Catholic voluntary schools. There was confusion, struggle, unease and resistance among the nuns. Yet, as the largest managerial body the CCSS proved also to be the most courageous in facing the rationalisation. There was also some opposition in the CHA: the new managerial structure that was envisaged would become the negotiating body for the Catholic schools and so the CHA would lose its long established role. It is also true that there was a greater identity problem for the CCSS and the TBA than for the CHA. In a sense, the CHA could be sacrificed because of the changed circumstances of the other two groups. In the end the greater need for a strong and representative managerial body for the Catholic schools triumphed. That was what both the bishops and the CMRS had wanted. The bishops would not make an issue of the changed role of the CHA.[102] A representative committee within the CMCSS considered any objections raised by the organisations - a necessary though time-consuming process.

In 1987 the JMB represented 62 per cent of the management of all secondary schools in the Republic of Ireland. That figure is virtually the same at the beginning of this century. The JMB is the main decision-making body for secondary school management. It works with the Department of Education and Science, ASTI, the National Council for Curriculum and Assessment, C and A, the National Parents' Council and all such groups related to the management of secondary schools. The CMCSS continues to deal with issues that are specifically denominational, for instance religious studies as an examination subject, just as the SEC and the ISA sometimes do for schools under Protestant management. However, it is important to emphasise the independence of each of the minority churches.[103] There is one other managerial issue that does not concern the JMB: the Scheme of Redeployment for Secondary Teachers agreed with the ASTI and the Department of Education in 1987 applies only to the Catholic schools. The JMB traditionally meets immediately after the CMCSS meeting but it is quite separate.

What emerged therefore by 1987 was effectively a simple, democratic structure with two supporting pillars - one related to religious denomination, the other to total management in the secondary school system. The re-structuring placed the emphasis on leadership, management, and regional representation. It provided a network and a system through which the denominational schools might function effectively.

In 1957, in so far as they were owners and patrons of the diocesan colleges, the Catholic bishops had the CHA as their managerial group. They themselves had little opportunity to be engaged in policy issues because the bishops' conference normally met only three times a year and from 1959 when Vatican II was called there were additional demands on them. Throughout the 1960s they made regular visits to Rome and on three occasions in the 1970s and 1980s attended Synods there. These visits put yet more demands on their time as they were exhorted to introduce changes in liturgy and practices. Thus their ability to respond to educational changes from the early 1960s in both primary and secondary level education was under pressure and by the early 1980s they were under severe stress from the shortage of priests and in the 1990s from a series of scandals revealed within the church.

Vatican II reminded the Catholic Hierarchy of their responsibility to ensure that Catholic education was available and supported, so the vision and mission that are essential components of effective management were clear. However, their own structures within their conference were inadequate to deal with the complexity that the managerial bodies were involved in as a result of issues such as free education and community schools. In 1974 the bishops' Council for Research and Development at Maynooth had identified 'the young, the urban dwellers and the better-educated' (*Report*, 1984:144) as becoming distanced from the church and by 1984 these groups were significantly more distanced. Although the research in the 1970s had revealed a desire by the laity for greater involvement in the church, that had not occurred by the mid-1980s. There was 'continued satisfaction with clergy and religious involvement in the management of schools but an even greater desire for parental involvement in this area' (*Report*, 1984).

The fact that Cardinal Conway found it necessary to appoint the EPG indicated that the Episcopal Commission for Post-Primary Education was insufficient to meet the pace of change. The EPG until 1977 was a bridge between the bishops and the CMRS; in addition it was sufficiently small in numbers to meet frequently[104] and the fact that the cardinal himself chaired it gave it a status within church organisations. After the cardinal's death in 1977 Dermot Ryan, Archbishop of Dublin since the end of 1971, became chairman. He was neither cardinal nor leader of the Irish Hierarchy. Moreover, a lot of the issues of concern to the bishops had been resolved: comprehensive and community schools, free education and the primary school boards of management. Perhaps the EPG had accomplished its purpose and had suited the particular leadership and management style of Cardinal Conway. It pointed out the need for unity among the managerial bodies and two of its members were important in bringing the CMCSS and the JMB to the centre of the managerial stage.

Two other factors in the 1970s contributed to a decline in the influence of the Hierarchy on the managerial bodies. Firstly, the two sections of the CMRS were developing a new sense of solidarity as they sought to have an impact on their own religious in all the renewal work demanded by Vatican II - they had learned from their lack of readiness for comprehensive schools, free education, community schools and a growing discontent among some religious about their role in schools.[105] Secondly, the bishops established a National Advisory Council on Education and this body produced a number of pamphlets the most noteworthy of which was one on home-school relationships (1974). The Council, however, lacked a clear mission, a clear sense of purpose, and a strong sense of identity with any of the existing managerial bodies, and so it had little impact.[106] In fact it was unhelpful at a time when the ASTI was negotiating payment for parent/teacher meetings (O'Flaherty, 1992:107).

The ways in which the various churches handled educational issues had an impact on the managerial bodies and here the difference between the two main churches is striking. The historical context in which secondary education developed in Ireland enabled the Catholic bishops to rely on the religious orders and part of that history too was the existence of the lay Catholic secondary schools as a separate group. But problems developed in the aftermath of the free education scheme. That period coincided with the beginning of a fall in religious vocations, so the bishops were forced to become more involved in secondary education. By contrast the Board of Education had existed since the nineteenth century and the Church of Ireland authorities were able to change and develop in the light of educational needs. The SEC has developed since 1965 as the conduit for the free education block grant and as a support to the churches in developing educational policy. In the 1990s the establishment of a 'committee on management' ensured that the SEC could rely on a group to deal with emerging legislative issues. The position of the minority churches is not analogous to the way in which the CMRS (now CORI), and the bishops where necessary, have become the springboard of policy-making in the voluntary secondary school sector. The CMRS development took on greater impetus after 1987 and by the end of the twentieth century there was clarity on the implications and possibilities of trusteeship (CORI, 1996; 1997; 1997a). Had the Catholic bishops attempted to establish a single board to deal with secondary education the sheer scale and autonomy of the historic involvement of the religious orders would have made it impossible.

The Church of Ireland's involvement in secondary education came from a different past. Therefore the role and style of church leadership was different. The General Synod of the Church of Ireland nominated to the SEC. Much of the work of the Board of Education has been with primary schools while the SEC has focused on secondary. The scattered nature of the membership of the minority churches partly explains why they entered into a process of review and rationalisation that was to prove a stable context for their involvement in 'the Protestant comprehensives' from 1966. Catholic bishops, even those who had been headmasters in diocesan colleges, tended to distance themselves from schools as they were faced with different demands in their new roles, but the SEC on the other hand ensured a close relationship between the ISA, the school governors and the education system. The changing culture in Ireland from the 1960s, diminishing numbers of religious and priests and the implications of Vatican II would ensure that the Catholic Hierarchy had a constantly shifting external environment to interpret and one that was more sophisticated than that of the 1950s.

The Protestant community in Ireland was dwindling since the early part of the twentieth century and has suffered 'a very substantial decline' (Sexton and O'Leary, 1995; *The Irish Times*, 16 December 1995). By the 1960s the schools under Protestant management were ahead of all the secondary managerial bodies in pursuing their process of rationalisation. In some places co-educational schools developed from amalgamations of small schools and this could mean relocating to a new site, e.g. Wesley College to Ballinteer, the King's Hospital School to Palmerstown, Dublin or the relocation of Alexandra College to Milltown, Dublin. At its largest membership the AIH had numbered seventy-seven though the majority were senior teachers not headmistresses, but by 1968 when they merged with the headmasters in the ISA there were very few female principals - the agenda for the final meeting of the schoolmistresses in 1981 noted the prevailing tendency to appoint male heads in Protestant schools. Some interesting notes in the records of the CCSS refer to the 'demise' of their 'Protestant colleagues' as 'a sign of the times'[107] although the nuns do not elaborate either on the 'sign' or 'the times'. The Irish Schoolheads' Association (ISA) has represented the men and women principals of the schools under Protestant management and continues to do so. When first the two groups merged in 1968 their title was the Irish Schoolmasters' Association though there were women in it. The more inclusive 'Schoolheads' was adopted in the 1990s. By 1987 the number of schools under Protestant management was slightly more than half what it had been thirty years earlier though their fifth comprehensive school was opened that year; the twenty-one secondary and five comprehensive schools remained viable up to 1995 (Kingston, 1995:48), and the existing twenty-one schools are represented by their eighteen male and three female principals in the ISA.

Unfortunately, little has been written on the philosophy of schools under Protestant management and researchers therefore tend to refer to Catholic Church documents on education (Kingston, 1995; Milne, 1995). A former secretary to the Board of Education highlights the importance of their schools in enabling young people to develop a sense of identity. He also points out that

> the Protestant minority's attitude to its schools owes something to the
> fact that it is, at best, a five per cent minority, whose continuing influence
> in the educational system is hard to envisage without its own institutions,
> given that the alternative is the Roman Catholic school, even allowing for
> the growing number of multi-denominational schools.
> (MILNE, 1995:14-22)

The schools under Protestant management and their managerial bodies have survived to the twenty-first century. They have come through the educational cutbacks of the 1950s, a process of rationalisation, developments in the state comprehensive school system, free education, community schools, the pressure to establish boards of management from the late 1970s, demands for involvement in curricular change in the 1980s and the economic recession of much of that decade. Despite the continuing decline in numbers in the four churches represented in the SEC, their denominational system of voluntary schools was in a relatively stronger position by 1987 than at any other time since the establishment of the Free State in 1922. To whom should go the credit? The SEC cannot be ignored but it was established in 1965 shortly after Dr Hillery's announcement of the comprehensive system. The representatives on the JMB from 1964 were alert to the possibilities for denominational models within the comprehensive system although such had never been intended by the state (Barber, 1989). But the JMB was not a maker of policy.

The minority church groups had the advantage of size: it was possible to establish the SEC where the four churches could work together and in time become a strong source of policy. Leadership for strategic management needs to interpret the 'external environment' (Goldring, 1997) of an organisation or school or managerial body. The SEC was apart from the schools, the boards of governors, the ISA and the JMB yet

> *Protestant schools are those defined as schools which*
> *are represented by the SEC at official level.*
>
> (KINGSTON, 1995:48)

The SEC was in position therefore to appreciate the wider picture of denominational education in the minority churches, in a state that valued and respected them. Their mission was clear to them. Thus they could make an impact on the comprehensive model in the sense of influencing it to meet their denominational need and they were less confused than the Catholic managerial bodies regarding acceptance or rejection of the free education scheme. Perhaps they were fortunate that their school fees could not 'fit' the scheme, and so in effect they created a separate scheme within the original O'Malley plan.

Another factor contributing to the success of the SEC was that the particular governance structures of the minority churches always included high levels of lay input. Possibly, therefore, they were accustomed to a more open approach to policy and decision making. Early on, and indeed in advance of free education, they recognised their need to address structures, finance, and size of school. It would not have been possible for all the Catholic schools to follow the example of the SEC. Even if the Catholic bishops had wanted a single board to oversee education, the sheer scale of numbers and the singularity of the religious orders, each with its own mission and charism, would have made it extremely difficult, if not impossible. And so the confused network of organisations and structures continued.

Organisations or Institutions? Leaders or Managers?

In 1957 there were five managerial organisations representing the private voluntary secondary schools, and by 1965 two more were added. The free scheme proved to be a type of initiation rite for the religious brothers in their new group - they showed leadership in their manner of responding. On the other hand, the managerial bodies that were longer in existence had greater problems in coping, the exceptions being the ISA and the AIH since they already had clear structures in place for the managing of their voluntary schools. The bishops associated with the twenty-six diocesan colleges were also able to clarify the position for their schools in 1966. Lack of leadership and confusion of roles in the CHA, the CCSS and the CMRS resulted in distress and uncertainty in the schools, though the imminence of the starting date for free education provided the necessary stimulus for action. Nevertheless, the 1960s was the decade that challenged the managerial bodies as organisations and found them wanting. Selznick (1992:233) describes an organisation as

> a special-purpose tool, a rational instrument engineered to do a special
> job, a lean no-nonsense system of consciously co-ordinated activities.

The ISA, AIH, Church of Ireland Board of Education and the CHA, all founded in the nineteenth century, would measure up to most of Selznick's definition. The CCSS, on the other hand, might have tried to embrace too much to be credited with that definition. It might more accurately be called an 'institution', which Selznick describes as

> a product of social adaptation, largely unplanned, often a result of
> converging interests (1992:133).

However, by the late 1950s its members were all in secondary or 'secondary top' schools; the junior private schools were a separate group. By 1973 the CCSS was more truly 'managerial' in membership though it was not until 1977 that the focus on management became clearer.

The FCLS and the TBA began as 'organisations'. The Department of Education had an impact on the lay Catholic group and the brothers, thus enabling them to become 'organisations' rather than 'institutions'. The JMB appears to have begun in 1964 as an 'institution' but it became a managerial organisation by the end of the 1970s and has continued to develop its role. It offers leadership through effective management skills that are used to support a shared vision and mission in education. The separate existence of the NAPD may prove a catalyst in encouraging the managerial organisation to define its leadership role for an unknown future where lifelong learning will be the norm. The potential for denominational schools to become 'schools *of* communities' is obvious. On the other hand, NAPD could almost replicate the confusion of earlier decades if it were to become involved in 'policy'.

How might the CMCSS and the AMCSS be described in Selznick's terms? The CMCSS evolved into a managerial organisation for Catholic schools. It included many principals, managers, bishops and major superiors whose leadership and organisational skills developed a number of 'institutions'. These were the Joint Committee of 1959, the Catholic Management Consultative Committee and the Catholic Managerial Committee of 1967, the Special Committee from 1967 to 1968, the Council of Managers of Catholic Secondary Schools from 1968 to 1987. The story of the managerial bodies individually and collectively is itself proof of the complex human activity that is management. Some learned to interpret the external environments more quickly than others. None of them pursued the development of a professional association for the secondary school principals.

The developments that resulted in the founding of NAPD in 1999 were not intended to be part of this book. What is important is that the professional association exists at the beginning of the new century. There is a delicate relationship between those who are charged with the daily leadership and administration of the schools and those who are responsible for leadership and management on behalf of the patrons or trustees. It is delicate because policy and its implementation are not always distinct in schools. The history of the managerial organisations has shown the struggle and at times the pain of clarifying what Bishop Fergus of Achonry called 'policy' and 'those other matters'. Only time will reveal if that history will prove a source of learning.

The schools under Protestant management must be acknowledged for remarkable leadership in their understanding of the demarcation line between 'policy' and 'those other matters' of the day-to-day operation of education. The AIH led the way in reviewing their function as an organisation. The CCSS was possibly less of a 'managerial' body than the other groups until 1977 when a new direction emerged. The nuns showed courage in reviewing their role in the 1980s even if it entailed their demise. Is there significance in the fact that it was the Protestant women and the nuns who ceased to exist as organisations? The CHA has not shown evidence of any review of their role perhaps because they have become an 'institution' - as more and more lay people are appointed as principals in that group of colleges, will the future bring a merger into the FCLS? The CMCSS includes a representative of the Catholic Hierarchy so the bishops are involved in management. Perhaps it is therefore logical to conclude that the CHA is an 'institution' that provides members with a supportive network of professional contacts.

The ISA continues to represent male and female heads of the schools under Protestant management. The CHA is a professional association of the male headmasters but it is not a negotiating body.[108] The FCLS comprises the lay men and women principals, managers and often owners of these private lay schools. The TBA is still made up of the provincials and teaching brothers. Macro-matters of interest to the management of the Catholic schools are the responsibility of the CMCSS. That Council, re-constituted as the Council of Management of Catholic Secondary Schools, is the 'national Catholic management group' which is the governing body of the Secretariat of Secondary Schools.[109] The word 'management' was a necessary inclusion because one-third of the schools by then had established boards. The managerial basis for the CMCSS is the Association of Management of Catholic Secondary Schools (AMCSS). This Association consists of ten regional groups where the lay and religious principals, unitary managers and chairmen of boards work 'to promote the interests and welfare of Catholic voluntary secondary schools in the Republic of Ireland'.[110]

The greater openness towards other faiths encouraged by Vatican II encouraged the managers in the 1960s to discuss a support structure for mutual interest in secondary education. Out of such a vision came the JMB in 1964. Membership then was open to the ISA, AIH, CHA, CCSS, the TBA from 1965 and the FCLS from 1967. The re-constituting of the CMCSS in 1987 affected the composition of the JMB. Each of the seven managerial bodies shared a vision of education in secondary schools but they did not always share a concept of management or leadership. Organisations that do not exist first of all for profit need people who have an outstanding sense of commitment and such commitment is evident in the story of each of the seven managerial bodies. After 1987 energies were directed towards a CMCSS and a JMB with a firm regional base in the AMCSS. It is important to note that members of the FCLS continue to play an important part in the regional structures and through those in the CMCSS and the JMB. The mission of voluntary secondary education is the shared vision in leadership and management of the sector.

The twenty-four members of the JMB include two representatives from each of the ten regions in the AMCSS; three people from the ISA represent the schools under Protestant management; the President of the CMCSS is also President of the JMB; the full-time General Secretary and the Principal Officer attend its meetings. The Secretariat of Secondary Schools implements policy decisions taken by the JMB. It is operated as a limited company in much the same way as the Secretariat of Catholic Secondary Schools that it replaced. The task of the Secretariat therefore is one of a management function. The In-service Development Council that was established in 1991 is directly linked to the management functions rather than to the CMCSS or the JMB. The representative of the bishops and the representative from CORI (formerly CMRS) on the CMCSS are not members of the JMB. That makes sense because their interest is the future of the Catholic secondary schools and they ensure a close working relationship between the management body, the bishops and the religious superiors and trustees. In that way the interaction of leadership and management is assured. CORI continues to emphasise the Catholic school as a counter-cultural influence, and identifies needs that have relevance for the work of the CMCSS:

> *First, the need to engage, with others, in the task of developing new structures*
> *to take over the responsibilities for schools currently held by religious*
> *congregations. Secondly, they need to identify new ways of being involved in*
> *education which will enable unmet needs to be identified and responded to;*
> *give rise to the empowerment of poor and marginalised groups and represent*
> *a counter-cultural voice promoting an alternative vision of society based on*
> *Gospel values.*

(CORI 1997a:32)

4

Salaries and Posts of Responsibility

SALARIES AND POSTS OF RESPONSIBILITY

The 1950s were years of economic stagnation and high emigration[1] though the end of the decade brought a rise in both agricultural and industrial output. The government Programme of Economic Expansion in 1958, the repeal of the Control of Manufacturers Acts (1932) in 1964, and the lessening of import duties through the Anglo-Irish Free Trade Agreements in 1965, heralded and promoted economic development.[2] A rise of 82 per cent in industrial output from 1959 to 1968 reflected that growth. Earlier high levels of emigration began to fall and there was a rise in the birth rate from 1961. Public health began to improve, though it would be some years before there was control over 'the other disappeared', those who suffered from tuberculosis or 'TB' as it was popularly called. There were indeed signs that a new Ireland was emerging (Murphy, 1979) and Ó Buachalla (1989) believes that 1957 was the watershed.[3]

Meanwhile, in education, the contentious issue of teacher pay had to be faced by the managerial organisations and the government. The ASTI was better organised to deal with their grievance than the managers who continued to function as separate groups. The growth in the economy raised union expectations and courage to pursue a promotional system for their members - by the end of the 1960s posts of responsibility were about to be introduced into all schools. But no sooner were the voluntary schools learning to cope with the implications of the free education scheme than principals and managers were being challenged to change their hierarchical management style.

Conciliation and Arbitration 1951

The Department of Education was responsible for the larger part of the teacher salary, that increased by steps or increments, and the managerial bodies had no control over this. From 1951 a government process of Conciliation and Arbitration (C and A) with three panels by 1957 for the separate teacher unions became the mechanism for dealing with teacher pay. Representatives of the Ministers for Education and Finance sat with the teacher unions on the Conciliation Council. Once a claim was lodged, explored and agreed, it could be processed and when there was no agreement the union usually sought a hearing at Arbitration. While the C and A Scheme meant that the Ministers for Education and Finance did not have to deal directly with teacher claims, the separate union panels created problems for the Department of Education. No sooner had one claim been dealt with than the second, and then the third union lined up for increases. Thus, in 1955 the INTO were ahead; in 1959 and 1965 the VTA was in the lead (Ryan Tribunal, 1968:6-7). It was a costly system in terms of time, personnel and money for the Department. When this temporary C and A Scheme was made permanent in December 1955, it must have seemed to the civil servants that the teachers had an unfair advantage.[4] There were eight increases for secondary teachers from 1951 to 1962 as compared with only three between 1922 and 1950 (Coolahan, 1984:195). The ASTI had sharpened its negotiation ability in securing the Liston award [5] that set a seventeen point incremental scale for all teachers in 1956, and it had a logical expectation that the managers should increase the basic salary proportionately with advances in the incremental salary.

Attitudes among the Catholic managerial groups differed in relation to C and A. The CHA saw participation as an opportunity to support their teachers in salary claims that cost schools nothing. The priests also acknowledged the fact that religious and clerical principals who were recognised teachers benefited from any increases won by the ASTI. Past experience had shown the managers that the union was more likely to pressurise for an increase in the basic salary when C and A failed to meet their demands. The CHA therefore joined the Conciliation Council in 1959 and encouraged the other bodies to do so, but to no avail.[6] The nuns did not think it was important for them to be involved since they had no interest in salaries at that time.[7] The fact that the Christian Brothers and the nuns continued to desist from taking managerial places on C and A was a source of annoyance to the ASTI.

In 1957 the Provisional United Trade Union Organisation (PUTCO) emerged, representing the trade union congresses, with James Larkin as secretary, and this organisation responded positively to a government request for a national pay agreement of ten shillings. In October, under the auspices of the Labour Court, talks between PUTCO and the FUE (now IBEC) emphasised the importance of collaboration for the sake of a developing economy and on 5 February 1959 their efforts eased the conclusion of the sixth round of wages increase. The ICTU was established in 1959 representing 77 unions and 94 per cent of total trade union membership. The ASTI re-joined the Irish Conference of Professional and Service Associations (ICPSA) with a view to building support in their struggle for better pay and conditions for professional workers. This development and strengthening of the ASTI position was celebrated at their Golden Jubilee on 31 October. Their commitment to education was the focus of President Nora Kelleher's address when she stated that their first objective was 'to promote secondary education in Ireland' and that 'the success or failure of any system depends on the teacher ... (whose) character, personal gifts and scholastic attainments ... are of primary importance'.[8] In the CHA records of 14 October is a statement that they 'would apply (for membership of C and A) and therefore their chairman would attend the ASTI Jubilee dinner'. Doubtless the chairman was pleased to report back that a previous CHA chairman, Archbishop McQuaid, was publicly acknowledged by the union for his contribution to the status of secondary teachers. The union had already tried to get the Archbishop to resolve their grievance with the basic salary but they were told that any change in the school payment was 'a matter for the individual school'.[9] By the time of the ASTI jubilee in 1959 the CHA had agreed that a resolution of the basic salary was essential.

The Basic Salary

As employer, the school manager paid the basic salary to every recognised secondary teacher - a salary that was always inadequate (Collins, 1980; Barry, 1989). It pre-dated the first grant for teacher salaries in 1914 and the introduction of the incremental salary scale and capitation grants in 1924-1925. In 1946 Tomás Derrig, Minister for Education, had discussed the issue of teacher pay with the CCSS.[10] The Minister agreed with the CHA that the basic rate should remain at £200 for men and £180 for women. The records indicate that up to the 1960s the prevailing attitude among CCSS schools was that the £180 would be paid 'if possible'. The Christian Brothers and the nuns seem to have been convinced that the capitation grant could not be used to pay the basic salary. In the meantime, the ASTI had to negotiate increases in the basic salary with each school manager because the £200 or £180 was not always paid. There was no mechanism whereby union claims could be processed, and there was no umbrella managerial body to facilitate communication. The hope that C and A in 1951 would solve the union problem was dashed when the managerial bodies failed to join.

It was a most unsatisfactory and at times frustrating situation for the ASTI. The union files through the 1940s and 1950s contain frequent accounts of visits to individual principals and managers by union officers, seeking an increase in the basic salary. Moreover, the Department of Education was responsible for the total salary of the primary and vocational teachers so neither the INTO nor the VTA experienced the problems of the basic salary - they had access to their separate C and A teacher panels to negotiate pay increases. It was inevitable, then, that once the mechanism to deal with incremental salaries was established in the 1950s, the ASTI would actively pursue a resolution of the problematic basic payment. Unlike his or her colleague in the two other unions, a secondary teacher had no expectation at this time of ever becoming a school principal: in the 1950s and early 1960s it must have seemed that the only promotional posts in the majority of the secondary schools would always be filled by a nun, a brother, or a priest. Anyway, the union had little interest in this matter, because only vocational school principals were paid an extra allowance for their managerial work; but from 1959 it began to use 'lack of promotional opportunities' as an argument for pay increases.

A few examples will give some insight into the experience of the ASTI in the 1950s. In 1951 they requested an increase of $12^1/_2$ per cent in the basic salary but the CHA 'could not interfere with individual schools'.[11] Unknown to the teachers, the CHA were feeling the pressure and they sought the support of the bishops for their refusal. After that, the bishops were frequently used as a delaying tactic, so for almost a decade the union was put in the undignified position of being refused first by the CHA, who referred them to the Hierarchy and secondly, by the bishops who told them to 'deal with the headmasters'. What might be seen as policy by inaction on the part of the managerial body resulted in individual headmasters giving in to ASTI pressure to increase the basic salary beyond the £200 that was frequently paid by the CHA schools. More money for the teachers meant increasing school fees and CHA schools appear to have been more likely to follow that course than either the brothers or the nuns. For a second time within ten years, the bishops asked the CHA for 'a statement of salaries *actually* paid to teachers'.[12] It was revealed that many schools were paying more than £200 'in order to keep good teachers' and at times even to poach 'good teachers' from other managers. Payments were sometimes given in the form of additional bonuses for efficiency or length of service.

Thus, in 1955 the ASTI wanted a basic payment of £350 for all teachers, though in December 1954 the Department of Education had directed that schools would pay £200.[13] At that stage, there were CCSS schools where the original £180 was not being paid. The average paid by the nuns was £209 but basic payments of £150 existed. The Christian Brothers paid an average of £249 and the CHA £269, though a few schools paid more.[14] As variations in the basic payment became more widely known within the union, there was reason for anger - a particularly vexatious aspect was the unreliability of information about the salary. When Máire McDonagh was appointed in 1958, she received the support of Standing Committee to ask the membership to lodge complaints in writing.[15] This was to enable her to build up records and to cut down on the number of occasions where ASTI officers reacted to a member's grievance by travelling to meet the school manager concerned.[16]

The problem for the ASTI was the inadequacy and variation of the basic salary. The fewer lay teachers the school employed, the lower the overheads for the manager. Orders like the Loreto, Sacred Heart Sisters and Dominicans where the majority of the religious worked in the schools, were in a position to offer a wide curriculum without employing large numbers of lay teachers.[17] By contrast, the Christian Brothers employed many lay teachers, charged low fees and therefore were less able to give increases. The ASTI made frequent requests to the Brothers for better pay and that involved dealing with two separate provincial administrations as well as individual managers in schools. A round of such meetings might produce very little for union membership. The exasperation of the ASTI was understandable while the difficult financial position of some of the schools was a fact.

In 1952 the ASTI asked the CCSS for a basic salary of £350 for its members, but it was eight years before they made the same demand of the CHA. There are no accurate records, but it is at least possible that the CHA basic salary was in the region of the amount sought. What emerged gives further insight into the workings of the managerial bodies at the time. Bishop Fergus of Achonry, and a member of the CHA, recalled a letter from Jack Lynch, Minister for Education, in 1959:

> While it is true that the Department does not provide direct building grants
> for secondary schools, it will in the financial year 1950-60 be providing
> £853,000 in capitation grants. Out of this sum the school authorities are
> not required by the Department to pay more than £200 basic salary to the
> some 3,000 registered teachers, that is, a total of about £600,000 to such
> teachers, leaving for building, maintenance, etc. a quarter of a million
> pounds . ... The secondary schools capitation grant is not required to cover
> more than the £200 of the teacher's total salary and emoluments, the entire
> cost of the rest of such salaries and emoluments falling on the Department.
> The amount concerned, including the recent 6% increase, which accrues to
> all recognised secondary teachers, will in 1959-60 come to £1,545,000. It
> may not be out of place here to mention that, when very substantial increases
> were made in the secondary schools capitation grants in 1954, the Department
> still continued to bear the full costs of the salary increases awarded, either by
> reference to cost of living or to status, to secondary teachers.[18]

The letter added that the CHA had no authority to decide the amount that individual schools should pay their teachers. In other words, the basic payment as laid down by the Department was to rest at £200 and it was the Department, not the managerial organisations or individual managers, who decided the amount. Obviously, the Minister's approach suited the managerial bodies. That the bishops appreciated the Minister's commitment to paying teacher salaries and emoluments is clear from a letter they sent to the annual general meeting of the CHA in 1961:

> *This concession had the great advantage that the campaign of the*
> *secondary teachers for higher salary was no longer between the teachers*
> *and the schools but between the teachers and the government, and that*
> *the responsibility for payment of adequate salaries rested on the government.*[19]

Thereafter, the CHA passed a resolution:

> *That any revision of the basic or school salary can only be negotiated if*
> *the Department is a party to the agreement.*[20]

The bishops discussed the basic salary at length and they subsequently issued an instruction through the CHA on the importance of united action by the managerial organisations:

> *It would seem that the CHA and the CCSS should give this matter their*
> *consideration and either revert to the terms of the original arrangement*
> *(i.e. £200 basic) or failing this, at least agree among themselves on a*
> *<u>rigidly uniform</u>* (sic) *basic salary for all teachers. If neither of these*
> *alternatives is now feasible, the bishops suggest that the CHA should*
> *open this whole matter with the Department and demand a complete*
> *revision of the system of paying secondary teachers.*[21]

Clearly, the ministerial statement of March 1959 was an escape clause for the managerial bodies though it was never intended as such. The CHA agreed that no further increases would be made in the basic salary in their schools.[22] Such agreement, even among the CHA schools, was unprecedented and is probably attributable to the involvement of the bishops whose diocesan colleges formed the nucleus of the organisation. The Catholic managerial organisations at the time were unaware of the letter from Jack Lynch, but it was relevant to the nuns and the brothers, many of whose schools were not paying the set amount because they believed that only the school fees could be used for salaries. This issue highlighted the lack of an appropriate structure for communication among the managers and helped to bring the managerial bodies together.

For the next two years John Hughes SJ, as President of the CHA, worked incessantly to meet the ASTI demand for a basic salary of £350 along lines that might be accepted by the nuns and the brothers. Eventually, all were in agreement that the basic should constitute a percentage of the incremental salary. However, when the bishops received the proposal in January 1963 they rejected it, not unreasonably, because 'it involved the managers in every increase granted by the Department'. They recommended 'a fixed non-varying sum', or alternatively, that the CHA request the Department to take on the entire salary charge.[23] On 30 April 1963 Dr Fergus wrote to John Hughes SJ on behalf of the bishops:

> ... get the brothers and nuns to agree, then see if the Department would fix a non-varying sum and all schools keep to it. This would have the desirable result of saving the clerical and religious headmasters from having to bargain with teachers regarding money matters.

The principals and managers had failed to see the weakness in their proposal. The ASTI suggested an alternative: the basic payment could commence at £260 and increase by eight increments to £400 over a period of ten years; after five years the scheme could be reviewed. The CHA rejected the proposal but urged 'that some part of the total salary should continue to be paid by the schools' on the basis that it was a sign that the manager, not the Department of Education, was the employer[24] - the Christian Brothers favoured a maximum payment of £200. In the absence of a workable and agreed solution the bishops were more direct in their advice to the CHA, CCSS and the Christian Brothers. They should:

> approach the Minister and try to secure such an arrangement. The bishops would not object to you making your offer even as high as £300 as long as that was an end of it, and as long as the schools kept strictly to it.[25]

A note of impatience is detectable in the reply from the bishops who were probably more concerned with the impending Second Vatican Council and its implications. In the event, the Minister Dr Hillery turned down the proposal from the CHA and there ensued endless meetings between the managerial organisations, and between the CHA (mainly) and the ASTI, until January 1964 when the bishops were informed that agreement was reached.[26] Eventually, there was to be a basic salary of £200 with an additional $12^{1}/_2$ per cent of the standard married salary, because the ASTI wanted to end the discrimination between married, unmarried, male and female in relation to pay. In fact, the brothers and the nuns had been most reluctant to agree, but the CHA stance prevailed.[27] Dr Fergus wrote to John Hughes SJ on 18 January 1964 that the bishops

> want <u>all</u> schools to pay the <u>same</u> salary to lay teachers and not to give increases under pretext of non-salary pay thus reverting to the old competition which was the chief reason why the bishops raised the question in the first instance.

The CCSS was unhappy about the agreement because of the number of small schools owned by the nuns, and the Christian Brothers held out even after the bishops' conditional approval. Finally, on 8 April 1964 at a meeting of all teaching brothers including the Christian Brothers, agreement was reached.

In a two-page letter to Dr Fergus and Cardinal Conway, John Hughes SJ expressed his personal misgivings about the agreement on a common basic salary. The astute Jesuit and experienced headmaster saw it as 'preventing recognition of exceptional and long service' of individual teachers. He admitted that it would prevent 'poaching of teachers amongst us', although 'good teachers may still go to non-Catholic schools and universities'. The suggestion was that the agreement reached between the ASTI and the Catholic managerial bodies could discourage motivation by failing to recognise quality performance by individual teachers.[28] Cardinal Conway sent a brief formal acknowledgement and a personal note:

> *I have noted its contents carefully. I don't think there was (sic) anything useful I can say except that I hope that things will turn out better than you fear. It would be a thousand pities if the Joint Body which has such valuable potentialities, were to founder so soon or if the CHA were to, in effect, be split.* Oremus omnes. *Kindest regards.*[29]

The 'Joint Body' referred to was the JMB that had quietly formed that same year. It was a mark of Cardinal Conway's stance that he did not refer to separate managerial bodies, being consistent as always in encouraging inter-church collaboration between the managerial organisations. He believed the managers needed to unite in order to be effective.

The basic salary issue brought the CHA to the fore and into closer contact with bishops, CCSS and Christian Brothers. John Hughes SJ clearly had misgivings about the final outcome and the ASTI failed to get the £400 they wanted. While the union had fewer problems with the schools under Protestant management [30] and those in the FCLS, the aim was to secure a uniform basic payment for their members. Therefore, the settlement was only temporary. The brothers and the nuns were unhappy too, but the nuns began to re-think their attitude to C and A and joined a few months later. All three managerial organisations learned to appreciate the leadership qualities of their two main protagonists, John Hughes SJ and Dr Fergus. The basic salary issue gave a new impetus to involvement by the bishops and the CHA was happy to seek the advice of the Hierarchy.[31] The CMRS assured the CHA that they would not be putting 'anything about schools on our agenda' and would let the activists 'on with it because the CHA's task of negotiating is already very difficult, and the entry of our body upon the battle-field would only impede your laudable efforts'. The CMRS followed a similar policy in relation to the 'graded posts'.[32]

Teachers' Salaries 1958-1968

A five per cent differential had traditionally existed between secondary salaries and those of the other teachers. The differential was designed to reflect greater responsibility in dealing with older pupils and in teaching subjects to honours level for the Leaving Certificate. The ASTI persisted in their demand that the differential be maintained, while the INTO campaign to end it led to the Minister for Education, Jack Lynch, setting up a group of fifteen as a Teachers' Salaries Committee on 8 December 1958. The ASTI was reluctant to co-operate with the Committee and reminded the Department of Education that the existing C and A Scheme stated that

> *Matters within the scope of the scheme will in future be dealt with*
> *exclusively through the machinery of the scheme ... (and appropriate*
> *subjects for discussion by conciliation council will be) principles*
> *governing the remuneration payable directly from state funds*
> *personally to recognised teachers in receipt of incremental salaries.*[33]

However, the union decided to participate in the Salaries' Committee while awaiting a $12^1/_2$ per cent cost of living claim already submitted to Conciliation in March 1958. Almost inevitably they had to go to Arbitration where they were awarded nearly half their claim (*Teachers' Salaries*, 1960:72-3; Logan, 1999:157-204).

It was a considerable victory for the union in a year when unemployment peaked at 78,000 and at 'a time of despondency and gloom that was reflected in national performance and aspiration' (O'Hagan, 1992:13).[34] The Christian Brothers and many of the CCSS schools saw levels of unemployment reflected in parental difficulties even where school fees were low.[35] Little progress was made by the Salaries' Committee, though issues were identified and the concept of differentiation through a 'basic school scale' and a 'basic personal scale' was explored (*Report*, 1960:84-106). As the economy improved, the determination of the ASTI to get a better pay deal grew. From 1960 they gathered information about 'graded posts' in schools in Northern Ireland in the expectation that these could offer a mechanism for promotional structures and further pay. By 1966 there were ASTI members in the new comprehensive schools and their entire salaries were paid by the state, so union attention drifted back to the inadequacy of the basic salary in the secondary schools. Finally, in the context of free education and increasing numbers of post primary teachers it made sense for the Minister for Education to sanction a major study of the salary issue.

The Ryan Tribunal 1967

On 6 October 1967 Donogh O'Malley announced the setting up of a tribunal to be chaired by Professor Louden Ryan, lecturer in political economy at Trinity College and chairman of the National Economic and Social Council (NESC). Louden Ryan who described himself to the author as 'the Dungannon man who came to Trinity as a student and never went back', was well suited to the task. Though Donogh O'Malley had not met him personally, the Minister had appointed an experienced man to lead a carefully chosen group. In addition to lecturing duties, Ryan had been bursar in the university and was the first chairman of the National Industrial Economic Council which had emerged from Ken Whitaker's economic planning for an integrated programme of national development (Kennedy *et al*, 1988:55-65). On extended leave of absence from Trinity College to work in the Department of Finance, Ryan was on the board of the Central Bank where in 1967 he headed up Money Management and was a director.[36] Possibly because of the existence of the three separate teacher panels in Conciliation, Donogh O'Malley decided that the Ryan Tribunal would not be representative: the five members were ministerial appointees. However, the presence of Maurice P. Cosgrave from ICTU recognised the trade unions, Cathal Ó Shannon the Labour Court, Earnest F. Benson came from the FUE and Louis M. Fitzgerald was head of Establishment Division at the Department of Finance; the secretary was Art Ó Callanáin from the Department of Education.[37] School managers and teachers would be invited to make submissions to the Tribunal.

Nine oral presentations were made following written submissions to the Ryan Tribunal: from the three teacher unions, the Departments of Education and Finance, the managerial bodies, the Association of CEOs, and the IVEA. The procedural rules of the Tribunal permitted the various groups to be present during the submissions though they could not intervene so this was the first formal occasion when the CCSS and TBA representatives listened to the frustration of their lay teachers. One grievance was salary; the UNESCO Conference two years earlier had emphasised the importance of pay as a factor in the recognition of teacher status (1966:82-3; Collin, 1980). The lack of promotional prospects in religious secondary schools was another issue.[38] Early in the deliberations Ryan was asked by the Minister's office to 'include the comprehensive schools in the terms of reference' and three teachers from Cootehill Comprehensive in Cavan made a presentation.[39] The Minister wanted an early recommendation from the Tribunal, whose first task was:

> *To recommend a common basic scale of salary for teachers in national,*
> *secondary and vocational schools.*

(RYAN REPORT, 1968:5)

chapter 4 | salaries and posts of responsibility

One of the first queries from Dominic Ó Laoghaire on behalf of the Department of Education, on 7 February 1968, was about the 12½ per cent agreed by the managerial bodies with the ASTI in 1964. A new basic salary had emerged without the Department's knowledge. If it was part of the teacher's total salary it was pensionable, though in fact neither the union nor the managers viewed it so. The VTA immediately claimed that the additional percentage gave secondary teachers an unfair advantage. Thus, four years after the bishops and the mangers believed they had a solution for the basic salary, it appeared again as a bigger problem. And Louden Ryan wondered why the managers had made no effort to relate special duties to the increases they had given in the basic salary.[40]

A means of 'not upsetting the differentials' between the three groups of teachers had to be found. The managerial bodies, the INTO, and the VTA recommended a common basic scale and that was what the Department of Education wanted. The ASTI had 'no rooted objection to a common scale of salary for all teachers' but these

> should have reference to their length of training, the nature and the academic
> standard of their qualification and the level of work undertaken. A graduate
> secondary teacher spends five or six years post-Leaving Certificate before
> he becomes a registered teacher.

(SUBMISSION, 31 JANUARY 1968)

The managers advocated working towards a 'common training for and common entry into the profession' (*Ryan Report*, 1968:40). The FCLS made a separate presentation to the Tribunal partly because they differed from the CHA and the CCSS on two matters - they wanted a common scale for married and single teachers and an end to discrimination on the basis of sex (*Ibid.*, 1968:37-43); and they did not agree that 'the state should in future pay the basic salaries of our teachers'. Louden Ryan noted that during the exchanges with the Tribunal the FCLS alone wanted to retain the school payment to teachers.[41] Mother Jordana OP repeatedly stated that 'a canonical status' should be accorded the secondary schools so that they would be 'free' of state interference. It was the first time that Ryan had heard that phrase and it did not appear in the final *Report*. He was also struck by the fact that the managerial bodies 'assumed that whatever cost was involved arising out of any recommendations we made would be paid by the Department of Finance'.[42]

The Tribunal had met in full deliberation on twenty occasions and there were many working sessions in between. When the *Report* was presented to Minister Brian Lenihan on 23 April 1968, a common basic salary scale for primary, vocational and secondary teachers was recommended. Additional allowances would be paid for degrees and diplomas. The customary difference between married men and women and single men was to be maintained. Louden Ryan said at the time that future legislative developments would adjust that imbalance and that did happen in the

1970s. One important recommendation was that the period of probation for a teacher should last only one year.[43] A cause of anger with the ASTI was the recommendation that the duration of the school year should be similar in primary and post-primary schools. Dr Hillery had also advocated a longer school year when he was Minister. Fearing the managerial bodies might have agreed to this, the ASTI had been seeking a five-day week and shorter working hours but the CHA was so opposed to the idea that they refused to meet the union to discuss it.[44]

The Tribunal (*Report*, 1968:15) considered the dual system of secondary teachers' salaries. The advice was specific:

> *Our belief that the Department of Education should be responsible for the total emoluments of secondary teachers, and that secondary schools should have no discretion in making supplementary payments to their staffs, is reinforced by the fact that fees have been abolished since 1 September 1967, in almost all secondary schools. This, together with the higher capitation grants which are now being paid by the Department, mean that current expenditures of these schools are now being met almost entirely from public funds, and it must be accepted that the manner in which such funds are used is a matter of legitimate concern to the public.*

The advice only served to unite the union and the managerial organisations in keeping the dual system. In fact, the managerial bodies were divided on the issue. For that reason, as stated earlier, the FCLS made a separate submission - the lay managers wanted to retain the basic payment. The nuns and the Christian Brothers wanted the Department of Education to pay the entire salary, but the CHA did not agree with this. It was because the religious groups would not present a divided front to the Tribunal that they decided not to mention the matter. The ISA and the AIH collaborated. However, the combined religious bodies asked the Tribunal to recommend payment for substitute and part-time teachers, in line with the practice in the vocational and comprehensive schools.

By the mid-1970s all the managerial bodies wanted to continue paying the basic salary. This was partly because the ASTI supported the practice. There was no logical or legal basis for the managers' policy until 1977 when the Secretariat of Catholic Secondary Schools obtained legal opinion. From the year of the Ryan Tribunal, the basic salary became a symbol of a relationship between the ASTI and the JMB. Time and a different legal opinion in the 1990s intimated that it was merely symbolic, and neither the managers nor the union made an issue of the matter. Since 1996 the Department of Education has paid the total salary and adjustments are made in the capitation payments. The manager or board of management continues to be the legal employer of teachers in the voluntary secondary schools.

Posts of Responsibility 1970

The issue of posts of responsibility was part of the fallout of the negotiations that followed the Ryan Tribunal. The posts proved a challenge, a frustration and a piece of quicksilver to those charged with the management of voluntary schools until 1998 when a new structure of in-school management was introduced.

It was the second task of the Ryan Tribunal that opened a way for posts of responsibility. Ryan was asked

> *to recommend what appropriate additions might be made to the basic scale*
> *in respect of qualifications, length of training, nature of duties, etc.*
> (REPORT, 1968:5)

The FCLS was in agreement with the other managers that a system of posts of responsibility with 'real and effective responsibility' should be introduced. The ASTI[45] argued their case:

> *No opportunities for advancement exist at present even though 80 per cent*
> *of all lay teachers serve on the staffs of schools conducted by Religious*
> *Orders. The prospects which the secondary branch of the teaching profession*
> *offers are far less favourable than those of other professions.*
> (SUBMISSIONS, 1968:10)

The members of the Tribunal held that one of the principles for allowances for posts was that people 'should compete' for them and 'the managers would have to manage'.[46] In the long run, the recommendation on graded posts had implications for the managerial bodies that few could have foreseen in 1968.

There were three main players involved with the posts: the teachers, the managers and the Department of Education. Initially the ASTI on behalf of its members was the lead player dealing with the Department. In 1972 the JMB came to the fore in making an agreement with the union regarding the operation of the posts in schools. The Department did not play a strong role at that stage, and the secondary school posts system thereafter was the concern of the union and the managers. The Department allocated the finance but did not participate in developing the structure of the posts or in seeking accountability. By the 1980s the JMB had realised the importance of including the Department if the posts were to provide middle management in schools. But many more years were to pass before that evolved and, in the process, the managers struggled to strengthen their own organisational structures. In retrospect, if the PCW in the 1990s revealed a new toughness and solidarity in the managerial organisations, the evolution of the system of posts of responsibility exposed their weakness and lack of unity.

The system of posts of responsibility (PORs) developed in the aftermath of dissatisfaction with the outcomes of the Ryan Tribunal in 1968. The common basic salary, with allowances for university qualifications at pass and honours levels and a common C and A Board for all teachers, was introduced in October 1968 (*Report*, 1968:10-15). The INTO and the VTA were happy with the new arrangements. The three separate C and A Schemes up to this point had facilitated claims and counter-claims by the three unions.[47] The ASTI rejected the joint C and A Scheme, arguing that a previous Minister for Education (Donogh O'Malley) had given them an assurance that they would retain their separate scheme. In September 1968 the ASTI pressed a salary claim and the INTO and VTA wanted to be part of the C and A Scheme that would consider the secondary teachers' claim. After some months of wrangling, on 27 January 1969, Minister Brian Lenihan made one final offer to appease the teachers. On reaching the tenth point of the salary scale, secondary teachers would receive a Special Functions Allowance (SFA) and the money would be provided from what had been intended to pay the principals and vice-principals' allowances. The Minister argued that by giving this allowance he was not interfering with the common basic salary for all teachers. The ASTI would not accept the SFA and the other two unions resented it. It is worth noting that the suggested allowances were to be linked to seniority in the teaching profession.

So, the ASTI efforts to dissuade the Minister from implementing the findings of the Ryan Tribunal had failed. As a result, the union withdrew their teaching services on 1 February 1969 and the strike lasted three weeks, until 24 February. The managerial bodies had supported the teachers at the Ryan Tribunal. In the face of industrial action they publicly acknowledged their indebtedness to lay teachers in their schools and the JMB agreed to close the schools in support of the ASTI claim for a separate C and A Scheme. There was also the fact that the opposition of the Catholic managerial bodies had been fuelled by the rationalisation of schools that had been taking place. As already mentioned, the publication of the controversial article in *Studies* in the Autumn of 1968 helped to fan fear and distrust of the Department of Education among the managers and secondary teachers. The CCSS records indicate the prevailing uncertainty among the nuns about government policy on education and on secondary schools in particular. The Christian Brothers were concerned and the TBA, established since 1965, was anxious about the future of voluntary education. All these factors contributed to uniting the ASTI and the managers in opposition to the Department of Education.

A solution seemed at hand when Minister Lenihan signed a salary agreement with the JMB and ASTI in March 1969. The seventeen-point incremental scale was reduced. In future all teachers would attain the maximum salary on the sixteenth point. Allowances for university qualifications and SFAs were to be increased. A basic salary of £400 was to be paid by the school to each teacher, thus ending a lengthy struggle by the ASTI to persuade schools to pay a higher salary. Adjustments would be made in the annual capitation grant from the Department of Education to cover this. Any future increases would apply to a teacher's total salary. In general, it was a worthy achievement by the ASTI but there was a lot of unfinished business. Neither the INTO nor the VTA were satisfied with the introduction of the SFA for secondary teachers and the two groups called a number of local strikes. Randles (1975:297) highlights the resulting embarrassment for the government on the eve of a general election that took place on 18 June 1969.[48]

A new majority Fianna Fáil government and a new Minister for Education, Pádraig Faulkner, could not ignore the situation created by the combination of the Report of the Ryan Tribunal, the ASTI strike, and the salary deal with Brian Lenihan. Faulkner was correct that the introduction of the SFA had contravened the common basic salary agreed for the three teacher unions. In May 1970, Faulkner introduced a change in the system. In future, only those in receipt of SFAs on 30 July 1970 would be paid these allowances. A two-tiered secondary teaching profession would be the result. But the ASTI could find itself representing two different groups in the profession, those appointed before and after June 1970 - and no trade union could agree with such an arrangement. Industrial action by the ASTI on this occasion took the form of a refusal to mark the Leaving Certificate examination papers of June 1970.

A Solution to Industrial Action

In July 1970 school authorities were notified of the decisions of Minister Pádraig Faulkner's and his offer brought an uneasy solution to the industrial action.[49] No new SFAs were to be given; teachers who had such posts on 30 June 1970 would retain them. The allowance was frozen at the 1969-1970 level and the money saved would be used to pay a new system of PORs. These posts would be open to all teachers and not necessarily on the basis of seniority. They were to be established in a manner to be agreed by the JMB, ASTI and the Department of Education. Three months later the ASTI Special Convention did not see the offer as a resolution.[50]

Four grades of PORs were to be introduced in primary and post-primary schools: principal, vice-principal, grade A and grade B posts. The new system applied only to registered teachers. For registration teachers had to have completed one year's teaching following the award of the Higher Diploma in Education. Each year the Department of Education would inform the manager of the 'points rating' allotted to the school.

This would be based on the number and age of the pupils enrolled. From that the Department would tell the manager the number and category of posts allowed. A pool of money was then to be allocated to each school by the Department. From what became known as 'the school pool' the various allowances were to be paid. The first charge on the pool would be the holders of SFAs; the next charge would be the principal's allowance, then that of the vice-principal. Only when these were paid would the holders of grade A and B posts receive their allowances.

An additional complication was the creation of another category of posts, called the Supernumerary grade B post. The intention was to cater for those teaching in secondary schools before June 1970 who were not SFA holders, or who had been appointed to a POR for which only some of the money or none was available. The registered teacher had to have completed one year of satisfactory service on the maximum of the salary scale without having been given a POR. This Supernumerary B allowance was to be paid outside of 'the school pool' and would therefore not affect other post holders. Initially, the Department of Education tried to insist that the holder of a Supernumerary B post would be appointed to the next available POR, thus saving money. However, once the Agreed Memorandum between the JMB and the ASTI was operative from 1972, this was not possible, unless the teacher was in fact next in line for a post. In other words, the reality of seniority on the list of posts prevailed. A teacher who could not be moved into the POR in this case was then deprived of the Supernumerary B post by the Department of Education and given instead a 'long-service increment'. The problem was that the 'long-service increment' was of less value than the B allowance. Neither managers nor union was satisfied with such an arrangement. A circular from the Department in 1975 (M20/75) was an effort to solve the problem of the Supernumerary B post allowance but two years later it was still a matter of contention with the managers.

In short, the system of PORs institutionalised a hierarchical structure in the schools. A school might have holders of SFAs, where teachers were at the required point on the incremental salary scale. But there would also be Supernumerary B posts, along with holders of grade A and B posts. If it sounds complicated, the experience of the managerial organisations and the ASTI bore that out, particularly in the early years of implementation.

There were inherent problems in the scheme. Clearly, post-primary schools would have an advantage over primary schools because of the age of the pupils. The personal and permanent nature of the SFA, based on seniority, could prevent the holder from moving schools. The PORs on the other hand, were not personal allowances. Therefore, if teachers moved to other schools they would lose the post and the allowance. Understandably, school principals and managers were extremely reluctant to employ an SFA holder because of the inevitable problems created for 'the school pool'. This also had implications for major superiors in moving religious from one community to another. Religious who were holders of SFAs would have a negative effect on 'the school pool' of the school to which they were moved. This happened in a number of CCSS and TBA schools during the 1970s. In most instances the religious manager put the equivalent of the allowance back into the school account to ensure that an ASTI member did not lose money, but at times this became a complicated arrangement with individual lay teachers.

Once the SFAs had been paid, the principal's allowance was the next call on 'the school pool', then the vice-principal's. Only then could holders of grade A and B PORs be paid. Thus, if a school had a number of SFAs it was possible that the pool would be exhausted and other post holders might get little or nothing. It frequently happened that a vice-principal's allowance was very small because of the number of SFAs. Where there was no money for a post, the post was described as a 'designated post'. Where this might occur, the JMB urged its members to name the holders of posts because allowances were linked to pensions and there was always a hope that the ASTI might succeed in redressing the issue of 'unpaid' posts. Understandably, teachers were unlikely to be interested in posts and duties without payment. The ASTI and the JMB agreed that a teacher would not be required to do extra work for a post if there was no money available. But it should be recorded that there were individual teachers who undertook extra duties without payment though management could not require such work.

The PORs were more of a mechanism for a salary increase for secondary teachers than a means of managing schools. The method of giving the increase could not disturb the parity between members of the INTO, the TUI and the ASTI - any apparent improvement for one group would inevitably lead to 'leap-frogging' by the others.[51] In 1970 when these arrangements were made the managers were more concerned with the lateness of the examination results and the consequent closure of the schools until 22 September to enable teachers to mark the scripts. The voluntary schools were coping with the demands of the early years of the free scheme and increasing enrolments. The role of the managers in allocating posts and duties was not thought through from the outset and lack of clarity about the new system prevailed. Many teachers saw the introduction of the posts as merely a means of giving a salary increase at particular stages in a profession that was inadequately remunerated and where there were few opportunities for promotion. However, at least one member of the ASTI held another view:

> How can anyone decide on a just payment for a post of responsibility which
> has not been defined? Surely the logical approach is to decide first what
> responsibility is involved, and then make a valuation.[52]

In retrospect, one managerial representative claimed that the Department of Education 'saw (the posts) as helping to provide a middle management in our schools at a time when numbers were growing rapidly',[53] but given the failure of the Department to become involved in the implementation of the PORs through a process of evaluation and support, it is difficult to agree with this point of view.

One of the most far-reaching consequences for lay teachers was the virtual immobility encouraged by the PORs. With the exception of the SFAs who had personal entitlement, teachers who were awarded a grade A or B post were most reluctant to move schools, the exceptions being those who secured jobs in the community schools as these opened from 1972. Teachers who held a post with money for two consecutive years were deemed to have a personal entitlement to that post as long as they remained on the staff of the particular school. The managerial organisations, individual principals and managers, the ASTI officials and individual members of the union were to suffer the consequences of a scheme that was so ill defined, but most of all, the PORs system had ramifications for the voluntary sector and the JMB.

The Agreed Memorandum

An Agreed Memorandum on Posts of Responsibility between the ASTI and the managers emerged in 1972. This was a sincere effort by the two parties to manage the new posts system and to achieve uniformity in implementation. The agreement was about the procedures to be followed in appointing teachers to posts, with the exception of that of the principal. Initially arrangements were to be reviewed each year and an existing agreement could not be changed unless both sides agreed. Three criteria were agreed for appointment to a post. The first was 'suitability and capability'. If more than one applicant was considered suitable and capable for a post, then the manager used the second criterion. This was 'length of unbroken service in the school as a registered secondary teacher immediately prior to the appointment of a post'. In other words, the post was given to the teacher who was senior in service in the school. Finally, if applicants had the same length of service in the school, the third criterion was used by the manager: 'absolute length of recognised secondary teaching service'. It was evident that a high priority was given to seniority and that was in keeping with trade union attitude, but in 1989 seniority was identified by the JMB as one weakness in the scheme:

> This model (based on seniority) came from the civil service and the Church and was a quid pro quo for lack of promotion among lay teachers.

The posts were allocated first. No job specification or even area of responsibility could be advertised: the manager's notice in a staff room invited written applications for whatever grade of post was stated in the notice. In the case of a grade A post, the attention of applicants could be drawn to the fact that duties for such a post 'are more extensive than those for a B post'.[54] Teachers on leave of absence had to be informed of the vacancy and be given a reasonable length of time within which to apply. In the case of a grade A post, the holder of the senior B post who applied was to be appointed. A further narrowing of options arose from the fact that only service in secondary schools was counted where the criterion of absolute length of service had to be used. This meant that no matter how much experience a teacher might have abroad or in the vocational, comprehensive or community school sectors, it was not relevant. This stipulation also helped make the system a cage in the voluntary schools, so while there was movement from the secondary schools to the community schools in particular, a contrary flow was rare.

Only when the posts were given to the relevant teachers was there any decision about duties and responsibilities to be undertaken and there were restrictions by the ASTI on the duties that might be performed. In spite of the fact that the idea of posts reflected good practice in schools in the UK including Northern Ireland, the ASTI would not include the duties of 'year head' where a teacher would take responsibility for all students in a particular group of classes. The duties of 'librarian' were also excluded, as was supervision. Yet, members of ASTI in the comprehensive and community schools undertook such responsibilities as part of their post work. There was some logic in the union position - they wanted to negotiate these particular duties in subsequent pay talks. But ASTI members in the voluntary sector were disadvantaged as a result. They rarely had opportunities to develop professional experience and expertise in a range of management duties, and their loss became apparent at times when individuals competed for positions in the state schools. Comparisons between the work of holders of grade A posts in community schools and secondary schools were often to the detriment of the latter: a claim at interview of notional or potential ability to do a job was not verifiable when the teacher had been prevented by union policy from fulfilling a particular role. From the church perspective, the posts failed to facilitate a parallel in the religious schools to that 'strong laity' that Cardinal Conway identified in the Catholic schools in Northern Ireland.

It is a tribute to the individual representatives of the ASTI and the JMB that they worked unceasingly until the late 1980s to implement an Agreed Memorandum that had been made under pressure and that lacked a sound educational or managerial basis. In effect, it was only as ASTI members complained of perceived injustices in the allocation of the posts that the details of the system were cobbled. Each review of the Memorandum heaped on to the structure the minutiae that were essential in avoiding a repetition of misunderstanding, disagreement and above all, industrial action. It was the least effective way to manage promotion in the workplace, but it is difficult to envisage how it might have been otherwise given the history of the posts system in the voluntary sector. Perhaps the posts were ten years too early for the managers.

The Department of Education did not see its role as encompassing accountability for posts in secondary schools. In fairness to the officials, they were consistent in their 'hands off' approach to the privately-owned schools. The assumption was that if the manager or chairman of the board submitted the names of post holders, allowances would be paid. It was up to the managers to negotiate the duties. There was a sense of helplessness about the management position, since they were hedged round by the context in which the posts were conceived in 1970. Even five years later, the secondary schools were more complex institutions in the sense that they were inadequately funded yet catering for increasing enrolments. In 1965-1966 there were 98,300 students in voluntary schools as compared with 34,400 in the vocational sector. In 1970-1971 barely three years after the beginning of free education there were 149,600 and 52,900 respectively. A further 1,600 were in the comprehensive sector. By 1975-1976 the secondary schools catered for 183,300 or 67 per cent of the cohort. Vocational schools provided for 74,000 and comprehensive and community schools for 15,700 students. Simple arrangements for part-time teachers and substitution that were provided in the state schools were not available to the voluntary sector at that time. There was a need for effective middle management structures such as were developing in the community schools. More often than not the very Agreed Memorandum to which ASTI and JMB were party, served to stifle creativity, effectiveness and opportunity for teachers. On the other hand, the very newness of the community schools enabled the first principals and boards to create structures - they were not handicapped by an inherited system.

The ASTI and the JMB agreed that work outside class hours or during holidays would not be a pre-condition for appointment to a post including that of vice-principal. The majority of the principals also taught classes and did administrative work after school hours and during holiday periods.[55] Analysis and design of time-tables in a pre-computer era was an essential part of the principal's role but vice-principals who were unavailable when such activities were done would be prevented from learning. The system was accidentally rather than deliberately minimalist.

A formal written contract was to be part of the system from 1972. This presented an opportunity for principal or manager and teacher to discuss duties and responsibilities. While this happened in individual schools it could never make up for the inherent weakness of the posts system for secondary schools. By 1977 there were many schools where a contract was not presented to post holders. It seemed a pointless exercise since the form simply stated that the person had a post. No reference was made to the category of post or to the duties involved until 1979 when these details were agreed after the annual review of the Memorandum. However, the changes did not give the JMB the right to advertise the duties of the post. From that year almost all school principals or managers presented the contract to teachers and, despite efforts again in 1984 to have the areas of responsibility advertised, there was little change out of that review.

Both parties to the Agreed Memorandum in 1972 had accepted that 'either the post of principal or that of vice-principal shall normally be filled by the promotion of a lay teacher'. It was a small but important gain for the ASTI that 'the lay teacher' in the voluntary school could aspire to one of the two most senior positions. In time, it would prove a disadvantage for some religious teachers when a lay principal was appointed. Unless the vice-principal was retiring or appointed principal, it was not possible to appoint a religious to the second most senior position in a school. In 1975 a clause, 'equitable distribution' of post allowances, was introduced into the Agreed Memorandum. This was partly to appease the union whose members then seemed unlikely ever to attain appointment as principals in the voluntary sector. The ratio of religious to lay teachers in a school was agreed as the basis of this distribution. Doubtless it was a form of discrimination against religious but it was a sincere effort by the JMB to acknowledge that the lay teachers might be similarly disadvantaged in schools where they formed the majority.

There was some discussion among CCSS members about possible injustice to 'well qualified and experienced teaching nuns', but as long as the post of principal was closed against lay people, and the ASTI refused to admit religious as union members, the CCSS could effect little change. That exclusion of religious from the union caused some concern among the JMB at the time of the 1975 review. The managers agreed that

> Since religious/clerical assistant teachers are excluded from membership
> of ASTI, and have not any active recognised representative body as a
> party to the negotiation of these interests, (they) are deemed to be the care
> of the Joint Managerial Body on which are representatives of the religious
> congregations of which these religious/clerical assistants are members. The
> ASTI has refused to allow any representatives of such religious/clerical teachers
> to be included in the negotiations.[56]

While the managers did not initially have a difficulty with including some representation of the teaching religious in future negotiations about posts, they did not press the union on the matter.[57] However, the JMB continued to be uneasy about the exclusion of teaching religious and the agreement that virtually excluded them from the posts system:

> In agreeing, as <u>managers</u> (sic) to the matters (of excluding religious) does
> the Joint Managerial Body contravene the constitutional rights of their
> religious/clerical staffs?[58]

The intention from 1972 had been that manager and/or principal, vice-principal and holders of posts and SFAs would form a committee to work out how the various duties would be discharged. As a management concept it had potential: the seeds of teamwork and a certain collective responsibility were there. In some schools this committee approach worked, but it was ultimately hampered by the limited area of responsibilities acceptable to the ASTI and subsequently enshrined in the Agreed Memorandum. There was also the reality that religious were unaccustomed to working closely with their lay colleagues. They were more likely to rely on members of their religious community when additional school duties were needed. It would be impossible to assess the extent to which this was a factor in the development of the PORs, but in human terms it was relevant.

In some schools it was found that procedures were ignored more through ignorance rather than design. This caused problems for the managerial organisations whose leaders were voluntary workers with the busy schedule of a principal or manager, or both. There was no Secretariat of Secondary Schools to call on; that too was a developing service until 1977.[59] In an attempt to address the problem of neglected procedures, the Memorandum of 1975 stipulated that the committee should meet 'at the beginning of each school year' to agree the posts. The list of post holders with the duties attached was then to be put in the staff room. Again, this was not always followed in the schools, so the 1976 Memorandum added that such planning should be done 'not later than 1 October'. Partly to appease younger members who were critical of the POR system, the ASTI established a sub-committee in 1976 to consider how teachers' administrative experience might be developed. The report called for 'duties and responsibility with authority' and for a diminution in teaching hours to enable post holders to do the duties (*Annual Convention*, 1976). The 1976 review resulted in formal advertising of posts within the school. However, while the category (grade A or B) of the post could be stated, no suggestion of relevant responsibility or work could be included. This was in total contrast to the experience of CMRS trustees in the comprehensive and community sector at that time.

The records suggest some confusion about the question of automatic promotion from a grade B to a grade A post. The management claim was that in 1984 'a literal interpretation of the criteria of appointment to posts', by the Appeals Board, conceded automatic promotion from grade B to grade A posts.[60] Individual managers had permitted automatic promotion since 1975 though the CCSS in particular regularly reminded the nuns to keep strictly to the procedures in the Agreed Memorandum. As far as the ASTI was concerned, promotion was on the basis of seniority and was therefore automatic. A letter from Máire McDonagh, ASTI to Brother Declan Duffy, General Secretary, on 30 April 1981 emphasised the need for accurate seniority records to ensure promotion. Yet in 1986 and 1989 the JMB seems to attribute automatic promotion not to any formal agreement with the ASTI but to inaccurate interpretations of the Memorandum by the chairman of the Appeals Board. In any event, by the end of the 1980s the promotional system was effectively locked in favour of the ASTI and seniority.

The union continued to counter any complaint from the managers by suggesting that the principal's post be opened up through competition. The trustees or owners of the schools retained the right of appointing the principal so that managerial bodies would not discuss the issue - that was a source of aggravation for the ASTI. The managers were under pressure in relation to the nature and cost of the appeals procedures that had been agreed by the JMB and the ASTI. A teacher would lodge an appeal; the secretary of the Board then informed the Department of Education; POR allowances likely to be affected by the appeal were then temporarily stopped. As one might appreciate, this led to tensions in some staffs even though it was part of the agreed procedure with the ASTI. While the allowances were small, an individual teacher might have budgeted on a particular income only to find part of it frozen. Decisions of the Appeals Board were final and binding on both manager and teachers. As soon as the manager was informed of the decision on an appeal, the amended list of post holders was forwarded to the Department and payment of allowances resumed and was retrospective. During the first four years of the system, individual and local arrangements were made in a few schools. The managerial organisations obviously decried such practices, knowing that deviations from the Agreed Memorandum could ultimately prove unhelpful. It was more difficult for a union to disapprove of an arrangement that had worked in favour of a member. The process was a learning one for principals and managers as they tried to meet the demands of running the schools.

By the 1980s demands on the Appeals Board were fewer in number but not in complexity. Claims were becoming increasingly litigious and the JMB had sought independent legal advice on a number of occasions. They desperately needed a review of the Agreed Memorandum 'in the light of the changing circumstances now obtaining or in prospect in our schools'. Their need coincided with the ASTI quest for a redeployment agreement with the CMRS, the CMCSS and the Department of Education. It seemed opportune, therefore, that the managers would seek to link any deal on redeployment with changes in the structure of the PORs.

> *The management side envisages that this review will need to be processed*
> *and put to both management and union sides before an ultimate decision*
> *can be reached by management in relation to a redeployment scheme for*
> *teachers which may emerge at Conciliation Council.[61]*

In 1979 it was agreed that date of birth could be a criterion in the case of more than one applicant for a post being 'equally qualified'.[62] Other slight adjustments made for greater transparency in the allocation of posts. Details of the points given to each school by the Department of Education were to be made known to staff.[63] The duties attached to a post could be changed during the year provided all post holders met and agreed. Arrangements for the appointment of a new vice-principal in a school were brought forward to the end of February before the teacher took up the position. But the areas of responsibility that were acceptable to the union continued to be very narrow: the controversial issues of the year head, librarian, supervision of students, and work in the month of June remained off limits in the voluntary schools. In the majority of schools the supervision of students, whether during breaks or when teachers were absent, was an issue of increasing concern. At national level the CMCSS and the JMB had become alert to the importance of adequate insurance coverage in schools - unsupervised students could prove a liability. The ASTI stand was that teachers might volunteer to supervise but could not be required to do so.

Schools with larger enrolments would have benefited from the appointment of year heads as was the practice in all comprehensive and community schools from the early 1970s. The leadership skills of an effective year head were not unlike that of a principal in a small school. The post of year head might therefore be a valuable experience in professional development. The right of the ASTI to refuse to accept such work was one matter but what it did to their members was another. There is no doubt that secondary school teachers throughout the 1970s and much of the 1980s were prevented from exercising the managerial and administrative skills associated with the work of year heads. On the other hand, as early as 1978 there were voluntary schools where grade A post holders and a few grade B post holders sought opportunities to become year heads. CCSS records show that 'local arrangements' were sometimes made to facilitate such requests. Obviously, these were also beneficial to the smooth operation of the schools. On several occasions in the 1970s, Cardinal Conway had pointed out to the EPG the very different system that prevailed in Catholic schools in Northern Ireland where there was a cadre of 'confident and experienced lay teachers' for the denominational schools. The issue of lay principals might have been more readily agreed if the POR system had been operable.[64] It must also be accepted that individual members of the ASTI deeply resented the caged POR system in which they found themselves.[65]

During the 1979 review of the Agreed Memorandum the managerial negotiators made a little progress on the issue of advertising posts. Managers could now state that the higher-grade posts would carry duties that reflected the different levels of allowances. The continuing opposition to the work of year heads made it difficult for principals in some schools to ensure that a distinction between the duties of an A and a B post was evident to all staff and at times this could be a cause of tension between teachers. Logic might have dictated that the JMB would include a job specification for principals. Under the Agreed Memorandum the principal was 'responsible for the day-to-day running of the school'. True, that covered everything in the role, and the fact that details were inadequate may well have weakened the position of the negotiators during the various reviews. But since the majority of the principals were members of religious orders or clerics, the idea of a 'job specification' was repugnant. Appointment as a principal was an exercise of religious obedience first of all - the unwritten expectation was that the job would be done, in some orders with actual support of other teaching religious in the community.

The review of 1979 helped to set in stone a promotional ladder whereby the holder of the senior grade B post would proceed to the next available A post. However, as pointed out earlier, the evidence is confusing and suggests that such a ladder operated from 1975. This approach earned the tag 'senility promotion' from an irate manager in the CCSS. In the late 1980s the JMB insisted that they had never agreed to automatic promotion, but custom and practice was otherwise. The existence of the SFAs for certain long-serving teachers and the introduction of a new grade, the Supernumerary grade B allowance, were additional complications in the voluntary school system of PORs. There were some SFAs who consistently refused to do any duties as part of the post, their attitude being that the allowance was a reward for service. In 1980 in a submission to the Review Body on Teachers' Pay the JMB complained about their 'strangled management position' regarding the posts. The three aspects they picked out to illustrate their complaint were: seniority, the 'ladder' of promotions, and the threat for individual managers of a teacher going to the Appeals Board.[66]

The introduction of an agreed Appeals Board in 1975 had revealed many anomalies in the implementation of the Memorandum by 1979. In fairness to the ASTI and the JMB, no model existed that might have informed them - they could only learn from the implementation. Managers and union were feeling the pressure of a structure that had been hastily developed and in which the Department of Education played virtually no role. In 1979 the Appeals Board included three representatives each from ASTI and the JMB and an agreed independent chairman who was often a retired official of the Department of Education.[67] That same year it was agreed that future reviews would be held every three years. There was a vain hope that the system might settle down. But the posts were not introduced as a means of managing a secondary school system that was in fact catering for the largest number of the age cohort in the country. Pupil enrolments and consequent demands on managers and especially principals continued to grow. In the religious-owned schools the effect of decreasing vocations was already being felt, as the FIRE Report (1973) and the Focus for Action Report (1974) had shown. However, dissatisfaction with the POR system was not solely related to the religious schools. As the representative of the FCLS on the JMB told the National Education Convention in 1993:

> Many of the problems currently experienced by schools run by religious
> orders have always existed for lay schools. I am referring to such matters
> as the absence of a properly remunerated middle-management system where
> teachers are constantly being relied on to carry out voluntarily extra
> responsibilities and duties beyond their teaching load. It is an unhappy
> situation for both teachers and the school managers.[68]

The system was a noose even though some principals and managers managed the rope. At the same time the absence of effective middle management structures in the voluntary schools was more and more evident as the pace of curriculum change increased.

The POR system meant that those teachers who stayed longest in a secondary school would be assured of promotion and the most senior of all was virtually certain of becoming the vice-principal. One result was to lock the school system and discourage teacher movement, an outcome that was never intended. It was possible for religious teachers to gain from the experience of working in a variety of schools, but that was less likely to happen to lay teachers whose chances of promotion would be lessened by moving, unless of course they were successful applicants for teaching posts or principalships in the new community schools. It was policy for many orders in the CCSS and the TBA to transfer religious after a specified number of years in a particular post. An established practice in the Christian Brothers, for example, was to move the brother who had been superior and manager and probably also school principal, after a term of six years. In some orders the basis of such moves would be religious community needs rather than the requirements of the school. Falling enrolments in a number of schools in the 1970s created difficulties for major superiors among the nuns and brothers - a religious might lose an incremental position by moving schools. Before the redeployment scheme was finalised in 1987 the ASTI kept a watchful eye on movement of religious staff.[69] If the religious were the holder of a grade A or B post the major superior sometimes sacrificed that allowance in order to transfer the person. The situation was more complicated in the case of the religious with an SFA, as already mentioned.[70]

The Post of the Vice-Principal

The original Agreed Memorandum (1972) made four statements about the most senior post, that of the vice-principal. These related to authority, reduced teaching hours, acting as the school principal, and the duties of the post. Throughout all the reviews up to 1984 a single sentence alluded to the power of the position: 'The Vice-Principal must have authority.' The Agreed Memorandum of 1984 elaborated and described the position as 'of vital importance in the administration and development of the school'. The authority was to be 'commensurate with the responsibilities involved in the position', and the expectation was that of 'actively' assisting 'the principal in the day-to-day running of the school'. All earlier versions presented the vice-principal as the person 'who will act as principal' in the case of absences. Any expectation of the most senior position was denied: the vice-principal 'will not have right of succession to the post of principal'. By 1984 a small number of lay principals had been appointed in the religious schools. The gradual introduction of boards of management from the 1970s and the attempts by the CMRS and CMCSS to develop a contract for lay principals in voluntary schools had helped to create a new climate, and was only a matter of time before a considerable number of ASTI members were appointed principals. Indeed, continuation of the denominational system could depend on union members. The Agreed Memorandum of 1984 reflected some of those attitudinal changes.

The clause about the reduction in teaching hours remained constant from 1972 to 1984. In reality, this was central to any development in the role of the vice-principal. It also depended on the ability and readiness of the Department of Education to provide for additional teaching hours. The CCSS records show that there were some schools where these teaching hours were fewer than what the Department required. These were usually situations where inventive principals recognised the importance of the role of the vice-principal and made a local arrangement. In some instances students of the Higher Diploma in Education provided the necessary teaching. In others, retired teaching nuns did the work. Clearly, such practices were rare and voluntary schools did not have funding for part-time teaching hours. In general, therefore, the role of the vice-principal in the voluntary sector never developed as did that of teachers in similar roles in the state schools.

One of the most significant contributions made by the managerial bodies in the pilot scheme from 1989 and again from 1992 was a requirement that principal and vice-principal would participate as leaders of a management *team*. Successive agreements about the posts specified that teacher discipline and redeployment of teachers could not be included in the work of a vice-principal. In other words, the vice-principal could not be involved in any exercise of accountability, 'although he may offer advice to a teacher'. A vice-principal might assist the principal but not take responsibility for allocating work or for 'redeployment of teachers' within the school. The reality was that vice-principals and teachers were usually members of the same union. The concept of a managerial role for vice-principals had not been explored and, in a sense, the role could be so narrow as to be unchallenging if not frustrating to the holder, offer limited assistance to the principal and almost no opportunity to practise leadership and management skills.

Each version of the Memorandum from 1972 included the following among the vice-principal's duties:
- *To be consulted on appointment of teachers to posts of responsibility*
- *To be involved in discipline of pupils*
- *To have overall responsibility for rolls (in co-operation with staff)*
- *To assist principal in day-to-day running of the school*
- *To advise on school time-table.*

It is fair to say that successive memoranda contained elements of a job specification for the vice-principal, though it was hardly couched in professional terminology. The draft Memorandum of 16 November 1989 showed some improvement at least in the wording of the post. There was greater acknowledgement of the status of the role by then, and of the importance of the team aspect of the relationship with the principal. Such thinking was reflected in the pilot training programme initiated by the JMB that year.

> *The vice-principal shares responsibility with the principal for the*
> *internal organisation, administration and discipline of the school ...*
> *(and) shall be consulted by the principal about the implementation of*
> *policy ... (and) shall undertake specific duties commensurate with*
> *the responsibilities of the position ... (and) shall be kept informed,*
> *as appropriate, by the principal, about the decisions of the manager.*[71]

There was no reference to work outside the twenty-eight hour school week and attempts to include it met with strong resistance from the ASTI. There were vice-principals who did not restrict their working hours to the teaching week. The weakness was the dependence on 'grace and favour', as the General Secretary of the managerial bodies described it. For established vice-principals to be asked to include a time clause was to introduce a new element in their contract - it could also be viewed as offensive and as minimalist in human resource management. The arrangement where-by the most senior grade A post holder almost inevitably became the vice-principal needed to be abandoned. In their discussions, the JMB were not excluding the possibility of such an appointment. What they sought was the community school arrangement where posts were open and not tied to seniority within a school.

A constant point of comparison by the CMCSS, some of whose religious orders were trustees of community schools, was with the exercise of the role of vice-principal in those schools. The bases for such comparisons were not similar. From the outset, the community schools were established under a Deed of Trust that ensured a board of management and in-school management structures. The funding mechanism meant that the state was responsible. The freedom to employ some part-time teachers enabled the principal to lessen the vice-principal's teaching hours so that the two had a greater chance of developing a team approach to the running of the school. The challenge of providing a 'green field' or completely new school added to the work atmosphere. The second highest post in the community school system was advertised in relation to a specific role. There was in effect little comparison between the roles of the vice-principal in the community school and the voluntary school. The community schools began with the appointment of two people whose job it was to administer and develop a new educational institution; there was something of a sense of mission about the challenge to work together. The secondary schools might be described as having the POR structure imposed on them without adequate reflection and preparation.

The subsequent activities around the Agreed Memorandum from 1972 to 1989 were genuine efforts by the JMB and the ASTI to make the best of an unfortunate structure.

Many individual managers inadvertently added to the problem by not finding ways of involving their vice-principals in the management of the school. Over the years the custom and practice in many CMCSS schools was for the vice-principal to superintend state examinations through the month of June and therefore to be unavailable to assist the principal. Precedents thus established would become hurdles for the JMB in renegotiating the Agreed Memorandum. By 1989 it was clear to the managerial organisations that only a root and branch approach to the posts structure could help in developing the in-school management that the voluntary sector lacked.

The Position of the Department of Education

The Department of Education had always been a reluctant collaborator in the POR structure that developed in the voluntary sector and any effort by the managers to secure greater involvement had failed. The attitude of the Department was credible: the managers were the employers. The records of JMB meetings with officials from the late 1970s until the middle of the 1980s show frequent reminders to the managers of their position. Contracts for PORs were between employer and post holder. The Agreed Memorandum was between the ASTI and the JMB, not the Department that merely allocated public moneys. If school authorities submitted the necessary list of post holders, the Department rightly presumed that duties and responsibilities were undertaken. The fact that the managers needed realistic middle management responsibilities was not the business of the Department, and improvements in managing the posts structure were matters for negotiation between the JMB and the ASTI. At a personal level, it was true that individual officials expressed sympathy with the predicament of the managers, but that changed nothing.

Throughout the 1980s the managerial bodies frequently discussed the question of posts and how the Department of Education might become involved so as to ensure greater accountability. There is little evidence to suggest that the introduction of boards of management in schools contributed to a more effective posts system. Custom and practice meant that the individual principals had been implementing the Agreed Memorandum. The fundamental changes that were necessary to create middle management structures in voluntary schools were beyond the power of the principals. The JMB was well aware of that fact in 1984. They also knew that ASTI and JMB representatives were devoting significant time to dealing with appeals. A greater number of cases emerged in the first ten years after 1972. The voluntary work of the Appeals Board was usually done after school hours, and the earnestness of the efforts of union and managers cannot be denied. But the need for legal advice contributed to a mechanism that was both costly and flawed in spite of the best efforts of all concerned. The managers wanted to end the system of automatic promotion and to apply the criteria of 'capability and suitability' to all promotions - open competition for posts would mean that the discrimination against teaching religious would cease. Additionally, the issue of a principal or vice-principal who chose to revert to a teaching post needed to be addressed, since it had not been included in successive reviews of the Memorandum. Union and management needed to work out some arrangement whereby such a person would not revert to the most junior position on the staff - the principle of entitlement applied only to the holder of a grade A or B post. Finally, by the mid-1980s the issue of supervision of students outside classes had become a matter of considerable concern to the JMB; yet the Agreed Memorandum still precluded it. The levels of managerial discontent with the system were at their peak.

New Management

Another attempt to review the Memorandum began in 1987, under the independent chairmanship of Seán Moriarty, a former inspector of the Department of Education.[72] Richard Daft (1998) explores the relevance of re-visiting decisions in the process of organisational development. There comes a stage when the pace of change demands initiative and a fresh approach. Daft shows that the difference between leaders and managers is that leaders recognise the time for doing something in a different manner; managers deliver it because they or other people have the vision of how things might be different. The voluntary school system had already reached that point, and the re-structured CMCSS and the JMB were poised for a new approach to negotiation. In 1988 the management position was made clear to the ASTI.[73] Automatic appointment to posts on the sole criterion of seniority would have to be examined 'with a view to a more open system of appointment'. The post of vice-principal needed to be 'redefined'. The duties of all posts should be included in the advertisements. A selection committee should be established for all appointments except where there was to be automatic entitlement. The earlier specificity of a narrow range of work that might be included in the posts should be replaced by 'all duties of an administrative, educational or pastoral nature in the school'. Holders of posts should be able to 'move from a higher post to a lower post in the school'. This would have financial implications and would therefore need the support of the Department of Education.

Three other aspects of the JMB position in 1988 are of interest. The managers and the ASTI should make a joint approach to the Department seeking 'equalisation of conditions of employment of post holders' in the secondary sector with all other types of schools. This would affect selection procedures, job specifications, and above all the time available to do the work involved. The Appeals Board should be radically reviewed with the possibility of 'a Rights Commissioner approach to this area'. Finally, the JMB sought a joint commitment with the ASTI 'to ensure adequate experience' and 'additional training for secondary teachers who aspire to promotion within the system'. The document from the JMB was a strong indication of things to come. The CMCSS and the JMB were determined to bring about change in the management of schools and to bring the Department into the frame.

A lengthy discussion at a JMB meeting on 21 June 1989 resulted in a clear statement to the ASTI that the managers

> *cannot accept automatic promotion from grade B to grade A posts. They hold this view which was always held by management that suitability and capability are criteria at every point of promotion within the scope of the Agreed Memorandum.*[74]

On the matter of the vice-principal's 'attendance in the school outside of school hours or during school holidays' the JMB was adamant. They would not remove that demand from their draft of the Memorandum. The letter shows up the confusion that often existed between what was held by the JMB to be policy in relation to promotion and actual practice in the majority of the schools. The difficulty was that the JMB or indeed the CMCSS had no binding authority on their members and it was much more likely that union members would adhere to ASTI policy. As expected, the Standing Committee of the union 'reacted with great annoyance' to the JMB letter and accused the managers of a breach of the Fourth Agreed Memorandum. By September 1989 the principals and managers were being advised by the Secretariat of Secondary Schools to adhere to that Memorandum pending a resolution of the difficulties. The strong stand planned by the JMB was not to be implemented while negotiations continued.

The managerial representatives on the Appeals Board were becoming increasingly aware of the seriousness of the issues involved in their work. Indemnity insurance was secured for the members while Liam Murphy was acting General Secretary for Brother Declan Duffy who was on a career break.[75] At the same time, however, the JMB refused to continue on the Appeals Board. The JMB and the ASTI negotiators subsequently resumed the review without an independent chairman, and they produced a new draft Memorandum that was rejected by the ASTI and the JMB. Further attempts to amend and agree the document were unanimously rejected by the JMB in December 1989. It was clear that the end of the era of the 1972 Agreed

Memorandum on PORs was approaching. Stalemate set in. The managerial representatives on the Appeals Board were unwilling to serve 'until the review of the Agreed Memorandum was completed'.[76] Meanwhile, the JMB was determined to introduce changes in middle management. And this was communicated to the ASTI in the hope that 'a satisfactory conclusion' would be found.[77] The union could only agree to minor changes in the review of the Fourth Memorandum. From a management point of view 'two essential ideas' were missing.[78]

> *The effect of one would be that capability and suitability would not be admissable at any point except when a person was getting a B post for the first time. It was our total opposition to this interpretation which occasioned the present review of the Memo.*

The second item that was unacceptable to the union concerned the need for the vice-principal to be 'available, if required, during the public examinations and during the holidays (in the absence of the principal)'. The managers were adamant that such availability had become essential 'because of insurance issues', among others. In June 1989 the JMB was realistic: there was no prospect of agreement on the Fifth Memorandum for the new school year. The managers insisted that their stand was a 'reasonable response to the exigencies of the school situation today',[79] a position that the ASTI found 'totally unacceptable'. But the union was uneasy at the determination of the JMB to ignore automatic promotion, to appoint new vice-principals only if they agreed to be available as required, and to cease to participate in the Appeals Board from September 1989. The ASTI sought a meeting with the managers prior to their Standing Committee session on 28 August.

The Beginning of the End of the Posts of Responsibility

A joint meeting of the Standing Committee of the ASTI and JMB, chaired by the President of the union, Éamonn Ó hAllmhuráin, took place on 2 October 1989. That the 1986 review was unfinished three years later was a sign of the determination of the JMB that 'the lack of middle management support for principals outside of school hours' should change. The context of the administration and staffing of secondary schools had changed considerably from 1972 when the Memorandum was negotiated. For the managers the agreement was 'an outdated and faulty instrument'.[80] A more effective middle management was essential.

A cause of great concern to the JMB is the expectation that a principal, particularly, a lay principal, should be expected to cope single-handedly during the public examinations without any support from the vice-principal.

The JMB may not have implemented their threats of June 1989 but they exhibited a determination to introduce change. Their attitude was that they were being more than fair to the union negotiators. The union, on the other hand, would find it impossible to get the support of their members for the kinds of radical changes sought by the JMB. There would need to be other elements in the deal if agreement were to be reached.

The issues of seniority, capability and suitability were debated. It was clear that the ASTI was concerned but unprepared to break with the principle of seniority. The management position was not completely opposed to seniority. Suitability for the work of a grade A post did not follow from ability to perform grade B post duties, but neither was that to claim that the senior B post teacher would never be a suitable candidate for the A post. It would probably depend on the responsibilities and duties needed by the school at the particular time. But the union would not accept advertising the duties before the post was given to the teacher. Kieran Mulvey, General Secretary, used the impasse to bring up the CMCSS position whereby the post of principal was not for negotiation or advertising. He complained at the slow growth in numbers of lay principals appointed in voluntary schools. The union had 'a vested interest in the good management of schools', but relationships between principals and staffs were not 'always positive'. Interestingly, there were religious in the CMCSS, especially among the nuns, who believed that the continual refusal to advertise the post of principal was unwise. They also questioned the justice of such a refusal.[81] Some of these orders had schools in the UK where religious were accustomed to being interviewed for school positions. But such a decision belonged to the particular major superior of the order that owned the school. At CMRS level there was a united refusal to advertise the post of principal. Those appointments were a matter for the trustees or owners and it was only when a lay principal was sought that there would be an advertisement.

Two important points emerged from the ASTI contribution. One was the possibility that a principal's inept leadership might be the main reason for lack of collaboration and competency among post holders. The second was the union belief that the posts system they had won in 1970 had been imposed on a reluctant management. The ASTI accused the managers of seeking to introduce 'a kind of meritocracy' in schools during a period of educational cutbacks in the country.[82] The union perspective was not entirely inaccurate. The managers had been ill prepared for the introduction of the posts in 1970. For decades the ASTI had dragged and at times forced the managerial bodies into agreements about the posts, issues related to teacher contracts of employment, parent/teacher meetings, pastoral care in schools. But the re-constituted CMCSS and

JMB from 1987 were in a better position to take responsibility for managing and leading the schools into the 1990s. That lengthy meeting of 2 October 1989 was important as an exercise in communication and an expression of solidarity among the managers. There was tacit recognition by the two parties of the seriousness of each other's position, though none of the issues was resolved at that stage. Each knew there was no going back to previously entrenched attitudes about the structure of the PORs. Union and JMB would somehow have to manage future change - time revealed the extent to which they were prepared to shift positions in order to find common ground on which to develop an effective middle management system in the voluntary schools.

The determination of the JMB to take a new approach in their negotiations is shown in their seeking legal advice from two sources regarding withdrawal from the Appeals Board. They were told that withdrawal would be counter to the Agreed Memorandum. It would also constitute a breach of normal industrial relations practice. Criticism of the managers would be inevitable in the face of what would be seen as industrial action by the employers, and might lead to litigation.[83] The Fourth Memorandum had dated from 1 August 1984. Even at the time of signing the JMB had reservations. Moreover, failure to complete a satisfactory review in 1987 [84] and the 'increasing frustration' of the managerial negotiators with the operation of the Appeals Board [85] resulted in a refusal to operate the Memorandum.

There were other problems that might vary from school to school, depending on relations between principal and local union steward. Strict adherence to the terms of the Memorandum meant that a range of essential school duties would never be part of the work of post holders. The interpretation of 'the school year' was too narrow to be helpful. Some 'rather loose drafting' in the Memorandum had led to 'serious problems' including litigation, and legal advice to the managers had alerted them to the inevitability of further litigation unless the Fourth Memorandum was changed. There were three successive drafts of a Fifth Agreed Memorandum in existence.[86] The documents reveal the pattern of the negotiations and the difficulties that each party to the Agreed Memorandum was experiencing at that time. One problem for the ASTI was the JMB insistence on linking the clause on 'capability and suitability' to the candidate's ability to discharge duties 'appropriate to the relevant post of responsibility'. That could exclude a grade B post holder from a specified A post or indeed the senior A post teacher from the post of vice-principal. By 24 November 1989 the JMB agreed to withdraw this demand.

One important development for the managers was the inclusion of an annual 'review' by the school principal with each post holder - this might have become the first example of professional appraisal, and appropriately placed the emphasis on the duties, not on the post holder. Another innovative proposal advocated by the managers was that the principal should deal with allocation of posts and duties. It would be a development of the principal's leadership role. This could enable the manager or chairman of the board to fulfil an appeals function. But it was perhaps too soon to expect that level of trust by the union negotiators and the suggestion did not survive into the third draft of the Memorandum. In what was otherwise a positive draft the managers proposed a contentious item about the annual meeting of post holders in each school:

> In the event of the meeting failing to agree the duties to be assigned to a particular post or posts, the principal should assign the duties on the next school day following the meeting of the committee.

The union may well have shown more awareness of the importance of collaboration and leadership on this occasion. The managerial negotiators were seeking to return to a hierarchical and almost dictatorial manner of managing. On the other hand, the JMB was keenly aware of the exasperation of many school principals, particularly those in larger schools, about the outdated Memorandum. In that third draft also is a reminder of how the roles of principal and manager were sometimes vested in the one person even as late as 1989. There was a suggestion that a dissatisfied post holder should have the right to 'discuss the matter with the principal and manager or chairman of the board'. If the individual's dissatisfaction prevailed a formal appeal could then be made to the manager or chairman of the board of management. Details of this procedure were explored, and it appeared to be a logical and workable approach. However, at the request of the JMB it was omitted. There were still many schools where the principal was also the manager. Duality of roles was clearly a negative factor in relation to an alternative solution to the Appeals Board.

A study of these three drafts of the Agreed Memorandum in 1989 suggests greater realism on the part of the ASTI about the work of the school principal. The union was prepared to accept that the vice-principal might need to be involved in the vexed area of 'teacher discipline'. It was a tiny but important development that 'the vice-principal's duties shall not *normally* include responsibility for teacher discipline'. Admittedly the context was 'when the principal was absent' and the vice-principal was in charge. The established exclusion of automatic succession to the principal's job was retained. The struggle of both union and managerial negotiators to get agreement on that one word 'normally' offers some insight into those who sought to bring about the change needed in the voluntary system in the last century.

The language about the Appeals Board began to change throughout the process of the three drafts of the Agreed Memorandum of 1989. The operation of the appeals system had grown in complexity. One reason was undoubtedly the outmoded nature of the terms of the Agreed Memorandum and the changing circumstances in secondary schools. Another was the body of employment legislation developing in Ireland.

What the managers sought in 1989 was a speedy resolution of any issue related to PORs. This made sense. The school year was short, and expectations of what secondary schools might contribute to students, parents and staffs were considerable. Delays in delivering decisions about contentious appointments to posts involved considerable investment of time and energy by managers and individual teachers. Hence, any method that resulted in speedier resolutions was worth pursuing. The JMB recommended replacing the Appeals Board by a tribunal where a strict time limit would be set. So, if a dissatisfied teacher lodged a complaint, an appeals tribunal would meet to consider the matter within fifteen school days or three weeks. All relevant documentation would be available to the tribunal, which then had twenty school days or four weeks to complete the investigation. In the early years of the Appeals Board there had been agreement that the findings were binding on both parties to the appeal. It is a sign of developing work practices that in 1989 the draft Memorandum included the following item:

> Without prejudice to the rights of any of the parties involved to have
> recourse to litigation, the decision of the tribunal shall be final and
> binding on the parties.

There was one other clause that did not survive beyond the third draft of the 1989 Agreed Memorandum. The JMB wanted a vice-principal who might be the acting principal 'to be in attendance in the school outside of school hours or during school holidays'. Individual ASTI negotiators had no problem with the reasoning behind the request; their difficulty was with writing it into the Fifth Memorandum. The managers, on the other hand, had long experience of the importance of documenting agreements and wanted the clause included. Failure to get agreement was another indication to the JMB that the days of the Agreed Memorandum must be ended - the issue was not 'when?' but 'how soon?' The union negotiators, on the other hand, feared written agreements. The struggle with the contract of employment throughout the 1970s had shown that it was not easy to get agreement within such a large organisational structure as the ASTI. Individual negotiators and even teams might accept the need for a particular agreement or clause because they appreciated the nuances of discussions, reasons and examples given by the managers. Those union members who had not been party to such exchanges might have greater difficulty in changing a Memorandum that had worked in favour of teachers since 1972.

The JMB fear at this stage was a return to the Fourth Agreed Memorandum for yet another school year. They strengthened their negotiating position by linking the review with discussions on the Redeployment Scheme for Teachers in Catholic Secondary Schools. At the time of the meeting with the ASTI on 2 October 1989 this Scheme was being reviewed.[87] The managers were familiar with the union demand for a supplementary redeployment scheme and the elements of a 'package' were being put together.[88] The union needed a Supplementary Panel for teachers who had temporary work. A panel would satisfy the younger members of the profession who were bringing pressure to bear because of the uncertainty of their position, but it would tie the managers' hands in future selection because they would be obliged to choose teachers from those on the list. However, if the managers could achieve a realistic development in the Agreed Memorandum, the effects on the voluntary schools might be worth the price of the second panel.

The Complexity of the Redeployment Issue

With the approval of the CMRS the managers had agreed a Redeployment Scheme in 1987 mainly because it offered a solution to possible redundancies from school closures or diminishing enrolments.[89] The CMCSS accepted this Scheme as a means of fulfilling their duty of care by ensuring that permanent teachers would not be made redundant. That Redeployment Panel became operative in 1988 for the Catholic voluntary schools, religious, clerical and those represented in the FCLS. It did not extend to comprehensive and community schools or to schools in the ISA. The vocational sector were catered for within each VEC and had nothing to do with the arrangement for the Catholic schools. As the Redeployment Panel came into effect, a once-off arrangement with the Department of Education was made for teachers employed on 1 August 1987. Without the Panel these teachers might have expected permanent employment. Under the terms of Circular M41/87 they were offered temporary contracts by Ministerial order. This put their names on a 'supplementary panel' until such time as they would be subsumed into permanent posts. By 1989 that unique arrangement ended because the teachers were then in full employment. However, it had given the ASTI the idea of seeking a national panel for temporary teachers. If the union succeeded, a second or Supplementary Panel would be added to the Redeployment Scheme agreed by the CMRS in 1987.

School principals were already familiar with the necessary bureaucracy surrounding the Scheme and realised that what could accompany the Supplementary Panel had significant implications for their role. Under the Supplementary Panel the principal would have to monitor the professional performance of every temporary teacher who taught for a minimum of eighteen hours per week. The principal would be required to certify to the administrator of the panel that such teachers had been satisfactory and, in the absence of a favourable report, that teacher would not be listed on the

Supplementary Panel. Many principals and managers were opposed to such a development. As employers they would be ceding their right to advertise jobs and select the most suitable person to fill a vacancy. As principals with inadequate middle management support, they would be adding to their workload. Some of the JMB believed that it would prove impossible to design or implement such a system. Therefore, there was no harm in exploring the proposal in order to gain time in negotiating with the union.

The JMB was reasonably sure that industrial action would not occur as long as talks continued. There were only two outstanding cases for the Appeals Board, so complaints from the schools would be few when the JMB refused to participate in the hearings.[90] It was likely that negotiations would not be finalised by the end of the school year in June 1990, so students would not be disrupted by any union action. The ASTI would not have secured the Supplementary Panel and the issue of the Agreed Memorandum 'would have been brought to the attention of rank and file ASTI members'.[91] The managers were aware that in some schools younger lay teachers who did not have PORs or reasonable prospects were often critical of a seniority system that seemed calculated to prevent their professional promotion. By agreeing to discuss a Supplementary Panel the managers had more to gain than to lose. The outcome of the protracted negotiations from 1989 to 1990 was to delay the operation of the established Redeployment Scheme. The people most affected were the ASTI members on the panel and the school principals who were prevented from finalising time-table arrangements for the new school year.

Managerial opposition to a Supplementary Panel was logical at that time. There were issues of concern to school management and to the principals who could find the job of planning the time-table hampered as a result of additional bureaucracy. Also there was no precedent for such a guarantee for temporary workers at that time in Ireland - fixed-term contracts were increasingly frequent in all sectors. Neither primary nor other post-primary teachers had rights to permanency as a result of being employed as temporary teachers. The fact that there were many temporary teachers throughout the school system related to the pupil/teacher ratio and that was a government decision not one made by school management. Many voluntary secondary schools chose to employ such teachers at their own expense in order to improve the pupil/teacher ratio and to provide a wider range of options for students.[92] The General Secretary of the CMCSS in 1990 noted that the introduction of a Supplementary Panel would discriminate against newly qualified teachers who would be unable to apply for a permanent post if a teacher with the required subjects was on the Panel.[93] There had been unofficial suggestions from the union that similar panel rights would be sought for part-time teachers once the Supplementary Panel was achieved. The ASTI was simply ensuring future membership, and therefore had to try to meet the needs of teachers who were not assured of permanent employment.

Agreed Memorandum and Trade-off

The records show that the managerial bodies had planned their strategy for negotiating the Fifth Memorandum with care and attention to detail. In some sense they were coming of age as a negotiating body. They were leading and managing. They focused on outcomes for school managers, boards and principals. As a result they were assured of considerable interest by the schools in the progress of negotiations. This was crucial because neither the CMCSS nor the JMB had the authority to insist on compliance from the school authorities. At best the JMB had and continues in the twenty-first century to have

> *a persuasive authority and that authority is greatly enhanced if it can be*
> *assured of the loyalty and co-operation of our members and of their*
> *willingness to show solidarity in times of crisis.*[94]

At this stage, 1989, the restructured AMCSS was two years in existence, and structures for communication were clearer. At local level the principals, individual managers and boards expected to be consulted, and the level of interest and subsequent attendance at AMCSS meetings reached a new high; the Agreed Memorandum rather than the Supplementary Panel had greater significance for the majority of the membership. Both the CMCSS and the JMB were conscious of the importance of consultation at regional level. They plotted a possible sequence of events to ensure success: a critical path analysis. Among many options considered by the CMCSS was that of refusing to grant a Supplementary Panel. That would create problems for ASTI with their own members. A breakdown in negotiations could coincide with the end of the school year. As always the JMB did not want to disrupt students' education. At that stage, the managers could decide that both the Fourth and Fifth Memoranda were unacceptable. They could refuse to participate in the Appeals Board until a new Memorandum was agreed.

Another option that had not previously been proposed was to enlist the help of the Department of Education and the Minister to resolve the issues. This suggestion marked another stage in the development of the AMCSS and the JMB. Interaction with the Department was traditionally about funding, curriculum and public examinations. Teacher salaries were dealt with through the C and A process of which the managers and Department were members. But now the JMB position would be strengthened if the Department could be persuaded to become involved in the implementation of the Agreed Memorandum on the Posts of Responsibility. The relegation of the Department to the role of paymaster and part financier of the system would have to be re-negotiated. The JMB realised that whatever success might be achieved in the implementation of the Memorandum would be the outcome of negotiation not of industrial action by the managers. In planning their strategy, they decided they would advise the schools on how to deal with appointments during whatever period was necessary, pending agreement with the ASTI. The final sentence of an internal managerial memo stated:

*We keep schools informed of developments and attach a lot of importance
to group solidarity.*

The JMB were consciously leading their membership towards the particular goal of
a more effective middle management structure. They were also striving to bring the
Department into the negotiations.

During November and December 1989 AMCSS and ISA at local level considered
the third draft of the Fifth Memorandum. It was rejected unanimously by the ISA.
Seven of the eleven AMCSS regions turned it down. Of the four who voted in favour,
one recorded 'under protest', and another had 'major reservations'. The reports from
the membership said that there was nothing of value for the managers in the proposed
Memorandum. Minutiae about the implementation of the Appeals Board would
have little effect on the daily administration of the schools and the work of the principals.
Verbal recognition of the status of the vice-principal did not give the managers assurance
that expectations of work outside the teaching week might be realised. At regional
level, it was the principals rather than the chairmen and individual managers who had
greater impact on decisions. Brother Declan Duffy on behalf of the managers wrote
to Kieran Mulvey, General Secretary, ASTI on 15 December:

> *There was a clear rejection of the Draft by the regions. After a long and
> detailed discussion on the issue, the JMB unanimously rejected the Draft
> Agreed Memorandum.*

Central to the dissatisfaction of the JMB with the Memorandum were 'conflicting
and inconsistent interpretations of some of (the Memorandum) articles by the
Appeals Board':[95] clarification therefore was needed on the precedents that had developed in relation to the work of the Appeals Board. The managerial bodies queried
their inability to have access to previous case histories and decisions of the Board.
The matter of legal indemnity needed professional advice. It was evident that membership of the FUE (now IBEC) was raising JMB awareness about employment legislation. But neither the General Secretary nor the members of the JMB were indif-
ferent to the need for concerted action by all school managers. The support of the
regions and of the ISA was essential to strengthen the JMB refusal to 'concede automatic promotion', to serve on the Appeals Board, and to appoint new vice-principals
'unless they agree to be available as required by the principal during periods when
there are no school classes'. The JMB did not have authority to insist on such support. It
was in that context that the General Secretary asked:

> *If we take the option (of refusing what the union wants) are we prepared
> against all opposition to continue with this stance, even if our own members
> weaken? Or will we cave in when opposition reaches a certain level of
> intensity?[96]*

Individuals on the ASTI Standing Committee might have differences but they spoke with one voice on official matters. On the other hand, the inherent independence of the religious orders, whose members constituted the majority of the JMB, could militate against unified action. Earlier in 1989 the JMB indicated to the ASTI their refusal to participate in the Appeals Board if a new Agreed Memorandum was not in place by September.[97] Clearly, such a decision could be made by the JMB, but a religious order that had a school with an appeal pending could raise a discontented voice at CMRS level and at a regional meeting. Individual principals could feel isolated in their schools. Lay principals might experience a different sense of isolation. They were part of the management of the schools yet they were ASTI members and therefore would be expected to show solidarity with teachers. Professional empathy between school principals would be likely to secure support for the beleaguered colleague and that could lead to discontent and possibly opposition to the JMB decision. Leadership and management were indeed complex activities.

In spite of uncertainties about their leadership role, the reasons why the JMB rejected the 1989 draft Memorandum were significant, and they help to explain the stand taken by the managers throughout the PCW negotiations in the 1990s when the same issues were at stake. Journalist John Walshe (1999) points out that by the 1990s a consensus approach to rationalisation was growing in the Department of Education.[98] That may have encouraged the Department to take greater interest in the issue of middle management of schools. The religious orders needed an effective middle management structure to ensure the future of Catholic schools. It was evident by 1989 that fewer religious principals would be in the schools and so lay principals would be under considerable pressure without the necessary internal management support. It seemed that union, managers and Department were being drawn together on a common issue, though not necessarily from a shared perspective on leadership and management.

In a letter dated 15 January 1990 to Kieran Mulvey, General Secretary of the ASTI, Brother Declan Duffy explained at length the JMB refusal to agree the draft of the Fifth Agreed Memorandum. The managers saw little change 'except for minor textual amendments'. The basis of the posts system since 1972 meant the 'absence of any real effective middle management' in voluntary schools. The only solution was 'a radical change in the allocation of posts' so that the schools might function effectively in the 1990s. Duffy summed up the thinking of the managers by stating: 'The philosophy underlying the present Agreed Memo belongs to the sixties.' The 'vulnerability' of the secondary schools was manifest in a decline in pupil numbers, inadequate resourcing compared to other sectors, unremitting change from religious to lay principals, growing competition between schools, ageing school staffs exacerbated by the redeployment scheme. The threat of further rationalisation and possible school closures was implied in Duffy's statement:

Only a strong cohesive top and middle management in schools will secure their survival.

While the tone of the letter was conciliatory, and acknowledged the 'good relations' between the union and the managerial organisation and the 'splendid service' given by many post holders, the JMB was forthright about the 'inherent inadequacies' of the Agreed Memorandum. The appeals system was 'flawed' and the posts system, 'over a long period, proved detrimental to the good organisation of our schools'. Six years later during the PCW negotiations, the Department of Education estimated that the posts system was costing IR£30m a year. In the experience of the JMB, education was getting poor value for money.

The communication between Duffy and Mulvey in 1990 revealed an invigorated JMB with

> *its determination to give leadership in the present situation, motivated by*
> *the belief that our schools will be better and the morale of our teachers*
> *enhanced through the changes which we seek.*

This was no mere war of words by the managers. Acknowledging the fact that the ASTI needed time 'to reflect and consult on this new situation' created by the JMB, the managers were asking the schools not to make any appointments to PORs 'for some time'. The hope was that the time lag would help 'to create a climate where realistic (*sic*) negotiations' could take place between the two parties. The managers' participation in future negotiations was conditional on a more realistic stance on the part of the union. The JMB intimated (but did not specify) a 'fixed period' of time within which a new posts structure must be agreed. They also spelled out the consequences of union failure to do so:

> *The JMB will be obliged to circulate to our schools, criteria for appointments*
> *to Posts of Responsibility.*

In effect, the Agreed Memorandum of 1972 and its four subsequent amended versions would cease to exist because the JMB would no longer be party to it. The implications for the ASTI were serious and the consequences for union officials could be unpleasant. But the essential premise was the ability of the JMB to keep the AMCSS and the ISA united at regional level behind organisational policy.

The revised posts structure sought by the JMB in 1989 is interesting in the light of what the managers achieved almost a decade later under the PCW. The changes sought in 1989 were fundamental and continued to be so in 1998. The managers in 1989 wanted the duties attached to each post advertised before interview - this made sense in any size of school. In addition, the post of vice-principal, which had the highest allowance, should be open to all permanent teachers within the school. For the ASTI, this was much more controversial than the issue of advertising the job. The duties, responsibilities and availability of the vice-principal should be delineated in advance and all candidates for the post should be interviewed. This would be the function of a selection board from the school board of management. The 'most suitable person' for any post should be appointed. The criteria of capability and suitability were to be established in interview before any new appointment or promotion would be made. Under the appeals system a manager had to prove a teacher's inability and unsuitability for a post. In essence, every member of the profession was deemed capable and suitable of any post, whether that of a grade A or B or vice-principal. The managers criticised the system where the Department of Education had paid teachers an SFA or Supernumerary grade B post allowance simply because they had remained in teaching for a particular number of years. Unlike the vocational sector and the comprehensive and community schools, the voluntary schools alone had an appeals system built into the Agreed Memorandum. The JMB was trenchant in its criticism: the appeals system needed 'to be radically changed'.

> At the moment, it is costly to operate (normal expenses, indemnity, legal opinions) and inconsistent in its rulings (as evidenced by the imminent High Court case relating to (school) appointment.

In 1989 and 1990 the managers were rejecting any form of Appeals Board. Instead, they would be prepared to consider 'a one-person Appeals procedure along the lines of a Rights Commissioner'.

The ASTI blamed the school principals for the failure to agree the Fifth Memorandum, the inference being that the principals rather than the boards of management had refused to process the review. The fact was that the CMCSS and the JMB had conducted a full consultative process with their members. It was only when the ISA and every region in the AMCSS had explored the possibilities and voted that the JMB had made its decision to reject the Memorandum. Liam Murphy in his role as Assistant to the General Secretary reminded the ASTI President, Éamonn Ó hAllmhuráin,

> As explained to you at a meeting here on January 10, the final decision on acceptance or rejection of the Draft was made by the Joint Managerial Body following consultation at regional level with chairpersons of boards of management, managers and principals, many of whom were present in their capacity as secretaries of boards of management ... there was an average attendance of over 90 per cent of all those entitled to be present, including chairpersons of boards of management, at these meetings.[99]

Following the unsuccessful negotiations to agree the Fifth Memorandum, a detailed report was sent to the AMCSS and the ISA membership. The principals were advised to present a copy of the JMB letter to the school steward in the event of queries about the Agreed Memorandum, and in February 1990 the JMB issued a 'guideline' on the filling of new or vacant POR 'during the coming months'. Appointments of new vice-principals were not to be made 'for the time being' until further information was provided by the Secretariat of Secondary Schools. The authorities of schools where the selection procedures were already in train were requested not to finalise the appointment of a vice-principal 'until further notice'. While this would cause unease and tension in schools, the selection of a vice-principal in February was a new practice - the appointee would normally not take up duty until the following school year so the principals in these schools would not experience disruption until the end of the 1989-1990 school year.

The second request from the JMB was that 'permanent appointments to A or B posts should not be made until further notice'. At the same time, the Joint Commission of the Episcopal Conference and the CMRS had consulted the Catholic managers about the Draft Agreement on Redeployment. The Redeployment Scheme had been in operation for one year and had been under review in September and October of 1989. In spite of serious reservations about the operation of the Scheme and the introduction of the Supplementary Panel, the CMCSS recommended acceptance. However, they asked that the new Scheme should not be signed 'until the situation about the pupil/teacher ratio for the coming school year was clarified'.[100] This would bring the Department of Education into the frame. It was the ASTI that had suggested linking the acceptance of the new Redeployment Scheme with the pupil/teacher ratio. It may seem confusing that there was no mention of using the Supplementary Panel as a lever to negotiate the Agreed Memorandum as had been discussed by the managers in 1989. This is an example of role clarification within the CMCSS and the JMB. Redeployment applied only to teachers in the Catholic voluntary secondary schools. It was the result of negotiations between the bishops, major superiors, ASTI and Department of Education to meet the consequences of decreasing enrolments and rationalisation. While the CMRS consulted the CMCSS in relation to the 1989 review of the Scheme and about the union demand for a Supplementary Panel, the final decision rested with the bishops and major superiors. The JMB had no part in the process. Earlier talk, therefore, of including the Supplementary Panel in a negotiating 'package' with the Agreed Memorandum, was indicative of that confusion of role that continued in the early days of the re-structured CMCSS and JMB after 1987.

The situation in 1990 was that the ASTI and the JMB had failed to agree the Fifth Memorandum. The JMB refused to operate on the basis of the unsatisfactory Fourth Memorandum. The ASTI reacted to the refusal with an unexpected statement in the *Irish Independent* on Monday 12 March 1990, threatening industrial action. All post holders, including vice-principals, would 'be directed not to undertake post duties from Tuesday 20 March until Easter'. If the dispute were resolved, the ban would be lifted; otherwise, the union directive would be reviewed after annual Convention (during Easter week). The possibility of 'banning all voluntary co-operation' would then be considered. Late on the evening of the newspaper announcement, a letter was delivered to the JMB giving full details of the industrial action.[101] The ASTI would direct its members not to participate in courses organised by the JMB for post holders. Further details were added:

> Standing Committee has also directed that a ballot be conducted of members on the withdrawal of their services for two days in the summer term on a regional basis on specified dates, as a protest against the decision of the JMB to unilaterally withdraw from the Agreed Memorandum and its refusal to operate the Appeals Board and to protest at the refusal of the religious authorities to include the supplementary panel for temporary teachers in the new Redeployment Scheme.

The JMB could not link the Supplementary Panel in a negotiating 'package' because that was CMRS business. The union, on the other hand, had the advantage of being able to target both the JMB and the religious owners of schools in their media announcement. The CMCSS issued a statement to their members that the Supplementary Panel could not be accepted. In that context the regions in the AMCSS were 'requested to co-operate' in a number of procedures. Regional officers were to ensure that 'the position of management should be clearly put forward' in the media. Every effort was to be made to avoid confrontation with post holders because 'the dispute will end and it will be important that good relations will prevail'. Thus, the action varied from school to school and on the whole it was low key. In the event a temporary resolution was found and the POR system continued uneasily and with little change, along the lines of the Fourth Agreed Memorandum though it was called the Fifth. The effect of the unhelpful negotiations was to make the JMB even more determined that change would take place.

Turning Point

The end of the 1980s marked a turning point in the leadership role of the CMCSS and the JMB. There would be a change in the managing of the schools.[102] Both on the level of articulation in talks with the ASTI and through the implementation of a new style of continuing education, the managers were clarifying their vision of change. From 1989 and the commencement of their pilot training programme, the Secretariat of Secondary Schools concentrated on developing models of 'middle management'. The legal definition of a trade union accepted by ASTI is 'an organisation which regulates the relationship between employers and employees'. From opposing sides of the ring, the two contestants were learning to spar, to fight, to mark territory and to seek accommodation in the interests of preserving the voluntary school system. In 1995 the ASTI agreed to include religious and clerical teachers on the seniority list in accordance with their chronological seniority in the school.[103] But both sides knew it was a temporary arrangement. Neither side was ready for change, though they were willing to face the need to negotiate. The next round of national pay talks would become the catalyst for a major organisational change in the JMB schools and the eventual ending of the Fifth Agreed Memorandum and the Posts of Responsibility.

5

Leading and In-School Management

*If the 1960s had been the best of decades it was also one of
upheaval and social turbulence (McCarthy, 1973; Tobin, 1984;
Horgan, 1997). The three teacher unions had contributed to the
unrest by their industrial action. The 1970s appeared more
promising. The salary issue was resolved in the context of such a
modest National Wage Agreement (1970) that one participant
said that 'its provisions were literally sketched out on the back of
an envelope' (Hardiman, 1994:147-58). Perhaps it symbolised
a door closing on a period when demarcation lines between
workers and employers generally, and between teachers and
the managerial organisations, had been clear and relatively
uncontested though not free of tensions (Nevin, 1980).
National Agreements throughout the 1970s were negotiated and
agreed by ICTU and the FUE.[1]*

*The teachers' common basic salary, operative since 1 July 1968,
was increased in proportion to general wage increases. The
managerial representatives at the Ryan Tribunal had argued in
support of salary increases.[2] Any special increases were agreed
within the terms of the National Wage Agreements and applied
from January 1972. The fourteenth round came in January
1975. From 1974 to 1979 when the twentieth pay round was
completed there had been an increase each year (Collins, 1980;
Nevin, 1980).[3] The basic or school payment had been settled at
£400 but the incremental payment kept a different salary scale
for women and single men and for married men. The difference
favoured married male teachers by 20 per cent, but membership
of the EEC in 1973 forced a move towards the equal pay
advocated by the CCSS in 1968.*

A Changing Economy

In sharp contrast to the 1960s when Ireland lived within its means and experienced an unprecedented rate of progress (Whitaker, 1986; Chubb, 1992), the year 1972 brought a government decision to run a deficit in the current budget. This was a reversal of policy and opened the gates for vast borrowing from 1974. Some attempt was made to control it in 1977 by an insistence on moderate pay settlements and by investing in job creation, but the practice was short lived. Borrowings escalated beyond control. The impact of the first oil crisis (1973) was not considerable but the second in 1979 exposed the weakness caused by the period of borrowing. The break with sterling currency that same year added to domestic costs and the escalation of wage claims in the absence of any structure for centralised bargaining. Meanwhile, inflation was catapulting more and more Pay-As-You-Earn (PAYE) workers into the income tax net and by the end of the 1970s

> *the government seemed to be approaching the limits of what it was politically and economically possible to tax and borrow to support employment and enhance and extend public services.*

(FOGARTY, 1986:114)

There was little room for manoeuvre to stimulate the economy at a time of genuine need (Whitaker, 1986; Kennedy, 1986; Lee, 1989). In the summer of 1985 the Central Bank, OECD and the ESRI expected economic growth in excess of two per cent in GDP for the year. State expenditure on education was considerable in that context, representing 10.61 per cent of total public spending (OECD, 1988). By 1986 GDP was less than one per cent (Lee, 1986:152-66). Employers and trade unions in general developed a new awareness of the relevance of tax to disposable income.[4] Employers wanted value for money and this was their stance on returning to pay negotiations at plant or enterprise level towards the end of the 1970s. But the CMCSS and the JMB could never wield power as paymaster, dealing as they did with teachers who were public servants.

The publication of 'The way the money goes' - an analysis of expenditure on primary and post-primary education - by a former inspector of the Department of Education, early in 1977, influenced the policy of the managers and the CMRS on the funding of their schools.[5] The CMRS and the Catholic managerial groups were concerned at suggestions that the state would take greater financial control of secondary schools and should pay the total salary of the teachers. In an internal Report on Religious as Employers (1978), the CMRS recorded conditions under which they

> *could seriously consider acceptance of the proposals relating to teachers' salaries (and) the operating costs of the school, with the proviso here that schools not in the free education scheme be paid an adjusted capitation grant.*[6]

Briefly, changes would be conditional on religious retaining ownership and employer status in their schools to enable them to provide denominational education. As early as 1973 the CMRS had been exploring ways of sharing the management of their schools. Their Report in 1978 was informed by legal opinion and clarity on the role of the congregations as owners of schools. At the same time, the Secretariat of Secondary Schools had begun the process of educating the managerial bodies in financial management, part of that work was the professional auditing of accounts in preparation for a major survey on the funding of voluntary schools.[7]

There was a sense in which the managerial bodies had begun to develop a new approach and not only in relation to the financial aspects of their role. A number of experiences contributed to this: participation in the C and A Scheme, the Ryan Report (1968), the resolution of the 1969 strike and the POR system, the inadequacies of the Agreed Memorandum (1972), the subsequent failure of the posts to meet the demands of the first decade of free education, insufficient state funding and the contrasting example of the new community schools, negotiations with the ASTI on the contract of employment. One might also add the unresolved issues of boards of management, parent/teacher meetings, pastoral care and redeployment. The Catholic bishops and CMRS were clearer than ever on the importance of their involvement in education. The Second Vatican Council, the FIRE Report, Focus for Action and the Report on Religious as Employers had set the context for a vision of denominational education. One result of the change of approach among the managerial bodies was that they sought to introduce elements of productivity into salary increases, and their first opportunity came in 1980 with a Review on Teachers' Salaries.

Review Body on Teachers' Salaries 1980

The threat of industrial action by the three teacher unions in January 1980 resulted in a special meeting of the JMB. The outcome was a statement to John Wilson on 21 January on behalf of the 530 voluntary schools.

> *The JMB calls on the Minister for Education to set up a Review Body to consider the salary and conditions of employment of teachers. They do so because they believe that major changes have taken place in the status of the teaching profession since the Ryan Report in 1967 (sic). It is alarmingly clear that teaching as a profession has become less and less attractive over the past few years. The pattern emerging among candidates for the teaching profession is a matter of serious concern. It does not augur well for the quality of education in Ireland in the future.*

This was quickly followed by a request that the Review would 'deal with the Management aspect' by affording them an opportunity to present 'all aspects of the problem which are involved in the employment of secondary teachers'.[8] The JMB carried out a comprehensive survey in preparation for their submission to the Review. The meticulous study of educational and administrative practices revealed the inadequacies of funding, allocation of teachers and posts of responsibility. A seven per cent gap between incremental teaching hours and what was needed to operate the schools was identified. Additionally, supervision for 'incidental absenteeism' was a problem that the managers hoped might be addressed in relation to the salary increase.

> The JMB survey indicates that management requires a minimum of approx.
> 0.75 hours of substitution from each member of the incremental teaching staff
> if it is to ensure that classes will not be unattended when teachers are absent.[9]

Supervision of pupils was necessary from the time the school buses dropped them in the morning, between classes, at breaks and while waiting for transport after school. The managers contrasted school needs before and after free education. One complaint was that vice-principals were often teaching so many hours as to be unavailable to assist principals in the managing of the schools. The JMB specified the problems of the POR system in voluntary schools in an effort to persuade the Review group to link productivity with the salary increase.

> It is no exaggeration to say that the present system of Posts of Responsibility
> in our schools is a major source of discontent and dissatisfaction to all the
> managerial bodies. It is clear from the submission made by the ASTI that
> their members are not enamoured of it either. The outline submissions made by
> the Irish School Masters' Association, the Teaching Brothers' Association and
> the Association of Irish Headmistresses all call for remedial action (1980:21-2).

Serious dissatisfaction of the managerial bodies with the appointment process, with seniority and automatic promotion, inability to specify jobs in advance or to advertise outside the school for the post of vice-principal were among the aspects itemised in the submission of forty pages. The JMB arguments for productivity were strong but they failed to achieve the desired end. They considered the Report of the Review Body on Teachers' Salaries at its meeting on 8 October 1980 and at an additional special meeting on 23 October. The Report reflected many of the items in the managerial submission. The IVEA was in agreement with the JMB that 'a productivity-linked increase' was essential and they sought a meeting with the Minister, John Wilson. The Minister chaired the final meetings in an effort to get agreement between unions and managers. The result for the JMB was disappointing:

> at the end of a nightlong session of bargaining, agreement was finally
> reached - thanks to the considerable concessions made to union demands.[10]

The ASTI position was that the salary increases were merited remuneration for their workload and therefore could not be linked to productivity because this agreement was negotiated outside the National Understanding. The dilemma for the JMB, as always, was their vote in Conciliation. Their opposition would 'kindle antagonism between management and unions with the possibility of a Ministerial Order being needed to carry through the proposed scale'.[11] The JMB decision was to meet with Liam Lane, secretary at the Department of Education in advance of Conciliation, in an effort 'to establish how far the Department will support management's demands'. What proved to be a somewhat acrimonious, unsympathetic and decidedly unproductive meeting took place on 20 November 1980.[12] The managers' efforts failed to improve the posts structure. However, one cannot ignore the growing solidarity among the managerial groups and the CMRS on the importance of middle management structures for the voluntary schools.

A year later the CMRS Education Commission pursued the 'eighteen hour rule plus certification of duties for posts of responsibility' with the Department of Education, but to no avail.[13] At the same time the JMB sent a copy of their Review Body submission to John Boland who was Minister for Education. The accompanying letter stated that

> One of the areas of greatest concern is the weakness of middle management
> in our schools. We drew the attention of the Review Body to the deficiencies
> which exist in the operation of the system of posts of responsibility and we
> indicated how school middle management would be improved by altering the
> criteria for appointment to these posts and by having an effective method of
> certification that these duties had been performed.[14]

The JMB repeated that the Review Body had validated the managerial submission in relation to the posts and in particular to the role of the vice-principal. Minister Boland was therefore asked to 'lay down more clearly the criteria for appointment' to PORs in secondary schools and to introduce

> ... a monthly system of certification that the duties attaching to these
> posts have been performed. This could be done by requiring the manager
> to send in such a statement each month with the salary form. Certification
> would then become a requirement for payment of post allowances each month.

Productivity

By the early 1980s, therefore, the managerial bodies were speaking openly about the inadequacies of the system of posts of responsibility. They were also indicating some solution through productivity within the pay structure. Ironically, the period from 1982 to 1987 when the JMB managed 524 of the country's 818 second level schools was one of severe financial problems in Ireland and in the voluntary schools.[15] Falling birth rates and high levels of emigration exacerbated the possibility of teacher redundancies and rationalisation of schools.[16] There were seven Ministers for Education during those five years and such a rate of change created further uncertainty for the managerial bodies. It was extraordinary, therefore, that the CMRS and the CMCSS managed to finalise the 'package' by 1987. Even more remarkable was the fact that by 1987 the ASTI had secured their biggest ever pay increase without any productivity clause.[17] Parent/teacher meetings were restored, boards of management were acceptable to the ASTI, and the Department of Education had become a partner with union and managers in a redeployment scheme for secondary teachers in the Catholic voluntary schools.

Acrimony between union and managers was inevitable during the process. The managers sought a solution for what they called 'the 1 per cent of unacceptable teachers' in their schools. There was no research evidence either from managers or inspectors for such a figure, yet all parties appear to have accepted the statement.[18] No solution was found. Further tension resulted from an article in the *Sunday Independent* on 12 February 1984 when the General Secretary of the ASTI, Kieran Mulvey, exasperated at the slow progress of the negotiations, questioned state expenditure on private secondary education.[19] To some extent he was expressing the impatience and the anger of some union members at the power of the religious who owned the majority of the voluntary schools.[20] However, the CMCSS and the ASTI had secured the support of the Department of Education to pay an administrator for the redeployment panel. Securing that financial support was significant for the managerial bodies. Neither union nor managers would have trusted each other or been trusted by the teaching profession to administer redeployment. The role of the Department was essential. This was also the first time that the Department funded an administrative structure for the private second level system.[21] It gave the state a new role in the private secondary system and one that it did not have in the comprehensive or community schools.

Scotford Archer in her study of education systems in England, Denmark and Russia found that

> *political manipulation is the main process through which educational change is pursued and produced in the centralised system* (1979:271).

Her statement may be applied to developments between the managerial bodies, the ASTI and the Department of Education in the 1980s. The state had become more involved in education in Ireland from the 1960s. Fear of the unfamiliar and distrust had helped to bring the managerial bodies and the ASTI together in certain levels of opposition to the Department of Education. Issues related to the posts of responsibility had served to distance the Department through the 1970s. The struggle of the JMB to get support from the Department for productivity in the 1980s did not result in an alliance, but it is possible that officials developed an awareness of the weakness in the voluntary school structures. It was the 'package' in the 1980s that brought union, CMCSS, Department and CMRS into closer collaboration, because each had something to gain.[22] Thus, the monopoly of the churches in post-primary schools was becoming balanced by increasing state involvement in education.[23]

Changing Times

For most of the 1960s when industrial production grew at the unusually rapid rate of 6.6 per cent (Chubb, 1992) the annual price rise had remained at three per cent. However, between 1968 and 1972 the annual average shot to eight per cent.[24] Industrialisation increased and with it urbanisation and this had enormous implications for the schools. In 1945 nearly half of all Irish people were involved in agriculture, but by 1990 the figure was fifteen per cent. In 1966 when the free education scheme was announced, the population was approximately half rural, half urban. By 1986 some two-thirds were urban dwellers and the demand grew for more widespread educational provision as a new class structure developed in Irish society (Breen *et al*, 1990). When Fianna Fáil and the Progressive Democrats formed the coalition government in March 1987, it was in a context of severe economic and social problems. The national debt was £256 million, one and a half times the GNP, and the country had one of the highest levels of unemployment in the EU at 18.5 per cent of the work force (Hyland and Milne, 1992:75).

Since the 1980s one outcome of national pay bargaining has been increased levels of change and flexibility in the workplace (LRC, 1997; 1998). By 1987 when the first national pay agreement, the *Programme for National Recovery* (PNR), was negotiated, it had become clear that having entered the world economy Ireland had to earn its own living there. There was a growing realisation that the country could not borrow its pathway to wealth and that enhanced competitiveness would deliver extra jobs. In the ensuing decade, successive social partnership agreements were among the key factors underpinning Ireland's economic performance, and it was inevitable that the teacher unions and the managerial organisations could not remain apart from such developments.

In the twelve years since the signing of the PNR there have been four further agreements. These were the *Programme for Economic and Social Progress* January 1991, (PESP), the *Programme for Competitiveness and Work* 1994-1997, (PCW), *Partnership 2000 for Inclusion, Employment and Competitiveness* (P2000), and the *Programme for Prosperity and Fairness* (PPF) in March 2000. With the exception of the Netherlands and Austria, Ireland was alone in pursuit of such national level agreements. Other economies, including the Scandinavian countries, were moving away from planned economies to deregulated economies with localised wage bargaining. At the beginning of the twenty-first century, the foresight of the social partners is evident in the success of the Irish economy. One commentator[25] has summed up developments:

> *These agreements have made a major contribution to the situation where we now have attained EMU membership and are regarded as a macro-economic success model by the OECD, EU and the IMF. We have attained a high level of prosperity, falling unemployment and rising employment against a background of population growth and net immigration. Irish living standards as a per cent of EU average have risen from under 50 per cent to 90 per cent and average percentage increases in take-home pay have risen from 3.5 per cent to 7.5 per cent per annum. Unemployment rates have fallen from 17 per cent to 5 per cent while the numbers in employment have increased by over 33 per cent. While the phrase 'Celtic Tiger' might seem slightly hackneyed now, we have been witnesses to an economic miracle over the past decade. In one generation we are in a position to make an economic journey from being one of the poorest countries in Europe to being one of the richest. Some dangers lie ahead, however. Rising levels of inflation, skills shortages and the need to upgrade rapidly our infrastructure will all place strains on the engine of growth. If we steer carefully, however, we will reach a place where the past really will have been another country.*

The public service sector and especially teachers have been slow to move - there was little evidence of change in work practices among post holders in the voluntary secondary schools before the finalising of the talks on the PCW in 1998. The JMB, as already shown, began to seek productivity in the 1980 pay talks. In fairness to teachers, the context of their job had changed. Free education was the first major factor. At second level, changes in curriculum began in the mid-1980s under Gemma Hussey as Minister for Education, and have been on something of a roller coaster ever since. But the absence of any systematic evaluation of the changes has deprived teachers of a sense of professional confidence on a national level. A basic principle of motivation is the need for human beings to *know* how well or otherwise they are performing. Societal pressures on family and students have ramifications for classrooms. One could add levels of literacy that are inadequate to cope with the secondary curriculum, an ageing profession with limited promotional prospects, and the growing entry of the Department of Education and Science and the Department of Health and Children into the work of schools. In the face of such shifting sands, perhaps the idea of worker ownership in educational institutions should not be dismissed without analysis, reflection and some creativity.

Managerial Expectations

The 1990s brought a rapid succession of papers and events that spurred on educational change. The Culliton Report (1992) on industrial policy proved unattractive to teachers and managers though it challenged the emphasis on academic senior cycle programmes. The Green Paper *Education for a Changing World*, published in June 1992, evoked an energetic response from the school authorities, mainly because it challenged the role and composition of boards of management. Under the coalition government between Fianna Fáil and Labour with their *Programme for a Partnership Government*, 1993-1997, a White Paper and a new Education Act was promised. Niamh Bhreathnach, Minister for Education[26] set up the National Education Convention in 1993. The Minister's plan brought together 42 organisations that had greater or lesser involvement in the education system. For the first time, the people who had the power to make decisions about educational policy were provided with a formal platform (Starratt, 1996) to state positions, to hear varying beliefs and perceptions, perhaps to be influenced by the process of interaction. The well established practice whereby each group, usually separately, sought to negotiate with the Department of Education and/or whatever Minister was in office, was put on hold for at least ten days. It was also evidence of further incursion by the state into the education system.

The JMB and the CMRS made significant presentations to the Convention. They were heady days. The teachers, principals, and students were at work in the schools. Their representatives were in Dublin Castle, enunciating realities, visions and dreams of what the experience of education might involve as the end of the twentieth century approached. If, as a result, Niamh Bhreathnach expected a smoother progression in changing management structures, she was disappointed. The publication of the *Position Paper on the Governance of Schools* in July 1994 back-tracked on the idea of school principals as voting members of boards of management. It also respected the stance of the owners of schools who wanted to retain their majority position on boards. The series of 'Round table' meetings on 12 and 13 September 1994 were an effort to clarify agreement between teachers, parents and trustees.[27] Journalist John Walshe (1999:106-10) expressed some surprise at the line taken by the churches at these discussions. He was correct in noting a change of approach. The bishops' representative had seemed to be more open to change during the National Education Convention.

But there is a difference between openness to *considering* alternative structures for the management of schools and *agreement* to change. It is often at the point of making the decision that representatives of institutions may hesitate. In view of the responsibility of ownership and trusteeship, it might have been more surprising if the churches had agreed the equal representation proposed by the Minister for Education. Nevertheless, when *Charting our Education Future*, the White Paper on Educational Development appeared in 1995, its recommendations had been tempered by the discussions, or rather presentation of positions, made by the education partners during the previous two years. The White Paper and the badly timed, 'Time in School' Circular M 29/95 (Walshe, 1999:13-14) in August 1995,[28] formed the backdrop to negotiations with the teacher unions and the managers under the PCW.

Managing Change

The management of change is challenging, complex and essentially collaborative if it is to be successful. The JMB and the CMCSS proved their ability to manage change on a macro-level in their handling of the PCW, but there was no precedent in the history of the managerial organisations for the stand they made on the issue of in-school management. However, if it took the Department of Education and Science and the teacher unions by surprise, it could have been foreseen in the presentations made by the JMB to the National Education Convention in 1993. In fact, as early as 1980 and again in 1986 and 1987 the CMCSS and the JMB had discussed the need for flexibility and change in relation to posts of responsibility[29] and the Green Paper (1992) had forecast some equalisation of post-primary management structures.

Liam Murphy, President of the CMCSS and chairman of the JMB, reminded the National Education Convention that 'equalisation of funding and resources' was essential.[30]

> *If principals are to fulfil their essential leadership role it is imperative that the middle management situation in secondary schools is addressed as a matter of urgency* (1993:7).

Referring to similar school systems in the United Kingdom, Murphy described the Irish situation as 'indefensible'. He called for a total review of the system of posts of responsibility and 'an immediate and significant investment in training for all who are expected to play a part in school management'. An effective middle management would necessitate a reduction in teaching hours for post holders and the addition of a second vice-principal in schools of more than 500 pupils. Moreover, the JMB was seeking higher allowances for principals and vice-principals, 'with serious consideration being given to establishing a separate salary scale on the British model'. Mrs Barbara O'Dwyer from the FCLS, the privately-owned lay schools in the JMB, described the reliance on voluntary work for the tasks of middle management as 'an unhappy situation for both teachers and the school managers' (1993:12). Alan Brook, then headmaster of the High School and one of the three ISA representatives on the JMB, echoed his colleagues:

> *The real issue in improving the management and accountability of our*
> *schools is generating rapidly the middle management structures essential*
> *to sustain principals in their over-demanding roles* (1993:14).

Some months later the research commissioned by the CMCSS on the role of the school principal in their schools was published. Leader and Boldt (1994) confirmed what the JMB representatives had said in Dublin Castle a year earlier. The voluntary school system was creaking along on an ineffectual structure that left principals giving considerable time to 'non-educational' issues. The White Paper (1995:155) raised the expectations of the JMB about improved middle management structures in the voluntary sector. It is also worth remembering that the CMCSS since 1989 had been actively extending their training programmes for new principals. They initiated the In-career Development Council (IDC) in 1991, which was representative of all second level school types and the Department of Education. The CMCSS two-year pilot programme in 1989 and subsequently again in 1992 on professional development for principals, became a more inclusive training for principals and vice-principals. At the next stage there was provision for other senior management and teachers. The aim was to create teams for management in the schools, and the Department of Education and Science supported the initiative. By the time the external evaluation was published in December 1996 (Leonard and Dundon) the inadequacies of the voluntary school structures had been discussed by a wide number of people in the system. Throughout the training programmes secondary school personnel had opportunities to hear from their counterparts in the community and vocational sectors where a more structured management system prevailed. The posts of responsibility system became more and more a focus of discontent and at times exasperation - an ageing teaching profession may also have been more aware of the lack of promotional prospects in schools.

The CMCSS had used the term 'in-school management' in 1989 when professional training programmes were organised for principals and vice-principals as 'management teams'. In 1992 when these programmes were moving into another stage the ASTI expressed some unease with the use of the word 'management'. The Secretariat of Secondary Schools subsequently referred to 'Staff Development Programmes', and 'Leadership Programmes' - titles that were retained until 1998. But if the union was unhappy about terminology, the managers were not going to impose it. Their underlying philosophy was unchanged no matter what terms were applied: the voluntary schools needed an effective middle management structure that was not feasible under the terms of the Agreed Memorandum. In 1998 the Secretariat was in a position to issue *In-School Management: Guidelines for the Establishment of In-School Management Structures* (ISM). By that time the ASTI had come to a fresh understanding of the concept of 'management'. Union and managers together had negotiated a new deal and on this occasion the Department of Education and Science[31] was a full and strong partner to the agreement to create a middle management structure.

The developments that led to the end of the Agreed Memorandum and the introduction of ISM structures began in earnest in 1994 as the PCW was being prepared. A three per cent productivity increase was part of the agreed protocol, details of which were being explored by teachers, managers, Departments of Education and Finance in Conciliation. It was Brother Declan Duffy, General Secretary, who first suggested that posts of responsibility should be included in the discussions. The union representatives agreed. To be accurate, the C and A process became an *ad hoc* structure to facilitate the talks. Each party was allowed to bring along an 'expert' to inform deliberations. The Association of Community and Comprehensive Schools (ACS), though not a party within Conciliation, was permitted to attend.[32] That meant that all parties had the benefit of reminders that the state schools already had a middle management structure through posts that were not hedged in by the limitations of an Agreed Memorandum.

Traditionally the C and A Scheme for Teachers dealt with pay claims. Over the years, the effects of membership of the EU and developments in industrial relations legislation contributed to a new national culture where government insistence on a link between pay, working conditions and productivity could be part of the PCW (1994-1997). Government and the trade unions had committed themselves in 1994 to negotiate wage agreements on the basis of the need for efficiency, flexibility and change, and the need to achieve savings and an improved quality of service in the context of an agreement. Since 1954, C and A was where primary teachers' claims for pay and emoluments were processed.[33] The scheme for secondary teachers was added in 1955 and for vocational teachers in 1957. These three separate panels then gave way to the common C and A scheme, though it was 1973 before the ASTI agreed to join. In 1970 a formal C and A Section was also established in the Department of Education. But in the context of the 1990s and the PCW local bargaining stage, C and A was not an adequate structure. Conditions of work were outside the scope of the Scheme; yet the elements of the PCW agreement had to be pursued by all parties.

During 1994 and early 1995 a list of claims was prepared. These included: early retirement, requests for pensions credit for those primary teachers who had taught under the capitation system, superannuation arrangements for part-time teaching service, the purchase of service for pension purposes, payment of a special allowance to teachers with 35 years service, a reduction of the salary scale by two points, payment of a degree allowance to non-degree holders, a Higher Diploma allowance for teachers with particular concurrent four year degrees, and improved allowances for principals and vice-principals. The talks broke down for a period over the summer of 1995 but resumed again in October. The JMB target in the negotiations was to improve 'the poor internal management structure' in secondary schools. They also wanted adequate salaries for principals and vice-principals 'on the basis that they would be fully functioning and a team member with the principal'. The essential requirement of the Departments of Education and Finance was 'flexibility and change' by teachers. The fact that nothing could be agreed until everything in the negotiating package was agreed intimated that progress might be slow, but the principle of flexibility and change in a national agreement was a source of encouragement for the managers in the context of local bargaining. The determination of the JMB since 1980 to pursue structures for middle management was informed by a clear vision of the future of denominational education.

Talks broke down in early summer but resumed again in October 1995 and early retirement, salary increases and consequent changes in work practices were under negotiation. Progress was slow because of the need to get all parties to agree. But Brother Declan Duffy, General Secretary, was hopeful that a satisfactory conclusion might be reached by November.[34] Progress was being made in relation to early retirement and it seemed likely that the three categories of need would be addressed. The principle of early retirement for more senior teachers in excess of the quota as a result of amalgamated schools, or 'an irreversible downwards trend numerically', met with little opposition, though the issue of enhancement of pension had not been settled. The second category was more complex. These were teachers who were unable to function 'at acceptable levels of professional performance'. There were two concerns: that of identifying the teachers and the possibility of professional support to enable them to cope. Compulsory retirement was not considered in the scheme. Agreement was reached on the need for an Early Retirement Advisory Committee (ERAC) with a representative of the unions, management and the Departments of Education and Finance. Again, the matter of enhancement of pension had not been explored in the PCW talks at this stage. The third category was that of teachers aged 55 years or more with a minimum of twenty years service, who could no longer function in the face of the demands of educational change. No more than 150 'retirals' would be permitted in this third category. The plan agreed was to support a maximum of 300 'retirals' each year.

Priority would be given to the first two categories and it seemed certain that ERAC would be responsible for processing all the applications for early retirement. Negotiations had not yet begun on the matter of salary increases for the holders of any post in the schools. Neither had the parties addressed the question of middle management though all were aware from the White Paper (1995:155) that a major re-organisation had to be debated. By the summer of 1997 the operations of the Early Retirement Scheme had been worked out. Implementation followed and a second offer was made in the first term of the 1997-1998 school year. Between primary and second level teachers a total of 153 availed of the scheme during its first year.

The New Posts

The process of negotiating the list of claims by the teacher unions and the managers under the PCW was described by one negotiator as 'the most complex and the most varied basket of claims that has been dealt with in any forum of negotiation in many years'.[35] The JMB concentrated their skills on securing an effective middle management structure for their schools. Clear job specifications of the responsibilities involved in all posts and a direct match with the needs of the schools were an essential. Enabling teachers to take on responsibility for 'instructional leadership, curriculum development, the management of staff and their development, and the academic and pastoral work of the school' was central to any negotiation of the posts. The managers were also seeking appropriate selection procedures for the appointments. Brother Declan Duffy believed that success would

> depend on how much money the Department is prepared to allocate in
> the short term to re-vamp middle management school structures.[36]

Negotiations were not finalised by November 1995 but continued through December when the historical evolution of the posts of responsibility in the three school sectors was explored. The JMB was encouraged. For the first time since the introduction of the posts in the early 1970s internal management was centre stage and described as 'an essential element of the package'.[37] By January 1996 an air of reality had hit the negotiators: these talks were complex and would take considerably more time than originally anticipated the previous year.

With agreement on an Early Retirement Scheme the parties turned their attention to the two remaining elements in the PCW proposals: In-School Management (ISM) and the principle of flexibility and change. Nothing could be implemented until everything in the package was agreed. While the managers were committed to all three, the crucial items for them were ISM and the issue of flexibility and change. They therefore voted in favour of the PCW deal in February 1996. They could see an end to the era of the posts of responsibility and the various editions of the Agreed Memorandum. George O'Callaghan, a member of the JMB team, described the proposals about the posts as 'a good package with open competition and a measure of seniority'.

The INTO supported the deal but both the ASTI and the TUI turned it down. Minister for Education Niamh Bhreathnach must have been disappointed that a government injection of IR£67.7m[38] in February had failed to resolve outstanding issues between union and management.

Negotiations resumed in April 1996 and lasted until December when the Department of Education decided to end the talks and refer back to C and A. Further proposals emerged on early retirement but the concept of 'flexibility and change' seemed to have been lost. Yet it was that element of the PCW that had been intended to lead to the productivity demanded by the national pay agreement. The JMB therefore refused to agree the outcome of the talks and began to put pressure on the Department about its position.

From January to May 1997 all parties in Conciliation went through a process of accepting the overall package. In a public statement, the JMB 'rejected the proposals by a majority of over 90% against to less than 10% in favour' because middle management in the context of flexibility and change had been ignored. The managers criticised the role of the Department of Education that claimed to pursue a major reorganisation in response to the government's Strategic Management Initiative while refusing to meet the needs of the secondary schools.

> The principle of appointments to promotion posts on the basis of merit
> rather than seniority has been strongly and consistently argued by the
> JMB throughout the PCW talks. These proposals mean that appointments
> to the posts of assistant principal and special duties teacher must go to
> the most senior suitable applicant. We cannot agree to this situation.
> For our schools to operate properly school management also requires an
> effective system of supervision and substitution as part of the professional
> non-teaching duties of teachers rather than relying on such assistance in
> a voluntary capacity.[39]

The Department of Education was accused of failing to treat the managers as 'an equal partner' in the PCW talks. It was a contradiction of the Department's claim in *Implementing the Agenda for Change* that school management was a partner in the change process.

At least there was agreement that there would be new titles and new posts. A deputy principal, assistant principals and special duties teachers would be appointed in all schools. These appointments were conditional on the willingness of existing post holders to agree changes. Post holders including the principals would receive an increase of 28 per cent on their allowances, provided they accepted new contracts for duties. This was the break sought by the JMB whose negotiating team at this stage was led by Brother Declan Duffy, General Secretary, and George O'Callaghan, then Princpal of Mercy Secondary School in Newport and a member of the CMCSS and

JMB. In September 1996 George O'Callaghan succeeded Brother Declan Duffy as General Secretary, the first lay appointment to the position.

In spite of their reservations, the managers were aware that movement would only be achieved through communication. They therefore agreed to take part in a series of discussions with the ASTI[40] on the details of new structures before finally rejecting or accepting. So, explorations that had begun in 1994 were still under discussion by the summer of 1997. At that stage the voluntary sector appeared to have gained nothing apart from whatever the Early Retirement Scheme might mean.

While the INTO supported the deal, both the ASTI and the TUI turned it down. In doing so 'a unique situation' was created.[41] The dilemma for the unions was to align their position with that of the INTO who had accepted the PCW proposals. In addition, the ASTI and the TUI now had need of a mandate from their membership and they had to agree some strategy for entering into negotiation again. Meantime a government arrangement with ICTU meant that an *ad hoc* arbitration process was available if Conciliation and facilitation failed to achieve agreement between the parties. The dissenting second level unions therefore had options. If they refused to avail of arbitration, under the PCW they could simply accept a straight, unconditional percentage salary increase for all their members. The problem was that the INTO would not be prepared to follow this route; they were anxious to stay with their acceptance of the PCW because of the advantages for their membership. It was unlikely that the ASTI and the TUI would happily cede the prospect of securing an early retirement arrangement for their members. Neither would they wish to lose the possibility of increased allowances for post holders and several other improvements for teachers. Negotiations resumed in April 1996 and lasted until December. By June the *ad hoc* facilitation process had begun with Seán Healy, Director of Advisory Services at the LRC, as chairman.

The principal issues for the parties were a better deal on early retirement, internal school management, the vexed question of seniority, the contentious 'Time in School' circular of August 1995. During the earlier stage of the PCW talks there had been 'provision for a consultation on the Time in School Circular prior to its amendment by the Department' and the JMB was interested in pursuing the matter.[42] In the last Newsletter before his retirement from the Secretariat of Secondary Schools, Brother Declan Duffy, General Secretary, outlined the position of the managerial negotiators:

> *The position of the JMB, in going into these talks is very clear. Our priorities are: We are seeking the maintenance of the increases for principals and vice-principals already indicated in the rejected PCW agreement. We are also (in line with the White Paper) seeking the retention of the agreement reached in relation to middle-management posts - both allowances and duties. Finally, we favour an early retirement scheme for teachers, with particular priority to those who have given all they have to give, and who wish to retire with dignity and some enhancement.[43]*

Once again, the JMB had planned its position with clear outcomes in mind. They would monitor progress in these renewed negotiations and they intended to break off negotiations if their 'legitimate needs and expectations' were not met. This was a definite management position. There would be no return to the inadequacies of the posts structure. The managers would manage the changing context of their schools by insisting on the introduction of middle management posts. At the annual conference of the CMCSS in Galway in June 1996 the AMCSS endorsed the JMB stand particularly in relation to middle management. The incoming General Secretary, George O'Callaghan, had a clear mandate from his members. It is worth remembering that at the time the JMB and the CMCSS was in a process of some change. However, through a cohesive Standing Committee they ensured that there was no shift from the objective of an effective middle management structure for the voluntary schools.[44]

By October 1996 there had been little progress in the negotiations and the position remained that the INTO and the JMB had agreed the 'package' since February. Of paramount interest was the implementation of any middle management structure. George O'Callaghan was specific:

> The cornerstone of such an effective structure is the principle of appointment on merit and not by seniority. We are committed to establishing effective and efficient structures within this sector and this commitment must extend to all the relevant partners in the education system. The management of individual schools cannot and should not be asked to shoulder the responsibility for the introduction of change and reform in the system by relying on a grace and favour situation particularly from staff of whom much is already demanded.[45]

Further proposals emerged on early retirement but the concept of 'flexibility and change' seemed to have been lost. From January to May 1997 all parties in Conciliation went through a process of accepting the overall package. This time the JMB voted against acceptance. However, they agreed to take part in a series of discussions with the ASTI[46] on the details of new structures before finally rejecting or accepting. So, explorations that had begun in 1994 were still under discussion by the summer of 1997. The voluntary sector appeared to have gained nothing apart from whatever the Early Retirement Scheme might mean to individual teachers and some schools. Nevertheless, in the early months of 1997 leading up to the General Election in June the CMCSS and the JMB galvanised their members into an educational campaign. 'Better Schools, A Lost Opportunity' was the heading of a series of newspaper advertisements in April when the annual teacher conferences were in progress.[47] The regions of the AMCSS and the ISA lobbied politicians in the weeks before the election - the voluntary sector made its historic role and its continuing contribution in Irish education a matter for politicians of the future.

The Standing Committee of the JMB, comprising the General Secretary, President Sr Marie Céline Clegg, Vice President Seán Burke, Vincent Foley, Harry Meyer and Dr Sinéad Breathnach began discussions with the ASTI on ISM structures. The discussions and negotiations were often fraught with difficulty and on a number of occasions the talks broke down. By late summer 1997 a kind of working relationship had built up between union and managers, according to George O'Callaghan. The JMB representatives had set a clear mandate. Having rejected the re-negotiated PCW, there were to be discussions and negotiations in respect of clarification, elaboration and interpretation of certain sections of the PCW agreement relating to the ISM structures. Following the completion of these discussions the outcome would again be put to the vote of members of the CMCSS/JMB.

At the tenth Annual General Meeting of the CMCSS in Waterford in May 1997 George O'Callaghan was in a position to give details of the in-school management agreement. There was a departure from the established practice of basing the number of posts of responsibility on enrolments and ages of students. In future the allocation of posts would be based on teacher numbers and no school would lose posts under the new structure. However, as O'Callaghan told the AMCSS,

> *If existing post holders do not opt for new contracts they will effectively block the filling of the full schedule of posts to which a school is entitled.*

Throughout 1997 and early 1998 talks continued between the ASTI and the JMB, between each party separately with the Department of Education and Science, and between all three. Every effort was being made to reach a workable agreement that had been made all the more problematic by the fact that Minister Niamh Bhreathnach in 1996 had authorised implementation before negotiations had been completed. However, the union had too much to gain for its membership by actively implementing the terms of the PCW to throw it away in favour of a mere three per cent of a pay round.

Compromise alone ensures the success of negotiation when the stakes are high for the parties involved. Contacts in between meetings became more frequent as each side strove to move towards resolution. The union had to concede that specific duties would be allocated in advance of appointments though the manner of doing so was less obvious than the managers had wanted. The managers failed to get the open field they desired in relation to seniority. The principle of seniority had been recommended by Healy and endorsed by the TUI;[49] however, an agreed set of national criteria was to be drawn up by the parties in conjunction with the Department of Education and Science. The union secured the independent chairperson for the interview panel. The managers had not wanted this because of the cost factor for schools, but there was agreement on the need for the additional impartiality of such a person. In return the managers sought detailed contract forms of agreement, and some slight leeway on the order of seniority was also achieved. The appointment of an agreed arbitrator for a fixed renewable period of two years was a considerable improvement. The ASTI and the JMB had come a long way from the Agreed Memorandum.

The union reluctantly agreed that the new post of deputy principal should be publicly advertised. The compromise arrangement was that schools of less than seventeen teachers would be confined to internal candidates. Nevertheless, it was a major breakthrough for the voluntary sector. Existing vice-principals would also be asked to upgrade to the newly defined post of deputy principal which was to include a broader managerial remit than vice-principal. Agreement was reached on the two categories of posts, that of assistant principal and the special duties teacher. By October 1997, after a long summer of negotiations that extended into the beginning of the school year, the JMB decided that the 'documentation offered a basis for agreement', and a series of regional meetings with the AMCSS and the ISA was planned. Members of the Standing Committee attended - this had been agreed as part of the strategy for managing change in the voluntary school system.

The stakes were high for the CMCSS and the JMB. Their vision of the place of denominational schools in the twenty-first century was the basis of their determination to work with the principals, managers and boards on implementation.[50] There would be no undue haste in the change process from posts of responsibility to the new ISM structures. The JMB negotiators had received a clear mandate from their membership in 1996 and again in 1997 to pursue the ISM aspects of the package, so the negotiators were exercising accountability as agreed in April 1997 by returning to the membership with details of the best possible package that they had secured after the protracted struggle right through the summer months. Following a series of detailed briefings by Standing Committee members to all of the Regions and the ISA through late Autumn of 1997, the final negotiated package on ISM was accepted by a large majority of the membership. In 1997 the AMCSS and the ISA had mandated the JMB to 'address their concerns about supervision and substitution and time for post holders to do their duties'; the management response to failure to make progress should be 'a policy of non-co-operation in regard to certain issues'.[51] The JMB had pursued those issues with the Department of Education and Science though little advance was made by the time the ISM was being implemented. There had been a ceaseless flow of documentation between the ASTI, the JMB and the Department of Education and Science, and all parties were committed to the best possible agreement under the 'flexibility and change' element of the PCW. The issues of supervision, substitution and time for duties were unresolved, though the 1998-1999 school year would bring in the ISM structures.

In-School Management: Implementation

To ensure correct interpretation and implementation it was agreed that the ASTI and the JMB would present examples, including specimen advertisements, to the schools - one member of the union suggested a parallel with the preparation of 'sample teaching lessons'. To strengthen the impact, the Department of Education and Science agreed to issue relevant circulars, giving details of the procedures to be adopted. This was public acknowledgement by all parties that the Department had a crucial role in the internal management of the schools. The advertisement would tell teachers that they 'should refer to the school schedule of posts to identify the duties required at this time.' Part of the communication process was the assurance to the AMCSS regions that the Secretariat of Secondary Schools would provide detailed in-service. This was in keeping with its role as the support agency for leadership and management in the denominational system. Early in 1998 the Secretariat issued *ISM: In-School Management: Guidelines for the Establishment of In-School Management Structures (ISM Guidelines)* to all members. The process from which this detailed volume resulted gives insight into the changed nature of the operation of the CMCSS, the JMB, and the Secretariat of Secondary Schools. Nothing was left to chance. Every detail was explored to ensure that the boards of management and managers who would be responsible for the implementation of the ISM development would be informed and supported.

The President of the JMB, Sr Marie Céline Clegg, a Loreto nun and former school principal, along with the General Secretary George O'Callaghan, established a 'Guidelines Advisory Group' and a 'Guidelines Working Party'.[52] The aim was to ensure that the highest standards of change management would inform the process because

> *The new procedures place a great deal of responsibility on individual boards of management.*[53]

The underlying philosophy of the CMCSS and the JMB is evident throughout the *ISM Guidelines* (1998). Clarification with the staff of the educational philosophy and current needs of the particular school would inform the process of the management of the changes consequent on the ISM. An emphasis on the school community, team leadership, collaboration and management is clear. In 'the old agreement' the vice-principal was seen 'in the same context as the other post-holders'. Under ISM there is a separate circular for principals and deputy principals because: they are 'clearly seen as the senior management team in the school'.[54] Like the principal, the new deputy principal is 'accountable to the board of management/manager'.[55] Nothing was omitted. Holders of SFAs and Supernumerary B posts under the old system could also have their allowances enhanced in line with the PCW, 'provided they opt for new contracts'. Boards of management were told that

> The duties offered and allocated should be commensurate
> with the appropriate category of post in each case.[56]

This documentation formed the basis of the regional in-service programmes organised by the Secretariat under Principal Officer Bernadette Kinsella. These programmes took place in 26 venues throughout the country. A detailed implementation process using the Circulars from the Department of Education and Science along with the management guidelines was planned. It was crucial that the preparation would ensure that the framework of an effective middle management was provided in each voluntary school.

Eight JMB constituents who had experience as principals or vice-principals in a variety of urban and rural denominational schools formed the Advisory Group. Led by the President of the CMCSS the Working Party was advised by Dr Séamus McGuinness from the Education Department at Trinity College and by strategist Tom Clarke from the Centre for Management and Organisation Development at the Department of Finance. Moreover, the in-service would be preceded by the *ISM Guidelines* on the implementation of the entire process. The undertaking was considerable. The process of change would be advanced by in-service for the largest group of second level schools in Ireland, catering for approximately 61 per cent of the student cohort or some 200,000 and the majority of the 16,000 members of the ASTI. What was described by the Principal Officer as 'a massive volume of calls, emails, letters and queries in person' developed as a consequence of agreement on ISM.[57] It was 'a very busy period for the schools and for the principals in particular'. Detailed preparations for the changeover meant that it was May 1998 before a relieved George O'Callaghan could write to his membership that they were unlikely to be able to complete all aspects of the implementation of ISM before the summer holidays on 5 June that year. Aware of criticism in some of the regions, the General Secretary clarified the situation on behalf of the JMB:

> *(The delay) has been compounded by the late arrival of Department of Education*
> *Schedules, some of which have contained errors. It may be necessary therefore in*
> *some instances to defer some appointments until September.*[58]

After what the JMB described as 'a considerable delay'[59] five circulars were issued by the Department to the school authorities. In fairness to the officials, the very titles of the circulars give some indication of the complexity of the issues involved. Given the history of the posts of responsibility system that was being abandoned in favour of the new ISM structure, it is little wonder that the Department officials took so much time to draft the circulars. Circular 3/98 was 'an enabling circular setting out the rationale for the new structure' while Circular 4/98 authorised the managers and boards to implement the ISM structures in relation to the posts of principal and deputy principal in secondary schools. Schools with 17 or more teachers would appoint a deputy principal 'on the basis of open competition'. Important principles of the ISM agreement were stated:

The principal, deputy principal and holders of posts of responsibility together form the in-school management team for the school.

More than anything else in the circulars that sentence summed up the thrust of the changed structure of posts in the voluntary schools. The emphasis on team introduced by the General Secretary and the CMCSS in 1989 as part of the strategy for that phase of management training was formalised in the Department's circular almost ten years later. This is not to claim that inclusion in a circular would create a team approach to management but it set the challenge and the requirement from the context of the 'flexibility and change' enshrined in the PCW. It will be a benchmark for future review and evaluation in the system.

The roles of principal and deputy principal are clarified in the circular and the appointment of the principal continues to be on the basis of the Articles of Management for Catholic Secondary Schools except where a school is not governed by those Articles. The traditional recognition by the Department of Education and Science of the rights of the trustees and owners of the private school sector pertains. Enhancement of the allowances for the principal and deputy principal are dependent on agreement to enter into the newly required contracts. Circular 4/98 appended a 'specimen contract' and 5/98 provided the full 'Contract for Deputy Principal'. For the first time in the voluntary sector there is a professional contract for the second highest paid post holder who 'acts as principal when the principal is absent, assuming the responsibilities and authority of the principal's role in accordance with the provisions of the Articles of Management' (5/98). Moreover, acceptance of the new contract that includes a review of duties 'periodically' or 'at the request of either party', was a pre-requisite of benefiting from the PCW deal.

In 'Schedule One' the Department of Education and Science provided an 'outline of specific professional duties, responsibility for which may be delegated, in whole or in part, to deputy principals'. Allowing for different needs in individual schools, the list is described as 'not exhaustive'. The thrust of the suggested areas of responsibility, however, is managerial and concerns areas of educational leadership. It could not be more different from the era of the posts of responsibility. The three parties to ISM had agreed 'a transitional period' until 30 September 1998. Following representations by the General Secretary to the Department the date was subsequently extended to allow schools to complete each phase of the ISM process without omitting vital and necessary components. The margin of human error in this historic change from the years of the posts of responsibility and the Agreed Memorandum was to be as slight as possible.

Union, managers and Department of Education and Science could be well satisfied with the outcome of the protracted PCW negotiations. However, it is the nature of such talks that no party is likely to be fully pleased. Principals, dealing with the demands of the school day, will be disappointed that the vexed issue of supervision has not yet been resolved.[60] But neither supervision nor substitution had been within the terms of the PCW. The acid test will be in the ability of managers and boards to continue to manage the process of change that has begun with the introduction of ISM in 1998 and 1999. To what extent will the new structures improve the quality of teaching and learning in twenty-first century denominational schools? Boards of management will need vision, energy, time and skill to ensure that maximum benefit ensues for all concerned. Acknowledging the 'needs of the school' as the basis on which duties are to be identified was a major factor negotiated by the management team. For the first time ever, the focus of allowances for posts was to be on the school. This in turn means that specific work for each post is identified in advance of the selection process. Insistence on a formal contract between the board of management and the individual teacher involves school management for the first time. Transparency is assured because the total staff is involved in the needs analysis, and management may exercise its role in accountability. Not only is there an agreed procedure to be followed but it is supported by the partnership between Department of Education and Science, board of management, and teacher union.

Crucial to development will be the manner in which managers or boards, teachers and union and the Department of Education and Science deal with the review of post duties. Circular 5/98 provides for 'a review of post duties at the request of either management or the post-holder'. Moreover, the written contract states that 'the duties attached to the post are subject to review' under the terms of the Department's circular. There is a mechanism for review and development that never existed in the old system of PORs. The implementation of the review has the potential to contribute to the status of the teaching profession and to a more effective middle management structure by ensuring that the posts are implemented in a professional manner. In March 2000 the parties to ISM have agreed to commence with a national review before the school-based reviews.[61]

The Agreed Memorandum 1972 and In-School Management 1998

The introduction of the system of posts of responsibility in secondary schools in 1970 was more about satisfying ASTI grievances than a strategic effort to create effective structures in the schools. Professor Louden Ryan's notes at the time of the Tribunal in 1968 show his impression that 'the managers would be unable to manage the posts system'.[62] Neither did the Department of Education attempt to manage what had been agreed with a Minister for Education. The history of developments after the Agreed Memorandum in 1972 suggests some variation in how individual principals and managers 'managed' PORs in their schools. It is true that the system itself was flawed from the outset. For the managerial organisations there was the problem of their authority as leaders of the schools. That authority was at best moral, at worst lacking in power to ensure a united stand. Even as the posts were being introduced in 1970 the secondary schools were in what proved to be a maelstrom of change. Demands on the voluntary sector were enormous and funding by the state totally inadequate. So the posts system was created in a present that had already become the past and the inadequacies became more pronounced with the passage of time. Subsequent efforts by the JMB to review and update the structures failed to meet the changing demands of the schools.

The fact was that for almost three decades the JMB and the ASTI negotiators had been trying to make an effective management tool out of an arbitrary and out-dated imposition. There were three parties to the PORs - management, union, and Department of Education. The historic independence of the voluntary sector, inherited attitudes of churches and civil servants to their roles in education, and lack of preparation for the impact of free education are relevant to an understanding of how the PORs developed. Thus the Department of Education was an almost silent partner in the matter. The process of bringing about change was arduous. In the end it achieved a degree of success mainly because the CMCSS and the JMB had assumed their leadership role and the religious orders knew that the future of Catholic education was in the hands of lay teachers, principals and boards of management. A help to the interaction between union and managers was the fact that CORI agreed to an ASTI demand for a change in the Articles of Management in relation to the selection of principals. From 1 September 1998 the number of people on the selection committees increased from three to five: there are now two nominees of the trustees, two of the board of management and an independent external assessor.[63]

The CMCSS and the JMB challenged the posts structures because they had a vision of how much greater the voluntary sector would need to become in the new millennium. That they succeeded in bringing the ASTI with them is as much a tribute to JMB determination as it is to the individual officials and negotiators in both organisations. The records show that issues related to the PCW and in-school management were the main focus of meetings by the CMCSS and the JMB for almost six years. As a result,

a clear and unambiguous process for implementation involving a step by step procedure was developed.[64] The process had emanated from a new premise. The allocations of duties to posts of responsibility under the Fifth Agreed memo was based upon a combination of agreement with post holders taking into account their skills and aptitudes and an historically based stratification and categorisation of duties. The new structures are based on a new premise. The duties and responsibilities emanate from the needs of the school with the objective of matching those responsibilities more clearly to the central tasks of the school.[65]

The role of the Department of Education and Science was inevitable in terms of the national PCW and emerging levels of transparency and accountability in the public service. Government policy after the Strategic Management Initiative provided Department officials with the power they needed to assert a role in the management of the voluntary school system. What emerged therefore was a tripartite agreement on ISM that has the potential to strengthen the privately-owned school sector in the twenty-first century. Time will prove its effectiveness.

In the first year of its operation from 1998 to 1999 more than 700 ISM posts were filled in voluntary secondary schools. Sixteen appeals (2.3 per cent) were lodged with the Arbitrator. Twelve appeals were concerned with 'suitability'. Eight were not upheld and three had to be re-advertised. There were four appeals on the grounds of 'seniority' but it was found that Circular 5/98 was correctly applied in three cases so the appeals were not successful. The fourth was referred back to the Arbitrator.[66]

New Conciliation and Arbitration Scheme

Since the reorganisation of the C and A Scheme for teachers in 1973 the three teacher unions, primary school managers, the JMB and the Departments of Education and Finance have tried to reach agreement on successive pay claims. When that fails the Conciliation Report notes the disagreement and the process moves to the Arbitration Board that includes an employer and a worker member of the Labour Court and is chaired by an independent arbitrator who hears the parties to Conciliation. The passing of the Industrial Relations Act, 1990 opened the way for a different culture in employee relations. It was clear that changes would have to be introduced into the operation of the Conciliation Council to allow discussion on such issues as conditions of service, industrial action and other grades of teachers such as people on secondment, although their employers may not be represented. The ASTI was aware that change was inevitable under the PCW (1994-1987).[67] For that reason the *ad hoc* arrangement was used. Since 1997 the P 2000 set the context for relations between the social partners and it also encouraged further developments in industrial relations. There was much emphasis on 'principles of co-operation and joint decision-making' between the partners (LRC, 1997:3). The teacher unions were assured of pay increases for their membership because the local bargaining negotiations were on schedule (*The Irish Times*, 30 July 1999).

The National Centre for Partnership established in the Department of the Taoiseach symbolised a new departure in pay bargaining.[68] The role of the Centre is to oversee the growth of partnership in private and public sectors. It is of interest that both IBEC and ICTU are represented on the Centre's Liaison Group. The Secretariat of Secondary Schools is a member of IBEC. The ASTI has been a long established member of ICTU.[69] The teacher unions and ultimately the schools have been drawn to the centre of the stage where economic success and aspirations have affirmed the importance of education and lifelong learning. *The Revised Scheme of Conciliation* and *Arbitration for Teachers* (2000) states that the following should be among the criteria taken into account at each stage of the scheme for dealing with claims:

> *the need for a high quality education service and, in this context, the need to ensure the recruitment, retention and motivation of staff with the qualifications, skills and flexibility required so that the education service can fully contribute to social and economic development* (2000:23).

The document includes the concept of flexibility and change so that the education service can continue 'to achieve greater efficiency and effectiveness'.[70] What the JMB was able to secure under the PCW, therefore, may be seen as the beginning of a new stage in employee relations and in the management of change in the voluntary secondary schools.

A New Context 2000

In 1998 a motion was passed at the AMCSS Conference

> *That AMCSS develop a vision for Catholic education which would address such issues as quality in education, loading of the curriculum and the place of religious formation.*

A sub-committee was appointed[71] and an interim report presented in 1999. The report was the outcome of consultations with a wide range of people including bishops and legal advisers. The role of management in the Catholic school is that of

> *guardian of the ethos and values and [its task is] to seek to foster and support a Christian spirit at management level and in all the working relationships within the school community.*[72]

In the context of a pluralist society, the three principals who prepared the draft report struck a note of realism:

A pressing question that emerges is the coherence between the assumed vision of school owners and the day-to-day lived reality of the local voluntary school in Ireland today.[73]

Three years earlier when a number of AMCSS regions had sought to meet their trustees because of concerns about ethos and the continuation of voluntary schools, CORI and the CMCSS issued a joint statement. CORI assured the principals and managers of its commitment 'to treating the continuation of the ethos of voluntary schools as a priority'.[74] Since then the Education Act, 1998 has provided a legal basis for denominational schools. The challenge to school boards is to:

> Uphold, and be accountable to the patron for so upholding, the
> characteristic spirit of the school as determined by the cultural,
> educational, moral, religious, social, linguistic and spiritual values
> and traditions which inform and are characteristic of the objectives
> and conduct of the school, and at all times act in accordance with
> any Act of the Oireachtas or instrument made thereunder, deed,
> charter, articles of management or other such instrument relating
> to the establishment or operation of the school (15.2(b)).

The continuing challenge to CMCSS and the JMB will be to ensure that the focus of their work as organisations will be on effective leadership and management. The ultimate aim is to enable pupils to experience denominational education of the highest quality. To that end it would seem to be essential that the managerial organisations lead the way in promoting a national discourse on social policy, education and church schools.

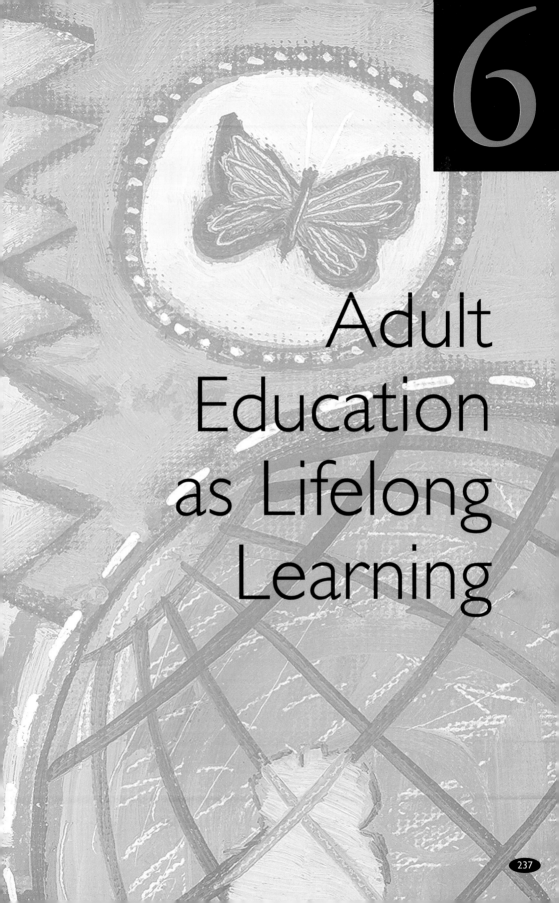

6

Adult Education as Lifelong Learning

Adult Education and the Voluntary Secondary Schools

Adult Education in an Era of Lifelong Learning (Green Paper on Adult Education) was published in November 1998 and brought the issue of adult education to the fore in Ireland. But the concept of education and training provision for adults is not new in Ireland. A strong tradition had been created by the Gaelic Athletic Association (1884), the Gaelic League (1893), and the Irish Agricultural Organisation Society (1894). There were also the United Irishwomen (1910), the Irish Countrywomen's Association (ICA) the same year, and the Irish Housewives Association (1942). The precursor of the Irish Farmers Association, the National Irish Farmers' Association, along with Muintir na Tíre, provided increased educational opportunities for men and women in rural Ireland. The passing of the Vocational Education Act in July 1930 established a framework of committees and helped to formalise provision. Each Vocational Education Committee was charged with the duty of

> *Establishing and maintaining a suitable system of continuation education*
> *in its area and of providing for the progressive development of such a*
> *system* (ACT, 1930:47).

The 1940s brought further development. University College Dublin and University College Cork[1] began to reach out to adults. The trade union movement established the People's College and in 1998 celebrated its fiftieth anniversary.[2] The provision of education programmes for shop stewards developed over the decades. The Dublin Institute of Catholic Sociology was founded in 1951 by Archbishop McQuaid and from the 1960s was attended by members of the CCSS. A significant development by the ICA in 1957 was the opening of an adult education centre with residential accommodation at An Grianán in County Louth. Economic growth in the 1960s influenced the establishment of the State Training Council, AnCO, in 1967, to increase the provision of vocational training. The County Committees of Agriculture (1931) and ACOT (1980) both of which provided training and education programmes were eventually replaced by the Agriculture and Food Development Authority, Teagasc, in September 1988. This new organisation was established under the Agriculture (Research, Training and Advice) Act, 1988. For the first time, a body charged with adult education and training had also a formal research remit.[3] Their new focus in 2000 on training and development for the food industry is a direct outcome of systematic research and close alliance with economic developments.

In May 1969 Brian Lenihan, Minister for Education, appointed a committee that produced the Murphy Report (1973) in which the work of the churches was acknowledged - what was recognised was the commitment of the religious orders and bishops to the education and training of personnel. The Report was an innovative way of looking at adult education, acknowledging the legitimacy of programmes both for work and for personal satisfaction. In this chapter, therefore, lifelong learning includes in-service and professional development as well as what has been done by the voluntary schools for adults since 1970.

From the end of the 1960s the Irish Management Institute (IMI) encouraged its members to avail of further education and training in management. An initiative of the Education Commission of the CMRS led to the IMI providing the first systematic adult education and training programmes for the voluntary school managers, principals and bursars as well as training courses for those working in adult education. As a result between 1974 and 1986 many members of the managerial bodies attended the IMI.

In 1978 the CMCSS held a two-day conference in Blessington to explore future plans for training principals. Attendance was by invitation only, to ensure that the thirty participants were representative of the mix of schools in the JMB. Bart McGettrick[4] from St Andrew's College of Education, Glasgow, worked with the group of principals and managers, and this event proved to be stage one in planning a systematic leadership training programme. What developed replaced the annual programme for new principals initiated by the CCSS in the early 1970s. The Secretariat of Secondary Schools is regularly in contact with CEEC, the European organisation of Catholic education and this connection also proved important in developing a policy on leadership training. In 1980 the General Secretary and members of the CMCSS attended a conference in Rome where the focus was on leadership and school planning. This was used in subsequent negotiations with the IMI in developing programmes. By 1984 the JMB secured agreement from the Department of Education to devote one school day per year to staff development, or lifelong learning. A second day could be taken with prior sanction from the Department. This was the first attempt to formalise professional development as part of the learning community.

The planning in Blessington had been purposeful. In 1985 and 1986 a total of 510 principals and teachers participated in school leadership courses there, organised by the CMCSS and the JMB. Preference was given to the 210 lay applicants and as a result 95 religious could not be accommodated on the programme. It was a recognition that the future of voluntary schools would be mainly in the care of 'the lay teacher'. It was also an effort to respond to *Lay Catholics in Schools*, a 1982 publication from the Vatican Congregation for Catholic Education. There was continuity and a developmental aspect in the design of these programmes; participants were encouraged to combine management theory with implementation in the schools. Review and evaluation was a regular feature of the work with the IMI.

Ten other courses for 600 principals and teachers from voluntary schools were provided in 1985-1986, while the National College of Industrial Relations (now the National College of Ireland) organised courses in industrial relations in schools from the late

1970s. Also, the last twenty-five years of the twentieth century saw a rapid growth in the rise of the outside consultant, consultancy firms providing expertise by individuals and teams, and the planning of organisational change (Starratt, 1996; Doyle, 1998). The IDC and the establishment of the ICDU in the Department of Education have created structures within which lifelong learning for teachers can progress. The Secretariat of Secondary Schools contributes to that work by systematic evaluation of all programmes. Alert to the role of the principal in the Education Act, 1998, Principal Officer Bernadette Kinsella has worked with new principals on an analysis of their professional development needs. That process of reflection and discourse with participants in programmes will ensure that adult education will belong to the participants.[5]

Vatican II challenged the Church to promote adult religious education. Within the women's section of the CMRS, the question of the continuing education and religious formation of nuns was frequently discussed. There was a preference among the larger orders to provide such education within and this prevented interaction among younger religious from various congregations. A significant development in 1966, however, was the organising of Saturday afternoon programmes in scripture and theology by the Jesuits in Milltown Park. More than a hundred young religious attended the two-year diploma courses there. These courses were repeated and approximately 500 religious women and men availed of them. When Archbishop McQuaid established the Mater Dei Institute of Religious Education in the late 1960s, the religious orders were encouraged to send members there. His aim was twofold: to train teachers of religion for secondary schools and to provide an Institute of Religious Formation for the many orders in his diocese (Cooney, 1999:380-83). At the annual general meeting of the CCSS in 1966, the Archbishop presented the promised Mater Dei Institute as 'a reward' for the nuns' hard work and devotion to 'the faith'.

In 1968 another Jesuit initiative resulted in the amalgamation of eight houses of theological studies, thus establishing the Milltown Institute. Initially, the programmes were offered to religious and clerics, but in the 1970s the first lay theology students were welcomed.[6] By the end of the 1960s it was clear that the Catholic Church authorities and the various religious orders of women and men had implemented a policy of adult education initially for their own members. For the smaller orders such a policy was enhanced by collaboration with other members of the CMRS. The work of the Focus for Action team from 1974 gave a new impetus to adult education. Courses on spirituality, personal development and psychology were organised in a variety of venues. At times, lecturers came from the US or from various colleges in Rome. Most of these programmes were part of the process of renewal of religious life that followed from Vatican II and contributed to the growing trend among religious orders to explore apostolic works other than teaching.

Aontas: National Association of Adult Education

In 1968 a priest of the Archdiocese of Dublin, Liam Carey, was Director of the Dublin Institute of Catholic Sociology and lately returned from the US where he had been studying developments in adult education. At the same time Archbishop McQuaid agreed to re-name the Institute as the Dublin Institute of Adult Education (DIAE), the aim being to broaden the scope of the work in order to provide

> *an adequate adult education service for adults of*
> *all ages, sexes, occupation and social classes.*[7]

Carey initiated the founding of a national association for adult education in Ireland with the support of Seán Ó Murchú, then director of the Adult Education Department at University College Cork (UCC). A special seminar on adult education was organised in Dublin in May 1968 and was attended by representatives of the various voluntary and statutory agencies, including the CHA. Contributors included personnel from the IMI, the European Bureau of Adult Education, the Inner London Education Authority, and an American university department of adult education. The range of issues addressed is worthy of mention, bearing in mind that it was the late 1960s. The same issues are relevant today and appeared in the Green Paper (1998): basic principles of adult education, adult psychology and adult learning, adult education and community change, new trends in programmes, the planning of adult education, co-operation in adult and community education.

What emerged from this historic seminar in the Royal Marine in Dun Laoghaire was agreement on the setting up of a National Association of Adult Education for Ireland. To ensure that it would happen, a special committee of twelve, including Carey and Ó Murchú, was appointed.[8] Their report was presented a year later at the first annual Adult Education Conference held in Athlone in May 1969. This was Brian Lenihan's constituency and as Minister for Education he presided at the launch of the National Association of Adult Education. The title Aontas or 'agreement' would encapsulate the aspiration of collaboration between the many organisations concerned with adult education, and the new Association agreed 'a basic adult education philosophy'.

> *This philosophy is expressed as the development*
> *of the full man, by man and for man.*[9]

Minister Lenihan used the occasion to announce the establishment of the committee that later produced the Murphy Report (1973).

From the outset Aontas had the support of the Churches and the interest of many principals and managers in the JMB that had been formed a year earlier (1968). Reliable statistics are not available for the very early years of the Association; however, in 1974 it had 30 individual and 90 corporate members including Aer Lingus which had joined in 1970, and in 2000 it has 182 voluntary members including Family Resource Centres, various women's groups, unemployment centres, networks, men's groups, advice centres, community development project groups and a range of policy groups. There are also 67 corporate members and 171 individual members. The Secretariat of Catholic Secondary Schools joined in 1977, though individuals among the Council of Managers and the CMRS were already members. The Secretariat continues its membership in 2000. The interest of the voluntary school sector was also evident from the early 1970s in the attendance by an increasing number of nuns and some TBA and CHA members at seminars and annual conferences. After 1972 when community schools began to be established the interest of the religious orders involved was reflected in Aontas activities.

Adult Education and the Schools

The introduction of the comprehensive schools in 1963 and the community schools in 1970 raised the awareness of the managerial bodies in relation to adult education, though the extent of that influence is difficult to assess. The Draft Deed of Trust for the new schools in 1966 made no reference to adult or community education (O'Flaherty, 1992:123-26). Four years later when the Document on Community Schools was published the structures envisaged were more developed in terms of management and provision for the local community (Ibid, 1992:127-35). The Document from the Department of Education in October 1970 stated that

> *There is growing acceptance throughout the world that education is a life-long process and that second chance education must be provided at all levels. It would seem clear, therefore, that there will be very substantial development of adult education facilities over the next decade.*

The Document also emphasised the importance of meeting local needs by giving the use of its facilities during out-of-school hours 'to voluntary and the adult community generally'. Facilities would be available

> *subject to reasonable safeguards against abuse or damage to buildings, equipment etc.* (Par. 4).

Over the years the 83 comprehensive and community schools have developed programmes of adult and community education. Internal management structures facilitated that development and there was also the contribution of the representatives of the VECs on the boards of management. The freedom to use adult education to increase the points rating of these schools encouraged principals and teachers to be creative in providing programmes. The voluntary sector has tried to get parity since 1981 but without success.[10] However, as a result of JMB negotiations under the PCW there is now a sub-committee of the Conciliation Council devising a structure for adult education. Voluntary schools will be able to appoint a director of adult education with reduced teaching hours (*ASTIR*, February 2000).

Neither the Model Agreement for Community Colleges nor the Articles of Management for Catholic Secondary Schools mention lifelong learning in relation to the schools. The agreement made initially by the Dublin Archdiocese and the County Dublin VEC by 1980 to establish community colleges did not need to allude to adult education. The colleges were established under section 21 of the Vocational Education Act, 1930 that empowered the VECs to appoint sub-committees. The boards of management of these community colleges, therefore, are sub-committees of the VEC. One aspect is that the VEC commitment to adult education is presumed. Indeed, from the outset the community colleges have provided adult education programmes.

The Articles of Management

The Articles of Management for Catholic secondary schools were first published by the CMRS in 1976 and updated as required. The Articles form the basis for joint training of boards by CORI and the Secretariat of Secondary Schools as the need arises. The last Articles (1989) continue to be the instrument of management in 2000, with the necessary amendments in relation to selection procedures.[11] The changes since the original document have concerned the composition of the board, but in general the responsibilities have remained intact. Unlike the community school instrument of management the Articles of 1989 contain no reference to adult or continuing education. In view of the interest of the CMRS and many individual managers of the voluntary schools in adult education, the omission is surprising. On the other hand, the lengthy struggle towards agreement with the ASTI on a move from a unitary management tradition has perhaps inevitably resulted in concentration on two sensitive areas: the composition of the board of management and the issue of teacher selection. However, two sections in the Articles offer possibilities related to adult education. One concerns managerial responsibilities and insurance coverage. The other refers to sub-committees. Subject to approval by the trustees of the school,

> *The board shall have power to sanction the use of school premises outside school hours by outside bodies. The board shall have discretion in determining such charges and conditions as it may consider appropriate for such use of the premises* (Section 15f).

Moreover, the 1991 revision of the *Manual for Boards of Management*[12] is more expansive regarding the use of premises 'by outside bodies'. While the emphasis is on the board's responsibility for adequate insurance policies,

> *... it should also be recognised that in allowing its premises to be used in this way, the school can serve the community by providing a location for a wide range of educational, recreational, social, cultural and youth activities* (1991:74).

In addition to the obligatory Finance Sub-Committee, a board may also 'delegate' any of its powers 'to a sub-committee or sub-committees of its own members' (Section 16a). Clearly, such a structure merits consideration in 2000 for those voluntary secondary schools that may be selected by the Department of Education and Science as centres for adult education and training. The management of the process of extending a voluntary school towards greater 'community' service should spring from the particular educational philosophy of the trustees or patrons. Ensuring such a focus will need research, review and development. It is essentially a management function that will demand particular skills.

The CCSS and the TBA

From 1973 the CCSS frequently discussed adult education developments at its meetings. There were Reports from principals and teaching religious who had attended summer courses and seminars organised by Aontas. While the emphasis was on local community adult education, the initial work of the CCSS was directed to parents of students in the schools. In a denominational system in the years after Vatican II it was appropriate that the themes of lectures, retreats and short courses were usually faith development, understanding the scriptures and relating to adolescents - methodology was rarely interactive and the long-established tradition of a preaching, teaching church prevailed until the mid-1970s. There was little contact between the managerial bodies and community groups before 1972 when the first community schools were opened but the inclusion of VEC representatives on the boards of management of these schools brought a long experience of apprenticeship training and adult education. According to Brother Declan Duffy, who was a pioneer of the community school movement in Ireland, the VEC representatives promoted the role of these schools in adult and community education. It was through such involvement that the religious orders and the CMRS learned to link educational services for adolescents with provision for families and local communities. They also became more familiar with the tradition of the VECs in adult education and appreciated the need for structures to enhance local provision.

The CCSS records show the nuns' interest in adult education in spite of the pressures resulting from the introduction of free post-primary education in September 1967, but at that stage their discussions were not about a broader or community-based process of adult education. The Document on Community Schools highlighted the concept of education as 'a life-long process' to which the new schools would contribute. It was the implications of that Document rather than the impetus of Aontas that were discussed at length by the managerial organisations and major superiors. The idea of a school system that served the 'community' was seen as problematic by many principals. The majority of the principals in the voluntary schools taught a full (and often six day) week - by 1980 they were still teaching on average six hours. Administrative duties were usually done after the school day and this was also true of the lay principals in the JMB. The post of principal was not 'recognised' by the Department of Education until 1974 though schools with sixty pupils could have a principal. Fear of unfamiliar structures for the community schools sometimes stifled reflection and discussion. The idea of a 'board' of management was not thought of in terms of democracy in action and a way of promoting *community* education. Some in the CCSS viewed it as unnecessary 'layers of officialdom' that would waste the time of the principals who were already over-worked. There was also a reluctance to have school premises used for any purpose other than the education of the pupils. Issues of maintenance, funding and personnel loomed large as deterrents. Similar issues were in fact identified in the evaluation of the ASTI-JMB pilot programme in adult education in 1999.

In the 1970s there were many schools where the religious, particularly the nuns, did not employ people to do the daily cleaning but did it themselves at the end of the school day. The traditional *horarium* of convent (and monastic) life was little changed by 1972. There was a time for work, for prayer and for duties within the religious community. Occasional evening meetings with parents of children preparing for the sacraments in the primary schools were exceptions. The same was true in relation to evening lectures for parents in the secondary schools. Even in the early 1970s it was not usual for CCSS members to change the 'custom and practice' of being in their convents for 9 pm when the Great Silence commenced.[13] Systematic provision of adult education would involve considerably more evening work. There was also the practical issue of securing school premises. The community schools were in a position to provide for caretakers and adult education organisers, whereas in 1980 the JMB were still requesting funding to employ school caretakers for the secondary schools.

Partnership Between Parents and Schools 1970

Although the Christian Brothers did not initially support community schools they made a unique contribution to adult and community education through their Federation of Parents of Christian Brothers' Schools from 1970. Brother Leo Canny was in the Christian Brothers' secondary school in Enniscorthy when he invited a group of parents to work with the school, and a number of brothers in Dublin schools then initiated parents' groups. The formation of the Federation was the outcome of identifying parents who were enthusiastic and willing to volunteer time and effort. The primary school parents formed one part of the development. By 1975 the Federation had helped the CCSS and other TBA schools to establish Parents' Committees, as they were called. Under Gemma Hussey, Minister for Education, the National Parents' Council was established in 1985. By that time the majority of the voluntary secondary schools already had Parents' Councils or Committees as a direct result of the work done by the Federation of Parents of Christian Brothers' Schools. The groups established in the CCSS and CHA schools combined to form a parallel to the Christian Brothers' Federation. It was called the Catholic School Parents' Association (CSPA). The parents' groups of the voluntary sector were continually involved in raising funds to supplement inadequate state grants to schools. In addition, many also organised a variety of self-funding adult education programmes. The Christian Brothers' Parents concentrated on raising awareness about curriculum issues and in providing opportunities for adults to study Irish, English and mathematics. In the 1980s all the parents of the voluntary schools were central to the lobbying by teacher unions and managerial organisations for increased government spending on education. By then, as a result of the initiative of 1970, a certain partnership between parents and schools had developed, though admittedly levels of involvement and effectiveness varied from school to school.

Although the Federation has been subsumed into the National Parents' Council in the 1990s, it shares the credit for an interesting initiative in adult education in 1987. This new development arose out of discussions between Mrs Jean Plunkett, a parents' representative on the Curriculum and Examinations Board 1984-1987 and Brother Canny of the Federation of Christian Brothers' Secondary Schools. Jean Plunkett, who was also an active member of the Federation, believed that VEC and community schools provided 'academic' programmes for adults, but that courses in aspects of family relationships, leadership, spirituality and communications were also needed. Thus it was that the Christian Brothers invested in developments that established the Marino Institute of Education in Dublin. Since May 1986 a number of approaches had been made to Brother Leo Canny by Liam Carey of the Dublin diocese, then in the Adult Education Department at St Patrick's College Maynooth, and Professor

John Coolahan of the Education Department at St Patrick's College Maynooth. The request was that the parents' programmes in the Christian Brothers' schools and the emerging developments in the Marino Institute would somehow be linked with Maynooth. The Catholic bishops were already urging Maynooth to make provision for such programmes and to forge links with parents and schools. The Marino proposal suited the two colleges and the outcome was that Maynooth provided certification for a range of programmes until 1989. Adults who had participated wanted additional opportunities for accreditation in family counselling. This was negotiated by Brother Canny with Iona College at New Rochelle, a university of the Christian Brothers, under the Board of Regents of the State of New York, the American equivalent to the National University of Ireland.

Since 1990, therefore, the Marino Institute continues to provide a range of training and education programmes in family counselling and addiction counselling, as well as a limited personal counselling service. To date some sixty people have completed a master's degree in family counselling. In 1994, the Year of the Family, two of the Christian Brothers from Marino made presentations at a conference on family values in Malta. Professor Heiko Steffens of Berlin University, who chaired the conference, recommended that the work of the Marino Institute be recognised by the United Nations.[14]

The Christian Brothers had viewed adult education in relation to their schools rather than to a wider community, but they recognised the importance of a framework to ensure continuity. The development of the Marino Institute of Education was no exception. The support of Archbishop Kevin McNamara of Dublin was sought, a board of management was established and later dis-established in favour of a more relevant structure that included CORI, and lay members. All the other orders of brothers that constituted the TBA were smaller in numbers of personnel and schools, and so there is a danger of neglecting their contribution to adult education. Among the first to become involved were the Marist Brothers, largely because Brother Declan Duffy, their provincial superior in the 1970s, was chairman of the Education Commission, one of the first religious trustees of a community school[15] and co-author of a CMRS report on adult education in 1977; from the mid-1970s he was responsible with John Shorrt for developing a comprehensive adult education programme in Moyle Park College in Clondalkin. By the end of the 1970s, the De La Salle, Presentation and other TBA members had introduced various adult programmes, usually in catechetics, personal development and family issues.

Several factors contributed to the involvement by the voluntary school sector in adult education. Religious women and men owned most of the secondary schools and were prepared to respond to the call of Vatican II for adult catechesis. The Document on Community Schools in 1970 and the positive response of a small number of teaching orders in the CMRS encouraged debate about the role of the Catholic school in a local community. Two publications in 1977 informed this debate. The first, *The Catholic School*, was published by the Sacred Congregation in Rome and the second was from the CMRS on Catholic schools and adult education.[16] From 1970 religious who were 'trained' catechists were graduating from the Mater Dei Institute in Dublin. They were familiar with the teachings of Vatican II and brought that to the schools and communities in which they lived. They were also trained in methodologies that were appropriate to the kind of interaction needed in adult education. Throughout the 1970s an increasing number of nuns, brothers and priests attended various postgraduate programmes in the US. Many of them were subsequently appointed superiors in Ireland, while some returned to teaching and other works. Additionally, since the early 1960s a number of orders had founded houses in parts of America. Such continual interaction gradually opened up a different culture where the Catholic Church and the bishops in particular were proactive in Catholic education, not only in schools. The CMRS was well established though still working in two sections, male and female. Finally, the falling numbers of religious vocations[17] was the catalyst that brought about a number of important reports, each of which, among a range of issues, dealt with adult education and the role of the voluntary schools.

The Future Involvement of Religious in Education

Between February 1973 and February 1977 there were four reports related to adult and community education. One was government commissioned: the Murphy Report, 1973. Two were not intended for publication - they were internal studies for the bishops and the major religious superiors. The fourth, *The North America Report*, was published by the CMRS and disseminated among its members and the managerial bodies of the voluntary schools early in 1977. Then, by 1983 the *Report of the Commission on Adult Education*, commissioned by the Department of Education, was published.

The FIRE Report has been mentioned a number of times in this book, and this report is also relevant to adult education. At a joint meeting in May 1972 the Episcopal Commission on Post-Primary Education and the Education Commission of the CMRS agreed to set up a working party to examine the future role of religious in education. Eight educationalists were invited to work on a committee chaired by Paul Andrews, the Jesuit headmaster of Gonzaga College.[18] Thirty-four eight-hour days of full committee work and 66 days in sub-committees produced a confidential document by February 1973. The FIRE Report was never intended for circulation outside the bishops and major superiors though it was frequently mentioned to the Department of Education and to ASTI at meetings throughout the 1970s. For the first time the religious themselves had access to statistical information about themselves and their educational institutions. Hitherto, there was a reluctance to share such data between the religious bodies. For some the sharing was the result of uncertainty about the future in the face of falling religious vocations.

The working party decided to concentrate on religious, including diocesan clergy, in post-primary education in the 26 counties. The problems that concerned the bishops and the CMRS were concentrated at that level: the drop in religious vocations, the state plans for developing the community schools, and pressure from the ASTI for access to school principalships. Indeed, the working party interpreted the development of community schools as the beginning of the end of denominational education. Their recommendation, therefore, was to concentrate all religious in a smaller number of schools so as to be able

> to maintain prayer, community life, health, links with parents, and a
> distinctive innovative style of schooling adapted to changing needs with
> a unified, tough negotiating posture with the Department of Education.

The aim was to ensure financial and other guarantees to secure the future of Catholic schools in 'a pluralist society'. Among the areas 'of special educational need' that the Report recommended were 'guidance, counselling, catechetics, third level and adult education'. Their concept of education for religious of the future 'would be considerably wider than the school-tied concept that has largely been the pattern up to now'. The emphasis should be on supporting parents in their primary responsibility for the 'religious and moral education of their children'. The FIRE Report explored a range of approaches to adult education:

> The most effective means of tackling this is likely to be in small groups or in
> the family. A link of this kind, provided by the religious through their schools,
> could help too in communication problems between parents and teenagers.

Religious and clergy would need 'special training in techniques of counselling (and) group work'. The thrust into adult education was to involve 'the laity and parish clergy'. The connection between the provision of adult guidance services and lifelong learning was emphasised.

Murphy Report on Adult Education 1973

The task of the committee appointed by Minister Brian Lenihan in 1969 was to investigate the provision of adult education and to advise on future developments. An interim report was prepared in 1970 and in November 1973, the final Report of the Committee on Adult Education was presented to Richard Burke, who was then Minister for Education. In their deliberations the Committee had explored the concept of 'the community school' where education would be available to pupils and adults. A prerequisite was a school structure that would support adult education. Such thinking would have been unlikely among religious in schools at that time. The school was a community responsibility where religious (and increasingly lay) teachers worked in the best interests of Catholic education. The hierarchical structure of the religious community was not a matter for discussion either in terms of its effectiveness or desirability for adults. The Agreed Memorandum on the Posts of Responsibility in the voluntary schools reflected the pyramid structure. The report presented to Minister Burke, known as the Murphy Report, is relevant to the managerial bodies of 2000 for a number of reasons: it presents a helpful approach to defining 'adult education'; the role of the churches is explored at length and sheds some light on early involvement in adult education; the potential for participation by the schools is emphasised. It is evident that the Committee had a vision of community education being widely available through all schools - a sample of primary and second level schools was surveyed in an attempt to estimate the extent of use of premises for adult and community education.

In the Murphy Report (1973:6) 'adult' is defined as a person who has completed formal schooling and is 'recognised and accepted by society as adult or as fulfilling an adult role'. The Report pointed out that people may assume 'the opportunities and responsibilities of adulthood' at many stages from as young as fifteen years of age. That reality is not unknown in the Ireland of 2000, whereas in earlier times twenty-three years of age would have been a useful demarcation line. A number of reasons indicate the need for the CMCSS and the JMB to initiate a debate on the meaning of 'adult' - these include school enrolment trends,[19] a voting age of eighteen, the effects on learning of information technologies, inadequate levels of literacy among the adult population, the inability of the school system alone to develop literacy skills, and the need for a proactive policy on lifelong learning.

In 1973 it was not possible for the Murphy Report to record accurate participation rates in adult education. However, the Committee found that adult learners tended to be aged 21 to 45 years with at least two years of post-primary education and from upper socio-economic backgrounds. The concept of education as 'life-long' and therefore from 'pre-school learning right through to the end of one's life' (Murphy, 1973:16) was central to the work of the Committee. Adult education provision should support people in interpreting, analysing and coping with change. It should also 'preserve basic cultural and Christian principles' in what Murphy described as 'this great storm of human, social and technological change'. An important principle was that youth work, community development and adult education should be inter-related and co-ordinated as well as supported by 'a really good and effective public relations programme'. What is noteworthy is that the Report urged collaboration and involvement by trade unions, credit unions, tenants' associations and every other type of local and community organisation of the early 1970s. The vision of Aontas was replicated in the thinking of the Committee.

The Murphy Report refers to the role of schools in general and to that of the new community schools in particular. The Department of Education issued the Community School Document in October 1970 when the Murphy Committee was into its second year. Members had visited adult education centres abroad and had seen the collaboration between various state schools and provision for adult learning. The Document was the first public acknowledgement of the potential of the second level system in Ireland to contribute to adult education. Advice from the UK[20] brought a relevant definition:

> *Physically a community college is a secondary school with additional facilities to meet the educational, cultural, social and recreational needs of adults and young people.*

A key factor was the use of premises. In the early 1970s school authorities in Ireland were not as alert to issues of insurance as they would become of necessity a decade later. But the Murphy Report did not relegate opportunities for adult education provision to the newly-emerging state schools. The recommendation was that

> *Present post-primary schools be encouraged and where necessary facilitated in becoming community schools or community learning centres* (1973:36).

This was in fact an imaginative proposal though it was ignored. For some unknown reason the 'recommendations' section of the Report did not accurately reflect the body of the text - 1973 was a pre-computer era. It also appears possible that the Committee decided to formalise only those recommendations that dealt with structures (1973:122-3). Indeed, all the items in that section deal with macro-structural issues. Only a detailed reading of the Murphy Report will reveal the extent of the discussion and deliberation that went on during the three and a half years of its existence. In fact, the Report opens up ideas, suggestions and recommendations that are relevant to adult education provision in 2000. Among the details were recommendations that the promotion of adult education needed structures at national, local and school level. Personnel needed specific training - a vital aspect to be noted in 2000. The full use of premises and resources was a key factor to the successful provision of a localised or community adult education service. All of this had obvious implications for the several religious orders among the managerial bodies that became involved as trustees and teachers in the community schools from the early 1970s.

A variety of approaches were considered in defining adult education. Put simply, education would enable adults to 'catch up, keep up and forge ahead' (Axford, 1969:6). A working definition was agreed:

> *The provision and utilisation of facilities whereby those who are no longer participants in the full-time school system may learn whatever they need to learn at any period of their lives.*

Acknowledging the absence of a distinction between 'formal and informal adult education', the Report emphasised that 'the process of adult education' should span 'every sphere of human development'. The greatest concern was with those adults who, for whatever reason, had not completed full-time education. At the end of the twentieth century a major national achievement was the fact that approximately 81 per cent of the age cohort were completing second level education and almost 50 per cent attaining third level (Green Paper, 1998:39). The voluntary secondary school sector played a vital educational and economic part in the achievement of that 81 per cent completion.

Even in 1973 the Murphy Report presented pre-adult education as a platform from which continuing learning would develop. The following quotation in the Report is notable because in 1996 an OECD group [21] would say virtually the same thing:

> *It is adult education which is the substantial and major part of the educational process - the part for which all the rest is at best ... a preparation.*[22]

There were and are two implications for the managerial bodies of the voluntary school system. One relates to curriculum and standards, the other to the nature of denominational schools. Obviously these are inextricably linked. The realisation of the potential of denominational education depends first of all on the clarity and commitment with which the underlying philosophy of education is informed. In 1973 the Murphy Report made a case for the complementary nature of liberal and vocational aims in education. By implication the Report warned against categorising any and every kind of programme as 'adult education'. Criteria were suggested: programmes should be 'purposefully educative', systematic and last for a period of time or a number of sessions; they should present evidence of appropriate guidance in learning and a continual process of evaluation (Murphy, 1973:4-5).

The Murphy Report acknowledged the work of the churches:

> *The Committee found that in Ireland the Churches have contributed notably to the general provision of adult education but found little or no evidence*

of religious adult education at local community level. The Committee notes the significant commitment of the Churches to residential adult ducation in the promotion of centres, retreat houses and the use of hotels as course centres (MURPHY, 1973:41).

Two criticisms were implied - firstly, that much of the provision by the churches was internal to members of religious orders, and secondly, that there was a lack of co-operation between the churches and local educational authorities, in other words, the VECs. In a survey conducted for the Murphy Report, national schools emerged as more likely than second level schools to be providing premises for adult education. Vocational schools and parochial halls scored best of all in utilisation for adult education purposes. Reluctance was noted on the part of school management 'in too many cases' to 'permit or encourage adult education activity in the buildings under their care'. Non-assertiveness on the part of adults themselves in demanding 'that facilities be provided' was acknowledged. The Report is gentle in its observations about the church owners of the majority of the second level schools: reluctance to provide premises is attributed to 'lack of awareness of, or interest in, the needs of the adult community'. What the Report did not record was the fact that the prime motivation of the churches in 1973 was the provision of education for young people. The challenge of adult education was distant for the majority of second-level schools faced with the stark reality of escalating enrolments and inadequate funding under the free education scheme.

An innovative observation in the Murphy Report merits mention: adult education did not need school-based facilities at all times. Outreach learning opportunities might take place 'in the canteens of factories, in homes, in lounge-bars, in libraries, in museums, in the open air, in sport-grounds, in churches, in short almost anywhere' (Report, 1973:45). A few CCSS schools experimented with using outreach facilities for meeting parents in the mid-1970s in an effort to include more adults in the education process. The nuns had come across such a service in the US. By 1977 two CCSS schools had appointed two religious as full-time Outreach Workers to develop educational contacts between school and home: the parallel in 2000 is the system of home school liaison teachers in the Department of Education and Science scheme. Organising adult education was part of the work of the Outreach Workers. By the mid-1980s there were approximately twenty nuns fulfilling that (unpaid) role. In February 2000 the Blessed Sacrament Fathers in Dublin had several hundred applicants for an adult education programme on 'counselling and suicide'. The outreach centre in this instance was their centre-city church. Members of the Murphy Committee had already seen such services in the US in the early 1970s.

Public libraries were 'the best-known but least appreciated adult education resources', according to the Murphy Report. As school and public library systems in Ireland continue to develop in 2000, a suggestion from the Report may be appropriate: the provision of a counselling service for adults within the public library service. It makes sense. An actual (possibly mobile) service within libraries might be supported by an on-line provision.[23]

Perhaps it is understandable that in the 1970s a committee on adult education saw fit to comment on the specific role of the churches. Certainly, the Murphy Report offered an opportunity to the managerial bodies to become much more involved in provision. By the time the Report was finalised the churches had already become members of Aontas, thus indicating their support for 'life-long learning'. What the Report advocated was that the churches would be represented on proposed County Education Committees and Adult Education Advisory Committees. But in fact what emerged was that the representation of the churches on the Adult Education Advisory Committees tended to be diocesan priests, not people who were directly involved in schools - one might suggest therefore that there was a gap. The presence of members of the JMB on the committees might have been more productive because it would have ensured school participation at a national level. The fact stands that the Murphy Report urged the involvement of the churches at every level in the provision of adult education.

One aspect highlighted in the Report was the long-established practice of the churches in adult education among their own members. That was especially true of the religious orders from the mid-1960s when the impact of Vatican II was becoming evident. Murphy correctly included in 'adult education' the growing investment of the religious in the education of their members. The coincidence of the drop in religious vocations meant that the Catholic bodies were slower to widen their vision of adult education to the laity though development did take place. The Report was accurate in identifying the weakness of adult education provision. It was the lack of

> A definite system, framework and organisation within
> which it can function, develop and give satisfaction.

Perhaps that is why the formal 'recommendations' section of the Report dealt entirely with structures. The pity is that readers might tend to focus on that section and ignore the body of the work where the more creative recommendations and those relevant to the voluntary schools are to be found. A role was acknowledged for the voluntary organisations, the schools and especially the new community schools, third level colleges and the various religious adult education agencies. The more important aspects of provision were identified as those pertaining to vocational and economic education, personal development including emotional, artistic, intellectual, remedial, and political in the sense of developing awareness about realising democratic structures and citizenship. Above all, the Report stressed the importance of research and development. As the voluntary sector becomes more involved in adult education and communication in the twenty-first century, the success of the CMCSS and the JMB might be measured by their commitment to the most professional levels of research for development. Without it one may envisage clones of adult education provision in denominational schools that show little vision, creativity or courage. Adult learners and communities deserve more from the managerial bodies that have survived to this millennium.

Focus for Action

As mentioned in Chapter One, the men's section of the CMRS was responsible for the Focus for Action Report. The intention was to develop a plan for 'appropriate action by religious in Ireland in the next six years'. The Report, presented in October 1974, was a systematic presentation that focused on possibilities for the Catholic Church to develop a greater partnership with 'the laity' through 'co-operative action' at parish level and at a more global level. Many religious interpreted it as being more optimistic than the FIRE Report of 1973. Perhaps people simply had time to become accustomed to the factual data presented in FIRE. The Focus for Action Report urged the development of a policy on adult education that was based on acceptance of 'the laity's co-responsibility and role in the mission of the Church in the world'. It was the first occasion on which the major superiors specified ways of using their power as a group to provide a more inclusive educational service. The seventeen members of the working party included four lay people.[24] The 'Focus for Action' was on the Church of the future and the importance of the laity. There was an honest recognition of the danger of alienation and the need to build trust. Most of the seventy-page Report explored ways in which church institutions might contribute to adult and community education: ' Education in the schools and adult education go hand-in-hand' (1974:11.21).

Involvement of parents 'and other adults' was encouraged and the development of summer schools would offer opportunities for collaboration with local communities. Contact with families and work with 'small groups' were ways of supporting adult education. The education of parents and other adults 'in personal growth and in religious and moral development' was to be central in the activities of the religious orders. Religious should be involved in all levels and forms of education and would need to carry our research with local communities to identify needs. The religious orders were urged to

> examine how economic and personnel difficulties might be overcome to make accommodation available for adult education, in service to the wider community (1974:11.26).

Methodology for Lifelong Learning

Awareness of the need for methodology appropriate to adults is evident in the Report. This was emphasised in the knowledge that 'many of those engaged part-time in adult education may be in full-time school teaching during the day'. The danger of treating adult learners like school children was to be avoided. One recommendation was for each religious institute to give responsibility for adult education to one member. This individual should then be sent for 'professional training in techniques, psychology etc. for the education of adults'. The local structure for adult education would include a cluster of part-time educators working with the religious who had been trained. Part of the leader's remit would be to establish a process of regular review of the programmes in conjunction with the adult learners involved. The CMRS would assist by setting up a resource centre and co-ordinating service for religious working in adult education.

A strong feature of the Report in relation to involvement in adult education and 'specialised apostolates' such as counselling, was the need for training of personnel, research with adult communities and co-operation with existing local services. In the late 1960s the Department of Education had introduced counselling in some schools through the provision of two preparatory summer courses for teachers. The Mater Dei Institute also provided a postgraduate diploma throughout the 1970s that was supported by many religious orders. The counselling service to be offered in adult education was seen by the Focus for Action committee 'as an important one, in which activity crosses and recrosses with lay specialists'. There should be 'joint and parallel involvement of both laity and religious' and the most rigorous selection for training was urged.

> Lay and religious counsellors should work together in close harmony, each realising the areas of their own least competence and providing for the other an understanding of a dimension in which the other has less knowledge and expertise. Here too, there should be activity in recruiting and training others to continue the work (11.47).

Duplication of Provision

The adult education envisaged in the Murphy Report included a range of services in local communities. However, duplication and overlapping was to be avoided by a policy of co-operation with existing social services. Initiatives to which religious orders might contribute would include work with 'the lonely, industrial workers, young mothers, married or unmarried, alcoholics, mentally ill, or handicapped, the disabled, drug addicts, youth work, senior citizens'. The role of adult educators in 'new housing areas' presented many opportunities for religious orders and the Report recommended the provision of a citizens' advice bureau where appropriate. An 'Open Door', centrally located possibly in a shopping centre, was also recommended where

> *people can walk in for a chance to talk about anything that is worrying*
> *them, where they will find a sympathetic ear and informed advice on*
> *where or how to get further information* (11.49).

A number of religious congregations might collaborate in providing such a local community service and 'some retired religious (or those approaching retirement) such as nurses, teachers' might be involved. The age structures of the religious indicated that many would be available: in 1973, 32 per cent of the nuns were aged 50 to 59; 28 per cent of the brothers and 27 per cent of priests in the clerical or religious institutes were in the same age bracket. And of course the decline in vocations was ongoing.

The Target

In 2000 it may seem strange to refer to certain aspects of a Report that was presented in 1974, but they are still relevant. Many aspects of Focus for Action are repeated in the Green Paper (1998) and may well figure in the forthcoming White Paper (2000): The importance of research to identify adult education needs and to evaluate provision, learning from pilot schemes, appropriate training, effective methodologies that include appraisal by adult learners, the emphasis on localised provision, the need for co-operation between state and voluntary agencies. None of this is new in 2000, but in 1974 it was visionary. In 1996 *Lifelong Learning for All* (OECD) pointed out that adult education cannot be imposed. Variation will inevitably result from an implementation policy that is informed by consultation, research and review.

The North America Report 1977

Arising from the Focus for Action Report the CMRS commissioned research into models of parent and adult education in the Catholic Church support services in North America. The joint CCSS and CMRS research was conducted over a six-week period in 1976 and the results were published in *The North America Report*, 1977. The objectives of this research were to learn from a variety of approaches to the organisation of adult education and to examine any connections between primary and secondary schools and adult learning opportunities. The CMRS remit was concerned with a range of issues related to future involvement by religious in adult education:

- *training and retraining of personnel*
- *the question of state involvement and the work of voluntary agencies*
- *varying levels and organisational frameworks whether diocesan, parochial, CMRS, managerial organisations or other*
- *day-to-day administration including programme methodologies*
- *possible priority areas for religious personnel* (REPORT, 1977:2).

By 1976 the Catholic Church in America had a sophisticated structure. Lay and religious personnel worked in a variety of adult education centres, religious education diocesan centres, area-based departments of home and school, parish pastoral centres, youth development agencies, Christian life centres some of which included the (North American) Indian and black communities. There were also counselling centres as well as state manpower services. Research was done with all of these groups as well as with people in various curriculum units where inspectors of schools and adult education organisers from the state education ministries worked. The approach taken was to meet those involved at organisational and implementation levels. Research was done in New York, Detroit, Chicago and Boston in the US and in Toronto, Montreal, Quebec and Newfoundland in Canada.

The preamble to the recommendations in the *Report* (1977:28) made a distinction between:

> *long-term and short-term possibilities. It must also be stressed that there is very little known in practical terms about continuing education: neither the voluntary organisations nor state-funded bodies have any clear vision of the direction adult education may take in the next ten years.*

Many of the short-term recommendations related to continuing education for religious and included areas such as spirituality, psychology and personal development, mental health, preparation for retirement, parish and local community development, pastoral care in schools. The need for adult education in the form of 'regular in-service training for teachers' including 'untrained catechists' and 'parent effectiveness' for families connected with the schools was emphasised. The CMRS was asked to 'seek the co-operation of the hierarchy' to stimulate parish development 'in those parishes where nothing has happened'. A priority was

> to encourage religious who have the talent to work with adults in a learning
> situation to co-operate with existing organisations for adult education.

A number of religious at that time were engaged in post-graduate studies in adult education in the US. It was recommended that better use would be made of such expertise in the form of training programmes for those interested in developing skills in working with adult learners. Such training was to be on a regional basis in order to encourage co-operation at local level. It was suggested that each religious order would train 'at least one religious for adult education' in any of the many qualifying courses available in the UK, the US and Canada; it was noted that a diploma course had commenced in Maynooth in October 1976. The IMI was already providing courses for the voluntary school sector. Schools were urged to appoint an outreach worker on a pilot base so that the most helpful model might be identified. The thrust of the recommendations was fully supportive of religious involvement in adult education at school and local community level and in collaboration with other agencies. A research and resource centre funded by the CMRS was to implement a policy of continual evaluation for future development. So what happened in adult education?

Many of the recommendations of *The North America Report* were implemented by the CMRS. Religious personnel were trained for adult education and relevant programmes were designed in conjunction with the IMI. A few religious orders appointed outreach workers who also helped to develop adult education in their schools. Principals and managers were encouraged to invest in in-service for teachers. Over a four-year period, approximately 100 teachers, mostly lay, from voluntary schools attended summer programmes in pastoral care, most of them in the University of Swansea. In 1978 using a 'training of trainers' model the CCSS and CHA organised a summer course in pastoral care. This week-long course took place in Carysfort College of Education and was attended by 500 teachers including a number from community schools. It was perhaps the first recognition that student support services needed to be structured in the voluntary schools where enrolments continued to increase. It was also a sign of the increasingly important role of ASTI members in sustaining denominational education. Most of the tutors on the course were lay teachers.

By 1980 nearly 300 schools in the voluntary sector were involved in some type of adult education, mainly of short duration and for parents rather than the wider local community. This figure does not include the use of school premises by groups or organisations. On two occasions after 1977 the Secretariat of Secondary Schools conducted surveys on the use of school facilities by outside agencies. Usage varied in relation to location, local population and plant facilities. In excess of 60 per cent of schools made some facility available to adult and youth groups though every school did not have a hall. Of 480 voluntary schools in 1981 only 22 had full-time and 30 part-time caretakers. Secondary school premises were used mainly for games including keep fit, concerts and drama, lectures, youth meetings, fund-raising activities, prayer meetings, hosting of competitions and senior citizen functions.[25] Financial charges were not exacted in all cases. However, by the mid-1980s when the cost of insurance was increasing rapidly, many religious orders sought professional advice on the cost implications of hiring out school premises. In spite of costs, numbers of the voluntary schools continued to provide some adult education, often at financial loss. Two orders in the CCSS set up provincial funding to offset such costs.

Lifelong Learning: the Kenny Report

The Commission on Adult Education was appointed on 29 October 1981 by John Boland, Minister for Education. *Lifelong Learning: Report of the Commission on Adult Education* was presented in June 1983 to Gemma Hussey, Minister for Education. Minister Boland had proposed the preparation of a national development plan for adult and continuing education, a plan that is only now, in 2000, expected to emerge.

Under Dr Ivor Kenny (IMI) as chairman, the Commission did useful work on the state of adult education in the early 1980s through the use of two surveys in 1982 and early 1983. This was some fourteen years after the first pupils had entered the free education scheme. The findings showed that

- *older people are less likely than younger people to have stayed on at school, after the compulsory school going age, and*
- *middle class persons have stayed on at school after compulsory school going age to a much greater extent than working class persons* (REPORT, 1983:81).

The data also revealed that 24 per cent of the survey population wanted to pursue further education after school but failed to do so. Some 46 per cent gave financial reasons as the deterrent. The other reasons give some insight into the provision for adult education at the time:

- No suitable course in the area (12 per cent)

- *Lack of appropriate qualifications (10 per cent)*
- *Had to look after dependants (9 per cent)*
- *Family would not allow it (8 per cent)* (REPORT, 1983:83).

The definition of adult education agreed by the Commission was clearly influenced by the Murphy Report (1973), in particular by the desire to include all schools in provision. There is no evidence that members of the Commission had studied the FIRE Report (1973), Focus for Action Report (1974) or *The North America Report* (1977). However, one of the earliest submissions to the Kenny Commission came from the combined Catholic Episcopal Commission on Education, the CMRS and the CMCSS. The submission for 'a national plan for adult education' came in November 1981 prepared by Brother Declan Duffy, General Secretary to the CMCSS. The Kenny Report reflects much of what the bishops and religious orders recommended. The church authorities expressed 'a keen interest' in particular areas, the first being parent education. Four aspects were highlighted in the church submission. Parents needed education in what the school seeks to do with their children.

> *This covers school policy, subjects, options, discipline, sex education, preparation for employment and for life, careers.*

The case was made also for 'home support programmes' including managing conflicts, health, relationships. The provision of second chance education was recommended as a means of meeting needs of individual parents. This would include:

> *Intermediate and Leaving Certificate courses, adult literacy courses, leisure, cultural and social activities ... physical fitness, socialisation needs in large urban areas, development courses and community caring.*

The fourth area of interest to the CMCSS and their partners was community education and community development where 'increasingly in Ireland the school is seen as the focal point' for taking the initiative. The influence of the experience of the religious orders involved in community schools is evident in this section of the submission. A special plea is made for parents in 'newly developing areas' to support them through a national programme of adult education and thus encourage the creation of 'a better environment' for families. The outline programme suggested in the submission is interesting. It included education in

- *how the country and the local community are governed, working in groups, how democracy works, interpreting local needs, leadership in the community, community caring, the people and their parish*
- *religion and how the faith is taught in schools*
- *faith education programmes including biblical studies, moral, social and ethical issues.*

In 1981 the voluntary school sector catered for almost 70 per cent of post-primary pupils. The bishops, CMRS and CMCSS therefore recommended to the Kenny Commission the potential of the resources of the Church for adult and community education. Those resources were buildings, personnel including those with 'a diploma or other qualification in adult education', the fact that many secondary schools 'have unobtrusively been running courses for parents and local people', and 'local knowledge'. The submission suggested that some of those qualified in adult education might become 'the resource person at local level' in the national development plan.

The Secretariat of Secondary Schools had carried out research through the CMCSS on adult education provision and found that two factors militated against greater involvement by the schools: financing and local management structures. On the matter of funding Brother Declan Duffy, General Secretary, pointed out:

> There must be adequate financing for teachers involved in these courses;
> the cost of heating, lighting and caretaking must be adequately covered.

The inequitable treatment of secondary as compared with VEC, comprehensive and community schools was stressed. The 'points and posts problem' was central to any real expansion of adult education courses around a secondary school. The voluntary sector could not avail:

> of the part-time points system to create A and B posts
> for managing local adult education classes.

It would be 2000 before a satisfactory resolution would emerge and the voluntary school sector would have an opportunity to play a role in adult and community education. Until then, involvement would continue to be sporadic and dependent on the good will and ability of principals and boards of management to provide adult programmes. That numbers of voluntary schools did so is a tribute to the vision, persistence and generosity of owners and individuals rather than to any national plan. The Catholic Church submission complained that the voluntary school sector was 'never offered an opportunity to be realistically involved in the structures for adult education which have existed in Ireland until now'. Any development should provide for local and national structures. The first would ensure that each part of the country would be adequately catered for and that the allocated finance was used to meet prioritised needs. At macro level an effective central organisation would direct the planning, financing and research. The Catholic Church wanted representation at both levels and the basis for the request was that they

> represent a very large section of our people, that they have significant
> resources and they would constitute an element of attraction in the
> promotion and development of an adult education plan designed to meet
> our people in their spiritual, human, social, personal, community and
> political development.

The Kenny Commission's definition of adult education was a development of that in the Murphy Report (1973). It also made special mention of the schools.

> *Adult Education includes all systematic learning by adults which contributes to their development as individuals and as members of the community and of society apart from full-time instruction received by persons as part of their uninterrupted initial education and training. It may be formal education which takes place in institutions e.g. training centres, schools, colleges, institutes and universities; or non-formal education, which is any other systematic form of learning, including self-directed learning* (1983:9).

One outcome was the establishment of the Adult Education Boards in 1984 under the VECs and the appointment of the Adult Education Organisers as secretaries to these interim boards (Kenny *Report*, 1983:156). The weakness was the unrepresentative nature of these structures as pointed out by Aontas (1999:26) in its response to the Green Paper (1998). Like the Murphy Report and the submission from the CMCSS, the Kenny Commission stressed the importance of local structures if adult educational needs were to be met. A schedule of implementation was suggested, culminating in legislation to establish a National Council for Adult Education. But the timing was misplaced by the economy. On 5 September 1983 at the opening of an Aontas Conference, Minister for Education Gemma Hussey 'had to give a fairly hard speech about money' (1990:55).

Adult Education on the Move to Lifelong Learning

The publication of the Green Paper on Adult Education in November 1998 represented the first real sign since the Kenny Commission (1983) that a national plan might be developed and implemented. The voluntary school sector had come through the frustrations of trying to maintain involvement in adult education in spite of lack of funding and support structures.

In 1992 the ASTI and the JMB were happy to collaborate in a pilot project in adult education. It was proposed by Aontas with the aim of promoting involvement of secondary schools in lifelong learning. Start-up grants of IR£5,000 were provided by the Department of Education and Science and ASTI provided in-service for the principals and co-ordinators. Schools were advised to adopt a broad definition of what constituted adult education. Each year 20 schools have been funded on a once-off basis. In 1998

IR£100,000 was allocated to provide grants for resources including fees. So, a mechanism had been found to direct some funding to the voluntary schools. The importance was not so much in the amount of money as in the principle that adult education was not the prerogative of the VECs, or of the comprehensive and community schools.

In negotiations arising from the old PCW on adult education structures JMB negotiators have also secured the right of voluntary secondary schools to have access to the establishments of paid posts of responsibility for adult education.

In 1999 an evaluation of 40 of the 80 voluntary schools involved was completed by the Centre for Adult and Community Education at Maynooth. All the schools met their objectives to varying degrees and the start-up grant was important (Evaluation, 1999:6). The highest number of courses offered was sixteen. Target groups were mainly parents (33 schools) and information technology (computers) accounted for 78 per cent of all courses offered. Problems identified were lack of funding and caretaker support.

OECD and Lifelong Learning for All

A meeting of the Education Commission at ministerial level in 1996 resulted in an inspirational report, *Lifelong Learning for All.* The importance of strategic directions points to the need for three conditions if lifelong learning for all is to be attained in any society. A system of lifelong learning cannot be imposed by governments and departments of education. The first need, therefore, is to seek a balance between national aspirations and desirable variations at local and even individual levels. Secondly, the role of government is to monitor and steer developments and to ensure that the distribution of resources support a system that is 'equitable, systematic, flexible and efficient' (OECD, 1996:97). The third necessary condition for lifelong learning is that a government would ensure co-ordination among the various policy sectors including those involved with economic planning and implementation and structural policies.

The history of involvement by CMCSS schools in adult education since the late 1960ss is testament to the view that schools have a role to play in lifelong learning for all. The danger is that undue attention on the adult learner may distract from the needs of primary and second level pupils. Ireland has the 'second lowest levels of literacy in the OECD International Adult Literacy Survey and the third lowest rate of participation in adult education and training (Green Paper, 1998:65). The necessity for responding to adult literacy needs on a national level should not become the focus of the voluntary school system. The findings of the Educational Research Centre (1999) on the literacy and numeracy levels of children leaving the primary school system are a challenge to primary and second level schools. Literacy levels are measurable. The priority in school planning may include the adult population but must detail aims and approaches to improving pupils' literacy levels where necessary. The measure of school effectiveness should not be adult attainment when there are pupils whose educational needs are not being met. Boards of management will need to provide for appropriate research for development in conjunction with school staffs. The need to change the school curriculum from 'near encyclopaedic information on disconnected subjects and items' (1996:100) to what the OECD describes as 'a source of intellectual instruments and strategies for learning' is a priority.

The privately-owned school sector will be a partner in future developments in lifelong learning. Will the voluntary schools simply replicate what is being provided in the other sectors? A national plan where a vision of adult education is informed by transparency in the evaluation of provision will be essential. And the JMB will have a role to play in that future.

Conclusion

The development of the managerial organisations involved in the voluntary secondary schools in Ireland has been charted in the course of this book, and the Conclusion therefore is an attempt to pinpoint their ethos and direction as we move into the new millennium. In summary, it can be said that the context in which these organisations have traditionally functioned included a strong and confident ASTI, a lengthy period of political stability, economic ups and downs, and increased interaction between Ireland and international political developments (Keatinge, 1982:225-38). By the end of the 1950s the ISA, AIH, CHA, CCSS and FCLS were in existence, with the Christian Brothers' Education Committee being a unique representative group. By 1968 however, the pace of educational change had resulted in yet additional organisations: these were the two separate and the Joint Commissions of the bishops and the major superiors, the JMB, the SEC, the TBA and the CMCSS.

It is not surprising, then, that the evolution of the managerial organisations has been marked by multiplicity, and by confusion in role, function, relationship and accountability. However, in 2000, as the result of a convoluted process of development, the CMCSS and the JMB have a clearer identity and vision of denominational education. Their partnership with the ASTI and the Department of Education and Science is tempered by the need to reflect on social policy in a pluralist Ireland and to find appropriate ways of developing the experience of education for pupils and local communities.

In the past, the autonomy of the religious orders affected structural developments among the managerial bodies because it was impossible to identify a leader who could persuade the organisations to take a common stand. That weakness is less obvious in 2000 although the leadership of the CMCSS and the JMB is more moral than mandatory. In 1959 the CCSS thwarted the attempt by John Hughes SJ to establish a united managerial organisation when they refused to work with the lay group. However, the bishops valued the lay Catholic schools and in 1967 insisted that the FCLS be included in the new managerial structures being planned.

The Federation alone among the managerial bodies showed leadership and an understanding of management at that stage, but they were hampered by their lay status. Once the TBA was established in the 1960s it influenced the salary issue, the EPG, the work of Focus for Action, the Report on Religious as Employers, the negotiations on the contracts, and the boards of management. From 1968 the JMB enabled the Catholic managerial bodies to have formal contact with the minority churches in education and in 2000 the JMB is the most representative and powerful of all the organisations, though the CMCSS continues as a distinct Catholic body.

Denominational Education

Before free education the power of the churches in secondary schools was unchallenged. But by the end of the 1960s the secondary schools were no longer the sole means of accessing the university system. Even if religious vocations had never decreased, the voluntary secondary schools would not have been able to meet the demands of free education. The state re-shaped though did not upset the traditional relationship with the churches by introducing comprehensive and community schools. A proof that these 'state' schools could be denominational in character was in the fact that religious orders and the Church of Ireland were willing to become involved. In 2000 there are five 'Protestant' comprehensive schools, and religious are involved in 55 of the 83 community schools. The churches were actively involved in the discussions on legislation in the 1990s and the Education Act, 1998 assured the future of the denominational schools.

Equality of Opportunity

Before the free education scheme the managerial organisations, being products of their time, did not promote an educational vision that encompassed equality of opportunity for all children. The CCSS disapproved of vocational schools but were unwilling to develop technical education in 1959 when encouraged to do so by Archbishop McQuaid. Until the mid-1970s the authorities of the voluntary secondary schools were preoccupied in teaching, administering and managing their schools and failed to articulate a vision of education. Members came to their managerial meetings after school on Saturdays and returned to their work in education. There was nobody with the freedom and mandate to stand back and consider the school system in terms of purpose, organisation and development, in the context of increasing political interest and investment in education.

The FCLS led the way in clarifying their vision but their *Investment in Education in the Republic of Ireland* (March 1962) was not welcomed by Dr Hillery. These lay managers were the first among the managerial bodies to suggest the payment of allowances for principals and a system of posts of responsibility as a means of managing the schools. The Federation was interested in working closely with the other managerial organisations. The CHA was willing, but the reluctance of the CCSS was a problem and delayed collaboration among the managerial bodies. By contrast, the schools under Protestant management could draw on the experience of the Board of Education and the SEC, and in 2000 a united CMCSS and JMB may be at the turning of another road in leadership and management with the emergence of NAPD. The challenge to sustain and develop the vision of denominational education may necessitate structural adjustments in these organisations.

In-School Management

The AIH and the CCSS were activists in curriculum development in their schools but by the end of the 1970s there was a significant gap in curriculum leadership in the majority of the secondary schools. There was an urgent need for heads of subject departments as in Northern Ireland. The system of posts of responsibility should have facilitated such a requirement, but the ASTI refused to allow it under the terms of the Agreed Memorandum in 1972. Moreover, the principals had no training for their roles and failed to create structures for effective delegation except in the area of religious education where the practice after Vatican II was to ensure that a lay teacher was adequately trained to be 'head' of that area of curriculum.

The system of paid posts was a lost opportunity in management and the ASTI failed to appreciate the potential for its members to develop managerial skills by accepting realistic duties. Professor Louden Ryan's conclusion that the posts were not 'managed' is hard to refute and there was no significant improvement until the 1990s when union, managers and the Department of Education worked in partnership on in-school management. The negotiations that lasted almost five years showed a new determination in the JMB to abandon the old system of posts of responsibility, although the issues of supervision and substitution for 'casual absences' remain in 2000 like carbuncles for the principals and boards of management.[1]

Social Policy and Education

If leadership, management and administration are about relationships and connections with sources of power, the CHA was traditionally in a more influential position than the other Catholic managerial bodies. The first full-time official of the CMCSS and the first Director of the Secretariat for Catholic Secondary Schools (1972) was a member and chairman of the CHA. All the bishops involved in education whether members of the Episcopal Commission on Post-Primary Education, the EPG, or the restructured

CMCSS (1968), were former CHA men; and relations were good with the FCLS and generally with the ASTI, many of whose members were past pupils of CHA schools. Recognition and acknowledgement are important in motivation. The bishops trusted the CHA to deal with the CCSS, and the protracted negotiations on the contract of employment, the unresolved issue of the basic salary and the administration of the bishops' religion examination were examples of that trust. The CHA initiated the move to establish the JMB, fully supported by the ISA, but the new organisation was in an uncertain position until the late 1970s because some bishops had reservations about allowing it to represent Catholic education. In the 1980s the CMCSS was determined to include the schools under Protestant management in the new managerial structures and sought legal advice on how to involve the ISA on matters of finance and policy.[2]

The challenge to the CMCSS and the JMB in 2000 is how to involve chairmen of boards of management in more dynamic ways at regional and national level. Membership of school boards gives people an opportunity to contribute to a local community but there is sometimes a fine line between voluntary work and the ability of individuals to devote time to managerial issues. The CMCSS will need to identify, implement and review creative ways of linking with the boards and a key factor may be the extent to which Council and JMB may succeed in promoting discourse on social policy and education. The ASTI/JMB participation in lifelong learning programmes will merit close attention and the role of the boards is crucial.[3]

It is worth noting that none of the 40 schools evaluated by Maynooth in 1999 offered courses in any aspect of religion or spirituality, though one offered a philosophy course. While programmes cannot be imposed, what is of interest to adult learners may give some insight into denominational schools and may therefore be helpful in future planning. The emphasis on lifelong learning is a fundamental shift in educational policy and may therefore deserve the attention of a sub-committee under section 16 of the Articles of Management. Otherwise, a board may run the risk of duplication of services and inappropriate competition with the VECs or other schools.

There is also the possibility that the denominational system could neglect the prime focus of church schools which is the quality of learning and teaching of a particular age cohort. The thrust of lifelong learning should be first of all with the teachers and parents whose energies are directed to enabling pupils to develop, and continual review within whole-school evaluation will ensure that the particular educational philosophy of the patrons is pursued in partnership. Falling enrolments in some schools may provide a different context for lifelong learning and that is an issue of significance for boards of management and trustees.

The Appointment of Lay Principals

The FIRE Report (1973) was the first attempt to evaluate the role of religious in education and it called for trust in the commitment of lay teachers to the Catholic voluntary schools. The subsequent decision of the CMRS and the bishops to pursue boards of management was the impetus for formalising a school 'statement of philosophy' which was a necessary preparation for the Articles of Management. Yet, only one religious order involved the teachers in articulating the educational philosophy.[4] The frequent misuse of temporary and probationary contracts showed that the religious were slow to admit that the involvement of lay teachers was essential to the survival of the 'family business'. Even in 1981 there were religious who wondered if lay principals 'could be in charge of the academic side and a religious in charge of ethos etc. (*sic*)' in the Catholic schools.[5]

However, within two years the CMCSS provided in-service on 'the role of the lay Catholics in our schools'. The evaluation by the participants showed significant levels of disinterest and even resentment and there were some members of the managerial bodies who understood the deep roots of the antipathy. Part of the reservation about lay principals related to making an appointment 'for life'. Religious principals generally served a term and could be removed by a superior if they were unsuited to the post. The reality in 2000 is that the appointment of lay principals has no fixed term and there is need for the CMCSS to work with the Department of Education and Science and the ASTI on humane alternatives to lifelong appointments.

Since 1977 the Secretariat of Secondary Schools has provided initial and continuing training for the principals and attempts were made in the 1990s by a number of orders to finance professional development for lay appointees.[6] The emergence of NAPD as a professional body has implications for the CMCSS and the JMB in relation to such in-service and the research done by Bernadette Kinsella in the Secretariat is relevant. Strangely, a study of the transition from religious to lay principals was never considered, perhaps because the setting up of a board of management and the appointing of a lay principal was a policy decision and therefore involved the major religious superiors as trustees of the schools.[7]

The Role of Research

The CMRS, not the managerial bodies, commissioned the various internal reports of the 1970s in the context of decreasing religious vocations and many positive suggestions emerged including the importance of strategic planning. The major superiors recognised the need for review and evaluation in relation to the future of denominational schools but, like the managerial bodies, they were slow to invest in personnel and money for the kind of research that was needed. When the Secretariat of Catholic Secondary Schools (1972) was established the budget was inadequate although a review carried out in 1978 led to more funding by the schools.[8] The additional finance facilitated research that informed the CMCSS and the JMB in their negotiations with the Department of Education. Membership of the FUE (now IBEC) and the use of professional consultancy services increased in the 1980s and the matters explored to date include legal aspects of posts of responsibility, boards of management, school insurance, the free transport scheme, the use of the school plant, contracts, funding, selection, middle management.[9]

In 1982 the CMRS were preoccupied with clarifying the difference between the CMCSS and the JMB.[10] Yet the major superiors established a new Office of Strategic Planning in January 1987 and within a year the Office was circulating documentation on staff development to schools, thereby duplicating the work of the CMCSS.[11] Similar duplication of activities happened in relation to requests to the Department of Education for funding for voluntary schools in the 1980s but this seeming disarray did not last. Rationalisation of the managerial bodies and clarification of role and function was pursued up to 1987 and the economic recession helped to unite teacher unions, parents and managers, thus enhancing the role of the CMCSS and the JMB. The development of the regional structures progressed in the 1990s and the determination with which the JMB pursued the in-school management negotiations was one indicator of the power of the CMCSS at local and national levels. That clearer sense of role and direction continues in 2000.

Increasing Lay Involvement

From the 1970s the daily managing of the secondary schools became more complex and demanding on the principals as larger enrolments under the successful state scheme of free education required a systemic approach to learning and teaching. By 1989 there were 62,000 young people aged between fifteen and nineteen years at work; it represented a 50 per cent decrease on 1979 (Ryan, 1996) and the majority of those who were not in employment had continued in the education system. In 1971 there were 71 per cent of fifteen year olds in school; ten years later it was 87 per cent, and in 1991 it was almost the full cohort when the OECD (1991) acknowledged that two-thirds of all second level schools in Ireland remained in the control of religious.[12]

The state supported this private system that catered for approximately 62 per cent of pupils, with building grants, capitation payments and teacher salaries. The system had lasted and the managerial bodies earned some of the credit although introducing necessary changes in their schools was less straightforward than making financial investment. From 1972 principals and teachers from CCSS and CHA schools attended pastoral care programmes in England and Wales and they subsequently ran summer schools in Ireland to promote the training of tutors and year heads for the bigger schools. The ASTI ban on 'pastoral care' was more related to trade union opposition to extra work than to professional disagreement with the need for a structural approach, but it was a setback that lasted almost three years. The CCSS introduced selection boards for the appointment of vice-principals in 1974 and this practice was followed for two years before the ASTI banned it in the context of the boards of management being proposed by the CMRS.[13]

The OECD (1991) recognised a growth in the level of 'state intervention' in Irish education since the 1960s and described the relationship between church and state as 'intriguing'. Moreover, 'change is only feasible through discreet negotiations and an unspoken search for consensus' (1991:37-38), perhaps because schools are mainly inward-looking and difficult to influence (Lewin and Riffel, 1997:147-67). The ability of the ASTI to dictate the pace of change was evident in the posts of responsibility system, the contracts, the basic salary, boards of management, pastoral care, home/school contacts, redeployment. However, by 2000 the involvement of the Department of Education and Science and the parents within the legislative framework of education and welfare provides a more level playing field where pupils are central.

The Department of Education and Science

Barrington (1982:89-112) described the Department of Education as 'a passive facilitator of spontaneous educational growth'. Sometimes forgotten is the fact that from the 1970s the civil servants of the Department became more powerful and were able to avoid supporting the managerial bodies in such matters as school inspection, rationalisation, posts of responsibility and the rule that allowed incremental salaries to be paid for an eighteen-hour working week, thereby giving the ASTI an easy means of threatening industrial action. By distancing itself from these issues the Department became increasingly a source of disappointment, annoyance and sometimes frustration to the managerial bodies. The traditional distancing of state and church might be desirable at the level of the bishops and major superiors but where the managers were concerned it had become a weakness.

Inevitably, the union threatened industrial action as a lever in negotiations for pay increases and was successful a number of times including 1980 when the managerial bodies were trying to introduce a productivity clause. The managerial bodies never refused to operate their schools and as a result had very little basis for negotiation with the ASTI or the Department of Education. It suited the Department to collaborate in the redeployment scheme in the 1980s when economic pressure helped to highlight schools with teachers in excess of the quota, though many of these were in vocational and community schools. There was no hope of the Department getting a redeployment scheme across the second level system but the secondary school scheme offered a beginning. When the Articles of Management were finalised in the 1980s, the CMRS and CMCSS included a reference to the role of the Department. It seemed to be an attempt to get the Minister or the Department to resolve a situation where a board of management might become problematic. There was no prior consultation with the Department or the Minister and the reference was an acknowledgement by the owners and managers of the voluntary secondary schools that they were inextricably linked with the Department.[14]

The Department was consistent in retaining the power to 'recognise' organisations as happened with the FCLS and the TBA, while the CCSS was formed at the suggestion of a Department official. At the end of the twentieth century this power was obvious in the process of recognising NAPD. In the past the outsider and even the managers and principals themselves were confused about the roles of the vast number of managerial bodies, but the Department and successive Ministers were always clear about who had power. It was as if they anticipated that stipulation from Bishop Fergus in 1967 that 'policy' belonged to the bishops and 'those other matters' to the managerial organisations. The difficulty for the managers and the CMRS was to separate the two. In 2000 roles are clearer and a healthy tension prevails.

A New Partnership

Traditionally, the focus of the managerial bodies and the CMRS was on the individual school or schools that they owned and not on the entire voluntary system. During the 1970s that focus began to shift because of the drop in vocations and the CMRS were energised into negotiations with the ASTI. The concern was the continuation of denominational and private schooling and the boards of management were believed to be the means to the end. The decision impinged on the managers whose fairly autonomous role was to be changed and, therefore, the collusion between principal and chairman identified in the ASTI survey of the boards in the 1990s may have been inevitable and needs to be borne in mind in the twenty-first century.

In the 1950s the structure and leadership style of the managerial bodies were the outcome of the historic context in which each of them began and subsequently developed. The process of gradual interaction among the organisations as well as with the ASTI and the Department of Education revealed the weaknesses of management and the lack of effective leadership. By 1987 a simpler managerial structure existed to support the voluntary secondary schools. The recognition of the weaknesses of the managerial bodies should not negate their achievements and all the time they were a source of support for individual principals and managers. Learning to lead is a process for the individual and the organisation. Leaders need to know where they seek to go and they must continually review and develop the means of bringing followers closer to the vision that informs the aim. The history of the CMCSS and the JMB is the story of some natural leaders and of many who were not but whose resilience paved the way for the structures that exist in 2000. The future will reveal the ability of the two organisations to pursue the values of denominational education in the context of lifelong learning for learners from all social groups.

Notes to Chapters

NOTES TO CHAPTER 1

1 The nuns owned 276 and the brothers 125 secondary schools; they catered for a total of 76,843 pupils.

2 See Maher *The Tortuous Path* for a detailed account of the events that led up to Ireland's admission into the EEC; the growth of international relations is traced from 1922, the preparation of the Irish application in 1961-1962 and the period of unease that followed are all chronicled in this book

3 The Twentieth General Council of the Catholic Church, known as the First Vatican Council, lasted from 8 December 1869 to 1 September 1870; it is remembered only for one of its two doctrinal constitutions: *Pastor Aeternus* on 18 July 1870 promulgated papal infallibility or the required acceptance by Catholics that the pope was infallible, not subject to human error when he spoke or wrote on matters of faith or morals; the disagreement among the 800 cardinals and bishops on the controversial belief in papal infallibility was ended by Cardinal Cullen, Archbishop of Dublin; he proposed a formula of words that was agreed by almost all the delegates; see Hennesey *The First Council of the Vatican*, 1963.

4 The task was not completed until 1983.

5 The first session lasted until 8 December 1962; a second full session was from 29 September to 4 December 1963; the death of John XXIII interrupted the council; Pope Paul VI was elected on 21 June 1963 and the work of the various commissions of the council resumed on 14 September.

6 Most Reverend John Charles McQuaid who was Archbishop of Dublin from 1940 to 1971 and who will be mentioned elsewhere in this book, was wont to quote this encyclical letter in support of his forbidding (*sic*) Catholics to attend non-Catholic schools or to pursue third level education in Trinity College Dublin.

7 The first 'Mass in the vernacular' (English) was celebrated in a CHA school, the Franciscans' Gormanstown College on 7 March 1965; the celebrant was Cardinal Conway.

8 There is inexplicable inevitability in the fact that the successor to Pope Paul VI was John Paul I who had been Patriarch Archbishop of Venice; a complete contrast to the more serious Paul VI, he was good-humoured and unassuming and died after one month in office; rumours of an untimely death followed but died down on the election of a non-

Italian, a Polish Pope John Paul II in 1978 at a time when one-fifth of the world was Catholic; drama followed him too, with a visit to Ireland in September 1979, an assassination attempt in 1981, the collapse of Communism and a policy of travel to all parts of the world, including Israel in March 2000, the first pope to do so in 35 years.

9 *Apostolicam Actuositatem* 18 November 1965; *Ad Gentes Divinitus* 7 December 1965; *Gaudium et Spes*, 7 December 1965.

10 Reverend Cecil McGarry, SJ, Rector of the Jesuit House of Studies at Milltown Park, Dublin, in a series of talks to the Religious Sisters of Charity, Mount St. Anne's, Milltown, Dublin, 1965-1966.

11 Cardinal John D'Alton had died in February 1963; Conway who had been his Auxiliary Bishop and at 45 years of age the youngest member of the Hierarchy, was appointed Archbishop of Armagh on 14 September 1963 and Cardinal in January 1964; a former lecturer and vice president in 1957 at Maynooth, he had worked in Rome and had an acute sense of the political system of the church; see Cooney, *John Charles McQuaid*, 1999:362.

12 He was appointed Cardinal on 13 June 1979.

13 A former philosophy professor at Queen's University, Belfast, and adviser to Cardinal Conway at the Second Vatican Council, Cahal Daly became Bishop of Ardagh and Clonmacnoise in 1968 where he remained until he was appointed Archbishop of Armagh on 16 June 1990; he became Cardinal on 28 June 1991.

14 The 1983 code of Canon Law presents the various canons on Catholic education under a separate heading, Title III; there are 29 relevant Canons and 793-806 relate to schools; by definition a Catholic school is one that is under the control of the bishop or operates with his consent; to use the term 'Catholic' it is essential to have the approval of the local bishop (Canon 803); accordingly, the right of the Church 'to establish and to direct schools for any field of study or of any kind and grade' (Canon 800) may be exercised through religious orders who provide education with the prior consent of the bishop (Canon 801); otherwise, the onus is on the bishop 'to ensure that such schools are established' (Canon 802).

15 The author recognises the fact that it was very rare for voluntary secondary schools to receive financial assistance from diocesan funds; in some situations a school chaplain was appointed by the local bishop; more often, parish clergy fulfilled that role; shortage of priests from the mid-eighties made

such appointments difficult; the bishops were already providing 'priest teachers', effectively chaplains, to the vocational schools.

[16] Records were in fact kept; Brother Declan Duffy, FMS, Provincial superior of the Marist Brothers, chairman of the CMRS Education Commission, a former headmaster, from 1970 a strong protagonist of religious participation in the community schools, and the first major superior to make a commitment to the new state schools, becoming chairman and trustee of the Tallaght Community School, one of the first two such schools in Dublin in 1972; Brother Declan was appointed general secretary of the CMCSS and the JMB in 1977 where he served until his retirement in 1996; the author is indebted to him and to a Christian Brother, A.P.Caomhánach for information on the workings of the EPG.

[17] The history of the founding of the Religious Sisters of Charity (often inaccurately called the 'Irish Sisters') by Mother Mary Aikenhead in 1815 is an example of such an order; she had to assert her autonomy as superior general and foundress with a number of bishops: the bishop of Cork in particular wanted to make the order subject to him as local ordinary or bishop, an event which would have stifled future development by the foundress who wanted to spread beyond Ireland.

[18] Officially this French-based order was the Congregatio Sanctus Spiritus (CSSp).

[19] Archbishop Dermot Ryan, former Professor of Semitic Languages at University College Dublin, had a sister in the Loreto order; named successor to Dr McQuaid in Dublin on 29 December 1971 he was installed on 13 February 1972; he declared his impatience with nuns who put an emphasis on 'teaching the poor': in a public address to nuns in the Mater Dei Institute of Religious Education, Dublin, 21 September 1972, he reminded his audience that 'the well-heeled also have *souls*'.

[20] See A. Sheppard, '60 years on', in *St. Conleth's College: 60 Years Revisited*, 1999:2-3; the school now has 300 students including a co-educational senior cycle; Ann Sheppard, daughter of the founder is Principal of the college.

[21] In May 1998 Mr Cannon the son of the founder announced the closure of the school in 1999 due to declining pupil enrolments; see P. Cannon, 'Denominational education in the Republic of Ireland', in *World Yearbook of Education*, 1966:330.
[22] At present the INTO has more than 20,000 members, the ASTI more than 16,000; the TUI has approximately 11,000 members, including 25 per cent at third level (Logan, 1999:238-9).

[23] In 1986 he succeeded Dr Fergus as Bishop of Achonry; he had unsuccessfully sought membership of ASTI before founding APPTI.

[24] Increasing enrolments in post-primary schools give some indication of the changing face of education within three years: from 148,000 in 1966 to 185,000 the following year, and 239,000 in 1968-1969.

[25] Strike action in 1969, when the union refused to assist in the public examinations, undoubtedly strengthened and encouraged membership.

[26] This was 98.5 per cent of all lay teachers in the secondary schools according to ASTI records of membership.

[27] See Education Commission Conference of Religious of Ireland. *The Trusteeship of Catholic Voluntary Secondary Schools: a handbook for the leaders of congregations*. Dublin: CORI, January 1996:viii; in 1992-1993 it was also estimated that more than 36 per cent of the religious working in secondary schools were within ten years of compulsory retirement and only 6 per cent were aged under 35.

[28] This Association published a pamphlet in 1904, *Secondary Education in Ireland: a plea for reform*, urging security of tenure and a proper registration system for teachers so as to encourage 'well-educated people' to join the profession; the Association merged with the Association of Secondary Teachers Ireland when it was founded in 1909.

[29] The immediate aims of the ASTI were to secure a system of registration of secondary teachers, a minimum salary with regular increases, security of tenure, pension rights; membership was open to all lay teachers; Chief Secretary Augustine Birrell had tried unsuccessfully in 1912 and more successfully in 1914 to improve teachers' conditions: he gave an annual government grant of £40,000 for lay teachers' salaries - the first direct Treasury grant for intermediate education according to Coolahan 1981; Birrell also paved the way for the establishment of the teachers' registration council which was finally agreed in 1916 although not operative until 31st July 1918: the outcome was the requirement for a teacher to have a university degree, a training diploma and a probationary year; see McElligott, 1966; see also Riordan 'The Association of Secondary Teachers Ireland, 1909-1968: some aspects of its growth and development' (MEd thesis).

[30] In Canon Law the term 'nun' is confined to enclosed religious women; the term 'sister' or 'religious' is used for all other women religious; however custom and practice in Ireland even amongst religious uses the term 'nun' for all religious women.

31 The first strike for improvement in teachers' salaries took place in May 1920; it was an expression of the frustration of the eleven year struggle by the ASTI; for a detailed study of the ASTI struggle see Collins, 'A Study of Some Aspects of the Status of organised Teachers within the Education System', unpublished MEd thesis.

32 Professor Corcoran, a Jesuit priest, professor of education, Education Department, University College, Dublin, a champion of Catholic education in a submission to Lord Justice Molony who chaired the Vice-Regal Committee, 1918, *Report of the Vice-Regal Committee on the conditions of Service and Remuneration of Teachers in Intermediate Schools and the Distribution of Grants from the Public Funds for Intermediate Education in Ireland*, cmd.66, H.C. 1919:41-42.

33 Church here means the Catholic Church authorities; the Church of Ireland bishops were favourable to the 1919 bill.

34 Capitation payments provided approximately 50 per cent of what trained teachers would have earned; the Christian Brothers and the Religious Sisters of Charity remained with the capitation system until the early 1960s; one advantage was the freedom to have untrained teachers; this meant that positions could be kept for a religious who might be in training college for three years; it also allowed religious to work in classrooms before attending college.

35 Exceptions were mathematics and art although a five per cent bonus was given to mathematics.

36 In 1929 University College Galway was designated as a university where a range of courses would be provided through the medium of Irish.

37 The majority of the secondary tops were in the girls' schools and in poorer areas; in 1956-1957 there were 87 with 6,081 pupils; see CCSS. Memo for discussion with members and with ASTI, dated 1962.

38 See chapter six of this book; the secondary schools did not become interested in adult education until 1970.

39 In 1930 when the Vocational Education Act was enacted the then Minister for Education, John Marcus O'Sullivan assured them that the new schools would not provide general education.

40 CCSS. Report of annual general meeting, 1960:32-35; the visitor was Professor Eoin Mac Tiarnáin who had spent a year in Ireland studying the education system.

41 Professor Ó Catháin, SJ wrote a series of articles in *Studies*, 1955-1957; Dr Peter Birch was professor of education at Maymooth at the same time; in his address to the annual general meeting of the CCSS, 25 June 1957 he told the nuns: 'as Irish schools are organised at present the Church has almost complete direction of secondary education'; he too was encouraging discourse about the inadequate system; as Bishop of Ossory, Dr Birch initiated the Catholic Social Services there; in 1962 and 1963 in conversations with the author, his impatience with the continuing involvement of so many religious orders in mainstream education was made clear; he advocated a radical change of direction by religious towards models of local and community based education.

42 It is probably true that the interaction of the JMB and the CMRS with Dr Don Thornhill who was Secretary in the 1990s has been important for the voluntary sector at a time when issues of funding and legislation were being worked out.

43 See John Harris, 'The policy-making role of the Department of Education', in Mulcahy and O'Sullivan. *Irish Educational Policy*, 1989:7-26 for the insights of a ministerial adviser (to Gemma Hussey) on influences on policy.

44 Literally, they were imbued with the Minister for Education's thinking. So, they could only guarantee a certain protection for the traditions and role of the Catholic Church; see Bonel-Elliott 'La politique de l'enseignement du second degré en république d'Irlande, 1963-1993' (PhD thesis) 1994:615.

45 Dr Hillery was Minister for Industry and Commerce from 1965-1966, Minister for Labour until 1969, worked in Foreign Affairs until 1972 when he was elected vice-president of the European Commission, a post he filled from 1973-1976; in that year he was elected President of Ireland and remained in office until he retired in 1990.

46 Bonel-Elliott, in 'Lessons from the sixties: reviewing Dr Hillery's educational reform', 1994; and PhD thesis, 1994.
47 Ibid.

48 Address to a Fianna Fáil meeting, 16 March 1965 just two days before he had dissolved the Dáil; his party was returned on 7 April with 72 seats which was half the total number of seats; the support of two Independents ensured Lemass a working majority; see Randles, 1975:173.

[49] Twenty of Jack Lynch's 33 years in the Dáil were in power; he died on 20 October 1999; the former leader of the opposition, Liam Cosgrave likened Lynch to Daniel O'Connell; Lynch was the bridge to the new Ireland of Europe and beyond, filling as he did the role of first leader of the post Independence generation.

[50] The author acknowledges former chief inspector Seán Mac Cárthaigh for this information supplied in 1998.

[51] Lemass (1891-1971) was born in Dublin, a founder member of Fianna Fáil, an experienced minister in industry and commerce, in supplies during the Emergency of 1939-1945, and *Taoiseach* 1959-1966 when he retired in November; his son-in-law, former *Taoiseach* Charles J. Haughey described Lemass as 'a man who had a sense of the fitness of things' and 'took Ireland by the scruff of the neck and set it on a new path' of economic prosperity; trade union leader Jim Larkin acknowledged that Lemass was 'very pragmatic' but 'had no vision': *RTÉ*, 25 March 2000.

[52] The members of the Duggan Committee were Dr M. Duggan, chairman, T. Ó Floinn, L. Ó Maolchatha, M. Ó Súilleabháin and Dr Finbarr Ó Ceallacháin who acted as secretary.

[53] The official title of the report was 'Tuarascáil Shealadach ón choiste a cuireadh i mbun scrúdú a dhéanamh ar oideachas iarbhunscoile', 1962.

[54] This has been confirmed to the author by Brother Adrian McGrath of the Christian Brothers' Provincial Council, 12 May 1998, and by Brother Declan Duffy, FMS, former General Secretary of the Secretariat of Secondary Schools, member of the EPG and a personal friend of Cardinal Conway's, 9 February 1998.

[55] In an article 'Education in the USA', in *Studies*, Spring, 1960:60-73, Dr Ó Raifeartaigh had written about a policy of anti-discrimination on social grounds; he was known to the author as a man with a keen social conscience and for that reason found Dr Hillery exciting to work for as Minister.

[56] Barber's research at that time showed that only nine of the 26 centres where community schools had been planned in 1970 had been provided with state schools; the remaining 16 continued to be served by two or three schools, the pattern being a nuns' school, a brothers' school and a vocational school.

[57] Bonel-Elliott. PhD thesis, 1994:312.

[58] CCSS. Minutes of meetings, 1964 and 1966.

[59] From the introduction of vocational education in 1930 there had been a number of priests on local VECs; one of the most vocal of these in the sixties was Canon McCarthy of the Elphin Diocese, subsequently parish priest of Sts Peter and Paul's Parish, Athlone in County Westmeath where he was also a member of the VEC; in 1963 he was president of the Irish Vocational Educational Committee (later Association); he voiced some opposition to Dr Hillery's comprehensive school plan but it was short-lived, giving rise to the rumour that his bishop had admonished him; in the 1970s Canon McCarthy was a frequent spokesman on primary education as the issue of boards of management unfolded.

[60] In 1998 agreement was reached on teacher representation on the comprehensive school boards of management.

[61] It is true however that the Minister had consulted Cardinal Conway.

[62] The five Protestant comprehensives as they were called were Raphoe in Donegal, 1971, Mount Temple and Newpark in Dublin in 1972, Ashton in Cork in 1972 and East Glendalough in Wicklow in 1987.

[63] It had taken six years to deliver and an additional two years before a translation into Irish was ready so that the report could be published; see Hyland and Milne 1992:198.

[64] *Dáil Reports*, vol. 216, col.955ff.

[65] The author who was then teaching a 'scholarship class' as the senior class in the primary school was often called, can remember the delight of principal and teachers at the ministerial announcement.

[66] The *Report* (1966) was presented under four headings, manpower, participation, curricula and use of resources; there were huge shortages of qualified workers at the time; aspects identified in the *Report* were considerable drop out rates especially from vocational education and the potential for drop out in the transition from primary to post-primary and before sitting the Intermediate or the Group Certificate examinations; participation rates revealed a very disturbing distinction between social classes and education; a lot of unqualified teachers of mathematics and science were in the system; curriculum was limited, little emphasis on continental languages and over emphasis on Latin; an imbalance in the pupil teacher ration in national schools was inevitable with the existence of so many small schools.

[67] In 1963 Dr Hillery as Minister for Education had already highlighted the need for state subsidised 'transport services' to the new comprehensive schools: pupils would have to pay 'a flat rate of so much per day' - Press statement, 20 May 1963; *Investment in Education* December 1965 also envisaged a limited subsidised school transport service - Hyland and Milne 1992:255-56; see also Randles, 1975:229, 247-48, 268-71; Hyland and Milne, 1992: 260-63.

[68] Bonel-Elliott. PhD thesis, 1994:380.

[69] CCSS. Minutes of meetings, November 1966 and January 1967; it is useful to note that the number of small national schools fell from 3,194 to 1,168 between 1962 and 1979 as a direct result of rationalisation; see Coolahan, 1981:169.

[70] *Dáil Reports*, 1966, vol.223, col.2152-56 and 2409.

[71] CCSS. Notes of meetings, October 1966; it is clear from the notes that some principals and managers had forgotten that it was Dr Hillery who had introduced the Common Intermediate Certificate programme three years earlier in the context of the comprehensive schools; see Press Conference 20 May 1963.

[72] Fine Gael *Policy for a Just Society* no. 3 *Education* 28 November 1966; a young Declan Costello and Garret FitzGerald are credited with the document.

[73] CCSS. Minutes, 1966; also Randles, 1975:238-42.

[74] Introduced as an optional examination at the end of sixth standard, in June 1929 the Primary Certificate examination covered Irish, English, mathematics, history, geography, needlework for girls; De Valéra as Minister for Education in the forties wanted the examination to be compulsory and from 1943 it became so; however, only three subjects were then examined: Irish, English and arithmetic until October 1967 when it was abolished; it was agreed with the INTO that a report and report card would replace it.

[75] In practice these examinations have continued, though in a decreasing number of schools; the author ascertained in 1998 that at least sixty schools in the Dublin area and twenty in Cork continued to hold 'entrance examinations'; however the schools contacted have stated that these examinations are to assist in placing pupils in suitable classes and not to exclude on the basis of academic performance.

[76] This was the introduction of the programme known as *Buntús Gaeilge* where the emphasis was on the communicative approach in language teaching and learning.

[77] The Minister's intention was that this change would commence in 1967; disagreement with the teacher unions and managers delayed the introduction; however from 1969 the change applied to both the Intermediate and Leaving Certificate Examinations.

[78] The Higher Education Authority was given a statutory basis in 1971 the same year as the National College of Art and Design was provided with a legislative framework that included teacher in-service.

[79] Possibly the best known case study was in Boyle where the local priest, school manager and member of the CHA, Canon Dodd became a focus of concern among the managerial organisations for his ready acceptance of common enrolment; the CHA and the CCSS feared that this 'local arrangement' might be more widely imposed.

[80] The union had developed a strategy by then and on 2 December 1974 prevented common enrolment in Cobh and Thurles; see ASTI. *Annual Convention*, 1975:25-27.

[81] The strike and related issues will be examined in chapter three of this book.

[82] This author was one of the small group of primary teachers involved in this pilot stage with the inspectorate of the Department of Education; *Curaclam na Bunscoile*, or the New Curriculum was published in two volumes in 1971 when it was introduced to all primary schools; it remained the primary school curriculum until the 1999-2000 school year when the NCCA began the process of introducing a revised programme published in twenty-three books.

[83] Under the terms of the School Attendance Act, 1926 (Extension of Application) Order, 1972, Statutory Instrument no.105 of 1972, that became operative from 1 July 1972 a young person must attend school from age six years and may only leave school at the end of the term in which the fifteenth birthday occurs; under the Irish Constitution there is provision for parents to provide alternative education; in 2000 the school leaving age is to be raised to sixteen or on the completion of three years of the junior cycle.

[84] It is interesting that Brother Declan Duffy who became General Secretary to the CMCSS and JMB in 1977 played a key role with the bishops, INTO and Department of Education in negotiating boards for the primary schools in 1975.

[85] Randles, 1975:314-15; see also Report of the Committee on the form and function of the Intermediate Certificate Examination *Final Report* (ICE) 1975.

[86] Since 1996 they are called Education Centres; in 2000 there are twenty with full-time directors, a further ten part-time; all have a central role in teacher in-service for curriculum development and evaluation.

[87] See chapter three for details of Mr Burke's interaction with the managerial bodies and the secondary schools.

[88] See chapter six on Adult Education as Lifelong Learning.

[89] CCSS. Records of activities, 1968-1971.

[90] The author recalls formation in religious life in the early sixties when the idea that 'planting cabbages upside down' could be an acceptable command under religious obedience; it is not recorded that any major superior ever requested such an act of 'blind obedience', but it gives some sense of prevailing attitudes before the effects of Vatican II were experienced in religious orders.
[91] See chapter four for a discussion on the basic salary and related issues.

[92] Secretariat of Secondary Schools to the Members of the Irish Hierarchy, 21 April 1978; it was drafted by Brother Declan Duffy, then General Secretary and member of the CMRS Education Commission and of the Joint Commission; the details were worked out in conjunction with Dr McKiernan, Bishop of Kilmore who from the late 1970s to the enactment of the *Education Act*, 1998, was deeply involved in policy developments for the church in education.

[93] The author was a member of a group who advised John Wilson when the Fianna Fáil election manifesto of 1977 was being prepared; it was at a meeting in a businessman's house in Lucan that the idea of an advisory curriculum council was discussed in 1979; *An Br Ó Súilleabháin*, Professor of Education at Maynooth and *An Br Eamonn Ó Beacháin* were also part of the group.

[94] CCSS. Notes of meeting with members of CHA, 1984 and 1985; the NPC held its inaugural meeting on 8 June 1985.

[95] In her *Cabinet Diaries*, 1982-1987, Gemma Hussey describes her first impression of meeting Liam Lane, Secretary of the Department, and the assistant secretaries: 'they seemed to me to be a group of rather elderly men, all with impenetrable Irish names' (1990:19).

[96] Kevin McNamara was then Archbishop; the fact that the cabinet decision on the closure was leaked did not help matters for the Minister.

[97] John Boland was Minister from 30 June 1981 to 9 March 1982; he had two special advisers, Gerry Cronin, acting CEO of the County Dublin VEC and Dr John Harris whom Mrs Hussey was to appoint.

[98] For her personal account of what happened see Hussey, *At the Cutting Edge: Cabinet Diaries 1981-1987*.

[99] The author was the vice-chairman of the CEB with chairman Dr Edward Walsh then President of the National Institute of Higher Education at Limerick, later to become the University of Limerick.

[100] *Department of Education,* 11 May 1984; *Department of Labour,* 11 October 1988; Doyle, 1990:19-32.

[101] CHA. Minutes, May and July 1985.

[102] CCSS. Notes of meetings, 1986 and 1987; the author was aware of similar concerns in the CHA, communicated to her as Education Adviser to the Archbishop of Dublin.

[103] The GCE, now called the General Certificate of Secondary Education (GCSE) is available in 2000 in three schools under Protestant management; Marymount Secondary School at Harold's Cross in Dublin where the author was principal until the closure in 1977, was in the free scheme and prepared senior pupils for the GCE.

[104] It is difficult not to record 1984 as a something of benchmark in public morality in Ireland; the year that Mary Manning, an employee in Dunne's Stores in Henry Street Dublin refused to handle South African goods; there were 3,026 abortions recorded in England on women with Irish addresses; on 19 September a committee of medical doctors at Calvary in Galway secretly signed an agreement at Bishop Eamon Casey's instigation, that no sterilisation operations for contraception purposes would be carried out in the hospital; the 'Kerry Babies' scandal was revealed on 14 April; in October 1984 a 5% rise in support of Catholics

for divorce since 1974, was recorded; the next year, 1985 legislation made it possible for adults (over 18 years) to get contraceptives in chemists, family planning clinics, health centres etc.: the Family Planning Act was passed on a vote of 83:80; in 1986 the Catholic bishops opposed any change in the ban on divorce; in 1987 the High Court banned the abortion referendum and SPUC won their injunction to prevent Trinity College students' union from providing information on abortion.

[105] See chapter six on Adult Education as Lifelong Learning.

[106] CCSS. Minutes of meetings, 1981 to 1986.

[107] See NCCA. *A Guide to the Junior Certificate, 1989; The Junior Certificate Examination: Recommendations to the Minister*, published January 1990, for details of the assessment proposals; and *The Curriculum at Junior Cycle: Curriculum Framework and Junior Cycle Requirements: a position paper*, June 1991; and *The Curriculum at Senior Cycle: Structure, Format and Programmes: a position paper*, June 1991; Mary O'Rourke also established the National Council for Vocational Awards on 29 October 1991 to structure modular courses and to develop forms of assessment for those not in mainstream education.

[108] Before the introduction of free education Archbishop McQuaid had tried to persuade the CCSS that 'some secondary schools should prepare pupils' for the Group Certificate Examination so as to enable them to become apprentices; strangely, there was very little discussion on the matter; CCSS file, Archbishop's House to M. Jordana OP, President, 28 February 1961.

[109] On 28 October 1987 a response by Mary O'Rourke, Minister for Education to parliamentary question no. 252 revealed some uncertainty regarding the exact payment by religious orders and the VEC; the VEC contribution would be paid indirectly by the State; the Minister indicated that the payment was 'not more than five per cent'; the author has ascertained that the maximum is two per cent; by 1987 religious in nineteen of the thirty-one schools had paid their five per cent of the local or trustee financial contribution, two other religious trustees were in the process of making theirs and ten more were to follow.

[110] Alvey (1991:49) makes the point that in a *Guide to Dublin Schools, 1989–'90*, only two schools advertised that parents and teachers played a role in management; Marian College Ballsbridge and Christian Brothers' College, a fee-charging school in Monkstown, were the schools.

[111] The Act clearly links parents with their school and not with the NPC as such; however, section VI,25 (4b) states: 'where a parents' association is affiliated to a national association of parents, the rules .... shall be in accordance with guidelines issued by that national association of parents with the concurrence of the Minister'.

[112] It should be borne in mind that until 1958 when Jack Lynch as Minister for Education lifted the ban, women had to leave their teaching posts (and civil service) on marriage.

[113] From the 1970s when religious orders sought to rationalise their involvement in schools, efforts were made to persuade the bishops to take over as trustees; in a very few situations that has happened to date; generally, the bishops were unwilling to get involved; the work of CORI since 1995 therefore, has researched alternative forms of trusteeship; a number of orders will benefit and Catholic education will continue as a result.

[114] Until Vatican II the orders of religious women had two 'social groups' within their membership; girls and women who entered these orders were put into one or other group depending on family background and education; the Mercy, Presentation, Loreto and others referred to such a group as 'the lay sisters'; the Religious Sisters of Charity used the term 'second degree sisters'; both phrases referred to women whose vocation was to do manual or domestic work as nuns; in the case of the Religious Sisters of Charity the majority made four vows: in addition to the usual three of poverty, chastity and obedience there was 'a vow of service to the poor'; the 'second degree sisters' were not permitted to make the fourth vow; domestic work (cooking, cleaning) in convents and schools was done by these lay sisters; it was only as numbers dropped that lay help was engaged; in the years after Vatican II the religious orders began the painful process of a more inclusive approach to membership with the objective of ending any form of discrimination.

[115] The author acknowledges that NAPD has neither a managerial nor a negotiation role; neither is it currently a trade union; it is a professional Association; but it is not always easy to separate managerial issues of policy from those who are charged with implementation in the daily running of the schools.

NOTES TO CHAPTER 2

[1] See Maurice Hime. *The Efficiency of Irish Schools*, Dublin: 1889; *An Apology for the Intermediate*, Dublin: McGee, 1899.

[2] Professor Corcoran, a Jesuit priest and a champion of Catholic education; his statement was part of a submission to Lord Justice Molony who chaired the Vice-Regal Committee on the conditions of service and remuneration of teachers in Intermediate Schools, 1918.

[3] Irish Schoolmasters' Association. Review of Agreed Memorandum on Posts of Responsibility, 18 January 1978.

[4] AIH. First Report, 1882.

[5] Much of this information may be found in the publications of the *Journal of Proceedings of the General Synod of the Church of Ireland*.

[6] JP of CI, 1959:195-96; in June 1999 Bishop Hodson School closed due to lack of enrolments.

[7] *The Irish Times*, 12 November 1970; 8 and 10 February 1971; 13 and 14 October 1971; 11 December 1971; 31 January 1972; 3 February 1972; Murphy, 1980.

[8] Report of the Advisory Committee on Secondary Education in the Republic of Ireland, 1965:18-22.

[9] Bishop Perdue served the diocese from 1957 to 1978; he died in New Zealand, aged eighty-seven years in August 1998.

[10] *JP of CI*, 1965:140-61; 1966:86-7.

[11] The author is not applying current standards of research and evaluation retrospectively; for an insightful reflection see Thomas Kelleghan, 'The interface of research, evaluation and policy in Irish education', in Mulcahy and O'Sullivan, 1989:191-218.

[12] The CMRS is now called the Conference of Religious of Ireland (CORI). The author will use either title as the context of the time dictates.

[13] These reports will be considered in later chapters of this book.

[14] CHA. Files, 1978.

[15] In later years the submission of the CHA to the Commission on Higher Education, 1961 also bore this out.

[16] As late as 1980 the average number of hours taught by the secondary schools principals was six hours; see chapter four of this book.

[17] Established in 1950 the Council reported on the primary system in 1954 and on the post-primary in 1960 but the report was published in 1962; see Randles, 1975:89-98; Coolahan, 1981:45-54, 80-1.

[18] Recommendations of Catholic Headmasters' Association to the Commission on Higher Education, 3 May 1961.

[19] CHA. Minutes, 28 April 1965.

[20] CHA. Extraordinary General Meeting, 28 November 1968; the resolution was unanimously passed.

[21] The success of these negotiations was due largely to McQuaid's ability: see Cooney, *op cit*, and CHA Minutes, 19 October 1939.

[22] CCSS. Notes: a subsequent law case in the Wexford circuit court where the State challenged parents for not sending their child to the certified junior school was won by the State; later appealed to the High Court where the decision was reversed in favour of the parents.

[23] *The Irish Times*, 4 and 6 April 1998; *Sunday Business Post*, 12 April 1998; *RTÉ1, John Charles McQuaid: What the Papers Say*, 9 and 16 April 1998; Cooney (1999:90-2) in the account of the chairman's success in getting the schools including the CCSS to boycott *The Irish Times* also illustrates the leadership role of the CHA at the time.

[24] Conversations with the author, 1974.

[25] Memorandum from chairman to CHA members, dated 11 October 1968 in which he refers to a meeting in September with Seán O'Connor, Assistant Secretary of the Department of Education.

[26] CHA. Regional reports, confidential to members of the CHA, 'management and control', 1973.

[27] CHA Reports: these were compiled by Reverend Thomas Finnegan, headmaster of Summerhill in Sligo who became Bishop of Achonry in 1986.

[28] *Mulloy vs. Minister for Education*, (1975) I.R. 88; the priest, Father Frank Mulloy was a member of the Holy Ghost Congregation and subsequently vice-principal of Templeogue College, Dublin.

[29] CCSS. Notes: In-service in pastoral care.

[30] CCSS. Files, proposed agenda item 6 for meeting of headmistresses, 1929.

[31] Circular letter, 26 March 1929, par.3.

[32] In fact in 1878 the O'Conor Don who was one of the Catholic Commissioners on the Board which administered the Intermediate Education (Ireland) Act had suggested that the heads of the convent schools should come together just as the headmasters did but there is no evidence to suggest this happened.

[33] Seven Ursulines came from Cork, Thurles, Waterford and Sligo; the St. Louis nuns came from Carrick-on-Shannon, Monaghan and Rathmines in Dublin; the five Dominicans travelled from Cabra in Dublin.

[34] CCSS. Minutes, 17 May 1929 when Rev. Fr Cullen the Vincentian priest was chairman.

[35] CCSS. Address of presiding chairman.

[36] The first President of the CCSS was Sr M. Reginald Lyons OP from Cabra Dominican Convent; she remained as President until 1942; there were eighty-four member schools in the first year of the Conference; see first recorded minutes of the 'Conference of Convent Secondary Schools Ireland', Friday and Saturday 17-18 May 1929.

[37] CCSS. J.J. Doyle, CM, Strawberry Hill to Mother M. Imelda OP Cabra; he referred also to the forthcoming celebrations for Catholic Emancipation in September 1929 when the training college would host a garden party.

[38] Since 1996 Sr Patricia Rogers, formerly President of the CCSS, presently a member of CORI, was elected chairman of the Northern Ireland Association of Grammar Schools which now includes the nuns' schools; it would be the parallel association to the JMB and has a high profile with the Library Boards which administer the education system in the north.

[39] CCSS. Report of annual general meeting, 1935; the relevant insurance act had been passed since 1930 but it looks as if the schools were only getting involved some years later; the nuns noted that for a payment of 3s. which would be about fifteen pence in 1998 per hundred pupils, a maximum indemnity of £300 was guaranteed for any one accident.

[40] CCSS. Accounts of discussions between the ASTI and CHA and between CHA and the Christian Brothers and then by the CCSS, 1937.

[41] 'The stop-gap profession', in *Cork University Record*, 1949:21-3; see also Coolahan, 1984: 157-58.

[42] CCSS. Discussions at various annual general meetings, 1948-1955.

[43] CCSS. Minutes, 18 June 1937.

[44] CCSS. Annual Report, 1937.

[45] Ibid. Annual general meetings, 1935-1937.

[46] CCSS. Report of the Commission, 1945; this was an internal report.

[47] Jubilee allocution of His Holiness, Pope Pius XII to the CCSS on the occasion of the silver jubilee, 1954.

[48] CCSS. Annual general meeting, 25 June 1952 where Moylan was quoting de Valéra's words to students at a preparatory college.

[49] CCSS. Address of the Minister for Education to the annual general meeting, June 1958.

[50] Lynch told the nuns that he was 'weary' on the doorsteps in the course of his campaign in Cork, of hearing 'the woman of the house' tell him that she did not know what way she would vote and that she 'left all that to himself': in other words, the image was one where married women voted as their husbands advised.

[51] CCSS. Notes of discussions on subjects, curriculum and education for girls 1949, 1953.

[52] CCSS. Committee on Education, 1943, 1947, 1951.

[53] More than thirty years later this was recommended by the *ICE Report* (1975).

[54] CCSS. One address at the annual general meeting, 1939 given by a male cleric spoke of 'this evil, the boy-friend'; see also annual general meeting addresses, 1-2 July 1942 and 1 July 1949.

[55] Ibid. Minutes of meetings, 1941-1943.

[56] CCSS. Correspondence, 1946.

[57] Ibid. Annual Report, 1948.

58 Ibid. Minutes and notes of discussions on courses, 1943-1947.

59 Ibid. address of the President of Strawberry Hill Teacher Training College, London and subsequent discussions, annual general meeting, 1951: 36-7.

60 The Council of Education was set up by the Minister for Education in 1950 to advise him on all matters pertaining to the role of the state in education; of the 28 members on the council five were women though none of them was a member of a religious order; the report was published in 1962.

61 The occasion was a celebration in the Clementine Boarding School, Rome, when Pope Pius XII addressed teachers and pupils.

62 Pope Pius XII, 14 September 1958, address to the Office of International Education, Rome Congress.

63 CCSS. 17 October 1955.

64 CCSS. Annual report, 1954.

65 CCSS. Notes of discussions at meetings, 1951-1960; report, 1960:8.

66 Ibid. 1958:10; Most Reverend Dr Fergus, Bishop of Achonry to the CCSS, October 1957.

67 CCSS. Report of the work of standing committee, 1959-1960:5-21; M. Jordana OP succeeded Mother Enda OP; she was an energetic Dominican and member of the standing committee.

68 CCSS to CHA, 3 May 1961.

69 The author is deliberately omitting the FCLS schools in an effort to focus on the CCSS at this stage.

70 CCSS. Annual Report, 1960:7.

71 Pius XII, 'Education and Modern Environment', an address to religious in education.

72 CCSS to the Taoiseach, 21 November 1957.

73 CCSS. Records of apostolic works, 1960:YODL.

74 Report of meeting of major religious superiors of women with Pope Pius XII in Rome, 1956, given by the superior general of the Religious Sisters of Charity, Milltown in Dublin, October 1958; the practice by women's orders of spending money earned or donated only on 'the works' was widespread and affected primary schools too: as a student in Carysfort Training College, 1962-1964 the author met many student nuns who had been waiting for up to ten years to attend the training college: this was not because they were inadequate students but because they had to wait in line in convents where there were so many young nuns that there was never sufficient money to pay for their training; this was particularly true of the Mercy sisters from country areas where they were organised on a diocesan basis; the advantage of these more mature students was that they had received 'training' from their seniors and had become very competent by the time they got their turn to attend the teacher training college.

75 As early as 1933 and 1934 a lay woman was invited to lecture on social work activities; the newly founded Legion of Mary was strongly supported by the nuns as worthy of promotion among their pupils because the founder was an Irish man, Frank Duff, and because it reflected the teaching of the Church.

76 In 1973 Marymount Secondary School in Harold's Cross in Dublin, owned by the Religious Sisters of Charity set a precedent for other CCSS schools by establishing a specialist room and facilities for the teaching of religion; it was an effort to accord equal status with science and other areas of curriculum.

77 The senior certificate of the Shannon Curriculum Development Unit was an alternative to the Leaving Certificate in the eighties; it relied heavily on CCSS schools.

78 The Irish Times, 31 January 1984: Ann Lovett, a pupil at the Mercy Secondary School, Granard died alone in a field having given birth to a child; RTÉ1, 7 February 1984; Sunday Independent, 5 July 1998.

79 JMB. Notes of discussions with the Health Education Bureau, 1985-1987.

80 Nothing could have been further from the truth; the author was one of those principals involved in training teachers in pastoral care and in the work of the Health Education Bureau; in fairness to Eugene O'Donoghue who directed the Bureau, there was no conspiracy to undermine Catholic education or to promote a 'value free' system for students.

81 CCSS. Annual general meeting, 1947; notes of discussions at meetings, March 1950.

82 Ibid. Notes of discussions, 1950, 1952.

[83] Ibid. Notes of discussions at meetings, 1951-1958.

[84] The protracted situation in Sligo was one such instance where the CEO, the vocational schools, the Marist convent schools and the Religious Sisters of Charity in particular experienced difficulties.

[85] Unofficially Rosary College, Crumlin in Dublin had run the vocational preparation programme from 1979; the Department of Education admitted the voluntary schools into the scheme in 1981.

[86] See chapter six.

[87] Doyle, 'Staff development as empowering and enabling', 1998:156-67.

[88] One such course was run over three successive summers in St. Anne's Convent at Milltown in Dublin to provide domestic science teachers for a variety of secondary schools and secondary tops run by the Religious Sisters of Charity: Religious Sisters of Charity, archives, 1956-1966.

[89] For the majority of the principals, handling the intricacies of the posts would always be associated with Sr Eileen Randles, a Loreto nun and experienced school principal and manager; she was involved in the Appeal Board, in the many reviews of the Agreed Memorandum and was ever available to all the managerial bodies to clarify issues.

[90] See chapter three.

[91] CCSS. Annual general meeting, 21-23 June 1983; the principal speaker was a Christian Brother, S.V.Ó Súilleabháin, Professor of Education at Maynooth.

[92] Ibid. Annual general meetings, motions, 1980-1984.

[93] In 2000 the issue of unsupervised classes remains unresolved; the JMB threatened to withdraw co-operation with the Department of Education in a range of areas unless the necessary funding is made available to resolve the issue; a joint letter from the JMB, IVEA and ACS to the Department demanded action: see *The Irish Times*, 10 March 2000.

NOTES TO CHAPTER 3

1 However the writer is aware from senior officials that inquiries were made in the 1950s and 1960s about individual teachers who sought to establish schools.

2 Their story was not unlike that of some of the religious schools as was pointed out in their presentation to the National Education Convention (1993): see chapter five of this book.

3 Federation of Irish Secondary Schools, *Investment in Education in the Republic of Ireland*, published by the Federation, March 1962, Table 17:27 cites the earlier capitation payments.

4 This phrase was often used by the chairman of the CHA and subsequently of the JMB in relation to negotiations about funding.

5 The first Apprenticeship Act in 1931 gave the Minister for Industry and Commerce power to designate a trade in a location that might then become a training place for that trade; the scheme depended on close collaboration between employers and workers; from 1935 the Department of Education set trade examinations but the weakness of the Act was that it did not oblige employers to train workers so there was potential for exploitation; see Ó Catháin, 'The first thirty years', in *Studies* December 1951:20-21 for a critique of the Act; The new legislation was passed on 15 December 1959; *An Cheard Chomhairle* or the National Apprenticeship Board was set up from 1960 with authority to decide minimum age of entry and educational requirements for trainees; the Board was to work with the VECs and could insist that employers released workers for training.

6 See chapter one where the author refers to the communication from Archbishop McQuaid to the CCSS President urging that 'some secondary schools *should* prepare pupils' for the Group Certificate Examination; his involvement in the first Catholic Social Services in Dublin made him aware of the connection between education and poverty, hence his request.

7 CCSS. Minutes of meetings, February, March and May 1959.

8 Dr James Fergus, Bishop of Achonry, Secretary to the Hierarchy, to the CHA, 29 June 1960; CHA Minutes, October 1959; on three earlier occasions in 1932, 1934 and 1938 the ASTI had tried to get CCSS agreement to establish an Advisory Council of Education: CCSS file on ASTI.

9 The meeting with the Minister was reported at the annual general meeting of the CCSS, June 1963.

10 The CCSS in their submission to the Council of Education (1963:22) had rejected the idea of secondary education for all because of the fear that it would lead to a lowering of educational standards; see also Minutes, June 1963.

11 JMB. File; the letter is written to John Hughes SJ, as 'headmaster' not in his capacity within the CHA and is all the more insightful for that.

12 Ibid. Files: correspondence September 1965 - March 1967.

13 Minute Book of the Schoolmasters' Association, 1964; Archbishop McQuaid encouraged the new JMB and shrewdly avoided critics of the inter-church group by insisting that as Archbishop he could whom he chose to 'afternoon tea': thus, the early JMB meetings were 'afternoon tea' gatherings.

14 Interview with Brother Declan Duffy, former General Secretary, April 1997.

15 *Constitution*, article 1 of the United Nations' Educational, Scientific and Cultural Organisation, founded as an off-shoot of the United Nations in 1946.

16 Dr James Fergus to John Hughes SJ, 26 June 1965.

17 Interviews with Brother Welsh, July 1977.

18 TBA. History and organisation; TBA to CHA, 10 October 1967.

19 Interview with Brother E.L. Gilmore, Christian Brother, member of the provincial council of St. Helen's province, May 1974.

20 Interview with Brother E.L. Gilmore and Brother Welsh, May 1974.

21 The author was assured that they knew about the interview between John Hughes SJ, Canon Mooney from the CHA and Dr Hillery; further evidence is available in the Memorandum presented to the Hierarchy by the Catholic Managerial Committee, 18 March 1967 and prepared by John Hughes, SJ.

22 CHA. Files, Catholic Managerial Consultative Committee, February 1966.

[23] Ibid. File, reference to meeting between the Episcopal Commission for Post-Primary Education and Mr Colley, 3 February 1966.

[24] Eight commissions were appointed to advise the bishops on the implementation of the teachings of Vatican II; two dealt with education as mentioned.

[25] TBA. Memorandum presented to An Taoiseach and An tAire Oideachais on points arising from the proposed scheme for free post-primary education, as presented to Dáil Éireann on 30 November 1966.

[26] The three officials were Seán MacGearailt who had been asked by the Minister to contact 'the TBA' on 8 December 1966 to arrange the meeting for the following day, Dr T. Ó Raifeartaigh and Seán O'Connor.

[27] TBA. Notes and memorandum of meeting with Minister, Donogh O'Malley, Friday 4.15 p.m. 9 December 1966.

[28] O'Connor was speaking on Education Forum, RTÉ1, 9 October 1986 and admitted that he was wrong in 1966 when he tried to dissuade O'Malley from proceeding.

[29] Catholic Managerial Committee. John Hughes SJ to the Hierarchy, 18 March 1967.

[30] Ibid. 1967:5.

[31] CHA. Account of the Meeting of the Managerial Associations with the Minister for Education, 16 December 1966; Letter, Reverend John Hughes SJ, to Dr Michael Mooney, Honorary Secretary, CHA, 20 December 1966; TBA Memorandum on the Free Books Scheme to the Department of Education, 12 April 1967; the brother was Reverend Brother Creed of the northern province.

[32] Since 1924 the Church of Ireland had been making provision for free transport; by 1933 there were some thirty-two van-schemes in operation: JP of CI, 1933:236; 1934:223; 1935:226; 1936:230; 1959:120; 1960:117.

[33] CHA. Memorandum from the Catholic Managerial Committee to the Episcopal Commission for Post-primary Education, 16 December 1966; notes of meeting 16 February 1967.

[34] Randles (1975:265-68) quotes the controversial letter from John Hughes, SJ, 24 February 1967 to the Minister; CCSS records do not enlighten further.

[35] Interview with Brother Michael Murray, provincial councillor, 1 May 1998: Oatlands College in Dublin and Christian Brothers' College in Cork were two schools of the southern province that would remain outside the scheme in 1967; a lot of publicised pressure developed in relation to Oatlands; the brothers had reason to believe that the pressure was 'orchestrated' from within the Department of Education.

[36] A detailed presentation of the scheme is not relevant in this book and may be found elsewhere; see Atkinson, 1969; Randles, 1975; Akenson, 1975; Coolahan, 1981; O'Connor, 1986; Ó Buachalla, 1988.

[37] JP of CI, 1967:92-93.

[38] Interview with An Br A.P.Caomhánach, May 1974.

[39] There was a huge burden on the brothers in terms of energy and time to provide buildings and facilities to cater for the additional pupils. A huge amount of time had to be given to raising money in addition to the meetings and planning sessions that were part of it all.

[40] Interviews with An Br A.P. Caomhánach, 1974, Br E.L. Gilmore, 1977, Dr M. Murray, 1997.

[41] In spite of the preponderance of brothers in the CMRS, the constitution required that only a priest could be chairman or president; in the early 1970s when Cecil McGarry SJ was transferred to Rome and a successor was needed as chairman of the CMRS, the Marist Provincial, Brother Declan Duffy was the suggested candidate because of his involvement in education which was high on the major superiors' agenda at that time; but he was not a priest; Dr Brendan Comiskey was then appointed.

[42] Interview with Dr M. Murray, August 1998.

[43] CHA. Dr Henry Murphy to John Hughes, SJ 21 June 1967.

[44] CCSS. Files, the bishops were Dr Fergus of Achonry, Dr Hanley of Elphin, Dr Ahern of Clones and Dr Murphy of Limerick.

[45] CHA. Notes of meetings of Special Committee, 29 August 1969.

[46] CCSS. John Hughes SJ, to Mother Fidelma, secretary to the new CMCSS, 3 October 1967.

47 There appear to have been five meetings.

48 The assistance of Seán MacCárthaigh, former Senior Inspector and member of the Development Branch who retired in 1988 and who had been present at the 'crisis meeting', is acknowledged.

49 CCSS. Notes of meetings, November 1968,

50 *JP of CI*, 1965:140.

51 CCSS. Minutes, December 1968.

52 CMCSS. Files, 1969-1972.

53 CMCSS. Annual reports 1969, 1970, 1971, 1972.

54 For its first three years the Secretariat was located in Veritas House in Dublin; it then moved to Milltown Park where it was beside the CMRS Secretariat; the need for additional space and facilities resulted in the move to its present location in Emmet House, Clonskeagh.

55 He was Eoin McCarthy who subsequently became a member of the working party on the FIRE Report (1973) and consultant to the Focus for Action Report(1974); his service to the CMCSS was voluntary.

56 CMCSS. Points made by Eoin McCarthy, 13 May 1972; see also Harris, 'The policy-making role of the Department of Education,' in Mulcahy and O'Sullivan, 1989:7-13.

57 Eoin McCarthy to CMCSS, 1972.

58 CCSS. Address of the Minister for Education to the annual general meeting, 26 June 1974.

59 Ibid.

60 Brother Declan Duffy remained as General Secretary until 1996; in an interview with the author he said that his post was not reviewed after the initial five years.

61 Founded in 1954, two years later the FCLS had 40 schools and 3,188 pupils; they had few ASTI members according to *Official Programme*, 1956:65-68; the union met representatives of the Federation on 1 December 1956.

62 ASTI to CHA, 18 November 1965.

63 According to Coolahan (1984:325) the union revived the contract issue in December 1966; the evidence is unclear.

64 ASTI. Files on dismissals; the author who acknowledges union access to all files, was given pause for thought in the face of the many incidents of 'dismissals'; some were stories of individual human misery.

65 The ASTI secured this agreement on 4 June 1966; CHA. Records, 1966.

66 ASTI. Minutes of Standing Committee, 24 June 1966; the TBA quarterly meeting took place on 25 June.

67 ASTI. Minutes of Convention, 1971, 1972, 1973.

68 Coolahan (1984) notes that as early as 1947 the union asked the CHA, the Christian Brothers and the CCSS to establish 'a negotiating body'.

69 CHA. Memorandum from chairman re. September meeting in Department of Education, dated 11 October 1968.

70 Interviews with Sr Patricia Rogers, CCSS and Liam Murphy, CHA members of the negotiating team, September 1999 and February 2000; the response of the union negotiators to the criticism that they had acted unilaterally was one of laughter: both they and the managers were aware of the position in schools where teachers were not teaching 26 or even 22 hours; both parties were alert to the fundamental issue that the Department required only 18 hours for salary purposes.

71 Interview with the author, 20 February 2000.

72 CMRS Education Commission to CMCSS, 12 September 1977.

73 See Glendenning (1999:359-45) for a full consideration of the unusual position in relation to teachers in voluntary schools in Ireland.

74 Brendan Comiskey, Secretary General CMRS to CMCSS, 27 September 1977: the managerial body was asked to pursue the matter with auditors and to get 'the best advice' on a system that would enable the CMCSS to gather facts about the funding of their schools.

75 Of 313 replies to the General Secretary's survey more than 50 per cent of premises were regularly available to outside groups; this data was communicated to the Department of Education on 21 December 1981.

[76] CCSS. Address to the annual general meeting, 20 June 1980; Dr Comiskey was appointed Bishop of Ferns in 1984; *Irish Independent*, 21 June 1980.

[77] Secretary General, CMRS on behalf of the Joint Commissions to CCSS, 20 November 1980.

[78] Interview with Sr Patricia Rogers, former treasurer, president and then member of the CCSS executive, June 1997.

[79] CCSS. Minutes 1981-1985; annual general meeting, 20-22 June 1984.

[80] Ibid. Annual general meetings, 1984 - 1987.

[81] The dismissal was subsequently upheld by Mr Justice Costello in the High Court in 1995: see *The Irish Times*, 9 February 1985; also Walshe. *A New Partnership in Education*, 1999:199-200.

[82] CCSS Minutes, 1929, 1961-1966, 1976; Reports, 1966:77; 1976:1.

[83] At the suggestion of the CCSS standing committee a separate organisation was founded *for* them in 1949.

[84] CCSS. Minutes of discussion regarding membership, November 1978.

[85] Ibid. Minutes, February 1981.

[86] CMRS. Meeting of Conference Education Assembly, 14-16 February 1985.

[87] CCSS. Notes of proposal, 1986; the nuns believed that this new Association could form the basis for both the CMCSS and the JMB to develop new structures.

[88] CCSS. Final annual general meeting, 23-25 June 1987; the organisation dissolved on Thursday 24 June; the Minister for Education, Mary O'Rourke, the Secretary, Declan Brennan attended.

[89] According to Liam Murphy, CHA, these matters were resolved by inviting past members of the CCSS executive.

[90] The Associationn of Vice-Principals of the voluntary schools was founded by Brian Cannon, as vice-principal in the Mercy Secondary School in Coolock; he is currently principal of Malahide Community School; the Association welcomed the principals to various seminars in the 1980s and Cannon was alert to the importance of a team approach by the two most senior posts in the schools; eventually by the end of the 1990s NAPD became the umbrella organisation into which the earlier Association moved.

[91] In 1993 Ray Kennedy, a former ASTI president, established an association for principals; by 1998 principals and vice-principals of all post-primary schools collaborated in the establishing of NAPD; funding was secured from Minister Micheál Martin and a levy from the schools; in 1999 a secretariat was set up and Mary McGlynn, principal of Mt. Anville, appointed Director; in 2000 the SSPAI continues to function.

[92] The contract of employment had stipulated 26 hours; the ASTI unilaterally reduced it to 22 hours in 1972; the Christian Brothers' separate contract retained 26 hours though in practice their teachers did not teach more than 22 hours.

[93] Sr Patricia Rogers to author, 13 March 2000.

[94] JMB. Notes, 1980; it is worth noting the teaser presented to the managers by the two professionals who asked the JMB 'to quantify the work of a teacher'.

[95] ASTI to JMB, 2 May 1980; effectively since 1974 parent teacher meetings had ceased in most schools because managers were unable to pay the £6.50 per hour demanded by the union; at their Convention the rate was increased to £15 per hour; the ban was to take effect from September 1980; see O'Flaherty, 1992.

[96] JMB to Michael Harrington, barrister and insurance consultant, 10 September 1982.

[97] Secretariat of Secondary Schools to FUE (IBEC since 1992), January 1982; membership cost £2,500 for the year and it opened up opportunities for attending courses on managerial issues; see chapter six of this book.

[98] Secretariat of Secondary Schools. Submission to the Department of Education on the National Parents' Council from the Council of Managers of Catholic Secondary Schools, December 1982.

[99] Other grants were subsequently withdrawn though incremental salaries continue to be paid; the ASTI supported the fee-charging schools at the time; the block grant negotiated by the SEC when free education was introduced was in contrast with the situation experienced by the Catholic voluntary schools in 1986; in 1999 the possibility of taking legal action was explored; see *The Irish Times*, 24 December 1999.

[100] An undated internal survey by Brother Declan Duffy, General Secretary suggested that membership of the ASTI by principals would be 'extremely difficult' and that future years might need to bring a separate union as in the UK; the author has ascertained from Brother Declan that the survey was in the late 1980s.

[101] It is interesting to note that in 1980 the secondary principals were teaching an average of six hours each week in addition to their administrative duties; this was partly because of the shortfall between pupil teacher ratio, the length of the school week and the 22 hour teaching week for teachers; see JMB Submission to the Review Body on Teachers' Salaries, 1980.

[102] Since the 1970s there had been continual communication between bishops, CMRS and the General Secretary of the CMCSS; a number of bishops contributed to this including Dr Fergus, Bishop Mulligan and in particular Bishop McKiernan; the 'CMCSS knew where they stood' and knew 'what the bishops would buy' were comments of two managerial representatives at the time.

[103] The establishment of boards of management in the schools under Protestant management is an example where the uniqueness of each of the minority churches is important; perhaps the most interesting example is that of Newtown in Waterford, a school of the Society of Friends; their approach is to achieve consensus and elections are not part of their traditional way of doing things.

[104] In addition to the Cardinal the core group included Bishop James McKiernan of Kilmore, Archbishop Ryan, Fr Cornelius Sayers, Education Advisor to the Archbishop of Dublin, Brother Declan Duffy, FMS, An Br A.P. Caomhánach; described as 'people who were united' they consulted with 'informed individuals from Northern Ireland and Ireland on issues including boards of management.

[105] Conversations with Mother Colmcille, SSL, Superior General of the St. Louis Sisters, and leader of the women's section of the CMRS, 1974-1977.

[106] CCSS. Undated items in files, possibly 1973 or 1974; these contain references to publications about home school interaction and some excerpts from the Advisory Council's report; one reference in the context of study methods subsequently quoted at a CCSS meeting is noted: 'The home and the school bear joint responsibility for a child's development. What happens to him in either place affects his total behaviour' (D'Evelyn, 1963; Welford, 1962).

[107] CCSS. Notes of meetings, 1981.

[108] In 1987 when the new CMCSS and JMB developed, it was agreed that 'old surviving organisations', specifically the CHA and the TBA could not give any information regarding CMCSS to members; the structure for communication, as agreed, was the AMCSS regions.

[109] Secretariat of Secondary Schools. *Manual on Procedures*, 1987:4.

[110] *Ibid.* 1987; 1988; 1993.

NOTES TO CHAPTER 4

[1] From 1951 to 1956 the emigration rate was three times as high as in the pre-war years; some 200,000 who emigrated included many small farmers, thus contributing to the depopulation of the west of Ireland; in the 1960s, before free education, when the author was teaching in a co-educational school in the west, more than half the fathers of the 220 students had emigrated to England in the 1950s; one impact was that most students helped the mothers with work on the small holdings before and after school.

[2] Ken Whitaker's work as secretary in the Department of Finance was a frank acknowledgement that protectionism had failed; by the 1950s 95% of Irish exports were to the UK, the same as in 1922; see BBC2, *Seven Ages: the story of the Irish State*, 25 March 2000.

[3] 1957 was also the year when the Common Market was set up by the Treaty of Rome.

[4] ASTI. *Official Programme*, 1956:45-54.

[5] Mr T.K.Liston, SC, chaired the arbitration council which sat from 12-23 September 1956; all teachers were to begin with £286 for married men to a maximum of £760; ladies and single men would commence at £218 to a maximum of £560; the honours degree allowance awarded was £48 and the increases were to operate from 1 August 1965; see ASTI. *The School and College Year Book*, 1958:89-92.

[6] CHA. Minutes, 6 May 1959; Fr Gaffney and Paul Andrews SJ were nominated to represent the CHA on the teachers' panel of the Conciliation Council.

[7] CCSS. Notes of meetings, 1955-1959.

[8] ASTI. President's address to members, 31 October 1959; Miss Nora Kelleher, MA, the speaker, was the second female to be a president of the union.

[9] CHA. Memo 46, undated but probably October 1962: Canon Mooney, St Jarlath's College, Tuam; for a detailed account from the ASTI reports to their annual conventions on this matter see Coolahan, (1984: 148-60).

[10] CCSS. Report of meeting, 1946:51-55; the Minister and three officials from the Department met the CCSS president, Secretary and two members of the Standing Committee at Dominican College, Eccles Street, Dublin in May 1946; he had already met the ASTI.

[11] CHA. Mooney to Hughes SJ, May 1951.

[12] The first occasion was referred to in chapter two and involved only CCSS schools; CHA to all members 11 August 1955.

[13] It is interesting to note that the value of the pound of 1955 in 1998 was £16.06; inflation in 1955 was less than 3 per cent; the author acknowledges the assistance of Ms Mary Smyth of the Department of Economic Analysis at the Central Bank, Ireland.

[14] CCSS. Correspondence, 1952-1954; Reverend Donal Cregan CM, who was a member of the CHA and would later be appointed President of St. Patrick's Training College in Dublin, gathered the information with the assistance of the three Catholic managerial bodies.

[15] Miss McDonagh served through 25 years the 27 presidents and varying committees of the ASTI; during her time, two presidents served two terms each (Coolahan, 1984:395-6); an MA of UCG, she was known to the author for 27 years until her death in 1997; her exceptional memory combined with professional integrity often proved a double edged sword in dealing with union and managers.

[16] There are copious records of these ASTI visits; in some CCSS schools the manager professed ignorance of the amount of the basic salary or was unaware that other 'local' convent schools were paying a higher basic salary than she gave; according to the CCSS records there was very little discussion of the basic payment until 1960: the attitude was that each superior would decide for her school.

[17] Large numbers of teaching religious did not necessarily mean equal numbers of incremental salaries; in the 1950s when efforts were made to get statistical information, the CCSS records suggest that less than half the nuns were in fact registered teachers.

[18] Department of Education to CHA, 2 March 1959; CHA. File, 4 May 1959; the letter came through the Minister's private secretary; Minutes of annual general meeting, 18 October 1961; CHA to ASTI, 23 October 1961.

[19] Most Rev. Dr Fergus, Joint Secretary to the Irish Hierarchy to CHA, 14 October 1961 and read at the annual general meeting of the CHA, 23 October 1961.

20 CHA. Resolution passed 18 October 1961.

21 CHA. Private letter from Dr Fergus to John Hughes SJ, October 1961.

22 Ibid. Report from John Hughes SJ, Chairman, on salary negotiations, 1960-1964, for circulation to all members before Special Meeting to be held 5 February 1964:par.1.

23 CHA. Files, 1960-1962; 1963.

24 CHA to the Standing Committee of the Hierarchy, March 1963.

25 Dr Fergus to John Hughes SJ for the attention of the CHA, April 1963.

26 CHA. Minutes, October 1963; Notes on files 1963 and 1964; one CHA memo states that the halving of the ASTI's original 25% was suggested by Brother Moynihan of the Christian Brothers; this fact is mentioned again in a note on a CHA file in 1969, the year when the final basic payment of £400 was agreed.

27 Sr Genevieve, OP to John Hughes SJ, 3 February 1964; CHA. Minutes, 8 April 1964; John Hughes SJ to Dr Fergus, undated: the author believes the letter was written in March or April 1964.

28 The ASTI records include letters of complaint throughout the 1960s from some teachers in Christian Brother schools; the cause of complaint was that some teachers were handed 'an envelope' by the manager and others got none; this bonus was recognition of long service or good teaching.

29 Since both the formal acknowledgement of Cardinal Conway and his personal note are dated 14 November 1964 the author accepts that John Hughes' letter may have been sent after April; however, since the Cardinal was in Rome for some time that year it is possible that the letter awaited his response for some time.

30 A certain sympathy is evident in ASTI records about these schools; the union told the Ryan Tribunal on 24 February 1968 that 'some of the lay Catholic secondary schools and smaller Protestant schools are not in a position to pay much in excess of the basic £200'; the union was aware that many of these schools were boarding and the majority of teachers were also remunerated for fulfilling duties after school.

31 In May 1963 despite Professor Patrick Lynch's clarification of twelve queries from the CHA about the questionnaire from the Investment in Education team, the headmasters consulted the bishops about the wisdom of responding; a rapid affirmative came on 3 July 1963 and the managers were to take care that 'only salaries actually paid to religious and priests would be included under the heading of salaries ... not salaries which would be paid if these posts were staffed by lay people': Canon Mooney to CHA.

32 Dr Joseph Dowdall, OSB, Glenstal, President, CMRS to John Hughes SJ, 27 January 1964; the Conference was only in existence in Ireland since 1960 and the nuns group did not form until 1966.

33 Cathal O'Gara and Daniel Buckley, Joint Honorary Secretaries, ASTI to An Rúnaí, Department of Education, 17 December 1957.

34 Many families experienced a sense of hopelessness during the 1950s in Ireland; living was beset with anxiety about money, jobs and food; jobs in industry had grown by 12,300 between 1946 and 1951 but that growth was cancelled by industrial job losses from 1951 to 1958; the Suez crisis and petrol rationing in 1956 was also a year of unusually bad weather and a strike in the building trade; problems with the IRA in Northern Ireland led to internment in 1957.

35 The author acknowledges information given by Brother E.L.Gilmore of the Christian Brothers' St. Helen's Province in 1977; see also CCSS. Correspondence with schools, 1958.

36 Louden Ryan was a director of the Central Bank until 1978; he was first chairman of the National Prices Commission and in the 1970s chaired the Commission of Inquiry into the *Garda Síochána*; from 1983 he was a member of the Court of the Bank of Ireland where he became a Governor from 1985-1991 when he retired.

37 In interviews with the author in 1997 and 1998, Louden Ryan quoted the advice given him by Louis M. Fitzgerald: 'No matter what you decide, don't given them the reasons'; according to Ryan, 'O'Malley was influenced by Charlie McCarthy (VTA), Dan NcAuley (FUE), Jim Larkin, John Convery, Donal Nevin and Ruairí Roberts, all with ITGWU and ICTU connections'.

38 The managers were represented by John Hughes SJ for CHA, Mother Jordana for CCSS, Brother Welsh for the Christian Brothers, Mrs S. Morgan, AIH and Rev. G. Miles for the ISA.

[39] Interviews with the author 1997.

[40] Ibid.

[41] Interviews with the author 1998.

[42] Ibid.

[43] The CCSS traditionally insisted on two years; the CHA had one year until the mid-1950s when the nuns persuaded them to extend it; the Christian Brothers had always used one year as probation.

[44] ASTI to CHA, 18 June 1965; the union argued that 'from a physical, mental and nervous point of view, teaching involves a good deal of strain, more so now than ever before because of the prevailing climate of opinion, the earlier (and sometimes precocious) maturity of pupils and the larger classes'; the union referred to Northern Ireland where the Ministry 'prescribes 200 days and allows ten days at the school manager's discretion which means a teaching year of 190 days'; throughout 1965 the ASTI pursued the CHA on the matter until the managers wrote on 20 October 'that the public image of the Secondary Branch of the Teaching Profession might suffer considerably if it were known that the members were seeking either a shorter work week or a shorter work year'.

[45] Louden Ryan told the author that the union had 'weakened rather than strengthened their submission by having it presented by what seemed to be a badly briefed counsel; the union team was D. Ó Broiméil, Dan Buckley, An Seanadóir D. Ó Conalláin, Cathal O'Gara, R. Barr, BL and Máire McDonagh; it was 'a classic example of the circus where they couldn't get a ringmaster'; it was also evident to Ryan that the ASTI 'couldn't make up its mind whether it was a professional association or a union'.

[46] Ibid. Ryan was unimpressed by the managerial input with the exception of the FCLS who seemed to have thought through issues of management more than the others.

[47] Dáil Report, cited in ASTI. Secondary Teacher, vol.4 no.8, February 1970:14-15 and 17.

[48] Louden Ryan was asked to reconsider the recommendations relating to posts of responsibility when the INTO and VTA called their series of strikes; the election overtook further development.

[49] Louden Ryan in an interview with the author, believed that the involvement of the managerial

bodies in the talks to settle the strike might have resulted in a better deal about the posts of responsibility; by the time the strike was settled, the Labour Court and then ICTU and the FUE had played their parts in bringing the three teacher unions together.

[50] ASTI. Secondary Teacher, November 1970:3-7.

[51] Years of such leap-frogging in the public sector may be coming to a close: in February 2000 a Bench Marking Review Body was established to seek ways of linking changes in work practices and pay to workers in the private sector; a report is due by October 2002 - The Irish Times, 8 February 2000.

[52] ASTI. Secondary Teacher, November 1970:14.

[53] Secretariat of Secondary Schools. 'Thoughts on the Agreed Memorandum', June 1989.

[54] CCSS. Guidebook for Principals, June 1977:29.

[55] Even in 1980 a survey by the JMB revealed that secondary principals were teaching an average of six hours weekly; see JMB submission in advance of the White Paper (1980).

[56] JMB. Notes: The Agreed Memorandum on Posts of Responsibility in Secondary Schools, 9 December 1975.

[57] The managers discussed the possibility of including a representative of the Association of Post Primary Teachers of Ireland (APPTI) a voluntary organisation of teaching religious and clerics; APPTI ceased to exist at the end of the 1970s.

[58] Notes of JMB meetings, 1975 and 1977.

[59] This was true of many CCSS schools as late as 1981; in a technological age this may seem hard to accept but one of the frequent problems encountered by the CCSS executive was a situation where school principals were using the 1972 Agreed Memorandum long after it had been amended; many principals had no secretarial support and the issue sometimes was one of mislaying the most recent Memorandum; see CCSS. Guidebook for Principals, 1977:29-32.

[60] Memo General Secretary to JMB, 21 August 1989; a former secretary of the Department of Education, Liam Lane, was the agreed chairman of the Appeals Board in 1984.

[61] Ibid.

[62] *The Employment Equality Act*, 1998 has alerted the Secretariat of Secondary Schools to possible discrimination on the grounds of age is such an approach is followed when there is more than one applicant for a post.

[63] In the 1970s as a result of human error in calculating the points, the JMB recommended to their members that principals should do their own calculations.

[64] In 1973 when the Cardinal was discussing this aspect with the members of the EPG, there were 87 Catholic secondary intermediate schools and 33 Catholic grammar schools in Northern Ireland: 20 of the grammar schools were convent owned and 13 belonged to the priests and brothers.

[65] Margaret Walsh, a former president of the union and in 2000 a deputy principal of a large school, told the author that she had been aware of the 'injustice' to union members of how the POR system had developed; she was not blaming either union or managers, simply stating a fact.

[66] JMB Final Submission to the Review Body on Teachers' Pay, 30 July 1980.

[67] One can only guess that the presence of such officials may have contributed to a greater appreciation within the Department of the inadequacies of the POR structure as compared with what had been developed in the community schools.

[68] Presentation to the National Education Convention from the AMCSS and the JMB by Mrs Barbara O'Dwyer, 12 October 1993:12.

[69] The ASTI attention usually focused on the type of contract given to their members; the union accepted the use of temporary contracts for up to three years, the time it would take for a religious either to complete novitiate training, or university education.

[70] The author encountered situations where two lay teachers sought to legally divest themselves of their special functions posts in 1978 in order to be free to move to other schools; it was not found possible to rid themselves of the post.

[71] Draft Agreed Memorandum, 16 November 1989.

[72] Moriarty had been proposed by the JMB to the ASTI: Brother Declan Duffy, General Secretary to Kieran Mulvey, General Secretary, ASTI, 27 August 1986.

[73] Memo to ASTI, 5 October 1988.

[74] JMB to ASTI, 27 June 1989.

[75] Liam Murphy, Acting General Secretary to Séan Moriarty, Chairman, 8 November 1988.

[76] Chairman of the Appeals Board to JMB, 14 May 1988.

[77] Brother Declan Duffy, General Secretary to Ms Kathleen O'Sullivan, President, ASTI, 18 May 1989.

[78] Secretariat of Secondary Schools. Circular letter to all members of the JMB, 6 June 1989.

[79] Brother Declan Duffy, General Secretary to Charlie Lennon, Assistant General Secretary, 27 June 1989; Lennon to Duffy, 25 July 1989.

[80] Brother Adrian McGrath, Christian Brother, negotiator on the Agreed Memorandum, to the joint meeting, 2 October 1989.

[81] Conversations with the author.

[82] Joe Costello (now Senator) was the ASTI representative who highlighted the issue.

[83] Federation of Irish Employers (now IBEC) to General Secretary, 29 November 1989.

[84] This was required under article 12 of the Agreed Memorandum.

[85] Secretariat of Secondary Schools. Notes, 13 March 1990.

[86] Secretariat of Secondary Schools, 5 May, 16 and 24 November 1989.

[87] Such a review was provided for in the Redeployment Scheme, par. 9.1.

[88] The earlier 'package' agreed in 1987 between the CMCSS and the ASTI had included three elements: boards of management, parent/teacher meetings (banned since 1973) and the issue of redundancy/redeployment.

[89] CMCSS and ASTI. Terms of the Redeployment Scheme for Lay Teachers in Catholic Secondary Schools under Religious/Clerical Management and those Catholic Secondary Schools under Lay Trusteeship, 1987.

[90] In fact, both cases concerned the same appointment.

[91] Notes: Proposed Strategy for Negotiation on Agreed Memo, undated.

[92] As a result of continual research by the Secretariat of Secondary Schools since 1977 on funding, and the auditing of school accounts, there were reports of commissioned studies readily available to the Departments of Education and Finance the evidence showed responsible expenditure and considerable private investment by the trustees and sometimes by parents in an inadequately funded voluntary school system.

[93] Secretariat of Secondary Schools. Fact Sheet, 16 March 1990.

[94] Newsletter, vol.16 no.9, May 1990:1.

[95] Brother Declan Duffy, General Secretary to Kieran Mulvey, General Secretary, ASTI, 15 January 1990.

[96] Ibid.

[97] Brother Declan Duffy, General Secretary to Kathleen O'Sullivan, President, ASTI, 18 May 1989.

[98] For an explotation of rationalisation see also Raymond Walsh. 'The issue of rationalisation in Irish post-primary education 1963-96: the perspectives of the Catholic Church and the State' in, *Oideas*, no.46, 1998:7-25.

[99] JMB to ASTI, 26 February 1990.

[100] Secretariat of Secondary Schools. Redeployment Scheme: Memo: CMCSS Minutes, 19 January 1990.

[101] ASTI to Brother Declan Duffy, General Secretary, 12 March 1990.

[102] *ASTIR*, vol.31 no.6, February 2000:10.

[103] Charlie Lennon, General Secretary to Brother Declan Duffy, General Secretary, 25 April 1995.

NOTES TO CHAPTER 5

[1] The Federation of Irish Employers was founded in 1942 to represent the interests of employers in Ireland in industrial relations and social matters; in 1947 their title became the Federation Union of Employers and they joined the International Organisation of Employers; this provided them with an effectie network of information on policy and workplace issues; following on the Unfair Dismissal Act; 1977 and the CMRS Report on Religious as Employers, 1978 the managerial bodies considered becoming a member and did so in 1982 on a trial basis for a year; however, they then continued to date; in 1992 when the FUE celebrated its golden jubilee they combined with the Confederation of Irish Industry under the present title IBEC; in 1994 IBEC established its schools-industry links programme to enable pupils to gain experience in local workplaces.

[2] Louden Ryan in interview with the author, 20 January 1998, had a clear recollection of Mother Jordana's 'incisive contribution' in support of salary increases for teachers; he described her as 'the memorable one' of the group.

[3] The first National Pay Round was in 1946-1947 when war time control of wages under the Emergency Powers Orders ended; the Industrial Relations Act of 23 September 1946 established the Labour Court which provided a mechanism for dealing with disputes; five pay rounds were agreed in the 1950s and five in the 1960s including the ninth which ended the eight week strike of construction workers and ensured a $41^1/_4$ hour winter week; eight rounds ensued in the 1970s; it is interesting that in the mid-1940s the Catholic bishops instructed the CHA to retain their lay teachers because of economic conditions.

[4] Collins (1980) shows that teacher pay kept pace with the consumer price index between 1969 and 1979; compared with average industrial earnings in the same period, teachers lost out; awareness of this discrepancy energised the unions to pursue pay claims through the 1970s.

[5] Kevin McDonagh left the Department of Education to spend two years as analyst in the Department of Finance; on his return to Education he worked on the analysis; see 'The way the money goes', in *Oideas*, no.17 Spring 1977:5-101.

[6] CMRS. Report of the Working Party on Religious as Employers in Secondary Schools, November 1978:28.

[7] See Nolan, John and Burke, Andrew. *The financing of Catholic Secondary schools in the Free Education Scheme: a survey of the period 1984-1989.* Secretariat of Secondary Schools, January 1991; the ESRI study by Dale Tussing in 1978 is relevant to investment in education by voluntary bodies; the third relevant study is that of Sheehan, Durkan and Thom. Report of a Survey of School Unit Costs: Primary and Post-Primary Schools by the Department of Economics at University College Dublin (1997) was commissioned by Niamh Bhreathnach as an internal document for her Department though it subsequently was made available.

[8] JMB. General Secretary to John Wilson, Minister for Education, 30 January 1980.

[9] JMB. Final Submission to Review Body on Teachers' Salaries, 30 July 1980.

[10] JMB Minutes of special meeting held in Milltown Park, 23 October 1980.

[11] Ibid.

[12] JMB. Minutes of meeting took seven pages, 20 November 1980; the Department line was consistent: the managers were responsible for their schools; complaints about inadequate supervision were unacceptable when 'managers sanction mid-term breaks, schools closing in May, school trips to the Seine'; the managers claimed that 'those who pay have the control' but the Department officials did not agree; the Review Body conclusion that salary increases should be accompanied with duties had been undermined according to the JMB.

[13] CMRS. Draft agenda sent in advance to Liam Lane for meeting with the Minister, 30 September 1981; increased capitation for secondary schools was also included.

[14] JMB to John Boland, TD, Minister for Education, 27 October 1981.

[15] In 1982 when government refused a five per cent public sector pay award a series of marches began; a half-day on 24 September and a full day on 1 October brought thousands of workers on to the streets and to Croke Park to demonstrate; the teacher unions were among them.

[16] The 'Partners for Education' idea emerged during these years; suggested by the Christian Brothers' Parents' Federation, it was the first concerted effort by the education partners to put pressure on government to increase educational expenditure;

from 1986 there were marches and from 17 February to 3 March 1987 the partners were urged 'to continue to meet and monitor events during the period when the new Taoiseach and cabinet will be selected and briefed. Consequently, strategic progress could be made by making approaches to the Taoiseach elect at this time': JMB. Minutes, January 1987.

[17] Conversation with Kieran Mulvey, former General Secretary, ASTI, 14 January 1997.

[18] CMRS, 6 April and 22 December 1981; CMCSS. Conclusion of redeployment, 9 September 1983.

[19] CMCSS to ASTI President, Raymond Kennedy, 13 February 1984; the subsequent meeting of the negotiators was 'coldly acrimonious': CMCSS. Redeployment, 17 February 1984.

[20] Interview with Brother Declan Duffy, General Secretary, CMCSS, 16 June 1996.

[21] CMCSS. Agreed criteria for the selection of the first panel administrator, 8 October 1982; the panel was to be country wide; the person appointed would be an acting or retired civil servant with full access to the records of the Department; the administrator would indicate the school to which the teacher would be redeployed and would issue a certificate where necessary to enable a school to advertise where the panel did not have a teacher with the required subjects.

[22] The gain for the Department of Education in redeployment of teachers was financial; there was also the hope that comprehensive and community schools might be brought into the scheme; to date in 2000 that has not happened although both systems have teachers in excess of the quotas.

[23] Archer (1984) in tracing the origins of educational systems in Europe has painted a similar picture of church monopoly becoming gradually balanced by greater state intrusion; this happened later in Ireland than in France or England.

[24] Through the 1960s the exports of goods and services on which Ireland relied strongly, averaged 36 per cent of GDP; in the 1970s it rose to 44 per cent and in the 1980s to 67 per cent.

[25] Interview by the author with Liam Kelly, of the Labour Relations Committee, March 2000.

[26] Niamh Bhreathnach was Minister from 15 December 1994 to 26 June 1997.

[27] The 'Round-Table Discussions' took place in Dublin Castle, the venue for the NEC in 1993.

[28] The unplanned shortening of the school year had been a matter of concern to the managerial bodies since the 1980s; eventually, the White Paper, 1995:61 had indicated that action would be taken to redress the issue; it was the manner of doing so in the form of an unexpected circular when the schools were closed that 'soured relations' as Walshe suggested.

[29] Author's notes of conversations with members of the managerial bodies, 1986 and 1987.

[30] Presentation to the National Education Convention from the Association of Management for Catholic Secondary Schools (AMCSS) and the Joint Managerial Body for Secondary Schools (JMB), Tuesday, 12 October 1993 at Dublin Castle, p.8.

[31] In 1997 under the Fianna Fáil Progressive Democrat government, the name of the Department was changed to include 'and Science'.

[32] Seán McCann, General Secretary, ACS, attended.

[33] In 1953 under the C and A for the Civil Service a Departmental Council was established in the Department of Education to deal with pay and conditions of service of the various grades within the Department; from that development came the three panels for the teachers; in 1967 two council schemes were implemented, one for clerical and administrative staff in the VECs and one for CEOs in the vocational sector; see White Paper (1980:95).

[34] Secretariat of Secondary Schools. Newsletter, vol.2 no.2, October 1995:1-2.

[35] Secretariat of Secondary Schools. Newsletter, vol.22 no.5, January 1996:1.

[36] Secretariat of Secondary Schools. Notes of PCW meetings, 1996.

[37] Ibid. Vol. 22 no. 5, January 1996:1.

[38] Department of Education, Press Release, 27 February 1996.

[39] JMB. *Press Release*, 10 March 1997.

[40] From 1996-1997 Charlie Lennon and John Mulcahy were the ASTI representatives; Mulcahy was replaced by John Hurley from 1997-1998.

[41] Newsletter. 'From the General Secretary's Desk': George O'Callaghan, vol.22 no.9, 1996:1.

[42] Brother Declan Duffy, General Secretary to Dr Don Thornhill, Secretary, 16 April 1996.

[43] Newsletter, vol.22 no.9, June 1996:2.

[44] The author acknowledges the comments of Sr Marie Céline Clegg, then President of the CMCSS and JMB and actively involved in the task on hand; along with the President and George O'Callaghan, General Secretary, were Dr Sinéad Breathnach, Vincent Foley and Seán Burke as a negotiating team.

[45] Newsletter, vol.23 no.2, October 1996:1-2.

[46] From 1996-1997 Charlie Lennon and John Mulcahy were the ASTI representatives; Mulcahy was replaced by John Hurley from 1997-1998.

[47] The Irish Times and the Irish Independent, 3 April 1997.

[48] Interview with author, December 1999.

[49] TUI News, vol.19 no.4, February 1997.

[50] The author acknowledges the comments of Sr Marie Céline Clegg, President, CMCSS and JMB, March 2000.

[51] AMCSS. General Secretary's Report to the Annual General Meeting, 1998:5.

[52] The members of the Advisory Group were the President, Seán Burke, Vice-President, Harry Meyer, Michael McCann, Mary McGlynn, Jack Cleary, Vincent Foley, Dr Sinéad Breathnach; the Guidelines Working Party were Noel Keating, Sr June Fennelly, Billy Gardiner, John Curtis, Donal O'Hanlon, Robert McCarthy, Dr Séamus McGuinness, Education Department Trinity College Dublin and Tom Clarke, Centre for Management and Organisation Development at the Department of Finance; the whole process was supported and organised by Bernadette Kinsella, Principal Officer assisted by Fionnuala Sheridan and Audrey Kane of the Secretariat of Secondary Schools.

[53] Secretariat of Secondary Schools. ISM Guidelines, 1998:1.

[54] Ibid. 1998:7.

[55] Ibid., 1998:8, par. 4.8; Circular 4/98, clause 9.

[56] Ibid., 1998:13, par.6.6.

[57] Bernadette Kinsella, Principal Officer, Secretariat of Secondary Schools in interview with the author, June and October 1998, July and November 1999.

[58] Newsletter, vol. 24 no.8, May 1998:1-2.

[59] AMCSS. Report of the General Secretary to the Annual General Meeting, 1999:6.

[60] Dr Michael Woods, Minister for Education in a recent comment on the ASTI demand for a salary increase of 30 per cent has said that extra pay might be available 'but only under the productivity terms of the new pay deal'; he was referring to the bench-marking mechanism of the PPF which links public pay to that in the private sector; given the level of opposition of the TUI that rejected it, and the ASTI who walked out of the negotiations on the basis of their demand for 30 per cent, the PPF negotiations will not be easy; see The Irish Times, 28 March 2000.

[61] The author acknowledges this information from Bernadette Kinsella, Principal Officer and Seán Burke who was a member of the negotiating team; one aspect that needs attention is the potential for delay in filling a temporary post; no doubt, in the first review this will receive attention.

[62] Author's interviews with Professor Louden Ryan in 1997.

[63] ASTIR, September 1998:13.

[64] AMCSS. Report of the General Secretary to the Annual General Meeting, 1999:4-7.

[65] AMCSS. Report of the General Secretary to the Annual General Meeting, 1999:6-7.

[66] Ibid., 1999:7-8.

[67] ASTIR, October 1998:12.

[68] Partnership 2000, chapter 9.

[69] The author is not ignoring the occasion in February 2000 when Charlie Lennon, General Secretary, ASTI, withdrew from ICTU because of union dissatisfaction with pay increases under the Partnership for Prosperity and Fairness (2000).

[70] The new scheme was signed in February 2000 and includes 4 management representative, the three teachers unions and 5 from the Departments of Education and Finance; included in the management group this time is ACS, not previously in C and A.

[71] The members were Sr Eithne Woulfe, Sr Anne Harrington and Fr James Cassin who was elected President of the CMCSS and the JMB in 2000.

[72] CMCSS. Vision for Catholic education and religious education in the voluntary secondary schools: draft interim report, 22 March 1999:3.

[73] Ibid, 1999:3.

[74] Secretariat of Secondary Schools. Newsletter, vol.22 no.7, April 1996:3.

NOTES TO CHAPTER 6

[1] A Department of Adult Education was initiated by Professor Alfred O'Rahilly and continued by Con Murphy who subsequently was appointed by Brian Lenihan, TD, to chair the Committee of 1969, referred to later in this chapter.

[2] The People's College was linked with ICTU and the International Federation of Workers' Education Associations.

[3] *Teagasc* is governed by an eleven-member Authority, five of whom are appointed by the Minister for Agriculture and Food; the remainder are appointed on the basis of nominations from designated organisations; eight research centres inform the work of *Teagasc* in its fifteen colleges and fifty local training centres; advisory services are also provided from about a hundred centres.

[4] He subsequently became the first lay head of the College of Education in Glasgow where he remains today; a leading figure in the development of the European Association of Catholic Faculties of Education, he recently collaborated in *Catholic Education: inside out* and outside in. Dublin: Veritas, 1999; he has worked with the managerial organisations and schools in Ireland over a number of years.

[5] Kinsella, Bernadette. '*Analysis of new principals' training needs*', 1999; among the specific in-service needs identified by the principals were training in communication, organisation, interpersonal skills, interview techniques, delegation and negotiation; Kinsella's analysis is a systematic, detailed study that is the basis of training programmes in 2000; as Principal Officer, she will review the programmes with the participants to ensure further development.

[6] The eight orders of men were the Jesuits, Augustinians, Calced and Discalced Carmelites, Camillians, Marists, Oblates, Passionists and Sacred Heart Missionaries; see Cooney, (1999: 403).

[7] Carey, Liam. 'The history of Aontas', in *Aontas Review: an Irish Journal of Adult Education*, vol.1 no.2, 1979:10-15; see also *Annual Reports* of Aontas.

[8] Members included: VEC principals (2), an inspector of the Department of Education, the Education Officer of ICTU, ICA (1), Muintir na Tíre, Macra na Feirme.

[9] Carey. 'The history of *Aontas*',1979:13; the DIAE was host to the fledgling Association until 1974 when the Irish Farmers' Association welcomed it to the Irish Farm Centre; a number of other moves followed since the organisation does now own premises; it is now located at 22 Earlsfort Terrace in Dublin.

[10] CMRS. Paul Byrne, Secretary General to Liam Lane, 30 September 1981 where he includes adult education on the agenda for a forthcoming meeting; Brother Declan Duffy, General Secretary and Liam Murphy President, CHA and CMCSS, pursued the matter from the late 1970s; under the terms of the PCW and P2000 the discrimination against the voluntary schools will end in the negotiations in 2000.

[11] See chapter five.

[12] CMCSS. *A Manual for Boards of Management of Catholic Secondary Schools.* Dublin: author, first edition, 1985; revised edition, 1991. For private circulation only.

[13] The tradition of the Great Silence was essentially monastic though it was practised by nuns and brothers; it was often recorded in their 'rule books' as mandatory; the idea of silence from 9 p.m. until after morning prayer, the Eucharist and breakfast next morning, was to create a quietness conducive to prayer and reflection; the teaching orders did not abandon the principle but quickly adapted before the end of the seventies as the demands of schools and works including adult education were being met.

[14] Steffens was economic advisor to the German Chancellor, Helmut Kohl; the Marino Institute in due course received a certificate from the UN in recognition of the work on the family.

[15] The Marist Brothers and the Holy Faith Sisters are co-trustees of the first community school in Tallaght; Brother Declan Duffy remains a member of the board of management in 2000.

[16] Doyle, Eileen and Duffy, Declan. *The North America Report: a study of what is happening in adult education and family life apostolate in some areas of the North American Church with suggestions for the Irish scene.* Dublin: Conference of Major Religious Superiors, February 1977; the report is explored later in this chapter.

[17] In 1973 there were 15,145 sisters in Ireland of whom 5,340 were teaching; numbers entering the orders fell from 592 in 1966 to 153 in 1973; of the 2,198 brothers there were 1,328 teaching in 1973 when vocations had fallen to 40 from 173 in 1973; vocations to the clerical institutes of priests declined from 390 in 1966 to 153 in 1973.

[18] The members of the working party were: Paul Andrews SJ (chairman), Sr M. Bede OP, Sr M. Cabrini (Mercy), Margaret Larminie (rapporteur, seconded from the Secretariat of Catholic Secondary Schools), Father James Lennon (later Bishop of Kildare and Leighlin), Brother Patrick McCann (De La Salle, Education Department, Maynooth), Eoin McCarthy (consultant), Mary Purcell (author), Matt Salters, Brother Victor Ward (De La Salle).

[19] The work of the Commission on School Accommodation, appointed in 1996 under Mr Frank Murray, principal of Springfield Community School, as chairman has produced comprehensive statistical data on every area in the country.

[20] Bernard Harvey, Advisor for Tutor Education, Leicestershire County Education Authority was consulted by the Committee (Murphy Report, 1973:35).

[21] OECD. *Lifelong Learning for All*. Paris: OECD, 1996:100.

[22] Adler, M.J. 'Adult Education' from a lecture. The Great Book Foundation, 1952 and cited in the Murphy Report, 1973:3.

[23] In 2000 the first on-line master's programme in counselling will be provided by the Newman Institute of Ireland, from Westport, County Mayo; possibilities for research and review will therefore be accessible.

[24] Margaret Larminie, the rapporteur and member of the Church of Ireland was described as having 'inclinations towards Christian reflection'; Angela MacNamara, a lay counsellor and 'agony aunt'; Louis McRedmond, a journalist and Dr John A. Cooney, psychiatrist.

[25] Secretariat of Secondary Schools. Survey of use of school halls/sports halls in secondary schools, November 1981:1; the survey was conducted in response to a query by Minister John Boland at a meeting with a deputation of bishops and CMRS on 9 October 1981.

NOTES TO THE CONCLUSION

1. The author is aware that negotiations continue in April 2000 and include these contentious issues.

2. The legal advice of 3 March 1987 was that there were two ways to ensure appropriate participation; the issues might be put on the JMB agenda as they arose; or the issues could be discussed on a more continuous basis with the three ISA representatives; the decision was to follow the second suggestion.

3. One aspect concerns EU legislation about hours of work; if teachers in a school are also involved in night classes under the lifelong learning programme in a voluntary school, the board may need to consider the implications.

4. The St. Louis nuns began the process of formalising the 'statement of the St. Louis education philosophy' with their teachers under the guidance of an outside facilitator; some other orders followed their example but did not work with lay teachers from the outset; the tendency at that stage was for the religious superiors to issue a 'philosophy statement'.

5. CMRS. Discussion on lay principals, 6 April 1981.

6. The readiness of community school boards of management to sanction time and funding for principals and deputies to attend a masters programme accounts for one masters programme in Trinity College Dublin; a few voluntary secondary school boards have followed that example in releasing principals to attend.

7. Inevitably, the experience in the school where policy is implemented differs considerably from that of major superiors who decide to establish a board and appoint a principal; a parallel was evident in school closures of which there were 37 between 1968 and 1972; the effects of the trustee decision were more keenly experienced at local level by the principal and manager.

8. Internal reviews had been done in 1973 and 1977 but the emphasis was on personnel not finance; in 1984 and 1987 the reviews were comprehensive; from 1978 the CMCSS and the JMB initiated research on school funding, administration of the free book scheme, the operation of a book loan scheme, school transport, pupil selectivity and first year curriculum.

9. From 1998 CMCSS/JMB took the decision to employ the services of an Education Development Officer having determined the need to fill a lacuna in the area of research and active policy development.

10. CMRS. Discussion on lay principals, at the 'think in' in Broc House, 3 December 1982.

11. Ibid. *Staff School Development: Consultative Paper*, vol. 1, CMRS Education Commission, 1988.

12. Expenditure on education more than doubled from 1961 to 1986 when it accounted for 6.6 per cent of GNP; by 1992 when there were 950,000 in full-time education between primary, second and third level, six per cent of GDP or twenty per cent of total government expenditure showed that Ireland valued education.

13. These selection boards were comprised of the school manager or representative, a member of the CCSS who was experienced in selection and an independent consultant who was always a lay person.

14. Interview with Brother Declan Duffy who was one of the negotiators of the boards of management.

Bibliography

PRIMARY SOURCES: UNPUBLISHED MATERIAL

ASTI RECORDS
Correspondence: files 1950-1989

Minutes of meetings of Central Executive Council

Minutes of meetings of Standing Committee

Redundancies, redeployment files

Reports of deputations: Department and others

Reports and submissions of sub-committees

Report (confidential) on the memorandum from the 1955 Convention on the claim for increase in the salary paid by the school

ASSOCIATION OF VICE-PRINCIPALS OF VOLUNTARY SECONDARY SCHOOLS
Newsletter, 1984-1987

CHA RECORDS
Minutes of meetings

Minutes of Catholic Managerial Body

CCSS RECORDS
Annual reports

Correspondence

Discussion papers

Minutes of meetings

Minutes of executive committee

Minutes of standing committee

Notes of discussions

Reports

Surveys

CMCSS / JMB RECORDS
Correspondence

Minutes of Council of Managers of Catholic

SECONDARY SCHOOLS
Minutes of Joint Managerial Body

Newsletters

Reports

Surveys

CMRS AND JOINT COMMISSIONS
Correspondence

Minutes of meetings

Reports

CORI
The trusteeship of Catholic voluntary secondary schools: a handbook for the leaders of religious congregations, for internal circulation only. 1996.

ISA RECORDS
Minute book

Journal of the Synod of the Church of Ireland, 1963-1990

Report on secondary education, 1965

RELIGIOUS SISTERS OF CHARITY
Records

Reports

TBA RECORDS
Correspondence

Reports

Surveys

SECRETARIAT OF SECONDARY SCHOOLS
Correspondence

Manual on procedures, 1st edition 1987; 1988; 1993

Newsletters

A Guide for principals of secondary schools, for private circulation only, 1992-1997

LEGISLATION

Vocational Education Acts, 1930 to 1994

Vocational Education (Amendment) Act, 1962 and 1970

Department of Education. Organisation of whole-time continuation courses, memorandum V40 (1942)

Memorandum V7 on the employment of teachers in vocational schools

Ministers and Secretaries Act, 1924

National Council for Educational Awards Act, 1979

Government of Ireland. *Bunreacht na hÉireann.* Dublin: Stationery Office

Apprenticeship Act, 1959, 39 of 1959.
Dublin: Stationery Office

Unfair Dismissals Act, 1977, no.10 of 1977.
Dublin: Stationery Office

Minimum Notice and Terms of Employment Acts,
1973 to 1991. Dublin: Stationery Office, 1997

Mulloy v. Minister for Education (1975). I.R.88

Education (no.2) Bill, 1997,
published 12 December 1997

Education Act, 1998

OFFICIAL REPORTS

Census of Population of Ireland, 1971.
Dublin: Stationery Office, 1975

Census of Population of Ireland, 1996.
Dublin: Stationery Office, 1997

Statistical Abstracts of Ireland.
Dublin: Central Statistics Office, 1989

Programme for Economic Expansion, 1958.
Dublin: Stationery Office, 1958

Teachers Salaries Committee, Reports and
appendices presented to the Minister for Education,
1960. Dublin: Stationery Office, 1960

An Cheárd Chomhairle. First annual report
for the year ending 31 March 1961. Dublin:
Department of Industry and Commerce, 1961

Report of the Council of Education on the Curriculum
of the Secondary School. Dublin: Stationery Office,
1962

Second Programme for Economic Expansion, part 1,
August 1963. Dublin: Stationery Office, 1963

Government White Paper on the Restoration of the
Irish language. Dublin: Stationery Office, 1965

Government of Ireland. Programme for National
Recovery, October 1987.

Government of Ireland. Ireland: National
Development Plan 1994-1999. Dublin:
Stationery Office, 1993

Government of Ireland. Programme for
Competitiveness and Work. Dublin: Stationery
Office, 1994

OECD Investment in Education: report of the Survey
Team appointed by the Minister for Education in
October 1962, 2 vols. Dublin Stationery Office, 1966

OECD. Reviews of National Policies for Education:
Ireland. Paris: OECD, 1991

OECD. Lifelong Learning for all. Paris: OECD, 1996

OECD/CERI. Staying Ahead: In-service Training and
Teacher Professional Development. Paris; OECD. 1998

OECD/ CERI. Parents as Partners in Education.
Paris: OECD 1999

OECD/CERI. Overcoming Exclusion: Adult Learning
Initiatives that Make a Difference. Paris: OECD, 1999

Commission on Higher Education. Presentation
and summary of report. vol.1. Dublin: Stationery
Office, 1967

Tribunal on Teacher Salaries. Report presented to the
Minister for Education. Dublin: Stationery Office,
1968

Report of the Public Services Organisation Review
Group. Dublin: Stationery Office, 1969

Report of Committee on Adult Education in
Ireland. Dublin: Stationery Office, 1973

Lifelong Learning: Report of the Committee on Adult
Education. Dublin: Stationery Office, 1983

National Council for Educational Awards.
Curriculum Development in Third Level Education.
Dublin: NCEA, 1974

Commission on School Accommodation. The
Rationalisation of Vocational Education Committees.
Dublin: Government Publications Office, 1996

Committee on the Form and Function of the
Intermediate Certificate Examination. Final Rreport
(ICE). Dublin: Stationery Office, 1975

Planning Committee Report to the Minister for
Education on the establishment of An Chomhairle
Mhúinteoireachta, Dublin: Stationery Office, 1977

Review Body on Teachers Salaries: Interim Report.
Dublin: Stationery Office, 1980

Report of the Pupil Transfer Committee. Dublin:
Stationery Office, 1981

Report of the National Youth Policy Committee.
Dublin: Stationery Office, 1984

Programme for Action in Education, 1984-87.
Dublin: Stationery Office, 1984

Department of Education. Tuarascáil Staitistiúil

Department of Education. White Paper on
Educational Development. Dublin: Stationery
Office, 1980

Department of Education. Report of the Committee
on In-service Education. Dublin: Stationery Office,
1984

Department of Education. Report of the Committee on
Discipline in Schools. Dublin: Stationery Office, 1985

Department of Education. *Partners in Education: Serving Community Needs*. Green Paper. Dublin: Stationery Office, November 1985

Department for Education. *Ages for Learning: decisions of government*. May 1985

Department of Education. *Education for a Changing World, Green Paper on Education*. Dublin: Government Publications Office, 1992

Department of Education. *Position Paper on Regional Education Councils*, March 1994
Department of Education. *Position Paper on the Governance of Schools*, July 1994

Department of Education. *Charting our Education Future, White Paper on Education*. Dublin: Government Publications Office, 1995

Department of Education and Science. *Adult Learning in an Era of Lifelong Learning. Green Paper on Adult Education*. Dublin: Stationery Office, November 1998

Department of Education and Science. *Report of the Steering Committee on the Establishment of a Teachers' Council*. Dublin: Stationery Office, 1998

Department of Education. Official circulars to schools

National Education Convention. *Report: National Education Convention*. Dublin: Government Publications Office, 1994

Curriculum and Examinations Board. *Issues and structures*. September 1984

Senior cycle: development and directions. Dublin: CEB, 1985

In our school: a consultative document. Dublin: CEB, 1986

Transition year programme: guidelines for schools. Dublin: CEB, 1986

National Council for Curriculum and Assessment. *Curriculum and Assessment Policy towards the new century*. Dublin: NCCA, 1993

NEWSPAPERS, PERIODICALS, JOURNALS

Administration

ASTIR

Business and Finance

Doctrine and Life

Economist

Education Times

Educational Administration

Educational Leadership

Educational Management and Administration

Furrow

Irish Ecclesiastical Record

Irish Educational Review

Irish Educational Studies

Irish Independent

Irish Press

Irish Times

Oideas

School and College Year Book

Secondary Teacher

Studies

Studies in Education

Tuarascáil

UNPUBLISHED THESES

Bonel-Elliott, Imelda. *La politique de l'enseignement du second degré en république d'Irlande, 1963-1993* PhD thesis, Université de la Sorbonne-Nouvelle, Paris III, 1994

Collins, Henry P. A study of some aspects of the status of organised teachers within the education system MEd thesis, Trinity College, Dublin, 1980
O'Connor, Daniel. Secondary education in Ireland, 1878-1969, MA thesis, St. Patrick's College, Maynooth

Riordan, Patrick J.N. *The Association of Secondary Teachers Ireland, 1909-1968*: some aspects of its growth and development, MEd thesis, University College, Cork, 1975

Sexton, Peter F. *The lay teachers' struggle for status in Catholic secondary schools in Ireland between 1878 and 1937*, MEd thesis, University of Birmingham, 1972

BOOKS: PUBLISHED WORKS

Abbott, W.M. *Documents of Vatican II*. New York: Corpus Books, 1966

Akenson, D.H. *A Mirror to Kathleen's Face*: Education in independent Ireland, 1922-1960. London: McGill-Queen's University Press, 1975

Alvey, David. *Irish Education: the case for secular reform*. Dublin: Church and State Books and Athol Books, 1991

Andrews, Paul 'The influence of university entrance requirement on second level curricula and examinations' in *University Entrance Requirements and their Effect on Second Level Curricula*. Dublin: Irish Federation of University Teachers, 1979

'Irish education transformed' in *Studies* 86 no.342 Summer 1997:149-55

'Ireland and the world educational crisis' in *Studies* Winter 1970

Aontas. *Making an Impact: Aontas response to the Green Paper: Education in an Era of Lifelong Learning*. June 1999

Archdiocese of Dublin. *Community Schools and Community Colleges in the Archdiocese of Dublin*. Dublin, 1982

Archer, Margaret Scotford. *Social Origins of Educational Systems*. London: Sage Press, 1984

Arnold, Bruce. 'Politics and the arts: the *Dáil* debates' in Frank Litton ed. *Unequal Achievement: the Irish Experience: 1957-1982*. Dublin: Institute of Public Administration (IPA) 1982:281-97

What Kind of Country: Modern Irish Politics 1968-1983. London: Jonathan Cape, 1984

Arupe, P. *Men for Others*. Rome: International Centre for Jesuit Education, 1973

ASTI. *The ASTI an Outline History 1909-1934*. Nenagh: ASTI, 1934

Response to White Paper, Dublin: ASTI, 1981

Schools for the 21st century: tomorrow's schools - today's agenda. Dublin: ASTI, November 1996

Staffing, Funding, and Facilities in Irish Second Level Schools. Dublin: ASTI, November 1996

Issues in Education. vol.2. Dublin: ASTI, 1997 and CMCSS. *Terms of the redeployment scheme for lay teachers in Catholic secondary schools under religious/clerical management and those Catholic secondary schools under lay trustee*ship. Dublin, 1987

Official Programmes for Annual Convention. Dublin: 1960-95

Atkinson, Dick. 'Towards self-governing schools' in *Studies in Education*. no.3. Institute of Economic Affairs, 1997

Atkinson, Norman. *Irish Education: a History of Educational Institutions*. Dublin: Allen Figgis, 1969

Axford, R.W. *Adult Education: the Open Door*. Pennsylvania: the International Textbook Company, 1969

Ball, Stephen J. *The Micro-politics of the School*. London and New York: Methuen, 1987

'Policy, social and critical social research: a personal review of recent education policy and policy research' in *British Educational Research Journal* vol.23 no.3, 1997:257-74

Barber, N. *Comprehensive Schooling in Ireland*. Dublin: Economic and Social Research Institute, 1989

'His Grace is not pleased', in *Studies*, Winter 1998:400-01

Barrington, T.J. T*he Irish Administrative System*. IPA, 1980

'Whatever happened to Irish government' in Frank Litton *Unequal Achievement*, 1982:89-114

Barrington, T.J. and T. Walsh. *Towards a New Democracy*. Dublin: 1983

Barry, C.H. and F. Tye. *Running a School*. London: Temple Smith, 1975

Barry, David. 'The involvement and impact of a professional interest group' in D.G. Mulcahy and Denis O'Sullivan eds. *Irish Educational Policy: process and substance*. IPA, 1989:133-62

'The ASTI and the development of the post-primary school structure' in *The Secondary Teacher* 13 no.1 Spring 1984:.2-5

Belbin, R. Meredith. *Management Teams: Why they Succeed or Fail*. Butterworth, Heinemann, 1981 and 1997, 15th edition

Birch, Most Rev. Dr Peter. 'The secondary programme and present needs' in CCSS *Annual Report*, 1957

Blackwell, John. 'Government, economy and society' in Litton, op. cit. 1982:43-62

Blumberg, A. and W. Greenfield. *The Effective Principal: Perspectives on School Leadership*. Mass: Allyn and Bacon, 1986

Bonel-Elliott, Imelda. 'Lessons from the sixties: reviewing Dr. Hillery's educational reform' in *Irish Educational Studies* 13, 1994

'The role of the Duggan report (1962) in the reform of the Irish education system' in

Administration, vol.44 no.3 Autumn 1996:42-60 'La représentation du systéme Èducatif dans les documents officiels en République d'Irlande, 1992-'95'. Communication au colloque de la SOFEIR, Centre d'Etudes et de Récherches Irlandaises de l'Université de Lille, 22-23 mars, 1996

Boyle, Richard. *Towards a New Public Service.* IPA, 1995

Breathnach, Pádraig. 'The introduction of the Junior Certificate: an overview' in *Issues in Education* 2. Dublin: ASTI, 1997:1-10

Breen, Richard, Damian F. Hannan, David B. Rottman, Christopher T. Whelan. *Understanding Contemporary Ireland: State, Class and Development in the Republic of Ireland.* Gill and Macmillan, 1990

Browne, Noel. *Against the Tide.* Gill and Macmillan, 1986

Bryck, A.S., Lee, V.E. and Holland, P.B. *Catholic Schools and the Common Good.* Cambridge MA:Harvard University Press, 1993

Bunreacht na hÉireann. Dublin: Stationery Office, 1975

Burke Savage, Roland. *Catherine McAuley: the first Sisters of Mercy.* Dublin: Gill, 1949

Bush, Tony, Ron Glatter, Jane Goodey, Colin Riches eds. *Approaches to Educational Management.* London: Harper and Row, 1980

Bush, T. *Theories of Educational Management.* Harper and Row, 1986

Bush, Tony and John West-Burnham eds. *The Principles of Educational Management.* Longman, 1994

Business and Finance. *Education: the real cost.* 22 September 1994:14-18

Byrne, E.M. *Women and Education.* London: Tavistock, 1978

Byrne, Kieran P. and Peadar Cremin. 'Ireland' in Colin Brock and Witold Tulasiewicz eds. *Education in a Single Europe.* Routledge, 1994:130-61

Byrne, Rev. P. 'The Irish Intermediate Education Act, 1978: before and after' in *Irish Ecclesiastical Record,* January 1915:16-17 and February 1915:126-44

Callan, Tim and Colm P. Harmon. 'The economic return to schooling in Ireland', Working paper, UCD: Department of Economics, August 1997

Campbell, J.J. *Catholic Schools: a survey of a Northern Ireland problem.* Fallon, 1964

Canavan, K. 'The quiet revolution in Catholic schooling in Australia' in *Catholic Education: a Journal of Inquiry,* vol.2, no.1, 1998:46-54

Cannon, Brian. 'The vice-principal: an identity crisis?' in *The Secondary Teacher,* vol.10, no.3 Autumn 1981:17018

Cannon, P. 'Denominational education in the Republic of Ireland' in *World Yearbook of Education.* 1966

Carey, Thomas. 'Roman Catholic bishops and the Education Reform' in *Education Today* 48 no.3, 1998:47-53

Casey, James. 'Law and the legal system, 1957-'82' in Litton, op. cit. 1982:267-80 *Catholic Encyclopoedia.* San Francisco: Harrap Collins, 1994

Cave, Ernest and Michael Connolly. 'Irish schools: managing' without 'management' in *Administration* 36 no.1, 1986:67-77

Charon, Marie-Claire. 'Protestant schools in Ireland: a French view' in *Studies* 87 no.345 Spring 1998:15-23

Chubb, Basil. *The Government and Politics of Ireland.* 3rd edition, Longman,1992

   FIE: Federation of Irish Employers, 1942-1992. Gill and Macmillan, 1992

Church of Ireland. Press release: 'Community schools: a statement from the Education authorities of Protestant denominations', 9 October 1979

Clancy, Patrick. *Who Goes to College.* Dublin: Higher Education Authority, 1988

   'The evolution of policy in third level education', in Mulcahy, and O'Sullivan eds. *Irish Educational Policy: process and substance.* 1989:99-132

   Access to College: patterns of continuity and change. Dublin: HEA, 1995

   'Investment in education: the equality perspective: progress and possibilities' in *Administration* 44 no.3 Autumn 1996:28-41

Clear, C. *Nuns in Nineteenth Century Ireland.* Gill and Macmillan, 1987

Coldrey, Barry. 'Church orphanages and industrial schools' in *Studies,* vol. 89, no.353, Spring 2000: 7-18.

Colley, G. 'Statement to the authorities of secondary and vocational schools 1966' in OECD. Reviews of National Policies for Education: Ireland. Paris: OECD, 1969

Collins, Stephen. *The Haughey File.* Dublin: O'Brien Press, 1992

   The Cosgrave Legacy. Blackwater Press, 1996

Committee of Post Primary School Principals. *Unemployment: a crisis for schools: Report of the Committee.* Veritas, 1984

CMRS. *Rationalisation of Schools: Report of the Working Party.* Dublin: CORI, 1986

Staff School Development: consultative paper 1 September 1988. CMRS, 1988

Inequality in Schooling in Ireland: a discussion paper. CMRS, 1988

Conference of Religious of Ireland. *Women for Leadership in Education.* Dublin: Conference of Religious of Ireland, 1994

Religious Congregtions in Irish Education: a role for the future? CORI, 1997

Education Bill, 1997: an analysis. CORI, 1997

The Future of Trusteeship: a review of some options for the way forward. CORI, 1997

Coogan, Tim Pat. De Valera: *Long Fellow, Long Shadow.* London: Hutchinson, 1993

Ireland Since the Rising. London: Pall Mall, 1966

Cooke, Jim. *Marley Grange Multi-denominational School Challenge,* 1973-1978. Dublin, 1997

Coolahan, John ed. *University Entrance Requirements and their Effect on second Level Curriculum:* Proceedings of seminar organised by IFUT. Dublin: IFUT, 1979

Irish Education: History and Structure. IPA, 1981 and reprints to 1991

'The fortunes of education as a subject of study and of research in Ireland' in *Irish Educational Studies* 4 no.1, 1984:1-34

The ASTI and Post-primary Education in Ireland, 1909-'84. ASTI, 1984

'Regionalisation of education: a recurrent theme', paper presented to seminar on the Green Paper, *Partners in Education serving community,* Tralee, 25 January 1986

Report on the National Education Convention. Dublin: Government Publications Stationery Office, 1994

Secondary education in Ireland. Council of Europe Press, 1995

Corish, P. *The Irish Catholic Experience: A Historical Survey.* Gill and Macmillan, 1985

Courtney, S. *Why Adults Learn: towards a theory of participation in adult education* Routledge, 1992

Cromien, Seán. 'Comment' in *Administration* 34, no.1, 1995:121-26

Cullen, L.M. *An economic history of Ireland since 1960.* London: B.T. Batsford, 1972

Cullen, Mary. *Girls Don't Do Honours Maths: Irish women in education in the nineteenth and twentieth centuries.* Dublin: Women's Education Bureau,1987

Daft, Richard. *Leadership: Theory and Practice.* Harcourt, 1998

Dallat, John and Joseph Sweeney. 'The reform of education in the United Kingdom and the Republic of Ireland: A comparison of Recent Policies, 1992-1993' in *Irish Educational Studies* 13, 1994

Declaration on Christian Education. Rome: 28 October 1965

Degnan, Sr Mary Bertrand. *Mercy Unto Thousands.* Dublin: Browne and Nolan, 1958

Department of Education. *All Our Children.* Dublin: Stationery Office, 1969

Department of Education and Science. 'Whole school evaluation: criteria', information sent to participating schools, 1998

Doctrine and Life. 'Irish laity: some findings of the 1984 natonal survey' in *Doctrine and Life* 36, no.5 May-June 1986:247-53

Dowling, Michael. 'The Ireland that I would have: development and the creation of an Irish national image' in *History Ireland* 5 no.2 Summer 1997:37-41

Downey, James. *Lenihan: His Life and Loyalties.* Dublin: New Island Books, 1998

Doyle, Eileen. List of alternative programmes/ projects currently in operation in JMB schools, 1984

Directory of inservice. Dublin: Secretariat of Secondary Schools, 1985

'The transition year' in Gerry McNamara, Kevin Williams and Don Herron.

Achievement and Aspiration: curriculum initiatives in Irish post-primary education. Drumcondra Teachers' Centre, 1990:19-32

'Curricular issues in the White Paper' in *Studies in Education* 11 no.2, Autumn 1995

'Staff development as empowering and enabling' in J. Matthew Feheney ed.

From Ideal to Action: the inner nature of a Catholic school today. Dublin: Veritas, 1998:156-68

and David Tuohy. 'New directions in Irish secondary education: some consequences of new programmes at second level' in *Studies* 83 no.332, 1996:436- 46

Dowling, P.J. *A History of Irish Education.* Mercier, 1971

Duffy, Brother Declan. *Adult Education and the Catholic School.* Dublin: CMRS, 1975

'Religious run secondary schools: a change in management' in *Secondary Teacher* 4 no.1 Autumn 1974:5-7

'Boards of management: the trustee perspective' address to Association of Vice-Principals of Voluntary Secondary Schools. 31 January 1987

Duffy, Patrick S. *The Lay Teacher: a study of the position of the lay teacher in an Irish Catholic environment.* Dublin: Fallons, 1967

Easterly-Smith, Mark. *Management Research: an Introduction.* Sage Publications, 1991

Education Commission, CORI. *The Catholic School in Contemporary Society.* Dublin: CORI, 1991

Considered Response to the Green Paper on Education: Education for a Changing World. CORI, 1993

Presentation to the National Education Convention. Dublin: CORI, 1993

Response to Position on the Governance of Schools. CORI, 1994

The trusteeship of Catholic voluntary secondary schools: a handbook for the leaders of congregations. Dublin: CORI, 1996

Religious congregations in Irish education: a role for the future? A reflection paper. CORI Education Commission, November 1997

Council for Research and Development. *Religious Beliefs, Practice and Moral Attitudes: a comparison of two Irish surveys, 1974-1984.* Maynooth, 1984

Egan, Owen and Joy O'Reilly. *The Transition Year Programme.* Dublin: ERC, 1977

Elliot, J. *Action Research for Educational Change.* OUP, 1991

European Commission. *Strategy for Lifelong Learning.* Brussels/Luxembourg: Office for Official Publications of the European Commission, 1996

EUROSTAT. Europe in figures. Luxembourg: Eurostat, 1989-'90

Fahey, Tony. 'The Catholic Church and social policy' in Falconer et al, 1985:411-30
Falconer, Alan, Enda McDonagh, and Seán MacRéamonn eds. *Freedom to Hope: the Catholic Church in Ireland twenty years after Vatican II.* Columba Press, 1985

Fanning, Ronan. *Independent Ireland.* Dublin: Educational Company, 1983

Farrell, Brian. *Seán Lemass.* Gill and Macmillan, 1983

ed. *The Creation of the Dáil: a volume of essays from the Thomas Davis Lectures.* Blackwater Press, 1984
'Politics and change' in Kieran A. Kennedy. *Ireland in Transition: conomic and social change since 1960.* Mercier Press, 1986:143-51

Farrelly, J. *Who's Who in Irish Politics.* Blackwater, 1990

Faulkner, Padraig. 'A friend of education' in *Studies* vol.87 no.348 Winter 1998:378-83

Federation of Irish Secondary Schools (FCLS). *Investment in Education in the Republic of Ireland.* Published by the Federation, 1962

Feeney, John. *John Charles McQuaid: the man and the mask.* Mercier Press, 1974

Fianna Fáil. *The Way Forward*, 1982

Fianna Fáil and Labour. *Programme for a Partnership Government,* January 1993

Fianna Fáil. *Education: a Fianna Fáil Position Paper*, May 1997

Fine Gael. *Policy for a Just Society.* Dublin: 1966
Action Programme for Education in the 80s. Dublin: November 1980
Building on Reality, 1985-'87. Dublin: 1985

Finlay, Fergus. *Snakes and Ladders.* Dublin: New Island Books, 1998

Fisher, Desmond. 'The church and change' in Kennedy, op. cit. 1986:133-42

Fitzgerald, Garret. *Towards a New Ireland.* Dublin: 1973

All in a Life: an autobiography. Gill and Macmillan, 1992

Flannery, Austin ed. *Vatican Council II: the conciliar and post-conciliar documents.* New York: Costello Publishing, 1975

Fogarty, Michael. 'The two faces of Irish industrial relations' in Kennedy. op. cit. 1986:112-19

Fogarty, M., L. Ryan and J. Lee. *Irish Values and Attitudes: the Irish report of the European value system study.* Dublin: Dominican Publications, 1984

Fogarty, M.P., D. Egan and W.J.T. Ryan. *Pay Policies for the 1980s.* FUE, 1981

Forrester, Duncan. 'Education and moral values - who educates?' in *Studies* 86 no.344 Winter 1997:347-79

Gaffney, Peter. 'The central administration' in Litton, op. cit. 115-32

Garvin, Tom. *The Birth of Irish Democracy.* Gill and Macmillan, 1996

Glendenning, D. *Education and the Law.* Dublin: Butterworths, 1999

Goldring, Ellen B. 'Educational leadership: schools, environments and boundary spanning' in Strategic Management. OUP, 1997

Grace, Gerald. *Education and the City: theory, history and contemporary practice.* Routledge and Kegan Paul, 1984

  School Leadership: beyond educational management. Falmer, 1995

  'Leadership in Catholic schools', in T.McLoughlin *et al* eds. *The Contemporary Catholic School: context, identity and diversity.* Falmer, 1996

Greenfield, Thomas B. 'Theory about organisations: a new perspective and its implications for schools' in Bush et al eds. *Approaches to School Management.* Harper Row for OUP, 1980:154-71

  And Ribbins, P. eds. *Greenfield on Educational Administration: towards a humane science.* London: Routledge and Kegan Paul, 1993

Grogan, Vincent. 'Schools under the Constitution', in *Studies* 59, Winter 1970:377-80

Handy, Charles. *The New Alchemists: how visionary people make something out of nothing.* Hutchenson, 1999

  'On the working of groups' in *Understanding Organisations.* Penguin, 1976:145-75

  Understanding Organisations. 2nd edition. Penguin, 1978

  Gods of Management. Penguin, 1979

  Taken for Granted? Understanding schools as organisations. Schools Council Programme I: purpose and planning in schools, 1985

Hannan, Damien and Richard Breen. 'Schools and gender roles' in Cullen. op. cit. 100-16

  Schooling and Sex Roles: sex differences in subject provision and student choice in Irish post-primary schools. ESRI paper 113, June 1983

Hannan, D. and S. Shortall. *Schooling Decisions: the origins and consequences of selection and streaming in Irish post primary schools.* ESRI, 1987

  The Quality of their Education. ESRI, 1991

Hannon, P. 'Church-state relations post 1992' in *The Furrow*, November 1997:587-95

Hardiman, Niamh. 'Pay bargaining: confrontation and consensus' in D. Nevin ed. *Trade Union Centuries.* Mercier Press, 1994:147-58

Hargreaves D.H. *Interpersonal Relations and Education.* Routledge and Kegan Paul, 1972

Hargreaves, D.H., D. Leask, M. Connolly and J. Robinson. *Planning for School Development: advice to governors, headteachers and teachers.* HMSO, 1989

Hargreaves, D. H. and D. Hopkins. *The Empowered School.* Cassell, 1991

Hargreaves, D.H. 'School culture, school effectiveness and improvement' in Harris, op. cit. 239-50

Hargreaves, D.H. and D. Hopkins eds. *Developing Planning for School Improvement.* Cassell, 1994

Harris, John. 'The policy-making role of the Department of Education' in Mulcahy and O'Sullivan, op. cit. 7-26

Healy Seán and Brigid Reynolds eds. *Social Policy in Ireland: principles, practice and problems.* Oak Tree Press, 1998

Heifetz, R.A. *Leadership Without Easy Answers.* Harvard University Press, 1994

Hennesey, J.J. *The First Council of the Vatican: an American experience.* New York: Costello Publishing, 1963

Hogan, G.W. 'Law and religion: church-state relations in Ireland from Independence to the present day' in *The American Journal of Comparative Law* 35, 1987:47-97

Hogan, Padraig. *The Custody and Courtship of Experience: western education in philosophical perspective.* Columba Press, 1995

  ed. 'Educational policy in philosophical perspectives' in *Partnership and the Benefits of Learning.* Maynooth College: ESAI, 1995.

Horgan, John. 'Educational policy and public interest' in *Secondary Teacher* 9 no.1 Spring 1980:9-10

  Sean Lemass: the enigmatic patriot. Gill and Macmillan, 1997.

Hussey, Gemma. *At the Cutting Edge: cabinet diaries 1981-1987,* Gill and Macmillan, 1990

Hyland, Áine and Kenneth Milne eds. *Irish Educational Documents.* vol.2. Church of Ireland College of Education, 1992

Inglesias, Teresa. 'Dignity of the Individual in the Irish Constitution' in *Studies* vol 89 no. 353, Spring 2000: 19-34

Investment in Education. *Studies in Educational Administration*. no.13. 1968

Irish Council of Churches: Board of Community Affairs. *The Churches' Rights in Education in Ireland*. Belfast: Irish Council of Churches, 1982

Irish Episcopal Conference. *New Ireland Forum*. Report no.12. Dublin: 1984

Irish Hierarchy. *The Work of Justice*. Veritas, 1977

Jessop, B. 'The transition to post-Fordism and the Schumpeterian workfare state' in R. Burows and B. Loader eds. *Towards a Post-Fordist Welfare State?* Routledge 1994

JMB. *Response to the NCCA Document Issues and Structures*. November 1990

Keatinge, Patrick. 'Ireland and the world, 1957-1982 in Frank Litton. op. cit. 225-42

Kelleghan, Thomas. 'The interface of research, evaluation and policy in Irish education', in Mulcahy and O'Sullivan. *Op cit*. 1989:191-218

Kellaghan, T. and M. Lewis. *Transition Education*. Veritas, 1984

Kelly, J.M. *The Irish Constitution*. Dublin: Jurist Publishing Company, UCD, 1984

    Belling the Cats: selected speeches and articles of John Kelly. Dublin: Moytura Press, 1992

Keogh, Dermot. *Twentieth Century Ireland: nation and state*. Gill and Macmillan 1994

Kerr, Robert. 'In-school management: a commentary on the White Paper's proposals' in *Studies in Education* 11 no.2 Autumn 1995

Kerry, T. and Murdoch, A. 'Education managers as leaders; some thoughts on the context of the changing nature of schools', in *School Organisation,* vol.13 no.3, 1993:221-30

Kingston, Stanford. 'Religious education in Protestant schools in the Republic of Ireland' in *Studies in Education* 11 no.1 Spring 1995:48-56

Kirkpatrick, W.J. 'Structures of the Leaving Certificate' in The *Secondary Teacher 2* no.1, 1967:6-7

Kotter, J.P. *Leading Change*. Boston: Harvard Business School Press, 1996

Laborem exercens: encyclical letter of Pope John Paul II on human work. London: Incorporated Catholic Truth Society, 1984

Labour Party Dublin. *Challenge and Change in Education*. Dublin: Labour Party, 1963

Labour Relations Commission. *Annual Reports*, 1997; 1998

Lane, Dermot. 'Education and moral values-who educates?' in *Studies* 86 no.344 Winter 1997:360-69

Lantis, M. 'Two important roles in organisational communities' in *Human Organisation* 46 no.3, 1987:250-89

Leader, Donal and Scott Boldt. *Principals and Principalship: a study of principals in voluntary secondary schools*. Dublin: Marino Institute of Education, commissioned by CMCSS, 1994

Lee, John J. *Ireland 1945-'70*. Gill and Macmillan, 1979

Lee, Joseph. *The Modernisation of Irish Society, 1848-1919*. Gill and Macmillan,1969

    'Worker and sociery and modern Ireland' in D. Nevin. *Trade Union and Change in Irish Society*. Mercier Press, 1980:11-25

    'Society and culture' in Frank Litton ed. op. cit. 1-20

    'Whither Ireland? The next 25 years' in Kennedy. *Ireland in Transition*. 1986:151-66

    Ireland: Politics and Society 1912-1985. Cambridge University Press, 1989

Leonard, D. and Dundon, P. S*chool Leadership Programme: evaluation of the school leaderhip and whole-school development programme provided by the Secretariat of Secondary Schools*. Limerick: Centre for Studies in Gender and Education, 1996

Lindsay, Noel. 'Concepts in post-primary school building' in *Oideas* 3 September 1969:33-40

Litton, Frank ed. *Unequal Achievement: the Irish experience 1957-1982*. IPA, 1982

MacCurtain, Margaret and Donnacha " Corráin eds. *Women in Irish Society; the historical dimension*. Dublin: Arlem House, 1978

McCarthy, Charles. 'The role of the teacher in a developing educational system' in *Oideas* 1 September 1968:36-39

    The Distasteful Challenge. IPA, 1968

    The Decade of Upheaval: Irish trade unions in the nineteen sixties. IPA 1973

    Trade Unions in Ireland 1894-1960. IPA, 1977

McCormack, Teresa and Peter Archer. 'Christianity, social justice and education' in *Studies in Education* 11 no.1 Spring 1995:11-26

    'Participation, empowerment and the White Paper' in ibid.11 no.2 Autumn 1995

    'The changing roles of trustees and boards of management' in J. Matthew Feheney. op. cit. 145-55

McDonagh, Kevin. 'The way the money goes' in *Oideas* 17, Spring 1977:5-102

McElligott, T.J. *Education in Ireland*. IPA, 1966

    This Teaching Life. Mullingar: Lilliput Press, 1986

    Secondary Education in Ireland. Dublin: Irish Academic Press, 1981

McGréil, M. *Educational Opportunity in Dublin*. Dublin: Catholic Communications Institute, 1974

McNamara, Gerry, Kevin Williams and Don Herron eds. *Achievement and Aspiration: curricular initiatives in Irish post-primary education in the 1980s*. Drumcondra Teachers' Centre, 1990

McQuaid, John Charles. *Higher Education for Catholics*. Gill and Macmillan, 1961

    Catholic Education: its function and scope. Gill and Macmillan, 1962

Maher, D.J. *The Tortuous Path: the course of Ireland's entry into the EEC, 1948-1973*. Dublin: IPA, 1986

Mankiw, N. Gregory, David Romer and David N. Weil. 'A contribution to the empirics of economic growth' in *Quarterly Journal of Economics* 107 no.2, 1992: 407-37

Member of the Congregation. *The Life and Work of Mary Aidenhead, foundress of the Irish Sisters of Charity: 1787-1958*. London: private publication, 1924

Meredith, David. 'The governance of schools: an evolutionary perspective' in *Studies in Education* 11 no.2 Autumn 1995

Milne, Kenneth. 'A Church of Ireland view' in *Studies* LVII, Autumn 1968
    'The role of the Protestant school' in *Studies in Education* 11, no.1 Spring 1995:14-22

Morrissey, Thomas SJ. 'Joseph Dalton, SJ: First Irish Jesuit mission in Australia' in *Studies*, vol. 89 no.353, Spring 2000: 62-70.

Mulcahy, D.G. *Curriculum and Policy in Irish Post-primary Education*. IPA, 1981

    and Denis O'Sullivan eds. *Irish Educational Policy*. IPA, 1989

Murphy, John A. *Ireland in the Twentieth Century*. Gill and Macmillan, 1975

    'Parties and elections, 1948-69' in J.J. Lee. *Ireland 1945-'79*, 1-15

Murray, Donal. *A Special Concern: the philosophy of education: a Christian perspective*. Dublin: Veritas, 1991

Murray, Donal. 'The role of the Catholic school' in *Studies in Education* 11 no.1 Spring 1995:1-13

National Advisory Countil on Education. *Home School Relationships*. Dublin: Veritas, 1974

National Economic and Social Council. *Educational Expenditure in Ireland*. no.12. Dublin: NESC, 1975

    A Strategy for Development, 1986-'90. Dublin: NESC, 1986

    Education and Training Policies for Economic and Social Development. October 1993 no.95. Dublin: NESC

National Industrial Economic Council (NIEC). *Report on Manpower Policy*. Dublin: Stationery Office, 1964

    Comment on Investment in Education. Report no.16. Dublin: Stationery Office, 1966

    Report on Full Employment. Dublin: Stationery Office, 1968

Nevin, D. *Trade Unions and Change in Irish Society*. Mercier, 1980

    ed. *Trade Union Century*. Mercier Press for ICTU and RTÉ, 1994

Nolan, John and Andrew Burke. *The Financing of Catholic Secondary Schools in the Free Education Scheme: a survey of the period 1984-89*. Dublin: CMCSS, 1991

Nowlan, K.B. and T.D. Williams eds. *Ireland in the War Years and After: 1939-'51*. Dublin, 1969

Ó Buachalla, Séamas. *Education Policy in Twentieth Century Ireland*. Dublin: Wolfound Press, 1988

    'Saothar suntasach oideachais gur mithid a aithint ina iomláine 1802-1994' in *Éamann Rís*. Christian Brothers: Johnswood Press Ltd., 1996:51-76

    '*Investment in education: context, content and impact*' in *Administration* 44 no.3 Autumn 1996:10-20

    'Education as an issue in the second Dáil' in *Administration* 25 no.1:57-75

O'Carroll, Michael. 'Inspired educator and ecumenist of sorts' in *Studies* vol.87 no.348 Winter 1998:365-71

Ó Catháin, S. *Secondary Education in Ireland*. Reprint of articles in *Studies* 1957-'58 Dublin: Talbot Press, 1958

O'Connell, T.J. *100 Years of Progress:the story of the INTO 1868-1968*. Dublin: INTO, 1968.

O'Connor, S. 'Post-primary education: now and in the future' in *Studies* 47 no.227 Autumn 1968:233-51

A Troubled Sky: reflections on the Irish educational scene, 1957-'68. Dublin: ERC, 1986

O'Donoghue, Martin. 'Investment in Education: the economist's view: great change, little change' in *Administration*, vol.44 no.3 Autumn 1996:21-27

O'Donoghue, T. 'The Roman Catholic ethos of Irish secondary schools 1942-'62 and its implications for teaching and school organisation' in *Journal of Educational Administration and History* 22 no.2, 1990.

O'Flaherty, Louis. *Management and Control in Irish Education: the post-primary experience*. Dublin: Drumcondra Teachers' Centre, 1992

'Religious control of schooling in Ireland: some policy issues in review' in *Irish Educational Studies* 13, Spring 1994:62-70

Ó Gráda, Cormac. *A Rocky Road: the Irish economy since the 1920s*. Manchester University Press, 1997

O'Hagan, John. 'The economy of Ireland' in B. Chubb ed. op. cit. 1992

O'Malley, D. 'Free education and after?' Address to public meeting of Fianna Fáil, Clontarf, 16 February 1967

O'Meara, J. *Reform in Education*. Mount Salus Press, 1958

Ó Muircheartaigh, Fíonán. 'Public expenditure in Ireland: evolution and prospect' in

Ó Muircheartaigh ed. op. cit. 68-99
Ó Muirí, An Br. Micheál. 'Scoileanna na mBráithre Críostaí: traidisiúin mar aon le hathraithí' in *Éamann Rís*. 1996:77-100

O'Neill, B. *Schools and Quality: an International Report*. Paris: OECD, 1989

Ó Riagáin, Pádraig. *Language Policies and Social Reproduction: Ireland 1893-'93*. Oxford: Clarendon Press, 1997

Ó Raifeartaigh, T. 'Education in the USA' in *Studies*, Spring 1961:57-74

Ó Riain, S. 'Boards of management' in *Secondary Teacher* 5 no.1 Autumn 1975:21-25

Ó Súilleabháin, Séamus V. 'School organisation: general principles' in *Oideas* 16 Spring 1976:98-105

'The profession and status of teachers' in *Oideas*, 3

'The concept of the community school' in *Social Studies* 1 October 1971

O'Sullivan, Denis. 'The ideational base of Irish educational policy' in Mulcahy and O'Sullivan eds. 1989:219-74

Osborough, W.N. 'Education in the Irish law and Constitution' in *Irish Jurist* 12, 1978:145-80

Owens, Timothy, J. 'Central initiatives and local realities, 1963-1983' in Mulcahy and O'Sullivan, *op cit*. 1989:163-90

Oxford Dictionary; the new edition for the nineties. Clarendon Press, 1990

Peters, T. and R. Waterman. *In Search of Excellence*. Harper and Row, 1982

Rafter, Kevin. *The Story of Clann na Publachta*. Mercier Press, 1996

Randles, Sister Eileen. *Post-primary Education in Ireland, 1957-1970*. Veritas, 1975

Raven, John et al. *A Survey of Attitudes of Post-primary Teachers and Pupils*. Dublin: Irish Association for Curriculum Development, 1975-'76, 3 vols

Rees, W. David. 'The manager and the unions' in *The Skills of Management*. 3rd Edition. Routledge, 1991:260-90

Rubenson, K. *Adult Education and Training: the poor cousin: an analysis of reviews of national policies for education*. OECD: University of British Colombia and Linkoping University, 1998

Ryan, Liam. 'Social dynamite: a study of early school-leavers' in *Christus Rex* 21 no.1 January 1967:7044

'Church and politics: the last 25 years' in *Furrow* 30 no.1 Jan. 1979:3-18

'Implications of social change for second level schools in Ireland', Address to the annual general meeting CMCSS 1996

Schultz, Theodore. '*Investment in human capital*' in American Economics Review 51 no.1, 1961:1-17

Scottish Office Education Department (SOED). *Effective Secondary Schools*. 1988

Management Training for Head Teachers. 1989

The Role of School Development Planning in Managing School Effectiveness. SOED: Management of Educational Resources, no.5

Secretariat of Secondary Schools. *A Handbook for Managers of Secondary Schools*. Published 1974, 1981, 1984, 1987, 1989

Access to Secondary Education. 1977

Evangelisation and the Catholic school. 1981

In-service in our Secondary Schools. 1984

A Directory of School Retreat Personnel. 1988

Manual on Procedures. 1988 and 1993

Submission to Department of Education on the Green Paper. 1992

A Guide for Principals of Secondary Schools. 1992

Discussion Document on Regional Education Councils. 1993

A Manual for Boards of Management of Catholic Secondary Schools. 1985 and 1991

In-School Management: guidelines for the establishment of ISM structures. Dublin: Secretariat of Secondary Schools, 1998

Selznick, P. *The Moral Commonwealth.* Berkeley: University of California Press, 1992

Sengé, P.M. *The Fifth Discipline: the art and practice of the learning organisation.* New York: Doubleday, 1990

Senior, Barbara. 'Team roles and team performance: is there 'really' a link?' in *Journal of Occupational and Organisational Psychology* 70, 1997:241-258

Sergiovanni, T. and J.E. Corbally. *Leadership and Organisational Culture: new perspectives on administration theory and practice.* University of Illinois Press, 1984

Sergiovanni, T. *The Principalship: a reflective practice perspective.* Allyn and Bacon, 1987

'Adding value to leadership gets extraordinary results' in *Educational Leadership* May 1990:23-27

Moral Leadership: getting to the heart of school improvement. Cassell, 1992

Moral Leadership. Jossey-Bass, 1992

'Why we should seek substitutes for leadership' in *Educational Leadership* 49 no.5, 1992:4-45

Building Community in Schools. Jossey-Bass, 1994

Sexton, J.G. 'Employment, unemployment and emigration' in Kennedy. op. cit. 1986:31-39

Sexton, Gerry and Richard O'Leary. Report commissioned by the sub-committee on obstacles in the south to reconciliation, presented to the Forum for Peace and Reconciliation, Dublin Castle, 15 December 1995

Sheehan, J. 'Education, education policy and poverty' in L. Joyce and A. McCashin eds. Poverty and Social Policy. IPA, 1982:63-74

Sheehan, J. and John Nolan. *A Report on the Financing of Catholic Secondary Schools. Dublin: CMCSS, 1982*

Sheehan, J., Durkan, J. and Thom, D.R. *Survey of school unit costs: primary and post-primary schools: report.* University College Dublin: Department of Economics, 1994

Sheppard, Ann. *'60 years in St. Conleth's',* in 60 years revisited, 1999:2-3

Starratt, Robert J. 'Building an ethical school: a theory for practice in educational leadership' in *Educational Administration* 27 no.2 May 1991:95-02

The Drama of Leadership. Falmer, 1993

Transforming Educational Administration. New York: McGraw-Hill, 1996

Statistical abstract of Ireland. 1965. IPA, 1973

Titley, Brian. *Church, State and the Curriculum of Schooling.* Gill and Macmillan, 1983

Tobin, Fergal. *The Best of Decades: Ireland in the 1960s.* Gill and Macmillan, 1984

Tooley, James. *Disestablishing the School: debunking justifications for state interaction in education.* Avebury, 1995

Troddyn, P. 'Editorial' in *Studies* 57 no.227 Autumn 1968:274

Tuohy, David and David Coghlan. *'Challenges of educational leadership: meaning community and excellence'* in J. Matthew Feheney. op. cit. 168-80

Tussing, Dale. *Irish Educational Expenditures-past, present and future.* ESRI, Paper no.92, 1978

'Irish educational policy reconsidered' Address to IVEA, 17 May 1983

Vatican Congregation for Catholic Education. *The Catholic School.* Rome, 1977

Lay Catholics in Schools. Rome, 1982

The Religious Dimension of Education in a Catholic School. Rome,1988.

Walsh, Brendan. 'The growth of government' in Kennedy, op. cit. 1986:60-70

'The economic return to education', Paper delivered to the Statistical Society of Ireland, Trinity College Dublin, 19 February 1998

Walsh, T.J. *Nano Nagle and the Presentation Sisters.* Dublin: M.H.Gill, 1959

Ward, Owen P. 'Why I voted against acceptance of the Ryan Tribunal Report' in *ASTIR* 1 no.8, 1968:7-10

Weafer, John. 'Change and continuity in Irish religion 1974-1984' in *Doctrine and Life* 36 no.10 December 1986:507-17

'Vocations: a review of national and international trends' in *Furrow* 39 no.8 August 1988:500-17

West, E.G. *Education and the State.* Indianapolis Liberty Fund, 1994 edition

Whitaker, T.K. *Economic Development.* Dublin: Stationery Office, 1958

Interests. IPA, 1983

Whyte, G.F. 'The White Paper: a lawyer's response' in *Studies in Education* 11 no.2 Autumn 1995 Whyte, J.H. *Church and State in Modern Ireland,* 1923-1970. Gill and Macmillan, 1971 edition and 1984

Williams, Kevin. 'Restoring education to vocational education. A role for evaluation?' in *Studies in Educational Evaluation,* 10 May 1984

'State support for church schools: is it justifiable?' in *Studies in Education* 11 no.1 Spring 1995:37-47

Yukl, G. 'Managerial leadership: a review of theory and research' in *Journal of Management* 15 no.2 1989:250-89

Index

Leabharlanna Fhine Gall

Sr. Marie Celine Clegg, President AMCSS and JMB, 1997-2000.

The first delegation from CMCSS to attend a Catholic European Conference held in Chantilly, outside Paris in Holy Week 1972. From left-right: Fr Aidan Lehane (CHA), Joe O'Dwyer (FLCS), Sr. Philippa O'Sullivan RIP (CCSS), Br. Bernard Doyle (TBA), Sr. Simone (CCSS), Fr. John Hughes (Director, CMCSS), Kevin Meehan (President, ASTI), Br. John Kelly (TBA), SR. Eileen Randles (CCSS), Liam Murphy (CHA), Rev. Tom Finnegan (CHA - now Bishop of Killala).

Miss Stella Mew (left), Brother Declan Duffy (centre) and Mr and Mrs Brian Cairns celebrating Brother Declan's retirement as General Secretary of CMCSS/JMB.

Brother Declan Duffy, General Secretary of CMCSS/JMB, 1977-1996.

Mr Liam Murphy former president of CMCSS/JMB with Brother Declan Duffy.

George O'Callaghan, General Secretary CMCSS/JMB who succeeded Brother Declan Duffy.

Mons. James Cassin, pictured after his election as President of the CMCSS/JMB, January 2000.

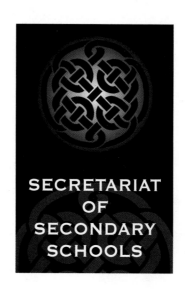

SECRETARIAT
OF
SECONDARY
SCHOOLS